Managing Natural Resources

Managing Natural Resources
Focus on Land and Water

(Felicitation Volume in Honour of Professor R.L. Dwivedi)

Editor

H.N. MISRA

Emeritus Professor
Department of Geography
University of Allahabad

PHI Learning Private Limited

Delhi-110092
2014

₹ 550.00

MANAGING NATURAL RESOURCES: FOCUS ON LAND AND WATER
H.N. Misra

ISBN-978-81-203-4933-9

Published by Asoke K. Ghosh, PHI Learning Private Limited, Rimjhim House, 111, Patparganj Industrial Estate, Delhi-110092 and Printed by Star Print-O-Bind, F-31, Okhla Industrial Area Phase I, New Delhi-110020.

Dedicated to

Prof. R.L. Dwivedi

Prof. R.L. Dwivedi with the Family

From L to R (Sitting): Samarth, Seema, R.L. Dwivedi, Gayatri, Deepa, Tarun
(Standing): Vivek, Akriti, Sudhir

Contents

PART III Water Resources

PART IV Natural Resources Management

List of Figures

List of Tables

Preface

Geography, as natural philosophy, is science of synthesis. It is integrative in nature and inter-disciplinary in approach. As a dynamic discipline, it is witnessing emergence of several new specializations cutting across the edges of traditional branches. Natural resource management and sustainable development has, of late, assumed great importance, especially because the ecological crisis and environmental danger are looming large. It has emerged as a new specialization and is being taught almost in all the colleges and universities at the undergraduate and graduate levels. The issues related to natural resource exploitation, consequences, their conservation, preservation and management leading to sustainable development have become the major thrust areas of research these days. Sustainable development is major goal which can be achieved only when resources are used judiciously. The resource use has to be need based rather than greed based. There are different types of resources. Some are replaceable, and some are non-replaceable. Obviously the non-replaceable resources are more difficult to manage than the replaceable one.

The focus of this volume is on *land* and *water* because they are vital for human survival and development. They provide the life support system but unfortunately both are under great strain and threat. They have wider and significantly varying implications in rural and urban settings especially in India where population has been multiplying and, therefore, the demand on land and water has been intensifying. Space occupied by agricultural land is getting reduced because urban areas are pushing forward to encroach upon the productive land. Common property resources, which used to maintain the ecological balance, are disappearing fast. Likewise, the availability of water, both in terms of quality and quantity, has been continuously declining. We may sooner face the water crisis. This situation, therefore, calls for a fresh look to handle these resources.

The volume has been divided into four parts. Part one presents a theoretical perspective on natural resources, especially on land and water. The dynamic relationship between increasing population and declining resources has been presented and the international efforts of maintaining the balance for sustainable development have been highlighted. Part two draws attention mainly on land resources. Several aspects of land resources such as land use, land utilization, morphometry, wasteland and land holding issues have been discussed in this part. Part three dwells upon water resources by focusing on river basins, hydrology and surface run-off. Part IV focuses on management of land and water resources.

The present volume aims at highlighting the problems of land and water in Indian context and suggesting remedial measures and policy prescriptions for sustained development of these resources. The students at the graduate level will find enough course material in the book; the thematic content will provide reasonably good food for cogitation to researchers. Even planners, policy makers and academicians may be benefitted while framing normative futuristic planning which may lead to sustainable development which is the ultimate goal.

H.N. Misra

Acknowledgements

The idea of this volume on natural resources having focus on land and water was conceived when I organized XXVIII IIG Meet in the Department of Geography, University of Allahabad. However, it could not take off due to some preoccupations. I am immensely thankful to my students Ashutosh and Anurag, who extended all possible help and endeavoured hard to expedite the process of preparing the volume for publication. I have full appreciation for them.

My thanks are due to contributors especially Prof. Graham Peter Chapman, Prof. Baleshwar Thakur and Prof. Harvir Sharma for being generous in allowing me to incorporate their papers. Prof. R.P. Misra and Prof. L.R. Singh always gave fruitful and productive advice and I am extremely grateful to them. I shall like to thank my colleagues Prof. Manorama Sinha, Prof. B.N. Mishra, Dr. Sudhakar Tripathi and Dr. Vandana Shukla for extending full cooperation and to Shri D.S. Lal, Dr. Savindra Singh, Dr. R.C. Tiwari, Dr. R.N. Singh, Dr. B.N. Singh, Dr. Alok Dube, Dr. S.S. Ojha, Dr. A.R. Siddiqui, Dr. Anupam Pandey and Shri Ashwajeet Chaudhari for their encouragement. Dr. R.C. Mishra, Assistant Director, Directorate of Higher Education also deserves mention on this occasion. Most of these have been students of Prof. Dwivedi and I am sure they will be very happy to see this felicitation volume in his honour.

My daughter Priyanka Misra and her husband Colonel Sunil Mishra read the typed manuscript and suggested necessary corrections. It is only too formal to thank them. I shall be failing if I do not mention Shangrila, Anamika, Ashish, Amit, Sanjana, Abhishek, Sangeeta, Dhruv and Tejas who always kept me in high spirits whenever I was in vacant and pensive mood.

My friend Mahamahopadhyay Dr. Onkar Nath Tripathi always encouraged me by his intelligent comments and enriched me by his thought provoking ideas. I shall remain grateful to him forever.

H.N. Misra

Professor R.L. Dwivedi
A Reine Geographer

H.N. Misra

A living encyclopedia and legend of Geography, Prof. R.L. Dwivedi belongs to the genre of Geography which believed in Puritan school of thought and, as appropriately described by one of his students[1], he is one of the reine kind of geographers on account of whom the pure geography survives in India. Amenable to new ideas, he has always been quite alive to the emerging research frontiers in Geography. Born on February 1, 1924 (Magha Krishna 11, Vikram Sambat 1980) in a very remote village called Sariyapur in Kanpur district of Uttar Pradesh, situated far away from any railway line or metalled road, he hails from a very large family of six brothers and three sisters from late Pt. Ayodhya Prasad and late Srimati Ram Shree. With meagre means and resources, life was full of hardships. Early education was a difficult affair in those times. However, Prof. Dwivedi was fortunate to have the patronage and guidance of his elder brother for his higher education. Having graduated from D.A.V. College, Kanpur in 1948 as a meritorious student, he joined the University of Allahabad for Master degree in Geography and passed the M.A. exam in 1st division with 2nd position in 1950.

Those were the days when for outstanding students, teaching was most sought after profession. Soon after the M.A. exam result was declared in June 1950, Dr. Dwivedi was literally called upon by late Kalka Prasad Bhatnagar, the then principal of D.A.V. College, Kanpur to join the permanent post of lecturer of Geography in the college. He joined the Department of Geography, D.A.V. College, Kanpur on July 27, 1950 and taught undergraduate and postgraduate classes. Young Dwivedi's quality as a teacher was rightly recognized by late Prof. R.N. Dubey, the then Head of Geography Department, Allahabad University. He subsequently got him appointed on the post of permanent Lecturer in Geography in July 1955. Those were the days when Allahabad University was known as Oxford of East. Naturally he was applauded by one and all on this achievement. As his career progressed, he was appointed Reader in May 1970 and then Professor in November 1977. In between he took over as the Head of Geography Department in August 1969 after the retirement of Dr. M.N. Khan and occupied the post for 14 years.

Kahlil Gibran, while describing quality of a teacher, remarks that a teacher who is indeed wise does not bid you to enter the house of his wisdom but rather leads you to the threshold of your

[1]Madhulika Mishra, Assistant Professor, Bangalore University in her Dissertation entitled Sustainable Development Planning of A Backward Region: A Case Study of Pratapgarh District, University of Allahabad.

mind. Prof. Dwivedi had all the qualities of a fine teacher. His lectures were looked forward to by the students. His simple solutions and easy explanations to different topics were much awaited.

The fact that he supervised as many as 17 research scholars for the degree of D. Phil., clearly speaks of his keen interest and orientation towards research in Geography. He, in fact, broke the tradition by supervising students in Urban Geography, Climatology, Population and Settlement Geography, Political and Electoral Geography, besides Micro Level Planning (Urban—5, Climatology—1, Population and Settlement—3, Micro Level Planning—2, Political and Electoral—4, Agriculture—2). In spite of the fact that he has been puritan in his approach, he did not hesitate in reaching out the new frontiers of teaching and researches in Geography such as quantitative methods, urban and regional planning, electoral behaviour, and micro level planning. He was a kind of supervisor who would see the thesis line by line and make his valuable comments for further refinement and improvement. In fact he ensured that nothing went unnoticed. A thesis supervised by him was sure to be awarded degree.

He has been a wonderful teacher, administrator and colleague. He maintained harmonious relationship with teachers and staff. Even the younger colleagues did not hesitate in approaching him because he has been very courteous, polite and benevolent. Although at times people got scared due to his frowning attitude but he has been honest to the core and he never allowed anything which was against norms, principles and ethics. He is a wonderful man and likes Sanskrit language of Bhavbhooti "*Nari Keli Fal Sammiti*". He is hard in appearance like a coconut shell but very soft from inside. As soon as Professor Dwivedi took over as the Head of the Department, he succeeded in providing the full strength of the teaching faculty due to his credibility in the university. He was known for taking quick, correct and appropriate decisions both in the academic as well as the administrative affairs of the Department.

Academic Achievements

As Professor Dwivedi's name was very well known in the field of Geography, he was appointed as member on various academic bodies of the U.P. Universities. He was a member of Faculty Board of Arts of Kumaun University and the Academic Council of Rohilkhand University. He was also member of the Executive Council of the Kashi Vidyapith for one term when Dr. Vidya Niwas Mishra, the Famous Hindi Scholar, was its Vice Chancellor.

The University Grants Commission appointed Professor Dwivedi as a Member of Geography Panel in 1997 of which Professor S.C. Gupte, a former Vice Chancellor of Poona University, was its Chairman. There Professor Dwivedi made valuable contribution in the revision of the syllabi of National Education Test, and in providing their Hindi translation.

Yet another valuable contribution of Professor Dwivedi to the advancement of Indian Geography which can never be forgotten is the publication of National Geographer by the Department which started in 1958, when Professor R.N. Dubey was its founder Head. But after the publication of volume five in 1962, National Geographer went out of publication. When Professor Dwivedi became the Head of the Department in August, 1969, he made commendable effort to restart this publication in 1971, which he had edited himself. He has published 27 creative articles and research papers (list enclosed), besides three books. His book on political geography is most sought after by students. Its updated version has come out in 2012.

Married to Gayatri ji, who was very caring and patronizing, Professor Dwivedi has two sons—Vivek and Sudhir. Both are engineers, and very well settled in life. He has already attained the age of 88 years. Let us pray to the Almighty that he has a happy long life of 100 years.

Creative Articles and Research Papers

1. The Discovery of North America, *D.A.V. College Kanpur Magazine*, **25**(1), Dec. 1951.
2. Soil Erosion in Kanpur District, *Daily Telegraph*, Dec. 25, 1953.
3. Bhugol—Ek Vrihad Aur Rochak Vishaya, *Dainik Vishwamitra*, Dec. 28, 1954.
4. Himalaya Ki Uttpatti, *D.A.V. College Kanpur Patrika*, **29**(1), Dec. 1954.
5. The Wandering Confluence, *National Geographer*, **1**, 1958.
6. Geographical Zones of Allahabad, *National Geographer*, 70th Anniversary Souvenir, Dec. 1958.
7. The Antiquity of Allahabad City, *The Allahabad University Magazine*, Nov. 1960.
8. Weather and Climate of Allahabad, *University of Allahabad Studies*, 1960.
9. Colonelganj, Allahabad: A Study in Urban Land Use, *Journal of Geography*, University of Jabalpur, Nov. 1960.
10. Allahabad: A Study in Industrial Development, *National Geographer*, **4**, May 1961.
11. Historical Introduction to the Urban Geography of Allahabad, *University of Allahabad Studies*, 1961.
12. Replanning an Existing City—Allahabad, *National Geographer*, **5**, 1962.
13. Origin and Growth of Allahabad, *Indian Geographical Journal*, Madras, **38**(1), 1963.
14. Delimiting the Umland of Allahabad, *Indian Geographical Journal*, Madras, **39**, Nov. 3–4, 1964.
15. Public Utility Services in Allahabad: A Geographical Analysis, *University of Allahabad Studies*, 1963–64.
16. Demographic Features of Allahabad City, *Geographical Review of India*, Calcutta, **27**(4), Dec. 1965.
17. Critique on the construction of the Conical Projection with Two Standard Parallel, *The Indian Journal of Geography*, Jodhpur, **1**, Jan. 1966.
18. Unrest in South East Asia: Its Geographical Background, *the Allahabad University Magazine*, Jan. 1966.
19. *Uttar Pradesh Ka Bhaugolik Paryavaran*, Gupta Abhinandan Granth, Lucknow, 1966.
20. On Delimiting the Urbanized Region, *Proceedings of the Autumn School in Geography*, Nainital, 1967.
21. Defining the Scope of Political Geography of A State; *Proceedings of International Symposium in Political Geography*, Nagpur, 1968.
22. The Concept of Conurbation: A Review, *The National Geographical Journal of India*, Varanasi, **15**(1), March 1969.
23. The Applied Political Geography as an Applied Geography Field, *National Geographer*, **6**, 1971
24. Uttar Pradesh, *Encyclopaedia Britannica*, Chicago, 1974.

25. Comparative Study of Evolution of Demographic Character of KAVAL towns of U.P., *Professor Anas Memorial Volume*, Geography Department, A.M.U., Aligarh, 1984.
26. The KAVAL Towns of Uttar Pradesh—A Morphological Study, *Concepts and Methods in Geography*, Institute of Geography, Burdwan University, 1984.
27. Geopolitical Stability in India: Some Reflections, *Annals*, NAGI, June 2002.

Books

1. *Manav Bhugol Ka Siddhant*, Kitab Mahal, Allahabad, 1956, Revised as *Manav Bhugol Ki Samiksha*, Kitab Mahal, Allahabad, 1966.
2. *Samajik Adhyayan*—Parts 1–5, Approved by M.P. Government, Tej Kumar Book Depot, Lucknow, 1959.
3. *Fundamentals of Political Geography*, Chaitanya Publishing House, Allahabad, 1990 (6th edition, 2012).

D. Phil. Thesis Supervised

1. O.S. Dwivedi (1966), Farrukhabad-cum-Fatehgarh: A Study in Urban Geography.
2. Sheela Roy (1972), The Changing Occupational Pattern of Population in Uttar Pradesh.
3. R.K. Srivastava (1973), A Geographical Study of Recent Drought Affected Areas of U.P. and Bihar.
4. H.N. Misra (1975), Urban Centres in the Umland of Allahabad: A Study in Urban Geography.
5. Niranjani Mishra (1977), Inter State Boundary Disputes in India: A Study in Political Geography.
6. Manorama Sinha (1979), Electoral Geography of India with Special Reference to Parliamentary Elections, 1971.
7. J.P. Misra (1980), Baghelkhand: A Study in Rural Settlement Geography.
8. R.C. Singh (1980), Land Utilization in Kadipur Tahsil of Sultanpur District.
9. B.N. Mishra (1981), Spatial Patterns of Service Centres in Mirzapur District.
10. Ramendra Babu (1981), Micro-Level Planning: A Case Study of Chhibaramau Tahsil (Farkukhabad District), U.P.
11. R.S. Tripathi (1981), Towns of Bundelkhand, U.P.: A Study in Urban Geography.
12. M.K. Srivastava (1981), Socio-Economic and Demographic Influences in Spatial Structure of Electoral Support to Indian National Congress in Lok Sabha Elections, 1952–77, U.P., India.
13. Krishna Kumar (1983), Rural Settlements in Bundelkhand (U.P.).
14. Raji Gopal (1984), Evolution of Administrative Boundaries of Madhya Pradesh.
15. Bhrigu Nath Pandey (1986), Allahabad: A Study in Planning and Development.
16. Smita Nigam (1992), A Comparative Study of Population Structure of KAVAL Towns in U.P.
17. Madhulika Misra (2009), Sustainable Development Planning of a Backward Region: A Case Study of Pratapgarh District, U.P.

List of Contributors

A.A. Ansari
Professor, Department of Geography,
M.S. University of Vadodara, Baroda.

G.P. Chapman
Visiting Professor,
The Open University (U.K.) and
Emeritus Professor of Geography,
Lancaster University (U.K.).

N. Charthad
Assistant Professor, Geography Department,
Vasantrao Naik Institute of Arts and Social Sciences,
Nagpur.

Arun Chaturvedi
Head, Division of Land Use Planning, Nagpur.

Amna Farooqui
Associate Professor, Geography Department,
Hamidia Girls Degree College, Allahabad.

Zubaida Farooqui
Associate Professor, Geography Department,
Hamidia Girls Degree College, Allahabad.

S. Girgaonkar
Associate Professor, Department of Geography,
LAD College for Women,
Shankar Nagar, Nagpur.

Vishal Gupta
Assistant Professor, Geography Department,
Carlrox Teachers' University, Ahmedabad.

Qutub Jahan
Geography Department,
Hamidia Girls Degree College, Allahabad.

Inder Jeet
Professor, Geography Department,
M.D. University, Rohtak.

Monika Kannan
Assistant Professor, Geography Department,
Sophia Girls College,
Ajmer.

S. Kant
Professor, Department of Geography,
Punjab University, Chandigarh.

Sandeep Kaur
Assistant Professor, Geography Department,
Science College, Jammu.

Ashwani Kumar
Deputy Director, Tourism and Civil Aviation,
Kullu, H.P.

A.K. Maji
Former Director,
National Bureau of Soil Survey & Land Use Planning,
Nagpur.

Ashutosh Mishra
Research Scholar, Department of Geography,
University of Allahabad.

S.P. Mishra
Professor, Department of Geography,
B.H.U., Varanasi.

H.N. Misra
Emeritus Professor, Department of Geography,
University of Allahabad.

Kavita Misra
Research Associate, Department of Geography,
Banaras Hindu University.

R.P. Misra
Formerly Vice Chancellor, University of Allahabad and Professor of Geography,
University of Delhi.

Ali Mohammad
Professor, Department of Geography,
A.M.U., Aligarh.

Mahamaya Laha (Mukharjee)
Assistant Professor, Geography Department,
Netaji Mahavidyalaya, Arambagh, Hoogly.

S.C. Mukhopadhyay
Formerly Professor of Geography,
University of Calcutta, Kolkata.

Damodar Panda
Associate Professor, Geography Department,
Utkal University, Bhubaneshwar.

A.C. Pandey
Scientist, Remote Sensing Division,
Birla Institute of Technology,
Mersa, Ranchi.

D.S. Pandey
Scientist 'D', Central Groundwater Board,
State Unit Office, Lucknow.

Reena Pradhan
Lecturer, Government Girls Inter College,
Allahabad.

Kalyan Rudra
Chairman,
West Bengal Wasteland Development Corporation.

Yasir Saeed
Research Scholar, Geography Department,
Aligarh Muslim University.

Abdul Shaban
Associate Professor of Geography,
Centre for Developmental Studies,
Tata Institute of Social Sciences, Mumbai.

D.D. Sharma
Professor and Chairman,
Geography Department, H.P. University,
Shimla.

H. Sharma
Emeritus Professor,
Department of Political Sciences,
University of Delhi.

S.K. Sharma
Formerly Professor of Geography,
Dr. H.S. Gaur University, Sagar.

G.B. Singh
Formerly Professor, Department of Geography,
University of Jammu.

Mridula Singh
Additional Director,
Land Use Board, Planning Department,
Government of Uttar Pradesh.

B. Thakur
Formerly Vice Chancellor, Mithila University and Professor of Geography,
University of Delhi.

P.S. Tiwari
Formerly Professor of Geography,
Madras University, Chennai.

Archana Tripathi
Sr. Lecturer, Geography Department,
C.M.P. Degree College, Allahabad.

Sunil Kumar Tripathi
Associate Professor, Geography Department,
Allahabad Degree College, Allahabad.

1

Introduction

H.N. Misra

Natural resources constitute the assets, which enable humans to realize their cultural, social, economic and spiritual goals. Ancient Indian civilization, rooted as it was in nature, it has always valued it and used it so judiciously that civilization advanced without destroying natural environment. Such was the relationship between nature and man that it could be called **symbiotic**. There was a deep emphasis on protecting and conserving the environment and natural resources. During the Vedic period, there was a very profound concept of conserving nature and its pristine beauty and wealth for posterity. This is quite explicit from the following **Mantra** of **Shukla Yajurveda**:

"ॐ द्यौः शान्तिरन्तरिक्षं शान्तिः
पृथिवी शान्तिरापः शान्तिरोषधयः शान्तिः।
वनस्पतयः शान्तिर्विश्वेदेवाः शान्तिर्ब्रह्म शान्तिः
सर्वं शान्तिः शान्तिरेव शान्तिः सा मा शान्तिरेधि॥
ॐ शान्तिः शान्तिः शान्तिः॥"

"Let there be peace in the sky, Let there be peace in the space, Let there be peace on the earth, Let there be peace in the water, Let there be peace in plants, Let there be peace in the nature, Let there be peace in all, let there be peace within peace, Giving Me the Peace which grows within Me"

This longing of our seers and sages for all pervading peace is dependent upon and conceivable only when there is sustained peace in the natural environment. This is possible only when there is no destruction, depletion and plundering of nature and natural wealth. The resources have to be need based instead of being greed based. The veneration ***Mata Bhumih Putro Aaham Prithivyah*** (The earth is my mother, I am her son) in Atharwveda not only reasserts the importance of earlier hymn, it also unfolds the concept of sustainable development which is currently in vogue.

Types of Resources

The resources are varied and manifold. In fact resources are not there, they become when they are used. While some of them are ubiquitous or universally available, others are non-ubiquitous and localized in nature; they occur only in a few areas/places. Likewise, there are two sets of resources: **exhaustible** and **inexhaustible**. The exhaustible resources are finite in quantity, which may be depleted if used continuously without managing properly. Such resources are not replaceable. The inexhaustible resources, on the other hand, are those that are not likely to vanish but such resources certainly are very few such as air, solar radiation and geothermal energy. There are some resources which are living and organic in nature such as forests, animals, birds and fish, etc. Even fossil fuels such as coal and petrol are also considered in this category because they have their origin from the decayed organic substances. These are called **biotic** resources. The **abiotic** resources have their origin from non-living and non-organic substances. These, for example, are water, air, ores such as gold, iron, copper, silver, etc. The resources are also classified based on the characteristics of their renewability. The **renewable resources** are those whose rate of replenishment/recovery is faster than the rate of consumption such as sunlight, air and wind, etc. The resources which once depleted have no chance of recovery are known as **non-renewable** from the human use perspective. Some resources can be recycled but some of them cannot. Based on the stage of development, the resources can also be referred to as (a) **potential**, (b) **actual** (c) **reserve** and (d) **stock resources**. The potential resources are those which can be used in future as they exist in a region. The resources which have been surveyed, and their quality and quantity known, are actual resources. The part of actual resources which can be developed in future are called **reserve resources**. The stock resources are known but cannot be used for want of technology, e.g., hydrogen.

Land and Water: The Crisis of Commitment

Nature as a resource for exploitation is primarily a western perspective. The industrial revolution set the stage for an augmented exploitation of natural resources for development and advancement of human society. Since then, so rapid has been the exploitation and plundering of natural wealth that today man stands on the brink of virtually destroying himself. Unless we understand the laws that govern nature and conform our own laws to the natural laws, we will take ourselves closer to a situation in which survival of the world will be impossible. Land and water are the two most basic elements of life support system on our planet. Life is not possible without them. No wonder that all great civilizations flourished in river valleys where these elements were available in abundance; and they declined or perished when these resources were depleted often because of shortsightedness of their end users, the human beings.

The man–environment relationships are precariously balanced because of large scale depletion and plundering of natural resources by man. This situation, thus, calls for sustainable development. Theodore Roosevelt, the former President of United States consistently emphasized that conservation of natural resources is the fundamental problem, unless we solve that problem, it will avail us little to solve all others.

During the last two centuries, the land and water resources of the earth have been put to great strain. They are no longer treated as indispensible for the very survival of humanity, let alone the great civilization that we boast about. Both are considered as resources for exploitation rather than the very foundation for life to exist and evolve further into higher level of consciousness. We appear to be heading towards a natural environment wherein land is no longer able to support life and water is so much scarce and polluted that even trees would wither away.

Of all the species of the earth, man is the chief culprit of this degradation. He looks at land as 'property,' he categorizes it as developed land, developable land, unfit for development, wasteland and so on. And he so uses the water, both surface and underground, that it gets depleted and thoroughly polluted. The deserts are expanding, temperatures are rising, glaciers are melting, rivers are drying and groundwater levels are going down. Potable water is a precious commodity in many places of the world. Water famine is no longer a problem of the future.

"There is enough on this earth for everyone's need but not for everyone's greed", said Mahatma Gandhi. Preserving, protecting and defending the land and water resources have been a sacred **Mantra** of all great civilizations. We are moving away from the age-old tradition of keeping our land and water resources in a healthy state. Man has become so confident of his scientific and technological prowess that he fails to see the limitations of both.

India constitutes 16.2 per cent of the world's population, 18 per cent of the livestock but only 2.5 per cent of land area, 1.0 per cent of forest area and 0.5 per cent of pasture land. According to NRSA, India has 75.5 million hectare of so-called wasteland much of which (58 million hectares) can be brought back to life. We are able to treat only 1 million hectare of this land each year while we make more than 1 million hectare of land inert each year. At the same time our food and water needs both in terms of quantity and quality are increasing incessantly as we 'modernize' ourselves.

Land without water is inert. Water, like land, is very unique gift of nature. The surface and ground water resources of the country play a major role in agriculture, livestock production, electricity generation, and industrialization apart from its use for drinking purposes. Water must be kept clean for drinking; it must be available for irrigation, industrial uses, recreation and navigation. Nothing should be done that would deplete and pollute our water resources.

India's water resources are large but not immense. We get around 4000 km^3 of water as rain or snow. The total average annual flow of Indian rivers is 1953 km^3; total annual replenishable ground water resources amount to 432 km^3. Of this, 690 km^3 of surface water and 390 km^3 ground water are available for our judicious use. But water is not evenly distributed spatially or temporally. And hence the strategies to tap water resources have to vary from place to place.

As we become more 'civilized' (i.e., westernized) we increase our water requirements while at the same time we increasingly waste and pollute it jeopardizing the life of the future generations. And, thus, it is not only the quantity of water that is declining but also its quality. It is estimated that per capita availability of water by 2025 will be 1000 cubic liters which will be reduced to 750 cubic liters by 2050 AD. A country is destined to face the crisis of water if its availability comes down to less than 1000 cubic liters per capita. Unregulated and uncontrolled commercialization of water by private agencies is further likely to accentuate the water crisis.

Natural Resources Management Approaches

There are several approaches of protection and management of resources. The ideas of *Conservation Biology* and *Habitat Conservation* have emerged from protectionists' view point. These call for land management practises that seek to conserve, protect and restore habitat area for wild plants and animals and prevent their extinction, fragmentation or reduction in range. Natural resource management is a complex process and it encompasses both environmental and ecosystem approaches. These approaches include (a) Top–down or command control, (b) Bottom-up or community based, (c) Adaptive or Plan-do-review-act, (d) Precautionary, and (e) Integrated. This is also sometimes referred to as **blue–green technology** or **land–water integrative approach**. The integrated approach is the most comprehensive as it involves all the stake holders and focuses on sustainable development through convergence of sustainable land use, participatory planning, integrated watershed management and adaptive management. The sustainability can be attained only when development is productive as well as environment enriching and friendly. This can be thought of through normative-futuristic planning—a planning which has long term vision of next 25 or 50 years.

Frame of the Volume

The present volume has been prepared keeping in view the importance of natural resources especially land and water in the current context. The papers are arranged into four sub themes. Thus, the volume has four parts. **Part I** presents the conceptual overview of the natural resources. There are five articles in this segment. Chapter 2 presents overall view of land, water and mineral resources by focusing on different dimensions. The paper highlights the impending ecological crisis due to over use of resources and attempts to discuss how human survival and development is greatly dependent on natural resources. It also focuses on the role of science and technology education in preserving and conserving the natural resources so that human survival and development continues unquestioned. Chapter 3 on Population Resources and Development by B. Thakur presents a review of conceptual approaches by examining the complex interrelationship among population trends, resource use, and developmental impacts at global as well as regional levels. It is an effort to relate the importance of natural resources to population and the paper highlights the major theoretical contributions in the field of population and natural resources. It focuses on the Malthusian and Neo-Malthusian, Marxist, Carrying Capacity, Limits to Growth, Global 2000 report and the resourceful earth, the earth summit and eco-feminism. The review of the relationship clearly indicates population and food imbalances, water scarcity, soil erosion, deforestation and plant and animal extinction.

Land is a major resource and there are not many theories which attempt to explain the theoretical background of land use. The paper entitled Revisiting the Classical Land Use Model of Von Thunen (Chapter 4) attempts to examine the applicability of Von Thunen's land use model in present day context especially when the landscapes have completely changed in view of transport facility, irrigation and variety of other services. In Chapter 5, Chapman and Rudra in their paper Water as Foe, Water as friend examine the utility of different approaches to explain disasters; particularly due to flood/water and in the process it attempts to search the most important truth. Highlighting the thesis of Himalayan Environmental Degradation (THED), it proposes the idea that the specific form of development that has taken place in Bengal since the mid 19th century, the standard road–rail and urban–industrial model has been transplanted into an inappropriate geographical setting. The result is that the urban sector has externalized its costs onto rural poor. In this context, it is suggested that the new 'open policy' on floods, also advocated elsewhere in the world, be seriously considered as more appropriate and sustainable for Bengal. Harvir Sharma, in Chapter 6, highlights the importance of managing resources in Indian Ocean besides focusing on its strategic importance in national security. He has enumerated economic resources as well as energy resources and focused the importance of ocean for drugs and pharmaceuticals and communication. The chapter attempts to portray that oceans provide alternative for land resources and unless the mankind is able to harness the bounty of maritime domain carefully and in a controlled fashion, the world population will be starved because resources on land may ultimately exhaust.

Part II, which is devoted to land resources, contains as many as seven chapters. These chapters attempt to explain different dynamics of land resources. S.K. Sharma, in Chapter 7, has presented the concept of natural resources and focused on land resources in Madhya Pradesh by highlighting the pressure of population especially the nutritional density. Arun Chaturvedi and A.K. Maji have tried to focus on land and land use planning in the Indian context in Chapter 8. They have also highlighted the national land use policy. They assert that scientific land use planning bases on soil and land characteristics, directed towards long term ecological and economic security which is need of the hour. Mridula Singh, in Chapter 9, presents national scenario of land resources with a focus on land resource management in Uttar Pradesh. Several recommendations which have been suggested are extension services, soil testing, certified high yielding variety of seed and restoration of degraded land.

The Chapter 10 is devoted to wasteland mapping and management for sustainable development. Waste land is that land which is lying unused or is not being used up to its actual potential due to some constraints. This chapter by Damodar Panda, while mapping different aspects of wasteland in Rushikulya basin of Orissa, attempts to identify different types of wasteland and suggests an urgent need for waste land reclamation. The author has used remote sensing technique for the purposes of mapping. S.P. Mishra and Kavita Mishra in their chapter on Geomorphic Mapping for Land Resources Management in Chapter 11 have selected the Chakia Tehsil of Chandauli District in Uttar Pradesh as an area of case study. They have used remote sensing technique to identify different kinds of geomorphic features. This kind of analysis not only leads to accuracy but it also has great value in sustainable planning of land resources. In Chapter 12, Ashwani Kumar and D.D. Sharma highlight the role of morphometric analysis in watershed management. Different aspects such as relief, slope, stream ordering, stream frequency and bifurcation ratio have been computed for a watershed lying in Lahul and Spiti District of Himachal Pradesh. This analysis is of great value in so far as sustainable land use planning in a cold desert area is concerned. Agriculture occupies the most important space in the spatial organization of the economic activities and Gurubaksh Singh and Sandeep Kumar in Chapter 13 attempt to identify the levels of agricultural development in a hilly terrain of Jammu district in the state of Jammu and Kashmir. The chapter is significant for its methodology being adopted for the ranking of agricultural regions.

The third part of the book (**Part III**) is devoted to discuss the water resources both at meso- and micro-levels. There are eight chapters in this segment. Water is an invaluable renewable resource without which any form of life is inconceivable. The very existence of biosphere is because of water and definitely the rivers play the role of lifeline in human survival and development. From times immemorial rivers have been the bases of human civilization and development. Unfortunately, however, rivers are shrinking in their size and volume on account of the paucity of water. In Chapter 14, H.N. Misra and Ashutosh, attempt to highlight the case of the Yamuna river which has been facing the crisis of non-existence, if not protected in time. The chapter discusses the causes of perils of this perennial river such as decreasing water flow, increasing pollution, deteriorating ecosystem and increasing encroachment of land around the river. The authors have also attempted to suggest the measures such as desilting the bed, arresting pollution, enriching ecosystem, defining territorial limits of river and finally watershed planning.

S.C. Mukhopadhyay, in Chapter 15, has attempted to focus on the water resource management of the Brahmaputra Basin. This chapter presents the hydro-geomorphological characteristics of the Brahmaputra which is the mightiest river in the world and which flows through a series of seismo-tectonic active zones of very complex nature. It highlights the concept of integrated water resource management and age-old water conservation practises also. The chapter discusses the need for effective use of modern methods and techniques combined with active participation of people and greater co-operation of the bordering states and countries for the water resource management of the Brahmaputra basin. The next paper (Chapter 16), is devoted to highlighting the problem of water scarcity in plenty by taking the case of Kashmir Valley. It presents the paradoxical situation, where there is a plenty of water but there is scarcity because adequate water is not being made available for irrigation, hydroelectricity production, drinking purposes and industrial use. It is not being utilized as desired and required and this situation calls for water resource management.

Ground water regime is a dynamic system wherein water is absorbed at the surface of the earth and eventually recycled to reach to the surface through the geological strata. Thus, there are various elements which influence the groundwater regime. In Chapter 17, Surya Kant and A.C. Pandey have attempted to map the hydro-geomorphology of Panchkula district in the state of Haryana for identifying the ground water potential zones by using high resolution satellite data. The ground water quality and its suitability for domestic and irrigation purposes have also been determined. A water resource development plan has also been suggested. The declining ground water level has become a cause of concern especially during summer season which has been very well highlighted by Archana Tripathi and Sunil Tripathi in Chapter 18, taking the case of Allahabad district. They have also pointed out the ground water recharge and discharge and suggested measures for efficient use of ground water. The author has highlighted the importance of mass awareness programs for conserving the water. Surface run-off is the most important source of the loss of rain water and this works as an impediment in rain water harvesting. By taking the case of Haryana, Inderjeet, in Chapter 19, has attempted to estimate the surface run-off. He has employed a simple methodology which can be easily used to measure the run-off. The areas characterized by hilly terrain have greater probability of run-off as compared to the plane areas and this, therefore, needs a considerable thinking as to how to control the run-off. Mahamaya Laha Mukharjee has portrayed the ground water resource situation in Eastern Barddhman (West Bengal) by highlighting the seasonal fluctuations and its agricultural use in promoting crop diversification in Chapter 20.

Part IV, which is the last segment of the volume, has nine chapters, and focuses on natural resource management. In Chapter 21, D.D. Sharma and H.N. Misra have attempted to suggest the management strategies for the sustained development of the land, water and forest. By taking the case of Solan district in Himanchal Pradesh, which presents a hilly terrain, the authors have discussed the state of these three resources and have suggested the management strategies which can go a long way in supporting the man–environment relationship in a vulnerable ecology and sensitive environment. In a mountainous terrain like Arunachal Pradesh, water resource is very much important and this aspect has been taken up by Gupta and Ansari in Chapter 22. Water resource management through hydel power projects could be the best solution in such terrains. The next couple of chapters are devoted to the problem of water supply in cities. In Chapter 23, the authors have attempted to suggest that peoples' perception needs to be taken into account to take care of sustainable water supply in the city of Nagpur. Yet another case study (Chapter 24) is based on the state of water availability and water supply in the city of Allahabad. This suggests the construction of collector wells besides rain water harvesting and educating people to change their attitudes towards this valuable resource. The integrated village development by combining water, environment and livelihood is the theme of discussion in Chapter 25. It highlights the role of NGO in transforming the village economy and points out the importance of Gandhian and Schumacherian models of development in rural transformation.

P.S. Tiwari, in Chapter 26, has highlighted several strategies such as change in cropping pattern, promotion of drip irrigation, reforms in pricing of water, comprehensive land care policy and watershed management and conjunctive use of water, strong organizational structure and national water grid to alleviate the problems of drought. The chapter focuses on the important role geographers can play in drought management. Monika Kannan tries to emphasize the role of remote sensing over conventional methods in mitigation of droughts in Chapter 27. In Chapter 28, Zubaida and others, present the ground water situation in Uttar Pradesh and highlight the ways and means of water resource conservation through rain water harvesting.

Realizing the need to conserve and better use and manage our land and water resources, geographers have laid great emphasis on watershed planning and development. This is rightly so because land and water, the two basic resources, have best interaction in a watershed and watersheds provide most homogenous environment for sustainable development planning. The Chapter 29 by H.N. Misra and Ashutosh present the watershed development model and pleads for its application for the development of Bihar which happens to be one of the most backward states of the country. Bihar has 19 river basins; each one of them may be treated a watershed for its comprehensive development as envisaged in watershed development model. This model could be easily replicated elsewhere in similar such situations to promote sustainable development by protecting land and water.

PART I

Conceptual Background
An Overview

2

Natural Resources and Development
Focus on Land, Water and Minerals

R.P. Misra and H.N. Misra

Abstract: The world is passing through a stage of impending ecological crisis mainly due to pressure of increasing population on natural endowments. The chapter highlights the problems related to the use of land, water and mineral resources and explores the possibilities of improving and reorienting science and technology education so that we from the very childhood are enabled to understand the symbiotic relationship between nature and man, and participate in the reconstruction of a new social and technological order more conducive to human survival and development.

Keywords: Ecosystem, Ecological Crisis, Land Resources, Operational Holding, Urban Land, Land Use Planning, World Water Balance, Ghost Towns, Oceanic Minerals, Economic Vulnerability, Universal Legislation, Science and Technology Education, Target Group

Introduction

We are passing through a stage of impending ecological crisis in the world. The crisis is the consequences of a number of factors and forces. Important among them are:

1. Our understanding of the nature and our attitude towards it;
2. Pressure of human population on natural endowments;
3. Mal-development of the international ecology leading to over-industrialization in some regions and no or under-industrialization elsewhere; and
4. Technological and scientific advances giving immense power in the hands of man to destroy things of lasting value.

Incalculable harm has already been done to our natural wealth. Agricultural land of lasting value has been brought under other uses; water is getting polluted, mineral wealth has been lost for ever, plant and animal species are dying. We are jeoparadizing our health and the survival of generations yet to come. We rarely realize that land is a finite resource and hence must be used judiciously. Our water resources are drying up fast and the technology to desalinate sea water at reasonable cost is not in sight. The rate at which mineral resources are being used by the industrialized countries will leave the rest of the world in the lurch in not too distant a future.

Our concept of nature has changed for the worse. We use the term 'exploitation' for the use of natural resources. We want mastery over nature as if we are outside the nature system. The ecosystem, of which we are a part, is too delicate to tamper with. It is not the fear of exhaustion that bothers us for we know that our technological ingenuities will help us develop alternatives and increase productivity in the farms and factory. What bothers is the serious implications of the current approach to the use of our natural wealth for the quality of the human life. Our task is now to prepare ourself for a new approach to interaction with the nature so that we can use our natural wealth without creating a situation in which it will stand exhausted because of over use or misuse.

Medicines do not make man healthy; technology does not make him happy. Outside the nature system man is 'dead'. Nothing should be done to destroy any element of natural system without giving full thought to its short as well as long term implications for human welfare.

The world population has been increasing at a very rapid rate during the present century. It stands at over 7 billion today and would reach 9.2 billion by 2050 AD (Figure 2.1). It so happens that much of the increase in population is in the part of the world which is economically poor and technologically backward (Tables 2.1 and 2.2). Because of these two reasons, the demand for natural resources in the third world countries has not increased at the rate at which the population increased. But this was more than balanced by the increased demand for natural resources in the industrially advanced countries of the world. The result is that the output of natural wealth has gone up in the developing countries and its use has increased in the developed countries.

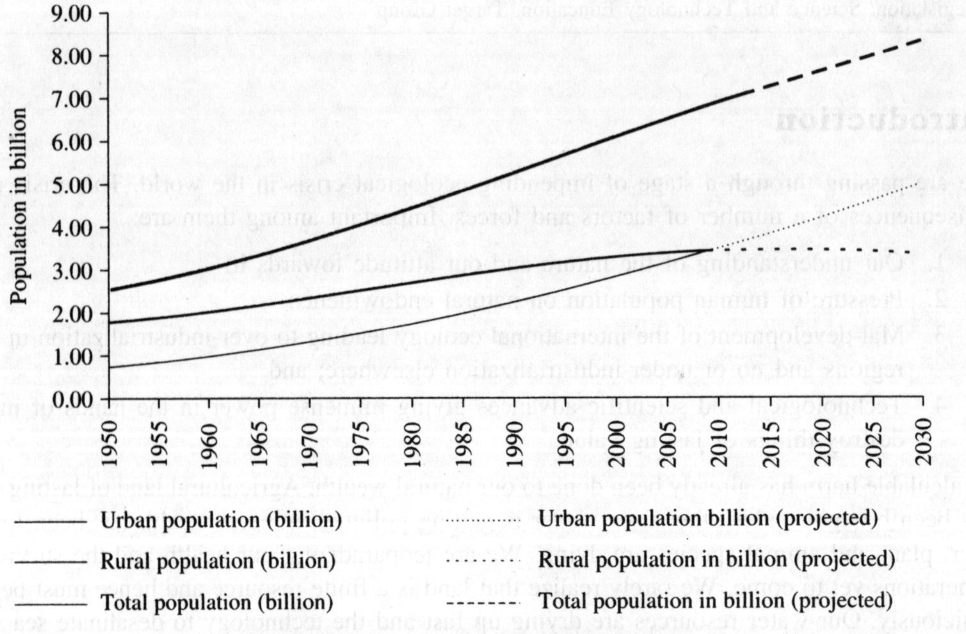

Figure 2.1 World population growth trend.

Table 2.1 Area and population of a few selected countries

Region	*Area* (1000 km²)	*Population* (million)			
		1982	1992	2002	2011
World	135,830.00	4586.00	5478.01	6276.72	6974.04
India	3,287.59	711.66	910.07	1,088.69	1173.97
Australia	7686.85	15.17	17.50	19.65	21.07
Bangladesh	144.00	92.62	110.23	134.27	143.96
Brazil	8511.97	126.81	154.58	179.29	189.80
Burma (Myanmar)	678.50	37.07	40.43	45.61	46.92
Canada	9984.67	24.63	28.52	31.36	32.93
China	9596.96	1020.67	1,164.97	1280.40	1317.89
Egypt	1001.45	44.67	59.01	70.17	76.94
France	547.03	54.22	58.81	61.80	64.01
Germany	357.02	61.64	80.62	82.49	82.27
Iran	1648.00	40.24	57.07	67.21	71.44
Israel	20.77	4.02	5.12	6.57	7.18
Italy	301.23	56.59	56.80	57.16	59.28
Japan	364.50	118.45	124.23	127.45	127.77
Kenya	582.65	17.86	25.04	32.93	37.49
North Korea	120.54	17.80	20.80	23.26	24.01
South Korea	98.48	39.33	43.66	47.62	48.60
Pakistan	803.94	87.13	118.01	150.41	164.45
Philippines	300.00	50.74	64.66	80.63	88.65
Singapore	0.69	2.47	3.23	4.18	4.59
Sri Lanka	65.61	15.19	17.43	18.92	20.04
Sweden	449.96	8.33	8.67	8.92	9.15
Thailand	514.00	48.49	58.23	64.64	67.80
United Kingdom	244.82	55.78	57.58	59.33	60.99
U.S.A.	9826.63	232.06	256.51	287.63	301.23
Russia (Formerly U.S.S.R.)	22,402.02	269.99	148.69	145.30	142.10

Source: World Bank Data 2010 and CIA Fact Book 2010.

Table 2.2 Population growth rate of a few selected countries

Region	*Annual population growth rate (%)*			
	1992	2002	2005	2010
World	1.53	1.22	1.19	1.13
India	1.86	1.55	1.37	1.40
Australia	1.22	1.17	1.18	1.60
Bangladesh	2.29	1.93	1.86	1.10
Brazil	1.57	1.42	1.35	0.90
Burma (Myanmar)	1.82	1.20	1.03	0.80
Canada	1.23	0.90	0.96	1.20
China	1.23	0.67	0.64	0.50

(*Contd.*)

Table 2.2 Population growth rate of a few selected countries (*Contd.*)

Region	*Annual population growth rate (%)*			
	1992	2002	2005	2010
Egypt	1.93	1.92	1.90	1.70
France	0.46	0.68	0.58	0.50
Germany	0.76	0.21	–0.06	–0.20
Iran	1.61	1.56	1.39	1.10
Israel	3.46	2.03	1.77	1.80
Italy	0.07	0.31	0.74	0.5
Japan	0.25	0.23	0.01	–0.10
Kenya	3.14	2.13	2.33	2.60
North Korea	1.26	0.62	0.46	0.40
South Korea	0.91	0.55	0.44	0.30
Pakistan	2.51	2.41	2.41	1.81
Philippines	2.29	1.88	1.75	1.72
Singapore	3.02	0.97	2.39	1.80
Sri Lanka	0.92	1.46	0.84	0.90
Sweden	0.59	0.34	0.36	0.90
Thailand	1.37	0.91	0.84	0.60
United Kingdom	0.28	–0.33	0.66	0.71
U.S.A.	1.39	1.06	0.96	0.81
Russia (Formerly U.S.S.R.)	–	–0.45	–0.51	–0.10

Source: World Bank Data 2010 and CIA Fact Book 2010.

According to Paul Ehrlich, a biologist, if the present population continues to increase at this rate, by 3000 AD every square metre of the earth's surface (land, sea and ice included) will be occupied by 2000 people (Haggett, 1975). We know that such a situation will not arise but we also know that rising living standards, high aspirations and expectations, improved technology, and rapid industrialization have increased the per capita demand for natural resources beyond the capacity of the ecosystem to maintain its balance. "The amount of most metals and ores used since 1930 is in excess of the combined amount used in all previous centuries" (Haggett, 1975).

Landsberg et al. (1964) estimate that the world will require three-fold increase in aggregate food and lumber output and five-fold increase in energy and iron alloys by 2001 AD. Similarly, the ratio between supply and demand for water is likely to drop from 8.3 in 1960 to 3.8 in the year 2000 (Keller, 1984). According to Central Water Commission and Central Water Resource Ministry, Government of India, the per capita annual availability of water is likely to be 1000 cubic litres by 2015 AD, but this will come down to 750 cubic litres by 2050 AD. Apparently, this will set the stage of water crisis.

The proportion of land area under cultivation is very small in some countries and this may encourage one to suggest further expansion of the cultivated land to meet the requirements for food. The suggestion based on the ample quantity of land waiting for reclamation may be highly misleading. The qualitative aspects of land should be given due importance along with the available quantity of land. In some cases the land use might have attained a stage of maturity and it might not be feasible to make much changes. The African countries, however, have great potential for extension of agricultural land in future provided that irrigation water becomes available.

The available land for cultivation is being consumed by other economic sectors at an enormous rate with direct and indirect impact on food supply and environment. "Worldwide more than hundred square kilometers of arable and virgin land are consumed for housing, industrial buildings and transport routes everyday" (Stein, 1984). We should think seriously about repairing the damage being done to environment.

Why are we failing? Why have we not been able to make a dent in the evergrowing problem of destruction and misuse of our natural wealth? Why do we not realize in operational terms the need to build a social order which will put science and technology to uses which enrich human life and put man in harmony with nature? The intension is not to go back to the 'good old days', but to use the potentials of science and technology to lighten the pressure of man on nature and thus save it from destruction.

The purpose of this chapter is to highlight the problems related to the use of land, water and mineral resources and to explore the possibilities of improving and reorienting science and technology education so that we, from the very early childhood are enabled to understand the symbiotic relationship between nature and man, and to participate in the reconstruction of a new social and technological order more conducive to the maintenance of the above relationship.

Land Resources

Since times immemorial land has played an important role in shaping the life of man. Early civilizations were essentially riverine. Even today, we depend on land for much of the food, fibers and shelter; land is non-renewable resource; it is finite in area (land including rivers and marshes cover 25.42 per cent of the earth's surface, oceans cover 71 per cent and polar ice and mountain glaciers cover 3.18 per cent. The share of continental lakes is 0.40 per cent). There is some scope for expanding the land area by filling up lakes, sea inlets and low lying coastal regions. Cases of Holland, Hongkong, Japan and Singapore may be cited as examples. The net gain from the global or continental perspectives is, however, marginal (Graves, 1985).

The global land use data (Ayres, 1964) reveal that the agricultural land, which is responsible for nearly 71 per cent of the total edible products, is only 2 per cent of the total area of the globe. Forests cover 8.6 per cent of the area, and contribute 10.4 per cent edible product per annum; grasslands cover 7.2 per cent of land and produce 15.3 per cent of edible product. Other lands including wetlands and swamps, tundra, hot deserts and cold deserts, extend over 10.4 per cent of the area and make only a marginal contribution to food. The remaining parts of the globe are covered by oceans and lakes (Haggett, 1975).

The optimum production potentialities of known resources are yet to be reached and vast tracts of land in various parts of the world are yet to be explored scientifically. But we do not know whether we can use these lands without inviting global ecological disaster. The nature does not recognize national boundaries and nations unfortunately have failed to recognize nature's unity.

It is this 2 per cent of the land already under agriculture which needs immediate attention for even this is being depleted at enormously rapid rate; soil erosion alone takes away thousands of hectares of land per annum. Add to this the land being diverted to non-agricultural uses.

Desertification and salinization of irrigated land mainly resulting from unscientific cultivation is too well known to be described here.

The problem of land is more acute in the developing countries where agriculture constitutes the main source of livelihood. Table 2.3 shows the dependence of economically active population in agriculture in the selected countries of the world. The dependence of economically active population on agriculture is phenomenally high in case of Bangladesh (59 per cent), India (51 per cent), China (40 per cent), Pakistan (45 per cent), Myanmar (57 per cent), and Sri Lanka (33 per cent). In African countries the dependence on land is much higher. In Kenya, Tanzania and Uganda more than 80 per cent of the population is dependent on land while in Burundi and Rwanda this is over 90 per cent (O'Conner, 1985).

While in North America the average annual agricultural output per person is 2.5 tons, it is less than 0.25 tons in Asia and 0.125 tons in Africa. This low productivity of land may be attributed to several factors such as lack of irrigation, poor technology and complex land tenure system, etc. The per capita arable land in developing countries is much less as compared to developed countries whereas opposite is true in case of economically active population engaged in agriculture. The data given in Table 2.3 indicates the very limited use of modern technology of crop production in these countries. The use of fertilizer is very small indeed.

Table 2.3 Man–land relationship in selected countries

Country	*Economically active population engaged in agriculture* (%)			*Per capita arable land* (hectare)		
	1991	2001	2009	1991	2001	2009
India	61.9	60.0	51.0	0.19	0.15	0.13
Australia	6.0	5.0	3.0	2.64	2.57	2.15
Bangladesh	66.0	62.0	59.07	0.08	0.06	0.05
Brazil	23.0	20.9	17	0.34	0.33	0.32
Burma (Myanmar)	70.0	62.8	56.9	0.23	0.21	0.23
Canada	4.0	3.0	2.4	1.62	1.48	1.34
China	60.0	50.0	40.0	0.09	0.08	0.08
Egypt	31.0	29.0	32	0.04	0.04	0.04
France	5.0	4.0	3.0	0.32	0.31	0.28
Germany	4.0	3.0	2.0	0.14	0.14	0.15
Iran	39.1	35.2	21.2	0.30	0.23	0.24
Israel	4.0	2.0	2.0	0.07	0.05	0.04
Italy	8.0	5.0	4.0	0.16	0.15	0.11
Japan	7.0	5.0	4.0	0.04	0.03	0.03
North Korea	29.7	22.2	18.6	0.12	0.12	0.11
South Korea	16.0	10.0	8.0	0.04	0.04	0.03
Mexico	27.0	18.0	13.0	0.28	0.25	0.22
Pakistan	47.0	48.0	45.0	0.19	0.15	0.12
Philippines	45	37.0	35.0	0.09	0.07	0.06
Sri Lanka	41.0	37.0	33.0	0.05	0.48	0.06
United Kingdom	2.0	1.0	1.0	0.11	0.09	0.10
U.S.A.	3.0	2.0	2.0	0.73	0.61	0.53
Russia	14.0	12.0	10.0	0.91	0.85	0.86

Source: World Bank Data 2010, CIA Fact Book, 2010.

So far, we have examined only the physical availability of land. What is physically available is, however, not necessarily, socially accessible. Land tenure is a social institution which mediates between man and nature. Who gets what, where, how much and when depends on the land tenure system of a country. Most cultivators consider land as property and, hence, it has been used as wealth to be owned by the privileged few. It does not necessarily belong to those who tilled it. As a result the land distribution among different sections of population in many countries is much skewed. While a few hold large chunks of land, millions of those who actually till the land own only a small or no holding at all. In countries such as India, Bangladesh and Pakistan the splitting up of land into small and uneconomic size of holdings is the result of laws of inheritance insensitive to changing man land relationship (Hodder, 1979).

The recent land reform measures undertaken by various governments to give land to the tiller are noteworthy but their total impact on the overall situation has been marginal. For example, in India Rural and Urban Ceiling Act, 1976 and the U.P. Zamindari Abolition Act, 1950 as also the U.P. Land Consolidation Act, 1952 were enacted to reduce the fragmentation and skewed distribution of land. But ownership pattern continues to be heavily skewed (Tables 2.4 and 2.5). The nature of medium and large holdings has been declining slowly and marginal holdings are at increase both in terms of number and area.

Table 2.4 Distribution of operational holdings and operated area in India

Size	*Number of Holdings* (%)				*Operated Area in Hectare* (%)			
	1980–81	1990–91	2000–01	2010–11	1980–81	1990–91	2000–01	2010–11
Marginal (Below 1.0)	56.39	59.44	62.87	67.04	12.05	15.04	18.70	22.24
Small (1.0–2.0)	18.08	18.84	18.92	17.93	14.15	17.42	20.16	22.07
Semi-medium (2.0–4.0)	14.01	13.06	11.69	10.04	21.15	23.19	23.96	23.59
Medium (4.0–10.0)	9.08	7.11	5.48	4.25	29.64	27.04	23.97	21.177
Large (10 and above)	2.44	1.55	1.02	0.72	23.02	17.32	13.22	10.92

Source: Agriculture Census 2010–11, Agriculture Census Division, Department of Agriculture and Cooperation, Ministry of Agriculture, Government of India, 12.

Table 2.5 Operational holdings in India, 2011

Size	*Number of holdings* (million)	*Operated area* (million hectare)	*Average area per holding*
Marginal (Below 1.0)	92.356	35.41	0.38
Small (1.0–2.0)	24.705	35.136	1.42
Semi-medium (2.0–4.0)	13.84	37.547	2.71
Medium (4.0–10.0)	5.856	33.709	5.76
Large (10 and above)	1	17.379	17.37

Source: Agriculture Census 2010–11, Agriculture Census Division, Department of Agriculture and Cooperation, Ministry of Agriculture, Government of India, 12.

Nearly 67.04 per cent of the holdings which spread over 22.24 per cent of the total are marginal holdings. The size of such holdings is below 1.0 hectares. Large holdings which vary between 10 hectares and above are only 0.72 per cent and cover nearly 10.92 per cent of the total cultivated land. The average area per holding in case of marginal group is 0.38, whereas in case of large holdings it is 17.37. In countries like Brazil, the multinational corporations and land speculators are buying tracts of land throwing away those small holders who cleared the land and cultivated for years. Even in high densely populated countries like India and Bangladesh landlessness is on the increase.

Urban Land

The problem of urban land is not less acute. True, it occupies only a small chunk of the earth's land, it is most valuable and has been expanding at a rapid rate encroaching the nearly agricultural lands. Urban land is most contested as well as congested land and provides examples of intense land use competition (O'Conner, 1985). The problem of urban housing in the third world cities needs no special emphasis. The mushroom growth of popular and squatter settlements is an indication of the failure of our social system to use land for the benefit of the poor. The complicated land tenure system, illegal sub-division and outmoded building codes and norms are the means by which the poor are kept outside of the land market. A study of popular settlements of Allahabad city (India) (Misra, 1988), reveals that city's complex land tenure system has encouraged the growth of illegal self-built housing units on government and other vacant lands as also on unclaimed land with disputed titles. Many of these settlements are located in marshy, swampy or low lying areas.

Land Use Planning

This brings us to the question of land use planning. This exercise has to be done in its total context (i.e., relief, soil, vegetation, climate, population, food, housing, clothing, energy and environment). Mechanization of agriculture in many developing countries has failed to meet the agricultural goal of maximum production. Yakuba observes that physically the land has been degraded (in Ghana) by uneducated use of technology on it. Soil erosion has escalated and the soil continues to be infertile year after year (Yakuba, 1985).

Land use planning should aim:

1. Making each piece of land for specific uses keeping in view the ecology and economic imperatives;
2. Indicating the potentialities of each piece of land given different levels of technological inputs;
3. Preserving and improving the fertility of land by appropriate conservation and management tools;
4. Advising governmental agencies of land reform including consolidation of holdings; and
5. Suggesting appropriate control over urban land use to stop speculation and to make urban land available to poor especially.

Water Resources

Water (H_2O) is vital for human life and is present as a major constituent in the cells of all animals and vegetative tissues and in the crystals of many minerals (Enclylopaedia Britannica of Social Sciences, 403). It is used for a variety of purposes: domestic, agricultural, industrial, transport, recreation, etc. Its social and economic importance cannot be over emphasized. It has political significance too because on many occasions water disputes between nations or between states within a nation have been the cause of continuing conflict.

World Water Resources

As a universal solvent the global water is found in liquid, gaseous and solid forms. Its purity or impurity depends upon the sources from which it is obtained and what is added to it subsequently. Snow is the purest natural source of water followed by rain water. Mountainous lakes, streams and wells are relatively free from organic impurities but contain some inorganic salts. Table 2.6 presents a detailed break down of the distribution of world water resources on earth. The earth's total volume of water is assessed about 1386 billions km^3 which will be

Table 2.6 The world's water resources

Zone of the resources			*Catchment area* (km^2)	*Volume of water* (km^3)	*Depth of stratum*	*Percentage of world's water resource related to*	
						Total resources	*Fresh water resources*
World's Ocean			361300000	1338000000	3700.0	96.5000	–
Land			148800000	47971710	322.0	3.5	–
1	Groundwater (gravitation and capillary water)		134800000	23400000*	174.0	1.7	–
	(a)	Fresh water	134800000	10530000	78.0	0.76	30.1
	(b)	Soil moisture	82000000	16500	0.2	0.001	0.05
2	Polar ice glaciers snow		16232500	24064100	1.483	1.74	68.7
	(a)	Antarctic	13980000	21600000	1545.0	1.56	61.7
	(b)	Greenland	1802400	2340000	1298.0	0.17	6.68
	(c)	Arctic islands	226100	83500	369.0	0.006	0.24
Mountains			224000	40600	181.0	0.003	0.12
Ice in permafrost			21000000	300000	14.0	0.022	0.86
Fresh water lakes			1236400	91000	73.6	0.022	0.86
Salt water lakes			822300	85400	103.8	0.006	–
Marshland			2682600	11470	4.28	0.0008	0.03
Water courses			148800000	2120	0.014	0.0002	0.006
Biological water			510000000	1120	0.002	0.0001	0.003
Water in the atmosphere			510100000	12900	0.025	0.001	0.04

Source: Applied Geography and Development, Institute for Scientific Cooperation, **24**, (1984).

sufficient to enclose the globe in a layer of 2718 m deep (Keller, 1984). Oceans constitute nearly 96.5 per cent (1338 billion km^3) of the total world water resources. The share of land water is 3.5 per cent (47,971,710 km^3) only. Yet another estimate (Strahler et al., 1977) suggests that the oceans share 97.2 per cent of the total global water storage and the remaining 2.8 per cent is shared by land which includes ice sheets and glaciers (2.15 per cent), ground water (0.62 per cent) and stream channels, fresh water lakes and other lakes, soil water and atmospheric water combined (0.03 per cent).

The water of land consists of:

1. Surface water: water flowing or ponded on the land.
2. Sub-surface water: water occupying openings in the soil or rocks.
3. Soil water: water retained by soil as soil moisture.
4. Ground water: water found in the bed rock.

The proportion of fresh water which is of greater consequences to human beings is 2.53 per cent (35 million km^3) only or 73 per cent of the total land water. The major proportion of the fresh water is found in frozen form and is under ground. The fresh water in its liquid form on the earth's surface constitutes only a small proportion (0.3 per cent of the world's resources and 0.0008 per cent of the global water). The lakes, marshes, river water and biological water (Keller, 1984) which are most frequently used by man represent only very small proportion of the earth's water resource. The quantity of water vapor in atmosphere which is responsible for all fresh water on land is also very small, that is 12900 km^3 or 0.001 per cent of the world's water resource. This inequitable distribution and limits imposed by nature have certainly great implications for future planning and development of world's water resources.

The notion that fresh water supply on the earth is unlimited is not based on facts. Water supply in areas of habitation is too precariously balanced to be misused. Much of fresh water is far away from human settlement. Even if technological knowhow permits us to use this frozen water, we may not utilize it for ecological reasons. We have to be contained with land water alone for years to come.

Hydrological Cycle and World Water Balance

Unlike land and minerals, water can be recycled and is renewable. It is true that the usable water available is only small fraction of total world's water, it gets renewed by global hydrological cycle. Water on the surface of the earth evaporates under the influence of solar heat and this returns back to the earth in the form of fresh water precipitation. "A particular molecule of water might, if we could trace it continuously, travel through any one of a number of possible circuits involving alternatively the water vapor state and the liquid or solid state" (Strahler et al., 1977).

This complex hydrological cycle tries to maintain the global water balance which may be explained by the formula:

$$P = E + R$$

where

P = precipitation
E = evaporation and
R = run-off.

According to one of the estimates (Strahler, et al., 1977) the evaporation from ocean and continents are 10900 cu mi. and 15000 cu mi. respectively. In turn, land surface receives 26000 cu mi. that is 11000 cu mi. more than what it lost through evaporation (Strahler, et al., 1977). This excess water is a surface run-off which reaches the sea. Thus, the continental water balance is 26000 = 15000 + 11000 cu mi.

Future Demands for Water

The water balance of world's land areas is expected to change (Table 2.7) in future due to various ecological changes resulting from indiscriminate use of land by man for agriculture, industry and settlement, etc. Table 2.8 compares the present and future demands upon the world's water resources.

Table 2.7 Estimated changes in the water balance of the world's land areas (km^3)

Elements of balance	*Balance*	
	1970	2000
Precipitation on land	110,000	110,300
Run-off from land (Total Run-off) excl. ice run-off form polar glaciers	38,800	37,500
Basic run-off (Stable Run-off) **Of which**	14,000	22,500
1. Ground water run-off	12,000	17,000
2. Controlled discharge from lakes and reservoirs	2,000	5,500
Surface run-off (Direct run-off from land surface, e.g., flood waves)	26,800	20,500
Total moisture stores on the land surface including superficial soil moisture	83,500	89,800
Total evaporation (evaporation + transpiration = evapotranspiration)	71,500	72,800

Source: Applied Geography and Development, Institute for Scientific Cooperation, **24**(1984), 8.

Table 2.8 Present and future demands upon the world's water resources (km^3)

Type of use	*Water extracted* (WE)		*Water consumed* (WC)	
	1970	2000	1970	2000
Water supply (settlements, industry, thermal power stations, livestock production)	600	1500	130	1050*
Agricultural irrigation	2800	3950	2100	4000**
Rain-fed irrigation (i.e., non-irrigated)	500	1200	500	1200
Hydropower and navigation	170	500	160	500
Fishing	65	175	15	85

*Excluding 450 km^3 of Sewage used for Irrigation.

**Including 450 km^3 of Sewage used.

Source: Applied Geography and Development, Institute for Scientific Cooperation, **24**(1984), 8.

It is abundantly clear that irrigation is the major consumer of water. But its unscientific use may prove to be detrimental as it may increase evaporation, salinization of soil and water logging.

Human settlements especially urban agglomerations and industries are the next important consumers of water. The demand for water by these two sectors is increasing due to rapid urbanization and industrialization. Two sets of problems have already cropped up: while the large scale use of water by industries and consequent discharge of affluent in the lakes and rivers is creating the problems of water pollution, the shortage of protected water supply in human settlements is responsible for diseases like jaundice, diarrhoea, dysentery, cholera, typhoid and worm infestations, etc. These diseases are the major killers of children in the third world countries. A study conducted recently in a community of 492 people in the city of Allahabad (India) reported more than 50 per cent of people suffering from worm infestations. The incidence was more that is about 55 per cent in the case of children below 14 years of age (Misra, 1990). The situation is no way better in the case of villages. Many villages do not have potable water supply in the dry season. Most of the rivers and lakes of the worlds are polluted. Efforts are afoot in many countries to clean these water bodies by treating the industrial effluents at the source. The creation of Ganga Valley Authority by the Government of India is a laudable effort in this direction.

Drying of the underground resources because of excessive use is another problem which has emerged in many parts of the world. The replenishment of underground water takes place at a rate determined by the rock structure, amount and periodicity of rainfall in the catchment area, etc. Modern bore wells can draw water with much faster speed than the natural replenishment. This leads to the lowering of the water table and in due course drying up of the source.

Water Resource Planning

The problems mentioned above call for a very judicious use of water resources of the world. Land and water are inextricably linked with each other. Land use planning, therefore, implies water resource planning. Land use should be such that it obstructs run-off allowing the water to percolate in the soil to recharge the underground and sub-surface water. We must give up the age old method of irrigation by flooding. It amounts to not only a callous misuse of water but also the destruction of the soil caused by salinity. We have to be frugal in the use of water to avoid water famine in the years to come. Many African countries are already in the grip of water scarcity. The day is not far off when the whole human civilization is threatened by water famine.

Appropriate steps are necessary to maintain the ecological nexus between land, water, minerals and trees. Soil conservation efforts should be speeded up all over the world. Barrages and storage reservoir should be built in drought prone areas. Only 5 per cent of the total world's water power potential is being used (Rao, 1975) at present. Wherever the ecological principles do not militate against the construction of dams, etc., this potential should be harnessed speedily. This will also minimize soil erosion and transportation of the silt to the sea. The two case studies, one by P.E. Spargo (1985) on the Orange River project and the other by E.G. Vedanayagam (1985) on Periyar–Vaigai project speak well of the benefits accruing from such projects. All these activities should, however, form part of grand design to harness the natural resources for the benefit of man.

Mineral Resources

Minerals like land and water are invaluable treasures of the earth. Without them, we cannot think about industrialization and hence the development of our economy. In many countries, they are the main source of the national income. Important among these are Nigeria, Brunei, Ghana, Mauritania, Zambia, Liberia and Venezuela. The most important characteristics of minerals which have bearings on our present and future well being is that they are practically lost once used. They are non-renewable resources. The mineral wealth being finite in nature, once depleted it cannot be replaced. Need to conserve these resources and to recycle them if possible cannot be overemphasized.

Among the many causes of the fall of the Roman Empire the depletion of the mineral deposit and erosion of soil is said to be one. Even during the recent past several mining towns turned into 'ghost towns' in many parts of the developed world. The Canadian Township of Elliot Lake which turned out to be "the first nuclear age ghost town" is the most recent example of this process. Built at an enormous cost in response to the discovery of uranium in mid fifties, its population declined from 25,000 in 1958 to 5000 in 1961 as soon as an alternative source was found by the U.S.A. (Knowles and Wareing, 1976).

Apart from the problem of depletion, mineral extraction has led to serious environmental damages. Mountainous areas which contain much of lime stone, coal, iron ore, etc., have been subjected to immense vandalism by man. Deforestation, landslides and floods have increased beyond the capacity of the ecosystem to control. Lack of appropriate conservation devices has made coal producing areas inhospitable.

Minerals should, therefore, be extracted only after a careful ecologically sound land use planning. Such a plan should include continuing prosperity of the area. The occurrence of minerals is a result of long term geological processes. It is associated with the formation of the earth's crust which is a composite form of minerals. When mineral matter is sufficiently concentrated, it is known as 'ore', unless adequately concentrated it does not warrant commercial exploitation. The mode of occurrence determines the relative cost of extraction.

Minerals Production and World's Reserves

The data pertaining to production, distribution and reserves of mineral wealth are still undependable. Tables 2.9 and 2.10 show the production and reserve situation of some minerals in the world. We note from Tables 2.9 and 2.10 that:

1. The total volume of workable mineral deposits is an insignificant fraction of 1 per cent of the earth's crust and once consumed there will not be a second crop (Lovering, 1969).

2. The production of all minerals has increased which is in consonance with the increasing demand for raw materials. It has been observed that despite recycling, the primary production of most of the raw materials has increased since 1950's (Schippers, 1982).
3. The production of developing countries has increased.
4. The life of world reserves has improved considerably in case of all minerals listed in the Tables 2.9 and 2.10 except that of manganese, tin, chromium and nickel, because of new explorations.
5. The percentage increased in proven reserves has been greater in developing countries. This implies that developing nations will assume greater importance in mineral output in future. This is also implied that mining activities will expand in those areas where infrastructural facilities are presently poor. This is bound to make mining expensive and this situation calls for public policy for adequate investment in the infrastructure of developing nations (Schippers, 1982).
6. The rate of extraction of all minerals has been far too high during eight years (2000–2008) as compared to 108 years during 1900–2008 (Table 2.10). This rate of extraction has only accentuated the processes of environmental damage.

Table 2.9 World's mining production of some mineral raw materials (in 10^6 tonnes) and their distribution (in per cent) between developed countries, transition countries, developing countries and least developed countries

Mineral	*World total production* (in 10^6 tonnes)			*Developed countries*		*Transition countries*		*Developing countries*		*Least developed countries*	
	2005	2009	*Change (%)* (2005–2009)	2005	2009	2005	2009	2005	2009	2005	2009
Copper	14.95	15.62	4.45	1.28	1.23	3.37	3.33	9.70	10.0	0.60	1.06
Lead	3.33	3.84	15.63	0.09	0.16	1.48	1.22	1.75	2.46	0.00	0.00
Zinc	10.13	11.33	11.85	0.58	0.69	3.66	3.43	5.88	7.19	0.009	0.02
Tin	0.30	0.28	–5.66	0.003	0.001	0.003	0.006	0.28	0.26	0.008	0.01
Iron	822.83	1125.47	36.78	106.29	107.20	235.02	301.16	474.51	710.44	7.00	6.68
Manganese	13.08	11.85	–9.40	1.97	1.71	1.89	2.17	9.23	7.97	0.00	0.00
Chromium	8.40	8.00	–4.70	1.98	1.74	0.32	0.17	6.02	6.04	0.82	0.41
Nickel	1.40	1.338	–1.29	0.29	0.28	0.42	0.32	0.69	0.78	0.00	0.001
Bauxite	176.45	184.93	4.81	12.26	11.51	62.79	67.67	82.15	90.03	19.25	15.73
Fluorspar	5.31	5.87	10.52	0.62	0.32	0.42	0.19	4.64	5.35	0.002	0.00
Phosphate	43.08	50.01	4.20	4.55	4.16	12.08	11.17	30.58	34.19	0.87	0.58

Source: World Mining Data, **26**, Minerals Production, Vienna, 2011.

Table 2.10 Oil, gas, and mineral reserves changes (Global, 2000–2008)

	Global	*Reserves*		*Extraction*	
		2000	2008	1900–2008	2000–2008
Energy	Oil (billion barrels)	1105	1333	1007	229
	Gas (trillions of cubic meters)	159	191	74	24
	Coal (billion ton)	984	826	157	49
	Hard (anthracite/bituminous)	509	411	121	41
	Soft (sub-bituminous and lignite)	475	415	37	8
Minerals	Bauxite (million ton)	24,640	25,200	4937	1480
	Copper (million ton)	3,935,00	5,40,000	5,26,298	1,28,423
	Gold (million ton)	45	48	133	22.9
	Iron (million ton)	1,42,600	1,62,500	57,096	13,115
	Lead (million ton)	64	79	217	29
	Nickel (million ton)	45,680	67,090	48	13
	Phosphate (million ton)	11,500	17,912	6711	1290
	Silver (thousand ton)****	420	570	820	175
	Tin (million ton)	7720	6072	19	2.5
	Zinc (million ton)	188	182	407	83
Other	Diamond industrial (million metric ton)	580	580	6.4	5.1
	Cobalt (million ton)	5475	6424	1.9	0.5
	Rare earth metals (million ton)	1,03,956	1,07,786	2.5	1

Sources: British Petroleum (2010), USGS Mineral Commodity Summaries (2010), USGS Historical Commodity Statistics (1990–2009).

Mining and Ecosystem

The eco-system can be adversely affected by the mining activity. It has already been discussed how mining has converted several settlements into 'ghost towns'. The working of minerals inevitably produces permanent scar on the landscapes through dumps of waste, surface subsidence and tailing ponds. It also results into chemical changes of soil and underground water, and water and air also get polluted. No matter what methods and or operation are adopted, the loss of useful land and vegetable cover is bound to occur unless appropriate scientific and technological measures are adopted to ward of the ill effects of land scarification and eutrophication.

Some Important Issues

A few basic issues which emerge from the discussion on land, water and minerals and which have very direct bearing on human survival and development are as follows:

1. Land, water and minerals are the important resources which satisfy basic needs by providing food, shelter and occupation.

2. While mineral is the most indispensable raw material for industrial development, land and water are put to variety of uses. Unlike water, however, minerals and land are limited and non-renewable.
3. All the three resources are interdependent and the problems emerging out of them are interrelated and therefore call for interrelated solution. They are not to be treated in isolation.
4. There are a host of factors—social, economic and political—which impinge upon the use and misuse of these resources.
5. All of these resources are being utilized to their maximum capacity. There is a kind of crisis on these resources and, therefore, their optimal use is to be sought for.
6. Indiscriminate use of these resources has given rise to the problem of ecological imbalances. Even water which is a renewable resource poses threat due to change in hydrological cycle. Similarly the prospecting and exploitation of minerals is causing loss of flora and fauna as well as the aesthetic damage to the natural landscape.
7. Some of the problems of the use of these resources have emerged due to widening gap in the level of demand and technological developments in the developed and developing world.

Priorities in this context may be as given below:

1. ***Assessment of Resources:*** Serious concern is being expressed regarding the availability of data at global, national, regional and community levels. This has to be given top priority and there is a need to have data bank for the information regarding land, water and minerals at different levels of territorial organization. Remote sensing techniques may be employed for global and national level assessment of these resources. At the level of the community and regions the college and university students should be deputed for collection of data. They, of course, need proper training in this direction and, therefore, this should be made part of the college and university syllabi. The data bank should be strengthened under a coordinated resources conservation policy. The coordinated resource conservation policy should be formulated and disseminated not only among the bureaucrats. The common mass should be made aware of it.
2. ***Level of Awareness:*** The level of awareness about the use and misuse of these resources and the resultant cost which mankind has to pay due to ignorance needs to be increased. It will indeed be of great value if steps are taken to increase the level of awareness by introducing course on land, water, mineral and ecology at primary, secondary and tertiary levels of education. Even school children should be imparted training to appreciate their surroundings and the changes being brought by mankind due to their day to day interference with the land and water. The dissemination of knowledge about these resources should be first step to organize and manage these resources for future.
3. ***Economic Vulnerability and Alternatives:*** There is a need for country level research to find out different types of substitutes which should act as alternatives to different types of minerals, nature of land use or water. Economic viability of alternatives should be determined with the help of cost–benefit analysis technique. It should be convincing

for the people to use those results. It should also consider how ecological destruction and damages can be restored and repaired.

4. ***Universal Legislation for Conservation of Resources:*** This should also be thought of seriously and the world organizations should take up the matter and provide the guidelines for implementation of such laws. The reckless exploitation, waste and wanton destruction can be controlled by such laws. This will lead to benefit of future generation.

Conclusion

Given the above perspectives how can we meet our basic, and developmental needs in the future is question that occurs to many of us from time to time. Land area is finite and non-agricultural uses of land would increase in future. Water resources are renewable if used judiciously. The mineral resources are fixed and inequitably distributed in the world. The limitations imposed by these resources can be partly overcome by science and technology. Productivity of agricultural land can be increased several fold, water can be recycled on a mass scale and new irrigation methods adopted to minimize its use, and metals can be substituted by plastics. And all the bounties of nature can be used without destroying the eco-system. Here lies the importance of science and technology education for future human needs–the needs which are so inextricably linked with natural resources of the world.

Science and technology education for future human needs should aim at:

1. Providing learning opportunities to various sections of people to understand the close relationship between nature and man; bringing home the importance of land, water and minerals for the present and future welfare of man;
2. Educating people in the use of scientific knowledge, appropriate technological know-how to get over the problems emerging from the use and misuse of the above resources.

Such an education has to be provided at various levels starting from the pre-elementary stage. How to interact with the nature must be taught from the very early stage in life. We need redrafting and reorienting of our curricula. Students are not to be taught; they have to learn partly by experience, partly by interaction with the teacher and partly by experimentation.

By the time, a pupil has passed the primary stage, he should understand the following aspects of land, water and minerals:

1. Origin,
2. Uses,
3. Current stage of utilization,
4. Importance in relation to future human needs,
5. Relation to overall ecological system, and
6. Role of Science and Technology to help solve the emergent and emerging problems.

Our target groups, however, include not only children but also adults. In most developing countries of the world, much of the adult population is illiterate and these countries do not have resources to build adequate number of schools and colleges to provide learning opportunities to all those who must be schooled. The use of modern technological devices to impart education through T.V., Radio. etc., thus, has acquired the considerable importance. New opportunities have, thus, been opened up for imparting science and technology education to the masses. We earnestly hope that the potentials of science and technology will be used more than hitherto, to regain the ecological balance and to enhance the welfare of man. Level of awareness, research for alternatives and universal legislation for conservation of resources will only help to maintain this ecological balance.

References

Ayeres, R.U. (1967), *Science Journal*, **3**(10).

Graves, N.J. (1985), The use of land, water and mineral resources, *Science and Technology Education and Future Human Needs*, CTS and ICSU.

Haggett, P. (1975), *Geography: A Modern Synthesis*, Harper & Row, New York.

Hodder, B.W. (1979), *Economic Development in Tropics*, Methuen, London.

Keller, R. (1984), The World's fresh water: Yesterday, today, tomorrow, *Applied Geography and Development*, Institute of Scientific Cooperation, Tubigen, **24**.

Knowles, R. and J., Wareing (1976), *Economic and Social Geography*, W.H. Allen, London.

Landsberg, H.H. et al. (1964), *Resources in America's Future: Pattern & Requirement and Availabilities*, 1960–2000, John Hopkins Press, Baltimore.

Lovering, T.S. (1969), Mineral resources from the land, in: *Resources and Man*, W.H. Freeman and Company.

Misra, H.N. (1988), Popular settlements in the city of Allahabad: Findings from Three Case Studies, *Cities*, May, 163–183.

Misra, H.N. (1990), Housing and health in three squatter settlements in Allahabad, India, in: J.E., Hardoy et al., (ed.), *The Poor Die Young*, Earthscan, London.

O'Conner, Anthony (1985), Studying the problems of land use in east Africa, *Science and Technology Education and Future Human Needs*, CTS and ICSU.

Rao, K.L. (1975), *India's Water Wealth*, Orient Longman, New Delhi.

Schippers, H.J. (1982), Mining and infrastructure in developing countries, *National Resources and Development*, Institute for Scientific Cooperation, Tubigen, Germany, **16**.

Spargo, P.E. (1985), The Orange river project: A case study, *Science and Technology and Future Human Needs*, CTS and ICSU.

Stein, Volker (1984), Mining and environment, *Natural Resource and Development*, Institute of Scientific Cooperation, Tubigen, **29**.

Strahler, A.N. et al. (1977), *Geography and Man's Environment*, John Willey & Sons, New York.

Vedanayagam, E.G. (1985), A case study of Periyar Vaigai project, *Science and Technology Education and Future Human Needs*, CST and ICSU.

Yakuba, J.M. (1985), A case study of technology in relation to land use in Ghana, *Science and Technology Education and Future Human Needs*, CST and ICSU.

3

Population, Resources and Development

Baleshwar Thakur

Abstract: This chapter highlights the dynamics of complex relationship between increasing population and declining resources such as land, water, minerals, forests and energy resources in the backdrop of several theories such as demographic transition, Malthusian, Marxist and Carrying Capacity, etc., related to population dynamics and resource utilization and attempts to bring out the different implications for sustainable development. The gender perspectives about natural resources have also been focused.

Keywords: Deforestation, UNEP, Neo-Malthusian Approach, Principle of Population, Carrying Capacity, Eco-Demography, Limits to Growth, Entering the Twenty-First Century, The Resourceful Earth, The Earth Summit, Eco-Feminism

Introduction

The relation between population and natural resources is quite complex and varied. The world's population is increasing with frightening rapidity which has reached unprecedented levels today. This will continue to grow 11 billion before it eventually stabilizes. This increase in population will take us into unknown territory and there is great uncertainty about the ability of the biosphere to accommodate this projected population increase. The risk is magnified when development moves large population groups into the high consumer life-style of the developed world. As population growth increases, in turn, the demand for goods and services also grow dramatically. Thus, the essential global question appears to be (a) What are the implications of rapid population growth for natural resources? (b) What are the resource implications of concentration versus dispersion of population? (c) How long can the natural resources of a finite world support growing populations at rising levels of living? Pressures on the natural resources caused by increasing population and their quest for high standard for living in the developing countries are growing at a rate that is increasingly difficult for the natural world to cope with. This chapter addresses the complex dimensions of the interrelations between population trends, resource use and developmental impacts including massive quantitative expansion of population size and their concomitant pressure on natural resources, penultimate problems of human survival and development impacts, opportunities and constraints.

Population Growth and Demographic Transition Theory

One of the noteworthy aspects of modern human history has been the spectacular growth of world population. The world population was hardly 8 million in 8000 BC, 550 million in 1650, 800 million in 1750 and 1200 million in 1850 which increased to 2.5 billion in 1950. The spurt of population growth which originated in Europe and spread to other regions on the heels of an economic development allowed production increases of a magnitude never before achieved. This extraordinary phenomenon reached at its peak in the 3rd quarter of the 20th Century. The world population rose to 6 billion in 2001 and is expected to be 8 billion in 2025 (Figure 3.1).

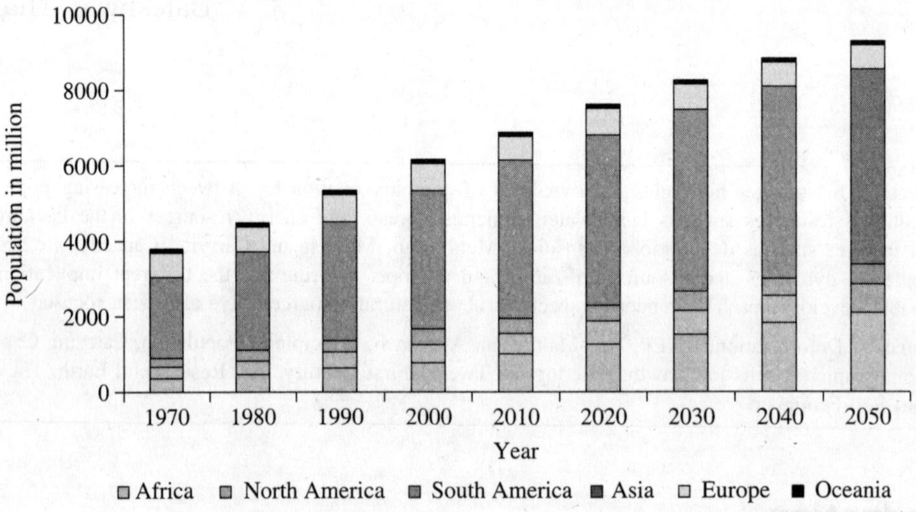

Figure 3.1 Continent's share in the world population.

It is increasing by a quarter of million every day, 3 or 4 people every second. The sixth, seventh and eighth billion will be spaced only 10 or 11 years apart (Word Resources, 1994–95:29). Nearly 93 million people are added annually and by 2035 it will still be growing by about 75 million annually (cc. 1991:60). The world population growth peaked at 2.1 per cent a year in 1965–70, the most rapid rate of increase in history; currently, it is expanding at a rate of 1.2 per cent a year as several countries have entered the transition phase. However, this rate is expected to decline to 0.95 per cent in 2025 due to enormous progress made in the reduction of infant mortality rates, increasing life expectancy and declining illiteracy in most parts of the world. The developing world, whose 4.3 billion people account for 75 per cent of global population, now supplies about 95 per cent of the annual population increase (World Resources, 95:29). Despite population control programmes, the population in developing countries continues to increase imposing ever growing pressure on its natural resources. The rapid growth is caused by two factors: (1) improved health conditions which brought down the death rate, and (2) an expanding population base (a population of 2 billion growing at 2 per cent per year will add 40 million people each year: a population of 5 billion growing at 2 per cent will add 100 million) (World Resources, 95:29) (Figure 3.1).

The contrasts in population growth are stark when both the developed and developing countries are compared. It would be interesting to note that during 1850–1950, the annual rate of the growth of population in the developed countries was 0.9 per cent and in the developing counties 0.6 per cent. Further, the annual growth rate recorded 1.3 per cent during 1950–70 in the developed countries characterized by a relatively high birth rate and a slowly declining death rate. However, this acceleration did not last very long (El-Badry, 1992:18). The average annual growth rate declined to 0.67 per cent in 1985 and is projected to decline to 0.24 per cent in 2025. Thus, acceleration seems to have given way to deceleration in the developed countries. On the other hand, the developing countries recorded an annual growth rate of 2.1 per cent during 1950–70 as a consequence of faster decline in the death rate than in the birth rate. The death rate declined in the developing countries after the Second World War at much faster rate than what was the case in the equivalent phase of earlier demographic transitions elsewhere in the world (Chandna, 1986:93). But, it is particularly striking to note that in the developing countries population growth has slowed down as fertility decline has become more effective (EL-Badry, 1992:18). Available estimates indicate that in the developing countries the annual growth rate is projected to decline 1.10 per cent in 2025.

An analysis of future population growth by major geographical regions reveals more intercontinental variations, with the likely appearance of Africa as the fastest growing region by 2025 from 626 million in 1989 to 1616 million in 2025, in spite of assumed substantial decline in fertility (World Resources, 1988–89:246: Findlay and Findlay, 1987). It is also estimated that Africa's share in the World's population will increase rapidly from 11 per cent in 1989 to 18.8 per cent in 2025. At the same time, Latin America will be the second fastest growing region over the next 30 years with a projected population about to double from 448 million in 1989 to 760 million in 2025. By comparison, the third major region projected to grow higher than world average is South Asia, where the population is expected to double from 1.4 billion to 2.8 billion in 2025, inspite of an assumed rapid fertility decline. However, the growth rate is expected to fall from 2.2 per cent in 1980 to under 1.0 per cent by 2025 (Findlay and Findlay, 1987). In contrast, China containing 1.15 billion population now (22 per cent of the global population) is heading for 1.5 billion by 2020 (World Resources, 1994–95:61). China is making remarkable strides in reducing the growth rate of its population. India's population has crossed the one billion mark at the turn of the century. By 2025, India is likely to overtake China as the most populous country in the world. More importantly, population in developed countries, now 1.2 billion, is projected to rise only to 1.4 billion by the year 2025, with virtually all of that growth occurring in the United States (World Resources 1995:27). Consequently, the share of the developed countries will shrink from 23 per cent in 1985 to 17 per cent in 2025. The decadal share of each continent may be gauged from Figure 3.1.

Fertility and mortality are the two most important components of natural population growth. From this has emerged the theory of demographic transition. This theory was first stated by Thompson (1929:959–975) and it was later reformulated by Notestein (1945:365) and it found wide acceptance among scholars such as Davis (1945:111), Wrong (1956), Peterson (1961:11–14) and Cowgill (1963: 270–274). This theory is concerned with the change from high to low birth and death rates and refers to the balance between them. More specifically, the theory describes the demographic change from high levels of mortality and fertility to low levels at or close to the replacement (Kim and Oever, 1992:57). In general, the demographic transition consists of four stages. The first stage is the primitive condition of high birth rates, high death rates and infant mortality. The second stage is that of transition and it is characterized by high fertility and declining mortality identified with low income developing nations. The third stage is characterized by declining fertility and low mortality, identified with middle income developing nations. Finally, this stage merges into a state characterized by low birth rates, low death rates and low infant mortality identified with high income developed nations. Because the decline of mortality precedes the decline in fertility, there is a period during which population grows rapidly (Figures 3.2 and 3.3). Davis (1991:13) indicates that as time goes by, fertility declines faster than mortality, with the result that the country's population growth stabilizes at a low or negative level.

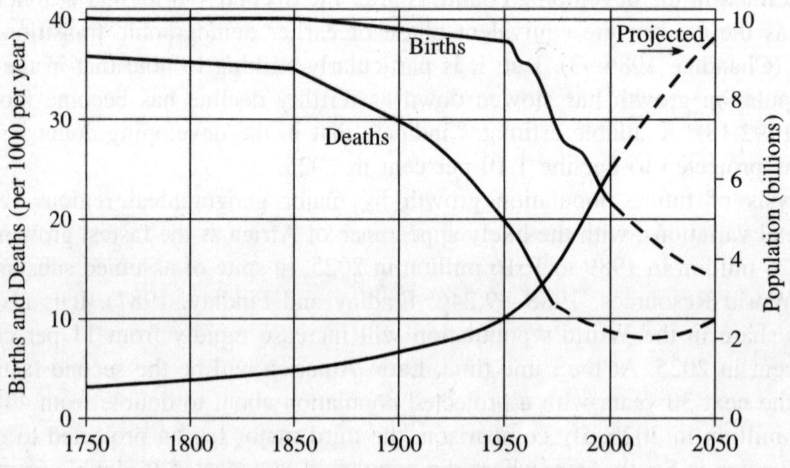

Figure 3.2 Demographic transition of the world.

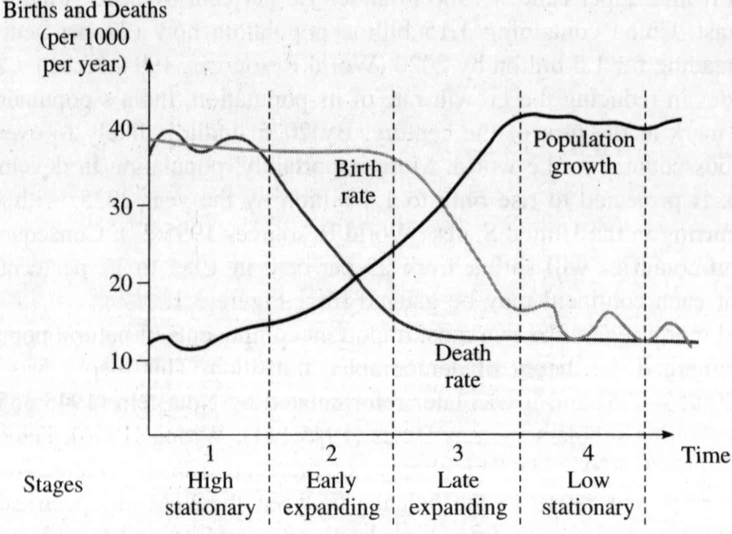

Figure 3.3 Demographic transition model.

Thus, the genesis of the theory of demographic transition is broadly related to the general theory of the economic change. Despite its applicability in both developed and developing countries, there are several disturbing trends. The theory is essentially temporal and inductive in nature based on empirical observations. The question is raised about the dynamics of the transition as to why does mortality decline first and fertility eventually comes down and then later stops falling; similarly, why does the demographic transition vary from one country to another? Even then, the theory provides a macro level of generalization of the world's demographic history and represents a powerful tool for connecting demography with outside factors in a process of change. The next section presents brief account of the implications of rapid population growth such as agricultural land shortages, limited water supplies, depleted forest resources, degraded soils and energy crisis.

Changing Patterns of Resource Use

The world's ice-free land surface is estimated to be approximately 13.4 billion hectares. In 1990, 10.0 per cent of the total land was devoted to crops, 22.0 per cent to grassland, 31.0 per cent to forests, 3.0 per cent to non-agricultural uses and the remaining 33.0 per cent to other uses. Arable land per person is lower in Japan, The Netherlands, Egypt, United Kingdom, China, Saudi Arabia, Zaire, India, Brazil, Nigeria, Tanzania, Sri Lanka and Pakistan. The corresponding figure for India is 0.14. Thus, land resources are very unevenly distributed, but the world as a whole has enough land to produce food for present and future populations. However, there are considerable areas where land resources are insufficient to meet the food needs of the present and future populations. The USA and Canada are rich in land on whatever basis one chooses to take. They have not yet felt the pressure of population on land, which is so severe in most of the countries of Europe and many parts of Asia, notably Japan, India and Pakistan have extreme shortage of cultivated land and unlike Great Britain and Japan, their productivity per acre is also low. Between 1950 and 1986, world grain output climbed from 624 million tonnes to 1870 million tonnes, a prodigious threefold gain that raised per capita grain production at an impressive annual rate of 3.0 per cent (World Resources, 1988:52). Never before had the world witnessed such an increase in food production within one generation. This growth in food production has been more significant in the developing countries (from 470 million tonnes in 1965 to 949 million tonnes in 1986) compared with that of the developed countries (from 535 million tonnes in 1965 to 920 million tonnes in 1986). This growth has outpaced population growth as per capita agricultural production has grown in developed countries by 21.0 per cent and in developing countries by 30.0 per cent (UNEP, 1993–94:135). This agricultural development has been caused by the Green Revolution which has occurred largely in response to world population growth and has operated through processes of intensification of agricultural production and expansion of agricultural land use (UNEP, 1993–94:135). However, there has been 10 per cent decline in grain output per person between 1986 and 1993, which is perhaps the most disturbing economic trend in the world today. By the beginning of the 21st century, there will be nearly one billion more people to feed. Already in Africa and Latin America, with the fastest population growth, per capita grain production has started falling. If action is not taken to arrest this trend, hunger and malnutrition will spread.

The major reason of slowing down the growth is environmental degradation along with emerging agronomic constraints. They are soil erosion, air pollution, ozone depletion, increased flooding due to deforestation, depletion of aquifers, losses in genetic diversity of various crops and the hot summers, which hinder the world's ability to feed ever growing numbers (Brown, 1994:1). In other words, this fall, is attributed to unsustainable use of soil and water. Prominent among these are the continual loss of top soil from croplands, conversion of cropland to non-farm uses, water logging and salting of irrigation systems, diversion of irrigation water to non-farm activities and now the possible adverse effects of climate change. Throughout the developing countries, mounting population pressure continues to push farmers onto steep sloping and semi-arid lands to sustain cultivation. They encourage erosion and land gradually loses its inherent productivity threatening the livelihood of those who depend on it. According to United Nations Environment Programme (1993:94) assessment, 4.5 billion hectares, or 35.0 per cent of the earth's land surface are threatened by desertification. Of this, three-fourth has already been at least moderately degraded, one-third has already lost more than 25.0 per cent of its productive potential and about 1.2 billion hectares of land—an area larger than India and China combined, have been seriously degraded in different parts of the world. Desertification reflects a deteriorating relationship between people and the land and also points out that peoples themselves are not only degradations' victims but its unwitting agents. It is estimated to affect about 25.0 per cent of the total land area of the world. As at present, half of these desert regions are in developing countries. The world's deserts are spreading continuously and almost every continent is affected by desertification. Arid lands (10–40 cm of average annual rainfall) amount to 12.0 per cent of the overall land surface of the world, inhabited by some 150 million people. This means that if land management remains unchanged, these arid lands will be turned into man-made deserts in less than 150 years and, most probably, within the next 50 years (Hourerou, 1994:2).

Northern Africa, Near and Middle East, Northwest China, the Sahel, East Africa, Southern Africa and ex-USSR countries are some of the examples where 0.6 to 0.7 per cent arid lands are depleted every year. Such expansion causes decreasing production and productivity, failing economies, impoverished biodiversity and, perhaps worst of all, decreased ability to combat the scourge (Hourerou, 1994:3). It hardly needs stressing that there can be any solution in the above countries where the demography grows faster than economy (Hourerou, 1994:3).

The developing countries, especially humid tropics, are the most thickly populated regions of the earth, where by the year 2021 almost one third of the world population will live. The poor productivity in food resources is in part due to the unusual ecological diversity of large parts of tropical climatic zone. It is also in part due to geologic and climatic factors which make many tropical soils (oxisols and ultisols) deficient in mineral nutrients and resistant to tilt as compared to those of the middle latitudes. It has been estimated that oxisols and ultisols account for 82.0 per cent of the total area in the American tropics, 56.0 per cent in Africa and only 38.0 per cent in Asia. Humid tropics represent the highest stage of natural vegetation in the world. But they are denuded of the forests which would be never replaced. Shifting agriculture plays havoc and forest resources is the main factor in the debasement of human living standards.

Soil erosion is occurring in developed and developing countries alike. The erosion has been severe from the earliest civilizations in the Middle East to the most recently cultivated lands in the Americas, Australia, and South Africa. In the United States and South Africa, soil erosion is a national disaster of first magnitude. Probably in no country in the world had such a short period of farming caused such tremendous soil wastage as in the United Status. In much of Asia, Latin America and Africa, change from forest to crop fields is accompanied by increase of surface run-off, arid and an acceleration of soil erosion. Since 1940's, the continued deforestation in the Himalayas and North-eastern Thailand has created serious soil erosion problems in the lower Ganga plain and Thailand. Soil erosion is making future production gains more difficult in China as well. The Yellow river is depositing 1.2 billion tonnes of soil in the ocean each year. Worldwide farmers are losing an estimated 24 billion tones of top soil from cropland each year (Brown, 1994:1). Thus, it is vital to conserve our fertile soil since this is a natural resource which is practically irreplaceable.

The escalation in the global population and the concomitant expansion of agriculture and industry has placed conflicting pressure on the world's water resources. There have been thirty-five fold increase in the amount of water withdrawal for human use during the past three centuries reaching to 3500 cubic km. per year (World Resources, 1991:170). Out of this, some 2100 cubic km of water are for consumptive use and the rest are returned to rivers and other water sources, frequently in a polluted condition (World Resources, 1991:171). According to yet another estimate made by United Nations Environment Programme (1993–92:142) recent decades have witnessed an annual increase in water withdrawal between 4 and 8 per cent with the highest rates in developing countries. On the other hand, in industrial countries water use is stabilizing.

The distribution of fresh water supply on the earth does not coincide with population concentration. Oceania, South America and North America are relatively water rich, because their per capita water use is small compared to per capita water availability. North America leads the world in per capita water availability, while Asia has the least amount of renewable water available per capita. In Europe, North America and former USSR, industrial and energy production use dominates and the consumptive use is relatively small. Conversely, in Africa and Asia, substantial withdrawals for irrigation result in greater consumptive use (World Resources, 1991:171). Globally, irrigated agriculture accounts for 70.0 per cent of the water used, industry 23.0 per cent and the remainder for domestic, recreational and municipal purposes. By 1950, irrigation had reached 94 million hectares but by 1993 irrigated land area nearly tripled to about 271 million hectares. This trend is likely to continue into the future. Thus, irrigation is the largest consumer of water and by far the most dominant. One-third of the world's food is grown on irrigated land, which comprises only 18.0 per cent of the total cropland. About 75.0 per cent of today's 271 million hectares of irrigated land is in developing countries. China and India lead the world in irrigated land. In China, this agricultural practice grew impressively to 52 million hectares between 1950–1990. India's net irrigated area in 1950 was about exactly the same as China's, though growth has been less rapid in view of the introduction of high yielding wheat and rice varieties that were both responsive to the use of water and more exacting in their demands. However, in less developed countries nearly two-third of the population do not have access to safe and ample supplies of drinking water. On the other hand, water logging and salinization of soils are the environmental problems caused by excessive input of water into systems with inadequate drainage capacities (UNEP, 1993–94:144). The world's affected areas include Egypt, Iraq, Syria, Iran, former USSR, Pakistan, India, Australia and South West USA. It is hardly surprising that for the world as a whole, supplies are relatively adequate for city dwellers in the developed nations, inadequate for the squatter settlements in the developing nations and thoroughly adequate for only half of the rural dwellers. The occurrences of major floods or widespread droughts are other major problems of water resources management. Similarly, the relatively sudden increase in the water withdrawals has depleted aquifers in many parts of the world. What is of particular importance, however, is the pollution threat to the world's vast supplies to groundwater.

Forests are looked upon as one of the great renewable natural resources of the world which cover nearly 30.0 per cent of the land surface and form the foundation of sustainable development. They are considered essential as they moderate local climates, reduce soil erosion, regulate stream flow, support extractive industries and afford unequalled opportunities for recreation and enhancement of human values (Haden–Guest et al., 1956:1). But, since 1950, the area under forest and woodland has changed tremendously in both the developed and the developing countries in response to the demands of the growing numbers of people. Most European countries including former USSR are characterized by an increase in forest extent and reduction in arable area, whereas most African, Latin American and Asian countries have shown an increase in arable area and decrease in forest (Grigg, 1970:104–110: Mather, 1986:108–109). Few countries show an increase in both the land use classes. China is the most notable example having doubled its forest area over the past three decades. Allen and Barnes (1985, 163–184) have found a statistically significant relationship ($r = -0.57$) between forest loss and population growth rates, increasing their forest area at the expense of arable area, while most developing countries with rapid rates of population growth were characterized by large reductions in forest area. Between 1980 and 1990, tropical forest areas have been shrunk on average of 15.4 million hectares (0.8 per cent) per year and over the past decade, 154 million hectares of tropical forests have been converted to other land uses (World Resources, 1994–95:131). However, in some of the developing countries, the problem of deforestation is acute. For example, Nigeria loses annually 5.2 per cent of its forest, Costa Rica 3.6 per cent, Sri Lanka 3.5 per cent, El Salvador 3.2 per cent. They may lose their forests by 2015. At the end of 1990s, tropical forests were estimated to cover 1756 million hectares, with 52 per cent (918 million hectares) in South America and the Caribbean, 30 per cent (528 million hectares) in Africa and 18 per cent (311 million hectares) in Asia, and the Pacific region (Word Resources, 1995:131).

Of particular concern here is that neither the rate of clearing nor its causes are uniform throughout the developing countries. The striking fact is that shifting agriculture and population density are the major factors causing deforestation in Africa, clearing for pasture in Central and South America, and commercial logging in Asia particularly in Malaysia and Indonesia. Perhaps most significant and overtly supportive of deforestation is the consumption of a large proportion of wood as fuel by the less developed societies. In the developed nations 20 per cent of all removals are used as fuelwood and 80 per cent as industrial wood, while in developing nations where fuel wood is still the major energy resource, the proportions are exactly the reverse. Fortunately, research has resulted in an increased awareness that rural dwellers are rarely the cause of large-scale deforestation through fuelwood cutting, rather they generally prefer to collect deadwood. Conversely, it is the urban and industrial consumers who cause much more extensive deforestation. Satellite data show clearly that deforestation in parts of Amazon is accelerating. In the Brazilian state of Rondonia, for example, the area deforested has grown at an exponential rate between 1975 and 1990. Another fact that requires attention is that of wood production in both developed and developing countries. Wood is a low value commodity and bulky. Therefore, most wood is consumed locally as the cost of handling and transporting them to overseas markets is correspondingly high (Bee, 1990:124). Hardwoods from the tropical rain forests dominate in tropical regions while softwoods from the coniferous forests dominate the removals of developed countries. The developed countries dominate world trade in wood products, accounting for 81 per cent of imports and 87 per cent of exports by value. The former USSR and North America alone supply over half of the worlds industrial wood.

Energy and mineral resources are central to all economic activities and are widely perceived as one of the key variables which determine the sustainability of the development process (UNEP, 1993–94:271). Indeed, throughout history, the questions of independence, wealth, equality, the survival or ruin of human society have been dependent on having access to energy (Khabeishvili, 1994:1). It is the energy which is the foundation of modern technology and has reached a crossroads in its development. Our economic development relies on a variety of energy resources including fossil fuels (coal, petroleum and natural gas), hydropower, nuclear energy, biomass fuels and exotic power resources. According to recent statistics, 82.0 per cent of all energy-consumed in the world is produced by burning fossil fuels, 7.5 per cent from biomass, 5.5 per cent from the use of hydraulic energy and 5.0 per cent from nuclear energy. Minerals are equally important as means for producing energy (atomic minerals, tar sands and oil shales), controlling some form of energy (ferrous and non-ferrous minerals) and conserving energy (non-metals). The five main characteristics of minerals as resource are that: (1) they are found in localized deposits, (2) they are very unevenly distributed both between and within countries, and over large areas the available mineral resources are insufficient to meet the needs of populations currently dependent on them, (3) demand for minerals is increasing at an increasing rate, (4) mineral exploitation leaves an indelible mark on the environment, and (5) most mineral deposits are short lived, and a mineral deposit once exhausted is gone forever. Therefore, it is a non-renewable resource. Energy derived from fossil fuels represents more than 80 per cent of the supply to the developed countries and are the important sources of energy. It has been estimated that there are 650–1000 billion tonnes of coal reserves in the world, out of which 300 billion tonnes are in the United States. It is for this reason that coal accounted for 30 per cent of energy consumption in 1991 in the world. USA, China and former USSR accounted for about 65.0 per cent of world's coal production. Petroleum is another most important and highly prized resource as a fuel. In 1991, it accounted for 40.0 per cent of world consumption of energy. The world's reserves of petroleum are estimated at 640 billion barrels. It has been estimated that 82.0 per cent of the world's petroleum is in Eastern hemisphere and two-thirds of it is held by the Middle East alone. Thus, it is quite clear that developed countries possess a major share of the world's coal, while a few developing countries contain the greater part of petroleum reserves. The consumption of petroleum figures prominently in the developed countries so much so that per capita consumption of oil in the United States is 8 times of the world as a whole. Demand is also increasing at faster rate in Western Europe, Japan and former USSR countries. Natural gas has emerged as the former USSR's fuel of choice, and domestic production grew 48.0 per cent between 1980 and 1990. The former USSR is estimated to control 42.0 per cent of the world's proved recoverable reserves of natural gas, with the Persian Gulf States controlling an additional 25.0 per cent (World

Resources, 1994–95:331). Since the first oil shock of 1973–75, per capita consumption has declined moderately in developed countries due to fear of hardship caused by this crisis (Word Resources, 1994–95:8). This brought about a change in their attitudes and efforts were directed at breaking free from this dependence, diversifying supply sources, perfecting replacement energies and promoting energy-saving programmes. In response to this, coal use has grown especially in the United States and Australia. Conversely, per capita consumption of oil has risen rapidly in developing countries driven by rapidly expanding economies, rising populations and increasing urbanization. However, per capita level in the developed world is still very high relative to those of the developing countries.

Biomass is the largest source of energy for developing countries (supplying roughly one-third of the energy needs) followed by coal, oil and gas as the next largest sources. Although important in some countries, hydropower and nuclear energy are relatively minor sources of energy. Both require massive investment and technical expertise. Hydroelectric power generation has more than doubled over the past two decades and supplied 21.0 per cent of electricity in 1991, which was less than coal or oil but more than nuclear power. Energy imbalance in the source of supply is the rule. For example, in Central Africa, 70.0 per cent of the energy consumed comes from wood; in Brazil, water power and wood account for more than 60.0 per cent of the total supply, in the former USSR, 45 per cent consumption is led by natural gas and in China coal is the primary fuel. The United States and France continue to be the largest user of nuclear power in absolute terms. Globally, less than a quarter of the world's richest population consumes almost three-quarters of the energy in the world. Per capita electricity consumption—symbol of modernity, therefore, corresponds to measures of development. For example, USA uses 10074 kW per hour, Argentina 1367, Pakistan 83, Haiti 49, Ethiopia 20 and Chad 14. Developing countries account for 75.0 per cent of world population, but consume only about 25.0 per cent of the global energy budget (about 26.0 per cent of all the commercial energy sources and 85.0 per cent of the traditional biomass fuels. The average annual consumption per capita in the United States is 26 times higher than in India, the average consumption of a Norwegian is more than thirty times that of a Guatemalan and that of a Japanese is 59 times that of a Nigerian.

It may be noted that though per capita energy consumption is very low among the developing countries, this climbs steeply with rise in their level of development. Projection for the remainder of the twentieth century suggests that total energy demand in the industrialized countries will double but that demand in the Third World will increase five-fold to seven-fold (Berry, Conkling and Ray, 1992:118). It is anticipated that for the foreseeable future it is doubtful whether the conventional energy supply can expand fast to cater to the needs of projected demand. At the same time renewable forms of energy (solar, wind, tidal and geothermal) are unlikely to offer economically viable alternatives to fossil fuels. There are no easy answers because a great variety of decisions have to be taken based on the following characteristics of energy use in developing countries: (1) rural and urban energy consumption differ vastly as the consumers in urban areas have access to commercial fuels, while rural dwellers rely heavily on traditional biomass fuels, (2) animal and human muscle contribute much of the energy for agriculture and transportation, (3) fuel wood is burned for cooking, heating and some industrial uses, (4) fuelwood is disappearing and people are burning more crop residue and animal dung instead of returning them to the soil, (5) energy supplies are inadequate in many sectors resulting into regular black or brown outs, (6) there is widespread inefficiency in energy production, distribution and use, (7) lack of proper maintenance and poor quality fuel erode the capacity and reliability of power plants, (8) power plants consume 15–30 per cent more fuel per unit of electricity produced than efficiently operated plants elsewhere, (9) losses between power station and customer range about 17.0 per cent and (10) lower energy prices and subsidies discourage conservation.

There has been rise in worldwide production and consumption of major metals as they are intimately related with consumption of mechanical energy. The United States, the former USSR, Australia and Japan are the important producers and the major consumers of world's metals. The United States, alone, is the outstanding consumer of metals although it lacks many essential metallic resources. At the global level, some of the metals like iron, aluminium, manganese, magnesium, chromium and titanium are plentiful, while copper, lead, zinc and nickel are the least plentiful. The use of non-ferrous minerals like aluminium and copper is growing most rapidly in developing countries—nine-fold growth for aluminium and five-fold for copper over 30 years as they are indispensable in electrical applications (World Resources, 1994–95:8–9). Its utilization in practically all sectors of the economy has shown a faster growth rate than that of any other metal (Blunden, 1985:129). With the exception of tin and mercury, both the production and consumption of metals have gone up continuously between 1977 and 1992 (World Resources, 1994–95:331). Over the past years the value of global mineral production has changed steadily from a focus on metallic minerals to a focus on non-metallic minerals. Therefore, the value of the non-metallic mineral production today is much greater than the value of the metallic mineral production. The trend is expected to continue as common commodities, such as sand, gravel, crushed stone and cement increasingly supplant the use of metals. In recent years, radical changes have been taking place in the global mining and energy resource industries. Tin producing countries of South East Asia, bauxite rich countries of Caribbean region, the phosphate producers of North Africa, and copper exporters of Zambia, Zaire, Chile and Peru are cases where exploration methods have been intensified. However, there is a need for participation of the international mining companies in many developing countries where many new sources of minerals are expected to be located which have not been well explored in the past.

Linking Population, Resources and Development

The relationship between population dynamics and the changing patterns of environmental resource use on which the survival and well-being of billons of people depend is at the centre of current debate in the world. The past two centuries, characterized by the emergence of modern science and rapid population growth, have witnessed a great interest in the relation of population to natural resources. A large number of scholars from a variety of disciplines have expressed concern about the gross imbalance between the rapid population growth and the increasing scarcity of natural resources. The various points of view on population, resources and development can be grouped into seven general perspectives: (1) Malthusian and Neo-Malthusian, (2) Marxist approach, (3) Population pressure and carrying capacity, (4) Limits to growth, (5) The Global 2000 Report and the Resourceful Earth, (6) The Earth Summit, and

(7) Gender-ecology and development. The issues that are raised, the specific questions that are asked and the proposed solutions to human problems vary with each approach.

Malthusian and Neo-Malthusian Approaches

The first scientific attempt to search for laws linking population and resources was stressed poignantly by Thomas R. Malthus (1766–1934), an English clergyman, historian and an economist in his famous essay on the *Principle of Population* in 1798, articulated over 200 years ago (Malthus, 1988). In this, he challenged the traditional view of economists that an increasing population was synonymous with wealth, and argued that numbers would increase until they met the constraint of limited food supplies. Drawing on the concept of diminishing returns, Malthus strongly expressed the view that population would grow in a geometric progression (2, 4, 8, 16, 32, etc.), when unchecked, doubling every 30–40 years, and food supply in arithmetic progression (3, 6, 9, 12, 15, etc.). According to Neurath (1994:82), man has the biological capacity to increase his own numbers faster than he can increase his food supply. The number of people to be fed will, thus, quickly overtake and exceed the food supply. Thus, Malthus doctrine of resource scarcity states that population tends to increase faster than the means of subsistence—mainly land and farm products, producing scarcity of natural resources due to mounting demographic pressure (Brown, 1987, Eckholm, 1976, Ehrlich, 1972, Ehrlich and Ehrlich, 1970;1990). He contends that the carrying capacity of the earth is finite and that resource distribution results when too many people intensify their efforts to extract food and other needs (Stonich, 1993:22). Consequently, Malthus foresaw the emergence of a chronic imbalance between population and resources unless prevented by some very powerful positive and preventive checks through which population is kept in balance with the means of subsistence (Harvey, 1970–41:9). He also stressed that this increasing gap shall ultimately lead to the point where misery and poverty shall become inevitable (Chandna, 1986:216). One of the most marked features of Malthus thesis was that population was growing quickly and that man was a biological as well as a social being depending on passion between the two sexes and food. Thus, he was the first scholar to propound population theory based on natural law and one might regard Malthus as the father of the modern birth control movement. His work has shown a strong propensity of maintaining a balanced relationship between population and means of subsistence. Regrettably, however, his views have been challenged as it is based on a number of simplistic assumptions and hypotheses that do not stand the test of empirical verification (Todaro, 1984:186). Perhaps the most important of these, and certainly the most elementary, is the principle that any theory of population and resources that overlooks cultural phenomena is very likely to be deficient (Davis, 1991:4). The role of cultural factors is either minimized or distorted.

Malthus failed to foresee the prodigious expansion in the technological means for the efficiency of resource use and in the substitution of new resources. It is equally amazing to find the invalidity of his two sets of ratios as questioned by his critics. Ricardo, in his major work on the Principles of Political Economy and Taxation (1817), accepted Malthus principle of population quite uncritically. He modified Malthus doctrine of scarcity by maintaining that the real threat was one of the progressive decline of resource quality because the richest farmland and beds of ore would be used first. As the higher quality more accessible resources are used up, we become increasingly dependent upon our technology to provide and develop resources (Burton and Kates, 1965:95). He was a normative rather than an empirical thinker. He constructed a model based on the law of diminishing returns and the differential fertility of agricultural land. However, it is with respect to social harmony concept that Ricardo's work contrasts most markedly with that of Malthus. John S. Mill (1848) in his work *Principles of Political Economy* accepted Malthus principle of population. He was an advocate of social reform and believed that social reforms and other improvements could lead to economic progress. He also broadened the scope of natural resource scarcity to include living space and the quality of life. The neo-Malthusian theory, led by Brown (1954), Osborn (1948), Cook (1951), Vogt (1948) and Huxley (1956:64–76) is a recent refinement of Malthusian view. The point of departure of the Neo-Malthusian school is that present rates of global population growth are far in excess of the carrying capacity of the earth (Brown, 1985:51–88, Ehrlich, 1972, Logan, 1991:40–57). It takes into account the great technological advances of the Industrial Revolution. Neo-Malthusians stress the rapid advances in productive capacity of technical innovation to overtake both population increase and deteriorating earth resources. Their views are common among the upholders of conservation and are usually strong among advocates of birth control and family planning. Thus, the neo-Malthusians advocate population reduction.

Marxist Approach

This approach has provided a distinctive method and some of the vital theory in the study of such a complex issue as the population-resources relation. Marx put forward a vigorous criticism on Malthus and Ricardo and arrived at the theory of surplus value. On the basis of this theory, Marx produced a distinctive theory of population emphasizing on relational rather than absolute concept. He defined resources in relationship to the mode of production which seeks to make use of them and which simultaneously produces them through both the physical and mental activity of the users (Harvey, 1974:265). The basic difference between Marx, Malthus and Ricardo is that Marx utilizes dialectical framework, while Malthus and Ricardo use the abstract analytics and logical empiricism. Marx used and developed the dialectical method of Hegel to understand the forms and processes of the emergence and decline of the society. This is a method of reasoning in which contradictions are synthesized. However, this method was no substitute for empirical analysis and the gathering of facts but a way of dealing with interrelations and dynamics. Marx accepts that the appropriate method to deal with the population–resources relation has to be holistic, system-wide encompass, and capable of handling dynamics, especially internal dynamic (Harvey, 1974:270). Marx focused on the class differentiations and the misery of the working class. He considers the society to consist of two major classes, i.e., the rich (the bourgeoisie) and the poor (the proletariat). The rich class is the owners of the modes of production and earns profit. The profit earned by the rich led to the process of capital accumulation with the rich (Chandna, 1986:221). The poor class on the other hand, accumulates labour through rapid population growth. In this respect, the poor becomes the exploited classes while the rich the exploiting classes. Marx insisted that the proletariat, the productive class, would replace the bourgeoisie and establish a socialist, exploitation-free society. As Harvey (1974:269) observed:

"Marx does not talk about a population problem but a poverty and human exploitation problem." He replaces Malthus concept of overpopulation by the concept of relative surplus population. He replaces the inevitability of the pressure of population on the means of subsistence (accepted by both Malthus and Ricardo) by a historically specific and necessary pressure of labour supply on the means of employment produced internally within the capitalist mode of production. Marx's distinctive method permitted this reformulation of the population-resources problem, and put him in a position from which he could envisage a transformation of society that would eliminate poverty and misery rather than accept its inevitability.

Population Pressure and Carrying Capacity

Another search for scientific-theoretical premises linking population, resources and development is the concept of population pressure and carrying capacity. It is generally recognized that equilibrium state between population and resources is a rarity but the maladjustments between population and resources in a region are more common, producing severe stress called population pressure. Population pressure is the concept which is considered important in the development strategies of Third World Countries. It's nature and degree of concern is best exemplified by Zelinsky (1966) who remarks that population pressure is a human–environmental crisis of increasing significance to low income countries. Such countries not only must face immense social and economic tasks in development, but also must contend with unprecedented rates of population growth and worsening balances between their citizens and the land which supports them. Thus, this concept illuminates man–land relationships and is an emerging area of concern to Third World planners and demographers. However, there is no universal definition of population pressure.

It has been conveniently defined as the situation in which there is a tension between the size of a population and the resources at its disposal. Taeuher (1970:56) suggests this to occur due to shakening of the equilibrium between population and resources. Similarly, Clarke (1972:305) is of the view that the pressure of population is caused by the imbalance between human numbers and their needs, and between natural and human resources of a region. Bernard (1970:44) notes that population pressure is a long-term process of deteriorating physical and human conditions occurring at many scales as a result of excess numbers of human or animals in relation to the ability of the land to support them. It also implies a reasonably well adjusted balance between the numbers of human and resources in a given area. This balance has been described by Steel (1970:4) as the optimum population density, and by Hart (1970:95) comfortable density. Whenever numbers exceed an optimum level in a region, population pressure may be said to exist and to grow more severe if population growth continues. Bernard (1970:44) states that the concept of optimum relates to the external needs and technical capacities of population as well as their perceived needs and expectations, and it has proved to be an illusory idea. As alluded to earlier, comfortable density has also attracted attention, which is defined as the maximum population size in a given area for perpetual, peaceful living without stress and without exhaustion of available resources. In addition, the focus has also been in relation to the living standards of the population. It is likely that the population pressure exists because excess numbers cause living standards to be lower than would be attainable with reduced numbers.

Instead of trying to determine optimum or comfortable densities, another closely related concept is to find out critical population densities or carrying capacities. It is within this context of ambiguities that the authors (Zelinsky et al., 1970:581–82) conclude by arguing that "the beast we call **PPR** (population pressure on resources) is too large, ambiguous and ambulatory to be simply catalogued. It is bigger than we suspected previously, it has too many appendages, angles, and wrinkles for comfort, and it may travel in herds. We have succeeded only in demonstrating that it is truly multi-directional, that it involves relationships among many different sets of variables—ecological, social, technological, psychological and historical. It is impossible to produce a simple, universal definition that subsumes all the kinds of pressure situations observed at different places and in different periods. But we are all uneasily aware that it exists". Mabogunje (1970:118) takes a more balanced and somewhat less pessimistic view: "that population pressure should be conceived as a result of interaction between three variables—resources, people and expectations". He points out that there are three principal conditions that form a concern for population pressure. The first is that resources and population are low but expectations are high. The second is that resources are low but populations and expectations are high. And the third is that resources and expectations are low but population is high. Mabogunje's final plea is that the product of high expectations may be better utilization of resources, permanent out-migration and change in social and economic attitudes, and a tendency towards breakdown of socio-economic conditions, where the pressure is the product of high population without high expectations.

From the foregoing section, it should be apparent that the perfect balance between population and resources, however non-existent, produces an equilibrium state which is often called **optimum population**.

The concept of optimum population has been defined as the population which gives the maximum income per head. It is also defined as that population which produces maximum economic welfare. Thus, it refers to the size of population enabling maximum per capita output and the highest possible living standard under given economic and technological condition. The measurement of such a population size is extremely difficult because the attributes and characteristics involved in its evaluation resist their precise measurement and mathematical simulation (Chandna, 1992:283). Perhaps the most distinguishing characteristics for assessing optimum population that emerge include per capita production, average standard of living, degree of employment, longevity of life, dependency ratio, social harmony, family stability, attainment of knowledge, per capita food consumption, proportion of expenditure on food, rationality of land use, balanced demographic structure and rational development of resources (Chandna, 1992:283). The deviations from the equilibrium state give rise to over-population and under population.

Overpopulation exists where there is an excess of population over utilized or potential resources. It reflects and also relates that it may result from rapid population growth with very high densities or resource depletion with low ecological capacity. More specifically, it is often viewed to occur when resource development fails to keep pace with population growth. Population pressure research now resembles a rapidly growing tree. The roots are spreading out in a large number of fields to assess and gain a clear and complete understanding of the nature of relationship. However, overpopulation thesis seems vague. It does not provide an objective and adequate index of population pressure. But, generally, it is characterized by low per capita income, low and declining living standards, high levels of unemployment, pronounced out-migration and high rural population density. Thus, it is clear that it is a relative term in the sense that improved exploitation of a country's resources would permit current population to be maintained at a higher standard of living, and this concept is only meaningful in conjunction with specification of a certain level of advancement in technology. Clarke (1972:165) has divided this concept into two parts; absolute overpopulation and relative overpopulation. The former is marked by low living standards even after the attainment of absolute limit of resource development and the latter is marked by a situation where the present level of production is inadequate for the population and greater production is still possible. In short it leads to the fundamental conclusion that relative overpopulation is more common than absolute as it is the product of limitations of technology and insufficient development of resources. Under population exists when a population is too small to utilize its available resources or where resources could support a larger population with no reduction in living standards, primarily found in developed countries. Clarke (1972) has divided this concept into absolute under population and relative under population. The former, according to him, occurs only in isolated areas where the degree of replacement of population is less than unity, and the latter occurs due to insufficient development of resources. Thus, the relative under population is more prevalent and occurs frequently both in developed as well as less developed economies, such as in the prairies and parts of Australia, New Zealand and Zambia.

Another closely related concept of population pressure is carrying capacity which has been borrowed from animal ecology by social scientists. Carneiro (1960:229–234), an anthropologist, elaborates this concept as referring to the theoretical estimate of number of people who can be supported by a particular environment with a particular technology for some period under a given system of land uses without deterioration of land resources. Davis (1991:4) discusses how this concept is an effort to build a bridge between demography and the environment. The concept has an intuitive appeal suggesting the existence of critical threshold beyond which serious problems are encountered (Mitchell, 1989:170). But the concept has important limitations. It applies best under stable conditions and over relatively short spans of time. In the real world, the carrying capacity also changes with the change in climate and the animals' adaption. Thus, the concept becomes more volatile because the threshold shifts significantly depending upon assumptions regarding future technological innovations, social values and variable standards of environmental quality. One implication of this expression is that there is considerable uncertainty associated with any carrying capacity estimates (Mitchell, 1989:170). Nevertheless, the concept can be very helpful for resource managers as it identifies possible futures in a variety of management situations. Cohen (1995:16–19) very succinctly expresses that the earth's capacity to support people is determined partly by processes that the social and natural sciences have yet to understand and partly by choices that we and our descendents have yet to make. Therefore, the interplay of natural constraints and human choices is the key to determine human carrying capacity. However, this concept has rarely been applied to Third World settings, Marten and Sancholuz's study of Mexico and Ramanaiah and Reddy's (1983:107–18) on India being a few exceptions.

Shrestha and Conway (1985:55–82) are of the opinion that since it is difficult to determine the carrying capacity of available resources, a clear theoretical understanding of population pressure requires a careful analysis of the issue in the context of resource scarcity rather than in the context of carrying capacity. Resource scarcity, according to them, is a much broader and more powerful concept than carrying capacity, which is limited and quite inadequate to explain population pressure; for it is only related to the availability of resources and technology and is virtually detached from any institutional context. Two concepts, namely, eco-demographic and socio-demographic relations contribute an understanding of the types and processes of resource scarcity and the nature of their relationships with population pressure. Eco-demographic relation views the relationship between people and their environments (nature) through linkages and feedbacks generally analyzed from a macro perspective in terms of absolute man–land relationships. Consistent with this conceptual eclecticism, population pressure becomes a function of two types of scarcity: (1) absolute or natural scarcity, and (2) technological scarcity. Absolute scarcity exists because of the paucity of resources necessary to sustain the population at an adequate level. Technological scarcity implies that full potential of the available resources are not realized due to the shortage of productive technologies called the **forces of production**. This implies that technological change involves increasing capital substitution for labour. Thus, it should be apparent that both resources and technologies are necessary for the existence and development of societies. At the same time, it should be made clear that population pressure is not a general problem, rather it is a specific issue-specific to only some classes (Shrestha and Conway, 1985:59). The implications of this are clear. There is an increasing realization that the problem lies in the socio-demographic relations as determined by the existing institutional forces. The socio-demographic relations are essentially the social relations of production, which reveal the social distribution of available resources and the roles and positions of different classes in the processes of production and development (Shrestha and Conway, 1985:60). In simplest terms, this is known as social or relative scarcity of resources, where class disparity in resources ownership is the main feature of the economy. The emphasis in this approach is that population pressure becomes a function of class relations, and the unequal distribution of resources has a tendency to become more unequal over time (Cassen, 1976). From this perspective, Shrestha and Conway (1985:60) suggest that relative population pressure results from the unequal distribution of resources. While individual studies contribute to a growing corpus of knowledge, their value is enhanced if they can be related to an emerging body of theory. Contributions are conspicuously absent toward developing a political economy perspective on population pressure.

Limits to Growth

Incorporating concepts of resource scarcity and carrying capacity specificity into our knowledge of population-resource linkage is likely to provide the level of understanding required at the micro-level. However, one important challenge that emerges is the need to raise and address questions about broad relationships on population and resources at the global level. Gains from broadening the range of enquiry in this manner are illustrated by Denis Meadows (1972). In the early 1970s, a slender volume *The Limit to Growth* but better known as *The Club of Rome Report* reported the findings of a team of scholars connected with the Massachusetts Institute of Technology and working under the auspices of a loose group intriguingly called **The Club of Rome**. The group made a dynamic world model linking five major variables as population, pollution, resources, land and capital generation. It examined how changes in one variable would affect changes in the others with the help of a computer during the period 1900–1970 and then project this under varying assumptions in the future. The model is based on the system dynamics model developed by M.I.T. Professor J. Forrester in his books; *Industrial Dynamics* (1961), *Urban Dynamics* (1970) and *World Dynamics* (1971). The authors (Meadows et al., 1972) indicate that they are concerned with accelerating industrialization, rapid population growth, widespread malnutrition, depletion of non-renewable resources and a deteriorating environment. The key finding from the behaviour of the dynamic model is that of an imminent collapse of the life supporting system on earth, unless mankind soon changed its ways of rapid growth of population, rapid depletion of resources and rapid pollution of the environment. This is expected to occur within about 120 years. However, this is not a prediction that the authors are making of things to come, but a warning of what would happen if mankind continues to grow its own numbers and its per capita consumption at the rate of which they are growing now and have been growing for the last few decades (Neurath, 1994:65).

The only way to avoid this outcome, The Club of Rome suggested, would be to pursue a deliberate policy of limiting growth before the population reaches a natural limit (Davis, 1991:11). According to *The Club of Rome* study, if population growth were stabilized by 1975 and industrialization by 1985, resource depletion and pollution would be sufficiently reduced to avoid collapse before 2100 (Davis, 1991:11). Five of the Meadows models illustrating this dilemma are: (1) the world model standard run, (2) world model with natural resources reserves doubled, (3) world model with unlimited resources and pollution control, (4) world model with unlimited resources, pollution control and increased agricultural productivity, and (5) world model with unlimited resources, pollution control, increased agricultural productivity and perfect birth control. The conclusion on global overshoot and collapse stood valid. Whatever variations in their assumptions were made: doubling natural resource reserves, cutting pollution to one-fourth of its present level, increasing agricultural productivity, and introducing birth control were each added as assumptions in the model simulations, but the general results remained the same. The Report has finally drawn attention to an immediate slowdown in economic growth for creating equilibrium between population and resources.

The book spread like wildfire and became a subject of debate in literally hundreds and hundreds of articles in newspapers, magazines, and journals and in books written about it by experts, journalists and others the world over. Criticism has been raised related to relationships among population and supply of resources, use of world averages rather than specific regional data, the growth of system components differing assumptions. "It did not allow for feedbacks, whether negative or positive, and to this extent it was a flawed analysis. I still think it served a valuable purpose in opening up a public debate and alerting us to the prospect that there could be all kinds of environmental limits to the way we live on Earth. Whatever its deficiencies, the book was certainly worth while" (Myers and Simon, 1994:139). Davis (1991:11) drew attention that its greatest weakness was not only that it dealt with the future, but that it dealt with future technology, which is notoriously unpredictable. The study has been further criticized for being unsound in its methods, biased in assumptions and extreme in its conclusions (Davis, 1991:11). Some of this, however, was later taken up by Mesarovic and Pestel in the so-called *Second Club of Rome Report, Mankind at the Turning Point* (1974). This report took account of a good deal of regional differences by dividing the world into ten major regions: North America,

Western Europe, Japan, Australia plus South Africa, Eastern Europe and the Soviet Union, Latin America, North Africa and the Middle East, Tropical Africa, South Asia and China. They also considered differences among three super regions: the developed world, the socialist world, and the developing world. In addition, they considered a much larger number of variables and the mutual relationships among them than did the Limits to Growth. The conclusions of the second report have emerged even grimmer than those of Meadows.

The Global 2000 Report and the Resourceful Earth

Ten years later, commissioned by the Carter Administration in 1980, an influential 3-volume study on Global 2000 Report to the President: Entering the Twenty-First Century, was published (Barney, 1982). This report is the first attempt by any government at a coordinated analysis of the probable changes in the world's population, natural resources and environment through the end of the century and to assess the government's foundation for long-term planning. It is an environmentalist document, which used the resources of 14 agencies to analyze all selected elements, such as land, food, water, fuel, forests, energy, fisheries, minerals, oil and air. It is an attempt to focus on the growing awareness of the interdependence of population, resources and environment and also recognizes their interrelationships. Barney (1982:1) summarizes that despite greater material output, the world's people will be the poorer in many ways than they are today. For hundreds of millions of the desperately poor, the outlook for food and other necessities of life will be no better, for many it will be worse.

The Resourceful Earth: A Response to Global 2000, edited by Simon and Kahn (1984) presents a bright global future. It explicitly contradicts and refutes the conclusions of Global 2000. Simon and Kahn (1984:63) conclude: "If present trends continue, the world in 2000 will be less crowded (though more populated), less polluted, more stable ecologically, less vulnerable to resource–supply disruption than the world we live in now. Stresses involving population, resources and environment will be less in the future than now. The world's people will be richer in most ways than they are today. The outlook for food and other necessities of life will be better (and) life for most people on earth will be less precarious economically than it is now".

The elaborated findings of the Resourceful Earth are as follows: (1) Life expectancy has been rising rapidly throughout the world, a sign of demographic, scientific and economic success. This fact—at least as dramatic and heartening as any other in human history—is fundamental in any informed discussion of pollution and nutrition. (2) The birth rate in less developed countries has been falling substantially during the past three decades. The rate of growth of the world's population has dropped from 2.2 per cent yearly in 1964–65 to 1.75 per cent in 1982–83, probably a result of modernization and of decreasing child mortality, and a sign of increased control by people over their family lives. (3) Many people are still hungry but the food supply has been improving since at least World War II, as measured by grain prices, production per consumer and the famine death rate. (4) Trends in world forests are not worrisome, though in some places deforestation is troubling. (5) There is no statistical evidence for rapid loss of species in the next two decades. An increased rate of extinction cannot be ruled out if tropical deforestation is severe, but no evidence of linkage has been demonstrated. (6) The fish catch, after a pause has resumed its long upward trend. (7) Land availability will not increasingly constrain world agriculture in coming decades. (8) In the United States, the trend is toward higher quality cropland suffering less from erosion than in the past. (9) The widely published report of increasingly rapid urbanization of U.S. farmland was based on faulty data. (10) Water does not pose a problem of physical scarcity or disappearance, although the world and U.S. situations do call for better institutional management through more rational systems of property rights. (11) The climate does not show signs of unusual and threatening changes. (12) Mineral resources are becoming less rather than more scarce. (13) There is no persuasive reason to believe that the world oil price will rise in coming decades, it may fall well below what it has been. (14) Compared to coal, nuclear power is no more expensive, and is probably much cheaper under most circumstances. It is also much cheaper than oil. (15) Threats of air and water pollution have been vastly overblown; these processes were not well analysed in Global 2000.

Thus, the Global 2000 reflects a trend toward eastern thinking in which every living thing is believed to have an intrinsic right to exist (Holden, 1983:42). Yet, equally remarkable is the notion that the report depicts a time of historical discontinuity in which traditional ways of doing things and the old supply–demand equations will lead eventually to pillage and desecration of natural resources and increasing human misery (Holden, 1983:42). On the contrary, Simon and Kahn share optimistic vision of the future of the globe. Based on historical trends, they powerfully suggest declining scarcity, lowering prices and increased wealth. Holden (1983:42), for example, points out that the free play of market forces—including natural ones—is fundamental to the Simon–Kahn vision. Thus, it appears that their views correspond in many respects to those of the Reagan Administration.

The Earth Summit

It has long been recognized that environmental problems do not respect national boundaries. It follows, therefore, that environmental management requires cooperation between states. Issues of environmental management are, therefore, being increasingly fought at the international level. The United Nations Environmental Programme has been a forerunner in this regard. In legacy of the Bruntland Commission, added to those of the World Conservation Strategy and United Nations Environmental Programmes' own conclusion, there arose a recommendation that an international conference be convened to review progress and decide on future action. In December 1989, the UN General Assembly passed a resolution agreeing to call the conference which Brazil subsequently offered to host. The decision to hold it in a less developed country had enormous political significance and symbolism.

The United Nations Conference on Environment and Development, also known as the "Earth Summit" drew representatives from 178 countries to Rio de Janeiro. During the two weeks in June 1992, it brought together over 100 Heads of State, wherein its official delegates numbered 10,000 and many thousands in other capacities. Governments were invited to draw and submit national reports on their policies and their hopes for UNCED. Aptly named the Earth Summit this became the largest conference ever staged by the United Nations. The outcome of Rio Conference can be seen in 5 key agreements:

(i) **The Framework Convention on Climate Change:** This convention was signed at Rio by 153 countries and the European Union. It established the principle that climate change needed precautionary measures that could not await the resolution of question about scientific certainty. The Convention reflected growing political concern for the issues of global warming. Following this, the more developed countries agreed to take steps to cut greenhouse gas emissions to 1990 levels by the year 2000.

(ii) **The Convention on Biological Diversity:** This convention was signed at Rio by 155 states and the European Union. It aimed at preserving global biological diversity through the protection of species and eco-systems. Since most of the threats were being experienced in the low developed countries and most biotechnology was based in more developed countries it hovered around attempts to reach a compromise.

(iii) **Agenda 21:** This is essentially an action plan for reconciling conservation and development for achieving sustainable development during the Twenty First Century. The Commission was established in late 1992 and consisted of ministerial representatives from 53 states.

(iv) **The Rio Declaration on Environment and Development:** This consisted of 27 principles guiding action on environment and development, building on the Stockholm declaration of 1972. Much debate in this focused over the low developed countries emphasizing development and global equity where the more developed countries emphasized environmental concerns.

(v) **The Forest Principle:** The principles were all that remained free from controversial attempts to draw a global forest convention in 1990–91. It emphasized the sovereign right of individual states to exploit forest resources but within general principles of forest protection and management.

The Earth Summit drew unparalleled levels of public attention of the problems of the environment. It brought national governments a step closer in agreeing to the underlying goals of their environmental policies. However, it lagged and suffered in many areas of achievement, common to most international agreements. Much of its declaration and conventions were couched in terms of vague commitments, general principles or guidelines rather than specific meaningful obligations. Certain issues were also beyond the economic feasibility of some countries. For example, the Rio Conference secretariat estimated that about $125 billion per year would be needed to implement Agenda 21. This sum itself is unlikely to be forthcoming, thus, highlighting the gap between words and deeds. Perhaps it is crucial to understand that dichotomy exists between interdependence of world ecology which recognizes no political boundary. Yet, it is the coming together and merging of heads of state alone which can dissolve the boundaries. Despite many critiques, the Earth Summit was a step forward in this direction.

Gender, Environment and Development

A more recent development in the study of population, resource and development has been the role of gender. Gender refers to culturally and historically specific concepts of feminity and masculinity and the power relations between men and women (Schrijvers, 1993). It is a fundamental concept in understanding human behaviour and social processes. Since 1980's the connection between gender, environment and development has become a special area of interest for researchers, policy makers and activists. Gender, in fact, has entered the rhetoric at the highest levels of international policy. It draws upon interdisciplinary roots within geography, sociology, anthropology and demography in seeking to understand the interrelationships between population, resources and development. It focuses upon how women live under environmental constraints, the roles women play as active agent in society, what decisions they make, and how they deal with the constraints imposed by larger social forces. It emphasizes that men and women deal with environment differently, and women in the South are called **day to day environmental managers** (Dankelman and Davidson, 1988). Finally, social scientists including human geographers recognize that women are the agents of change towards sustainable development. There is now increasing empirical evidence that in their role as managers of natural resources, women play key roles on the quality of environment in many countries. Thus, it is the gender which is a fundamental parameter of creation and alteration of environment. Both men and women act in gender-structured ways; as they do, they change themselves, altering their ways of working and oppressing one another. These alterations in the patterns of women's and men's activity are a profound and prognostic source of environmental change (Ghai, 1994:5). An innovative atlas of women (Seager and Olson, 1986:7) provides excellent illustrations of spatial variation in the lives of women, both globally and within a North American context: "The similarities and differences, the continuities and contrasts among women around the world are best shown by literally mapping out their lives. What we do see, however, is that everywhere women are worse off than men: women have less power, less autonomy, more work, less money and more responsibility. Women everywhere have a smaller share of the pie, if the pie is very small (as in poor countries) women's share is smaller still. Women in poor countries are nowhere equal to men". These differences of gendered perspectives on environmental problems have addressed a number of intellectual issues; (1) eco-feminist, (2) feminist environmentalist, (3) socialist feminist, (4) feminist poststructuralist, (5) environmentalist, and (6) feminist political ecology (Rocheleau, Thomas-Slayter and Wangari, 1995:3). Eco-feminists postulate a close connection between women and nature, while feminist environmentalism stresses on gendered interest in particular resources and ecological processes. Socialist feminism has concentrated especially on the incorporation of gender into political economy using concepts of production and reproduction to delineate men's and women's roles in economic systems. Feminist post-structuralism has started to examine gendered experience of environment as a manifestation of situated knowledge's shaped by class, age, race and ethnicity. A few environmentalists have looked into gender within a liberal feminist perspective to treat women as both participants and partners in environmental protection and conservation programmes. A quite different perspective is emerging from those writers concerned with the political ecology. They have focused on the uneven distribution of access to and control over resources on the basis of gender, class and ethnicity. Gender is treated by feminist political ecology as a critical variable in resource accessibility, in shaping the processes of ecological change and the struggle to sustain ecologically viable livelihoods.

Conclusion

The above review has examined the complex interrelationship between population trends, resource use and developmental impacts at the global level and more specifically developing countries. It has offered a synthesis of conceptual and theoretical approaches to their relationships from Malthus onwards in terms of resource adequacy. It has investigated and assessed seven historical efforts to conceptualize the relationship like Malthusian and Neo-Malthusian, Marxist, Carrying Capacity, Limits to Growth, the Global 2000 Report and the Resourceful Earth, The Earth Summit, and Gender, Environment and Development. The review has revealed that during the last four decades and particularly during the 1980s and 1990s, the population and resource relationship foreseen by scientists has begun to emerge in a number of guises: population and food imbalances, water scarcity, soil erosion, energy scarcity, tropical deforestation, pollution, hazardous wastes and plant and animal extinction the World has known. Many experts think that the provision of sufficient amounts of resources in the future is bleak with expanding population and rising per capita consumption. The review has also reflected that if demographic and economic increase is not checked, the Earth will become choked with people and pollution. Therefore, there is a need to probe the dynamics of complex relationships between population and resources.

References

Allen, J.C. and D.F. Barnes (1985), The causes of deforestation in developing countries, *Annals of the Association of American Geographers*, **75**(2).

Barney, G.O. (1982), *The Global 2000 Report to the President: Entering the 21st Century,* Penguin Books, New York.

Bee, O.J. (Ed.) (1990), *Natural Resources in Tropical Countries*, Singapore University Press, Singapore.

Bernard, F.E. (1970), Population pressure: a preliminary assessment with special reference to kenya, *East African Geographical Review.*

Berry, B.J.L., E.C. Conkling and D.M. Ray (1993), *The Global Economy: Resource Use, Locational Choice and International Trade*, Prentice Hall, Englewood Cliffs, N.J.

Berry, B.J.L., E.C. Conkling and D.M. Ray (1993), *The Global Economy: Resource Use, Locational Choice and International Trade*, Prentice Hall, Englewood Cliffs, 118.

Blunden, J. (1985), *Mineral Resources and Their Management*, Longman, London.

Brown, H. (1954), *The Challenge of Man's Future*, Viking, New York.

Brown, L. (1985), The state of the earth: 1985, *Natural History*, **94**(4).

Brown, L.R. (1994), Food, *Environmental Education Dossiers*, All of Us, No. 9 On Food, Centre Unesco de Catalunya, Barcelona.

Brown, L.R. (1987), *State of the World*, W.W. Norton, New York.

Burton, I. and R.W. Kates (Eds.) (1965), *Readings in Resource Management and Conservation*, University of Chicago Press, Chicago.

Carneiro, R. (1960), Slash and burn agriculture: A closer look at its implications for settlement patterns, in: A.F.C. Wallace (Ed.) *Men and Culture*, University of Pennsylvania Press, Philadelphia.

Cassen, R.H. (1976), Population and development: A Survey, *World Development*, **4**(10/11).

Chandna. R.C. (1986, 1992), *A Geography of Population*, Kalyani Publishers, New Delhi.

Clarke, J.I. (1972), *Population Geography*, Pergamon Press, Oxford.

Cohen, J.E. (1995), How many people can the earth support? *Span*, **37**(12).

Cook, R.C. (1951), Human fertility: The modern dilemma, *Soil Science*, **72**(1).

Cowgill, D.O. (1963), Transition theory as general population theory, *Social Forces*, **41**.

Dankelman, L. and J. Davidson (1988), *Women and Environment in the Third World: Alliance for the future*, Earthscan, London.

Davis, K. (1945), The world demographic transition, *Annals of the American Academy of Political and Social Sciences*, **237**(1).

Davis, K. (1991), Population and resources: Fact and interpretation, in: K., Davis and M.S. Bornstan (Eds.), *Resources, Environment and Population: Present Knowledge and Future Options*, Oxford University Press, New York.

Eckholm, E.P. (1976), *Losing Ground: Environmental Stress and World Food Prospects*, Pergamon, Oxford.

Ehrlich, P.R. (1972), *The Population Bomb*, Pan, London.

Ehrlich, P.R. and A.H. Ehrlich (1970), *Population, Resources, Environment: Issues in Human Ecology*, W.H. Freeman, San Francisco.

Elrlich, P.R. and A.H. Ehrlich (1990), *The Population Explosion*, Simon and Schuster, New York.

El-Badry, M.A. (1992), World population change: A long-range perspective, *Ambio: A Journal of the Human Environment*, **21**(1).

Findlay, A. and A. Findlay (1987), *Population and Development in the Third World*, Mothuen, London.

Forrester, J. (1961), *Industrial Dynamics*, Wright-Allen Press, Cambridge, MA.

Forrester, J. (1970), *Urban Dynamics*, Wright-Allen Press, Cambridge MA.

Forrester, J. (1971), *World Dynamics*, Wright-Allen Press, Cambridge MA.

Ghai, D. (Ed.) (1994), *Development and Environment: Sustaining People and Nature*, Blackwell Publishers, Oxford.

Grigg, D.B. (1970), The growth and distribution of the World's arabic land, 1870–1970, *Geography*, **55**.

Haden–Guest, S. et al. (1956), *A World Geography of Forest Resources*, The Ronald Press Company, New York.

Hart, J.F. (1970), The adjustment of rural population to diminishing land resources, in: W. Zelinsky, L.A. Kosinski and A.M. Prothero (Eds.), *Geography and A Crowding World*, Oxford University Press.

Harvey, D. (1974), Population, Resources and the Ideology of Science, *Economic Geography*, **50**(3), 256–277.

Holden, C. (1983), 'Simon and Kahn versus Global 2000', *Science*, **22**.

Huxley, J. (1956), World Population, *Scientific American*, **194**(3), 64–76.

Khabeishvili, S. (1994), Renewable energy, *Environmental Education Dossiers, No. 8*, Centre Unesco do Catalunya, Barcelona.

Kim, O.K. and P. Van Den Oever (1992), Demographic transition and patterns of natural resource use in the Republic of Korea, *Ambio: A Journal of the Human Environment*, **21**(1).

Lee, R.D. (1991), Long-run global population forecasts: A critical appraisal, in: K. Davis and M.S. Bernstam (Eds.), *Resources, Environment and Population: Present Knowledge and Future Options*, Oxford University Press, New York.

Logan, B.I. (1991), Overpopulation and Poverty in Africa: Rethinking the traditional relationship, *Tijdschritt voor Economische en Sociale Geografie*, **82**(1).

Mabogunje, A.L. (1970), A typology of population pressure on resources in West Africa, in: W. Zelinsky, L.A. Kosinski and R.M. Prothero (Eds.), *Geography and A Crowding World*, Oxford University Press, New York.

Malthus, T.A. (1988), *Essay on the Principle of Population*, Reeves and Turner, London.

Mather, A.S. (1986), *Land Use*, Longman, Hong Kong, 108–109.

Meadows, D.H., D.L. Meadows, J. Randers and W.W. Behrens, III (1972), *The Limits to Growth: A Report for the Club of Rome's Project on the Predicament of Mankind*, Universal Books, New York.

Meadows, D.M., D.L. Meadows and J. Randers (1992), *Beyond the Limits: Global Collapse or A Sustainable Future*, Earthscan Publications, London.

Mitchell, B. (1989), *Geography and Resource Analysis*, Longman, London.

Myers, N. and J.L. Simon (1994), *Scarcity or Abundance? A Debate on the Environment*, W.W. Norton, New York.

Neurath, R. (1994), *From Malthus to the Club of Rome and Back: Problems of Limits to Growth, Population Control and Migrations*, M.E. Sharpe, New York.

Notestein, F.W. (1945), Population: The long view, in: T.W. Schultz (Ed.), *Food for the World*, University of Chicago Press, Chicago.

Osborn, F. (1948), *Our Plundered Planet*, Little Browns and Company, Boston.

Petersen, W. (1961), *Population*, Macmillan, New York.

Ramanaiah, Y.V. and N.B.K. Reddy (1983), Carrying capacity of land in Andhra Pradesh, *Indian Geographical Journal*, **58**.

Rocheleau, D., B. Thomas-Slayter and E. Wangare (1995), *Gender and Environment: A Feminist Political Ecology Perspective*, Routledge, London.

Schrijvers, J. (1993), Motherhood Experienced and Conceptualised: Changing Images in Sri Lanka and the Netherlands, in: Diane Bell, Pat Caplan, and Wazir Jahan Karim (Eds.), *Gendered Fields: Women, Men and Ethnography*, 143–158, Routledge, London.

Schrijvers, J. (1995), The violence of development: A choice for intellectuals, quoted in: H. Van Den Hombergh, *Gender, Environment and Development: A Guide to the Literature*, Institute for Development Research, Amsterdam, Chapter 1.

Seager, J. and A. Olson (1986), *Woman in the World: An International Atlas*, Simon and Schuster, Now York.

Simon, J.L. and H. Kahn (Eds.) (1984), *The Resourceful Earth: A Response to the Global 2000 Report*, Basil Blackwell, New York.

Shrestha, N.A. and D. Conway (1985), Issues in population pressure, land resettlement and development: The Case of Nepal, *Studies in Comparative International Development*, **20**(1).

Steel, R.W. (1970), Population pressure in tropical Africa, *Transactions of the Institute of British Geographers*, **49**.

Stonich, S.C. (1993), *I am Destroying the Land: The Political Ecology of Poverty and Environmental Destruction in Honduras*, Westview Press, Boulder.

Taeuher, I.B. (1970), Population dynamics and population pressure: Geographic-demographic approaches, in: W. Zelinsky, L.A. Kosinski and A.M. Prothero (Eds.), *Geography and A Crowding World*, Oxford University Press.

Thompson, W.S. (1929), Population, *American Journal of Sociology*, **34**, 959–975.

Todaro, M.P. (1984), *Economic Development in the Third World*, Longman, New York.

United Nations Environment Programme (1993–94), *Environmental Data Report*, Basil Blackwell, Oxford.

Vogt, W. (1948), *Road to Survival*, Sloane, New York.

Wrong, D.H. (1956), *Population*, Random House, New York.

World Resources Institute (1988), *World Resources 1987*, Basic Books, New York.

World Resources Institute (1991), *World Resources 1990–91: A Guide to the Global Environment*, Oxford University Press, New York.

World Resources Institute (1995), *World Resources 1994–95: A Guide to the Global Environment*, Oxford University Press, Delhi.

Zelinsky, W. (1966), *A Prologue to Population Geography*, Prentice Hall, New Jersey.

Zelinsky, W., L.A. Kosinski and R.M. Prothero (Eds.) (1970), *Geography and A Crowding World*, Oxford University Press, New York.

4

Revisiting the Classical Land Use Model of Von Thunen

H.N. Misra and Reena Pradhan

Abstract: The only model or theory which partially or fully attempts to explain the spatial organization of land use is Von Thunen's Agricultural Location Model. This classical model was propounded nearly 200 years ago and since then several changes have taken place in the spatial organization and land use pattern. This chapter attempts to evaluate the relevance of this model in the contemporary context by studying the 12 sample villages located at the vicinity of Allahabad, a metropolis. The similarities, associations and differences in the theory and practice have been identified and an effort has been made to propose a land use model more relevant in the present day context.

Keywords: Traditional Knowledge, Perishable Product, Production System, Farm Produce, Zoning Mechanism, Locational Information, Dairying, Intensive Farming, Timber and Firewood, Ranching

Introduction

The world population has been continuously increasing and according to UN estimates by 2030 AD, the population of world is likely to be about 8.2 billion. Increasing population naturally necessitates more food, more water and more power, which are the three basic ingredients for the smooth functioning of the metabolic system. Interestingly with the increase of global population, the population of poor people has also been witnessing a phenomenal growth. It is estimated that nearly 25 per cent of the world's poor population will be living in the Indian sub continent. There is, therefore, the need to enhance the agricultural production processes in order to meet the challenges of the increasing population. Land, thus, happens to be the most viable resource that the man has at his command. But what is most critical is the type of land use that is practiced to sustain the humanity. Obviously, thus, agriculture occupies the vast expanse of land and plays the most dominant role in spatial organization. Even though it is purely a geographical issue, yet there has been no serious effort to deal with the spatial organization of the agricultural space. The only theory which partially or fully attempts to explain the spatial organization of land use is that of Von Thunen's Agricultural Location Model. Thus, there is a great substance in saying that geography has a long tail with a short body. There are a very few theories, and the applicability of these theories is even lesser.

Since times immemorial man has been trying to organize space, which is divided based on the different forms of activities such as agriculture, industry, rural settlements, urban settlements and commercial activities, etc. Of all these, agriculture represents the most dominant sector of spatial organization especially in developing countries. There are several theories dealing with spatial organization pertaining to industrialization, urbanization and commercialization. However, the theoretical explanation of agricultural space has been conspicuous by its absence from the very beginning. It is in this context that Von Thunen's Agricultural Location Model (1826) has great relevance as it is credited for its singular contribution in the field of agriculture. The concept of this theory was, however, put forth more than 200 years ago by an Italian—Giovanni Vico who gave the radical idea that human society was not just random collection of rather remarkable happenings, but was in actuality an ordered and lawfully structured. The Von Thunen's theory has, however, been further clarified and made more exciplicit by Hoover (1937), Isard (1951), Losch (1954) and Dunn (1955). Among the contemporary geographers who have attempted to explain and apply the land use theory of Von Thunen, the mention may be made of Garrison and Marble (1957) who presented the spatial structure of agricultural activities by propounding a model based on the modification of Von Thunen's model. This model is highly technical as it is based on mathematical equations. Yet another research paper which has attempted to explain the rural settlements and land use pattern, besides focusing on agriculture, has been presented by Chisholm (1962). He emphasizes the basic importance of land use competition and allocation process and chooses to examine those aspects that relate to the function of relative location. Thus, he places greater emphasis on distance. Birch (1963), while reviewing the rural land in relation to location theory, observes that comparatively little attention appears to have been paid by geographers concerned with land use studies to the development (from existing knowledge or from their own deductive reasoning) of a theoretical frame work. Such a framework has seldom been employed in order to embrace case studies as empirical evidence for testing, modifying, rejecting or extending existing generalization (Birch, 1963).

Peet (1969) has been discreet and distinct in presenting a very profound review and application of Von Thunen's model in the context of Britain, Western Europe and north-east North America. He has also presented different variants and strands of the theory of location of crop production. In so doing, he has attempted to remove some of the simplifying assumptions by introducing some complicating conditions such as: (i) No complexities, (ii) Influence of a fertile area or land, (iii) Influence of a subsidiary town, (iv) Influence of non optimal behaviour and (v) Influence of several complexities.

The present paper aims at filling this void by trying to see the applicability of Von Thunen's theory in the current context. The current context is particularly significant because much water has flown since the theory was propounded.

Objectives, Database and Methodology

A few assumptions and hunches can be made as under:

1. The economic rent is not the basis for spatial organization of agriculture.

2. Traditional knowledge/human behaviour based on seasons and soils play significant role in bringing the deviation in Indian context.
3. Irrigation plays the most significant role in spatial organization of agriculture.
4. The nature of demand and supply and change in technology influence land use pattern.

These are some of the hunches which have been explored to test the applicability of classical land use model in the present day context.

The analysis is based both on primary and secondary data. While secondary data has been tapped from census and tahsil records, the primary data is based on the field work conducted in 12 sample villages. The applicability of the model has been tested by randomly selecting villages at different locations and in different directions from the city of Allahabad. Altogether 12 villages have been selected. The selected villages are distributed in seven zones or concentric rings which have been drawn by taking Allahabad city as a centre. First circle has a radius of 5 km, the second circle has the radius of 10 km, the third circle has the radius of 15 km, the fourth circle has the radius of 20 km, the fifth circle has the radius of 25 km, the sixth circle has the radius of 30 km and the seventh circle has the radius of 35 km. The first circle is purely urban and, therefore, there is no sample village in this circle. In order to identify similarities, differences and association between the theory and practice, simple regression and coefficient correlation techniques have been used.

Von Thunen's Isolated State Model

The first attempt of agricultural land use model in relation to spatial pattern of a city and it's surroundings was made by John Heinrich Von Thunen, a German. His classical work on the locational agricultural land use zone was first published in 1826 in the form of "Der Isolirte Staat in Beziehung Auf Land Wirtschaft". He was the first to have laid the foundation for refined analysis of the location of agricultural land use. Indisputably, this has been the first solid work which also helped in much broader area of locational analysis. In 1810 at the age of 27, Von Thunen acquired his own agricultural state known as Tellow near the town of Rostok in Mecklenburg on the Baltic coast of Germany. For about 40 years until his death in 1850, he continued supervising the cultivation of the Tellow state and, thus, acquired not only lot of experience but also huge data base to support the model/theory which he subsequently proposed. Even though this model is mainly based on empirical observation, it has assumed the status of a normative model due to analytical base provided by Dunn (1955). The original model of Von Thunen was inherently descriptive and based on some assumptions. He made six basic assumptions while proposing his model.

These assumptions are as mentioned under:

1. The existence of an isolated state cut-off from the rest of the world.
2. The domination of this state by a single large city that served as the sole urban market.
3. The setting of the city in a broad, featureless plain that was equal everywhere in fertility and in which the ease of movement was the same everywhere so that production and transport cost were the same everywhere.

4. The supplying of the city by farmers who shipped agricultural goods there in return for industrial produce.
5. The transport of farm produce by the farmer himself, who hauled it to the central market along a close, dense trail of converging roads of equal quality at a cost directly proportional to the distance covered; and
6. The maximizing of profits by all farmers, who automatically adjust the output of crops to meet the needs of the central market (Haggett, 1975).

The land use pattern so proposed by him has been shown in the Table 4.1. This table clearly brings out the following:

1. More perishable products would be grown closer to market.
2. Products with higher economic productivity per land area will be grown closer to market.
3. Products that are more difficult to transport will also occur closer to market.

Table 4.1 Land use rings based on Von Thunen's model

Zone	*Percentage of state area*	*Relative distance from central city*	*Land use*	*Major product marketed*	*Production system*
0	<0.1	–0.1	Urban industrial	Manufactured goods	Urban trade centers of state; near iron and coal mines
1	1	0.1–0.6	Intensive agriculture	Milk, vegetables	Intensive dairying and trucking; heavy manuring; no fallow period
2	3	0.6–3.5	Forest	Firewood	Sustained-yield forestry
3a	3	3.6–4.6		Rye, potatoes	6-year intensive crop rotation; rye (2), potatoes (1), clover (1), barley (1), vetch (1); no fallow period; cattle stall-fed in winter
3b	30	4.7–34	Extensive agriculture	Rye, animal products	7-year rotation system: field grass with an emphasis on dairy products; pasture (3), rye (1), barley (1), oats (1), fallow period (1).
3c	25	34–44		Rye, animal products	3-field system: rye, etc. (1), pasture (1), fallow period (1)
4	38	45–100	Ranching	Animal products	mainly extensive stock-raising; some rye for on-farm consumption
5	–	Beyond 100	waste	none	None

Source: P. Haggett (1965), *Locational Analysis in Human Geography*, (St. Martin's press, New York, and Edward Arnold, London, 165.

There are two shades of the model- pre-modified model and modified model. In pre-modified model river has been introduced as the source of transportation and the land use zones form the concentric rings and in case of modified model due to role of river as a connecting network the concentric rings are distorted (Figure 4.1).

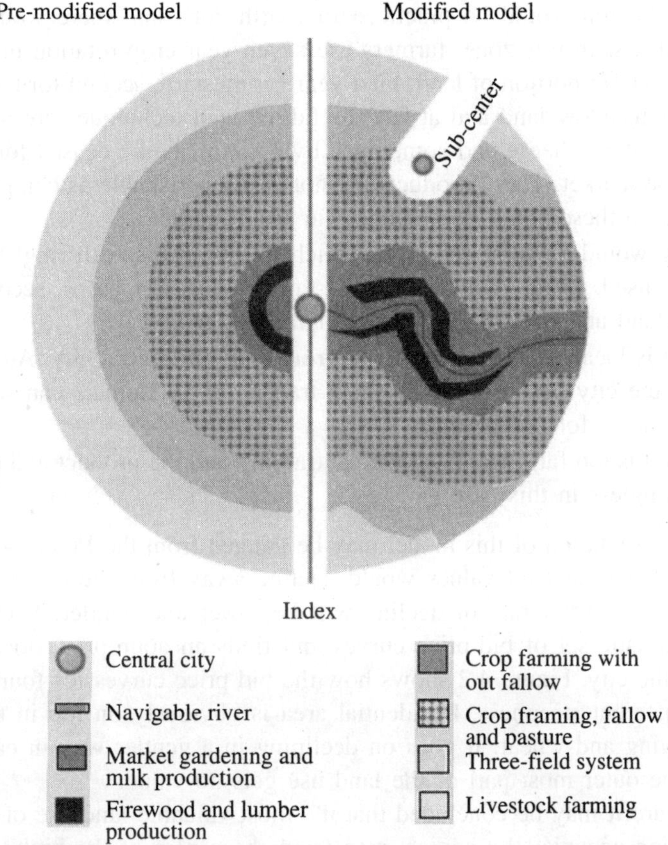

Figure 4.1 Von Thunen's pre-modified and modified model.

Spatial Organization of Agriculture as Conceived by Von Thunen

As it is evident from the aforesaid model, there are as many as seven land use zones which have been conceived by Thunen. These are as under:

1. Dairying and intensive farming occur in the ring closest to the city. Since vegetables, fruits, milk and other dairy products must get to market quickly, they would be produced close to the city as they are perishable and can not travel longer distance.
2. Timber and firewood would be produced for fuel and building materials in the second zone. Before industrialization, wood was a very important fuel for heating and cooking. Wood is very heavy and difficult to transport hence it would be located as close to the city as possible.
3. The third zone consists of extensive fields crops without fallow land, such as food grains. Since grains last longer than dairy products and are much lighter than fuel, the transport cost would be less and they would be located further from the city.

4. Crop production would be practiced in fourth zone and there would be fallow land and meadows. In this zone, farmers use seven year crop-rotation in which mustard is cultivated at 1/7 portion of land. First year for mustard, second for barley, third for oat, fourth for meadow land and at last the fallow land techniques are used in cultivation. Mustard, butter, cheese and sometimes living animals are ceased for meat are used to send to the market. These products are not easily perishable as compared to vegetables and milk, so these could be practiced far from market.
5. Fifth ring would be for three crops which means in the fifth ring three farm systems would be used. In this belt 1/3 part of farm is used for crops, second 1/3 part is for meadow land and remaining is used for fallow land.
6. Ranching is located in the final ring surrounding the central city. Animal can be raised far from the city because they are self-transporting. Animals can walk to the central city for sale or for butchering.
7. Waste land is too far away from the central city and the product and production system are meaningless in this case.

The graphical representation of this model may be gauged from the Figure 4.2. This pattern of land use reveals that rural land values would decline away from the central city in the same way as urban values do but rate of decline will be lower and gentler. Each agriculture land use has a characteristic set of bid-price curves and finds an appropriate location with respect to distance from the city. Figure 4.2 shows how the bid price curves for four types of land use have slopes of different steepness. Residential area is obviously on top in terms of bid price followed by dairying and wheat. It goes on declining in a gentler way in case of grazing but waste which is the outer most part of the land use gets no value.

From this figure it may be concluded that the most valuable land use of market gardening and milk production occupies the nearest ring from the centre of the highest rent and so on. This means that the land within the closest ring around the market will produce product that are profitable in the market, yet are perishable or difficult to transport. As the distance from the central market increases, the land use shifts to producing products that are less profitable in the market, yet are much easier to transport. These land use zones were arranged in a concentric circle fashion since one type of land use was homogenously away from the centre.

Thunen's model places too much emphasis on locational rent which has been explained mathematically by Dunn (1955). The location may be understood by the following equation:

$$L = Y(P - C) - YD(F) \tag{4.1}$$

where

L = the location rent (in \$/km^2)
Y = the crop yield (in ton/km^2)
P = the market price of the crop (in \$/ton)
C = the production cost of the crop (in \$/ton)
D = the distance to the central market (in km)
F = the transport rate (in \$/ton/km).

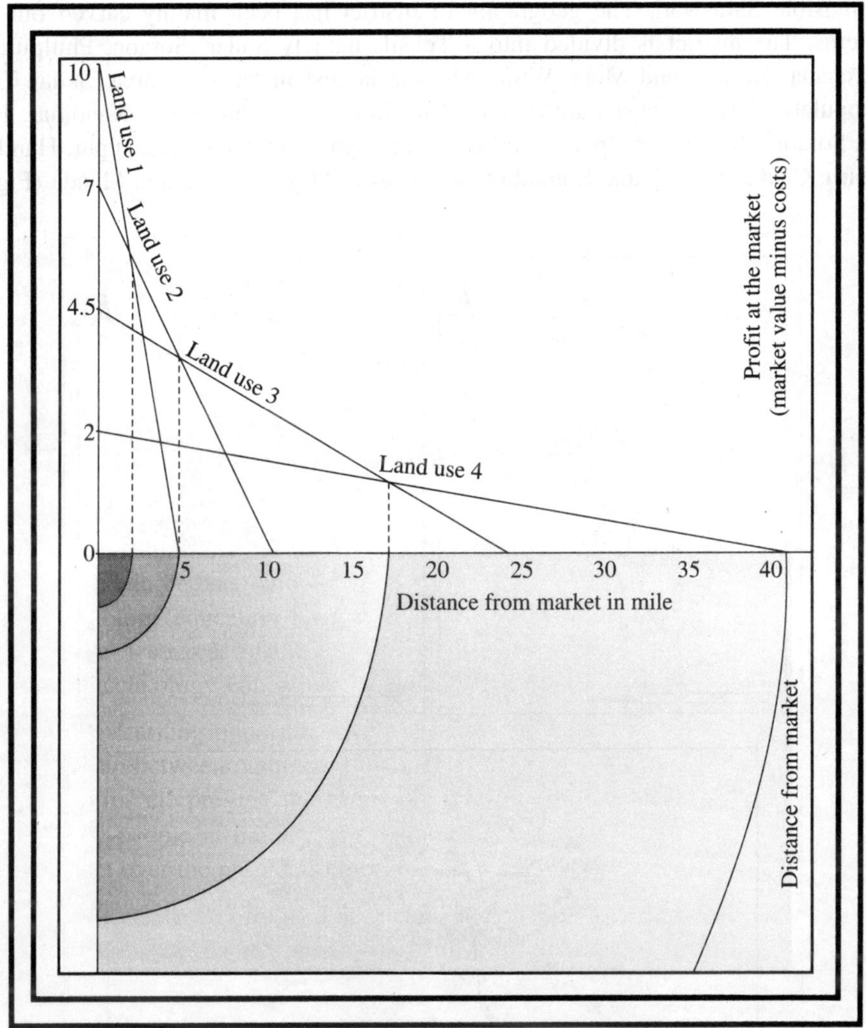

Figure 4.2 Zoning mechanism by Von Thunen.

Study Area

The district of Allahabad, which has been selected for study, is located between 24°27' and 25°45'N latitudes and 81°35'E and 82°22'E longitudes. It covers an area of 5246.22 sq. km. The extent of the district is 63 km. from east to west and 109 km. north to south. The study area is surrounded by districts of Bhadohi and Mirzapur in the east, Kaushambi and Banda in the west, Pratapgarh and Jaunpur in the north and, Banda of Uttar Pradesh and the district Rewa of state of Madhya Pradesh in the south. This represents 1.8 per cent of the total land area of Uttar Pradesh and stands 7th in the state in the areal extent. The famous city of Allahabad, which is of great antiquity, is located at the confluence of three rivers—the Ganga, the Yamuna and the invisible Saraswati. The geography of district has been mainly carved out by these river systems. The district is divided into 8 Tehsils namely Sadar, Soraon, Phulpur, Handia, Bara, Karchana, Koraon and Meja. While Meja is largest in terms of area, Sadar Tehsil has highest population. These tehsils are divided into 20 development blocks-Kaudihar, Holagarh, Mauaima, Soraon, Baharia, Phulpur, Bahadurpur, Pratappur, Saidabad, Dhanupur, Handia, Jasra, Shankargarh, Chaka, Karchhana, Kaundhiyara, Uroowa, Meja, Koraon and Manda (Figure 4.3).

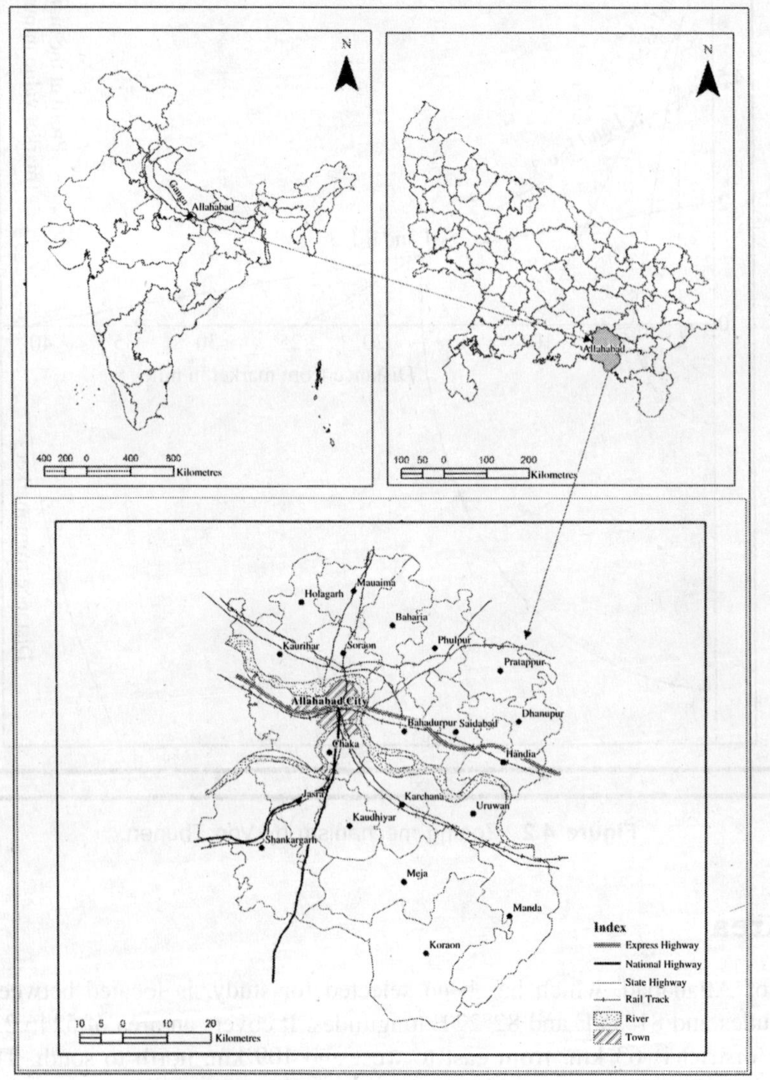

Figure 4.3 Location map of Allahabad district.

The applicability of the model has been tested by randomly selecting villages at different locations and in different directions from the city of Allahabad. Altogether 12 villages have been selected. The selected villages are distributed in seven zones or concentric rings which have been drawn by taking Allahabad city as a centre. First circle has a radius of 5 km, the second circle has the radius of 10 km, the third circle has the radius of 15 km, the fourth circle has the radius of 20 km, the fifth circle has the radius of 25 km, the sixth circle has the radius of 30 km and the seventh circle has the radius of 35 km. The first circle is purely urban and, therefore, there is no sample village in this circle. The location of villages according to zones has been shown in Figure 4.4.

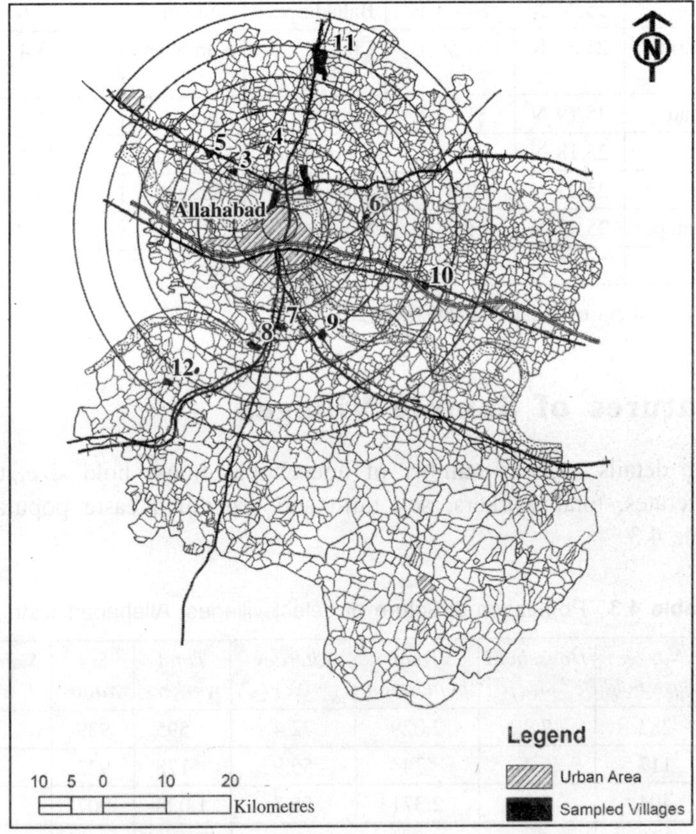

Figure 4.4 Location map of sample villages.

The sample villages, their astronomical location, straight line distances from the city besides the blocks and tehsils in which they are located, have been shown in the Table 4.2.

Table 4.2 Locational information of select villages, Allahabad district

Sl. No.	*Name of villages*	*Astronomical location*		*Blocks*	*Tehsils*	*Distance from Allahabad city (km)*	*Major connectivity*
		Latitudes	*Longitudes*				
1	Singramau	25,31 N	81,53 E	Soraon	Soraon	10.5	Rail, road
2	Tiwari Kala	25,30 N	81,50 E	Soraon	Soraon	11.0	Rail, road
3	Kashipur	25,34 N	81,50 E	Kaudihar	Soraon	13.8	Road

(*Contd.*)

Table 4.2 Locational information of select villages, Allahabad district (*Contd.*)

Sl. No.	*Name of villages*	*Astronomical location*		*Blocks*	*Tehsils*	*Distance from Allahabad city (km)*	*Major connectivity*
		Latitudes	*Longitudes*				
4	Krishnapur	25,33 N	81,47 E	Soraon	Soraon	15.3	Rail, road
5	Parwejabad	25,19 N	81,51 E	Kaudihar	Soraon	22.4	Rail, road
6	Roodrapur	25,34 N	81,44 E	Bahadurpur	Phulpur	22.6	Rail, road
7	Malak Harihar Uperhar	25,59 N	81,59 E	Chaka	Karchhana	23.4	Road
8	Markhamau	25,19 N	81,54 E	Jasra	Bara	25.2	Rail, road
9	Gauhania	25,18 N	81,48 E	Karchhana	Karchhana	26.1	Rail, road
10	Bendo	25,23 N	82,04 E	Saidabad	Handia	30.3	Rail, road
11	Aswa Dautapur	25,42 N	81,53 E	Mauaima	Soraon	30.9	Rail, road
12	Kishora	25,15 N	81,40 E	Shankergarh	Bara	41.6	Road

Source: Statistical Bulletin of Allahabad District (2010).

Salient Features of Sample Villages

The demographic details such as number of households, house hold size, total population, literates and illiterates, total workers, sex ratio and scheduled caste population have been presented in Table 4.3.

Table 4.3 Population structure of select villages, Allahabad district

Name of villages	*No. of house hold*	*Household size*	*Total population*	*Literacy (%)*	*Total workers*	*Sex ratio*	*Scheduled population (%)*
Singramau	283	7.2	2,029	72.4	595	939	27.25
Tiwari Kala	117	6.4	744	55.9	178	922	25.53
Kashipur	404	5.9	2,371	55.7	1,028	907	27.03
Krishnapur	140	5.8	813	56.0	365	988	53.75
Parwejabad	123	6.0	737	52.9	181	945	32.83
Roodrapur	221	7.5	1,665	56.6	471	903	17.47
Malak Harihar Uperhar	736	6.8	4,981	65.2	1,755	888	13.53
Markhamau	429	6.3	2,697	64.3	1,103	942	21.31
Gauhania	330	6.5	2,147	60.7	528	843	4.14
Bendo	556	7.3	4,079	53.5	1,200	843	4.16
Aswa Dautapur	555	6.5	3,631	39.3	1,625	937	18.45
Kishora	184	7.5	1,389	54.2	556	857	10.22

Source: Census (2001).

There are four categories of villages:

1. Large villages (more than 4000 population): Malak Harihar Uperhar and Bendo.
2. Medium sized villages (2000–4000 population): Singramau, Kashipur, Markhamau, Gauhania and Aswa Dautapur.
3. Small villages (1000–2000 population): Roodrapur and Kishora.
4. Very small villages (below 1000 population): Tiwari Kala, Krishnapur and Parwejabad.

The sex ratio in Malak Harihar, Kishora and Gauhania is very low. This is less than 900. This indicates that these villages are the victim of migration. The postal economy is playing very important role in these villages and this has an impact on the land use as well. The literacy rate in these villages varies between 55–60 per cent. The notable exceptions are Singramau and Aswa Dautapur. In Singramau it is 72.4 per cent where as literacy rate is exceptionally very low in Aswa Dautapur as it recorded the literacy rate of 39.3 per cent only (Table 4.3).

The scheduled caste population varies between 4 and 14 per cent among Bendo (4.16), Gauhania (4.14), Kishora (10.22) and Malak Harihar (13.53). The villages such as Roodrapur, Markhamau, Tiwari Kala, Kashipur and Singramau record scheduled caste population between 17 and 28 per cent. The two villages where the scheduled caste population is exceptionally very high are Parwejabad (32.83 per cent) and Krishnapur (53.75 per cent). The composition of scheduled caste population in Krishnapur is unusually quite alarming and this reflects on the land use pattern of this village.

The major chunk of the area of these villages is devoted to agricultural land use. The net sown area in these villages varies between 62 and 98 per cent. The unculturable barren land is insignificant except in Malak Harihar and Markhamau. Fallow land keeps varying and the pasture land is also non-existent.

In some of the villages horticulture has emerged as a significant alternative to agricultural crops. These villages are Singramau, Markhamau, Bendo, Kishora and Aswa Dautapur. The culturable waste is present almost in all the villages. The villages where area under culturable waste is excessibly found are Tiwari Kala, Malak Harihar, Kashipur, Roodrapur, Parwejabad and Gauhania. The presence of this type of land shows that these villages have great potential for development of area under food crops as well as horticulture.

This land use pattern does not, however, in any way conform to the land use pattern conceived by Von Thunen, e.g., there is no livestock farming. As a result organized milk production does not take place. This is further corroborated by the paucity of pasture land. All the pasture land has been converted into cultivable land. There is so much pressure of population on land that hardly any area is left for forest and, therefore, the concept of fuel production through forest resources is also not a very tenable proposition in the contemporary context. Horticulture is gradually emerging as a ray of hope in diversification of agriculture.

Cropping Pattern of the Selected Villages

An effort has been made to study the cropping pattern of sample villages lying in different zones. This exercise has been especially done to see if there exists any pattern close to the one conceived by Von Thunen in his model. In this exercise, therefore, the cropping pattern of the selected villages has been presented in the Table 4.4.

Table 4.4 Land use of sample villages Allahabad district (2010) (Area in hectares)

Villages	*Total area*	*Food crops*	*Cash crops*	*Vegetables*	*Other uses*	*Double cropped area*	*Irrigated area*	*Cropping intensity*
Singramau	569.61	256.58 (45.04)	86.94 (15.26)	193.5 (33.97)	32.59 (5.72)	237.02 (41.61)	237.02 (41.61)	144.14
Tiwari Kala	238.93	123.3 (51.61)	4.9 (2.05)	57.32 (23.99)	53.41 (22.35)	18.43 (7.71)	117.44 (49.15)	109.93
Kashipur	157.59	76.39 (48.47)	8.2 (5.2)	63.1 (40.04)	9.9 (6.28)	76.64 (48.63)	87.13 (55.29)	151.89
Krishnapur	118.78	73.76 (62.1)	5.24 (4.41)	31.58 (26.59)	8.2 (6.9)	73.19 (61.62)	106.77 (89.89)	166.19
Parwejabad	224.23	168.71 (75.24)	0.76 (0.34)	51.07 (22.78)	3.69 (1.65)	142.37 (63.49)	141.92 (63.29)	164.56
Roodrapur	175.05	86.8 (49.59)	4.05 (2.31)	60.94 (34.81)	23.26 (13.29)	49.76 (28.43)	139.67 (79.79)	132.78
Malak Harihar Uperhar	250.04	59.27 (23.7)	2.2 (0.88)	168.12 (67.24)	20.45 (8.18)	27.85 (11.14)	123.11 (49.24)	112.13
Markhamau	174.96	113.99 (65.15)	2.11 (1.21)	15.58 (8.9)	43.28 (24.74)	165.77 (94.74)	161.27 (92.18)	225.89
Gauhania	183.17	92.13 (50.3)	20.13 (10.99)	1.57 (0.86)	69.34 (37.86)	132.44 (72.3)	161.41 (88.12)	216.35
Bendo	117.18	79.96 (62.24)	0.22 (0.19)	27.17 (23.19)	9.83 (8.39)	23.12 (19.73)	32.05 (27.35)	121.54
Aswa Dautapur	343.88	202.93 (59.01)	41.32 (12.02)	15.75 (4.58)	83.88 (24.39)	97.35 (28.31)	102.3 (29.75)	137.44
Kishora	138.32	103.49 (74.82)	0.59 (0.43)	25.07 (18.12)	9.17 (6.63)	103.02 (74.48)	110.13 (79.62)	179.77

Source: Agriculture Department, Allahabad (2010) values in parenthesis show per cent.

From Table 4.4, it may be gauged that the area under food crops is predominantly very high in all villages. This clearly explains the fact that this activity is purely at the subsistence level where in food crop production is necessitated for survival and, therefore, this occupies the first priority in the agriculture production process. This honestly does not, in any case, take into account the transport cost factor as Von Thunen has mentioned in his theory. Vegetable production gets obviously the second priority as a supporting food product and, therefore, the area under vegetable production is next only to the food crops. Among the vegetables the main products are potato, onion, egg plant (brinjal), okra, cucumber, gourd, pumpkin, tomato, etc. The production of vegetable is, by and large, done at a small scale at the household consumption level. There are few patches around the city of Allahabad where it is produced at the commercial scale but certainly it does not follow any zonation. It does, however, follow the rule of accessibility. It is grown in areas which are close to road-rail network. The cash crop occupies the third priority as it is grown in much smaller area in all the villages. Among the cash crops sugarcane is most important. Since it requires irrigation, it is grown in those areas where there is reasonably a good availability of water. The water sources—canals and tube wells have started playing significant role in irrigation as against wells which were common sources of irrigation a decade ago. Thus, it may be concluded that the necessity of food at the household level and irrigation are the dominant factors in dictating the land use pattern. The accessibility–road–rail network also plays vital role but not at the scale as conceived in the classical model.

Testing the Applicability: Similarities, Associations and Divergences

The aforesaid analysis helps in testing the applicability of the model in question. An effort has, therefore, been made to see similarities, associations and divergences between the theory and the ground situation. The intercorrelation matrix (Table 4.5) based on the variables mentioned in Table 4.4 clearly demonstrates that out of 21 correlations, sixteen are insignificant. Only five correlations are significant. Area under vegetable and food crop is significantly negatively correlated (r = –0.68). So is the case with area under vegetables and cropping intensity (r = –0.61). Interestingly area under irrigation and double cropping have significant positive correlation (r = 0.74) which is self-explanatory. The cropping intensity and area under double cropping are also very highly correlated (r = 0.96). So is the case with cropping intensity and area under irrigation (r = 0.74). There is spontaneity in all these positive correlations. What is most important is that distance does not appear to play any significant role in this correlation matrix. This appears to be quite natural in an emerging economy where several innovative changes are taking place.

Table 4.5 Inter correlation matrix among seven variables

	Distance from city	*Food crops*	*Cash crops*	*Vegetables*	*Double cropping*	*Area under irrigation*	*Cropping intensity*
Distance from city	1						
Food crops	0.43	1					
Cash crops	–0.27	–0.26	1				
Vegetables	–0.36	–0.68*	–0.27	1			
Double cropping	0.27	0.58	0.01	–0.52	1		
Area under irrigation	0.09	0.27	–0.21	–0.24	0.74*	1	
Cropping intensity	0.27	0.45	0.11	–0.61*	0.96*	0.74*	1

Source: Computed

*Significant at 99 per cent.

The scatter diagrams have been drawn to show the relationship between the cropping pattern and distance. These diagrams are based on the data procured from sample villages. As many as six such diagrams have been prepared. From these diagrams the following conclusions may be drawn:

1. *Food crops and distance:* Food crops such as wheat, paddy, barley, pulses, and oil-seeds occupy very little importance in the area close to city (Figure 4.5). The area devoted to food crops increases with increasing distance which is evident from the positive correlation (r = 0.43) between the two variables. Even though this relation is not significant, yet it is indicative of the fact that food crops are grown in the areas away from city.

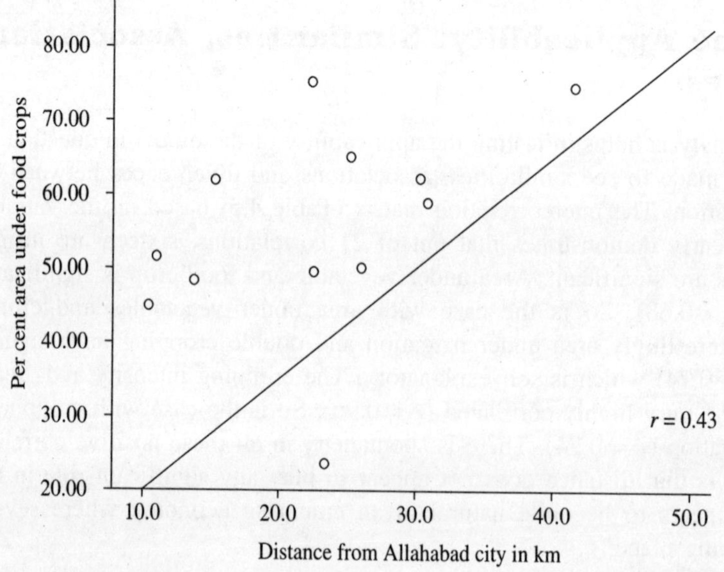

Figure 4.5 Relationship between area under food crop and distance from city.

2. *Cash crops and distance:* This is a very revealing pattern and it very closely conforms to the assumptions of classical model. The classical model emphasizes the importance of rental value of land and transportation cost. The analysis of the relationship between area devoted to cash crops and distances reveals that cash crop occupies the most significant land use in the vicinity of city. The area under cash crops goes on declining with the increasing distance, i.e., the villages located close to city have larger area under cash crops and villages located away from the city have lesser area under cash crops (Figure 4.6). Presumably the farmers are fully aware that they will get better price by producing the cash crops near by a city. This indicates the importance of accessibility as well as that of rental value of land. The correlation coefficient between two variables is negative (r = –0.27).

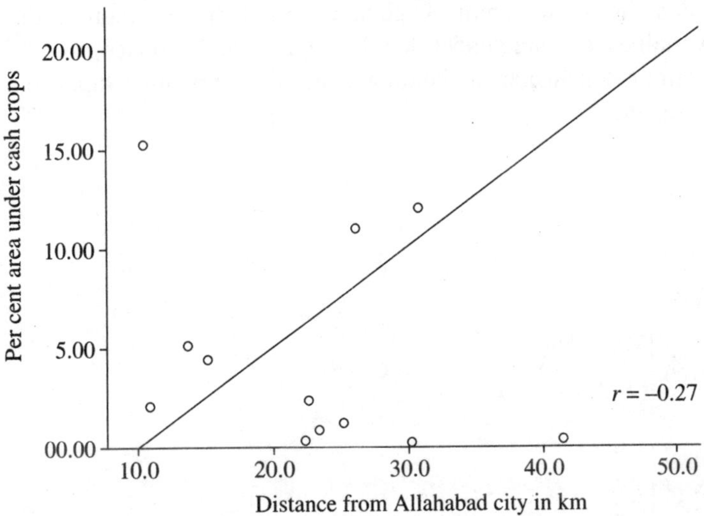

Figure 4.6 Relationship between area under cash crop and distance from city.

3. *Area under vegetables and distance:* The villages which are close to the city give much importance to vegetable produce. The villages which are closely located along the roads have devoted larger area to vegetables (Figure 4.7). The relationship between the two variables—area under vegetables and distance from city centre are negatively correlated (r = –0.36). This nature of land use pattern very closely corresponds with the classical model.

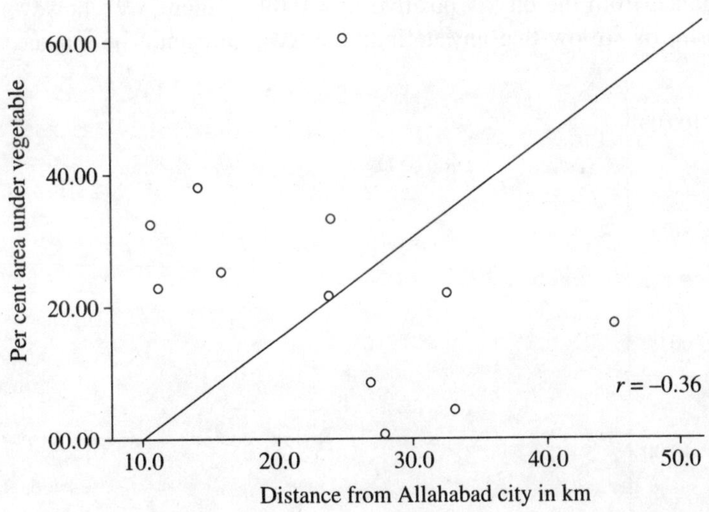

Figure 4.7 Relationship between area under vegetable and distance from city.

4. *Double cropping and distance:* The land devoted to double cropping is the characteristic features of those areas which are a little far away from the city (Figure 4.8). This is

very evident from the pattern of relationship obtained by plotting the scatter diagram of two variables, i.e., area under double cropping and distance from the city ($r = 0.27$), but no definite conclusion can be drawn because the relationship, even though positive, is insignificant.

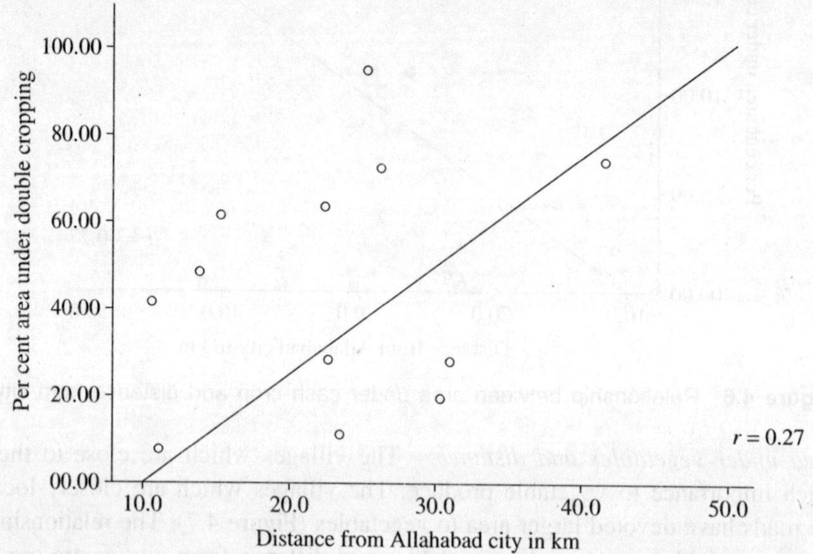

Figure 4.8 Relationship between area under double cropping and distance from city.

5. *Area under irrigation and distance:* The relationship between area under irrigation and distance from the city is positive ($r = 0.09$) (Figure 4.9), however, the degree of relationship is so low that any definite observation cannot be made.

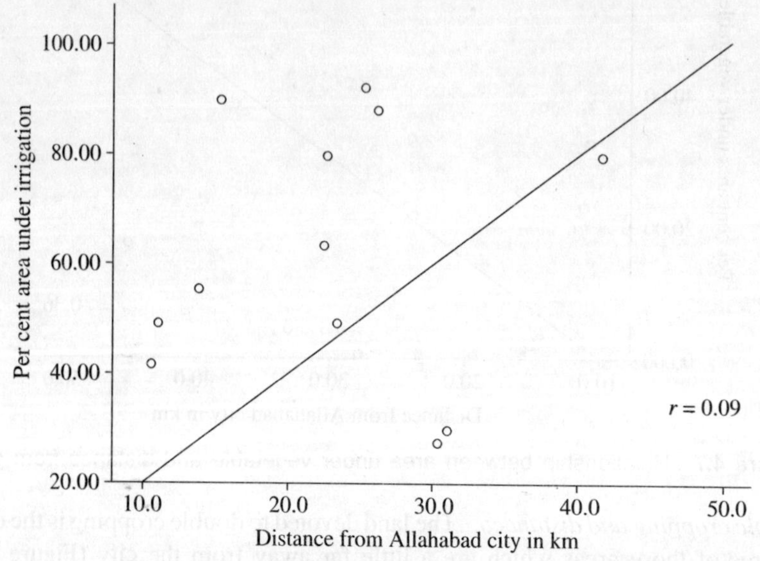

Figure 4.9 Relationship between area under irrigation and distance from city.

Undoubtedly irrigation plays a very dominant role in determining the land use but the villages under sample have subsistence level of living and, therefore, they are not able to take full advantage of irrigation facility either on account of their poverty or on account of small land holdings. The demographic pattern of the villages reveals that in some villages, the scheduled caste population is less than 5 per cent and in other villages (Singramau, Kashipur, Parwejabad and Krishnapur) it varies between 27–53 per cent. This clearly indicates that the majority of the sample villages are inhabited by extremely poor people. This has a great bearing on the land use pattern. In a situation like this they have not been able to get away from the traditional type of farming and they continue with the old practice of cultivation. Much of the agricultural innovations currently in vogue have not been adopted by the farmers.

6. *Cropping intensity and distance:* The relationship between cropping intensity and distance from the city is positive ($r = 0.27$) and it is clear that the cropping intensity increases with increasing distance (Figure 4.10). However, the relationship is evidently insignificant and therefore it is not possible to draw any conclusion.

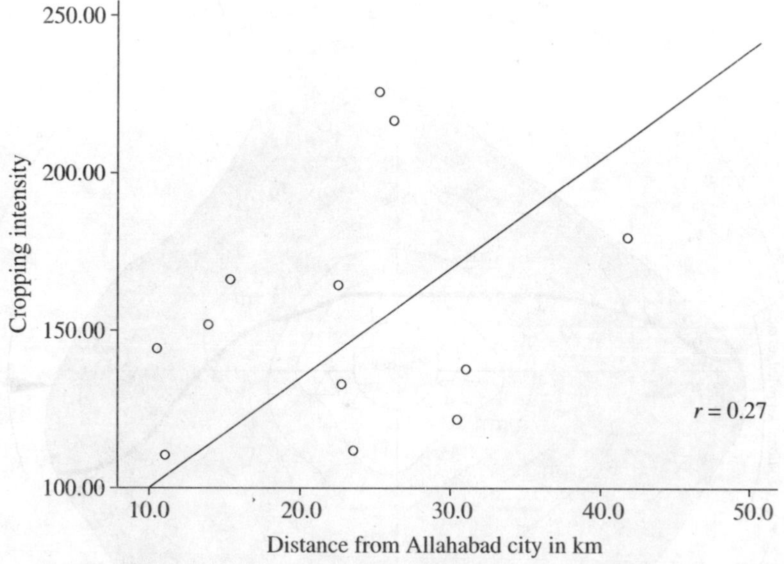

Figure 4.10 Relationship between cropping intensity and distance from city.

Some Observations

It may be pointed out that the there is a great difference in between the reality and classical model in view of the changed circumstances through time and space. This necessitates proposing a new model of land use. The model is basically an abstraction of reality and works like a bridge in between reality and abstraction. There are different forms of model such as iconic, analogue and symbolic. The models are also classified as deterministic and stochastic and also sometimes as graphical and mathematical. In the present case the graphical model of land use is being proposed which is basically a modified version of the classical land use model. There are two parts of the model (Figure 4.11):

First Part attempts to summarize the factors which impinge upon the land use process. These are;

1. Physical factors such as temperature, rainfall, soil characteristics, slope and seasons such as winter, summer and rainy seasons.
2. Social factors/human factors such as family size, family belief, family compulsion, traditions and values, education, labour, human perception and cognition.
3. Economic factors such as per capita income, accessibility to resources, technology, transport, demand and supply and price factor.
4. Political factors such as public policies. Of late, this has become very important element in decision making process and, thus, plays very significant role in determining the land

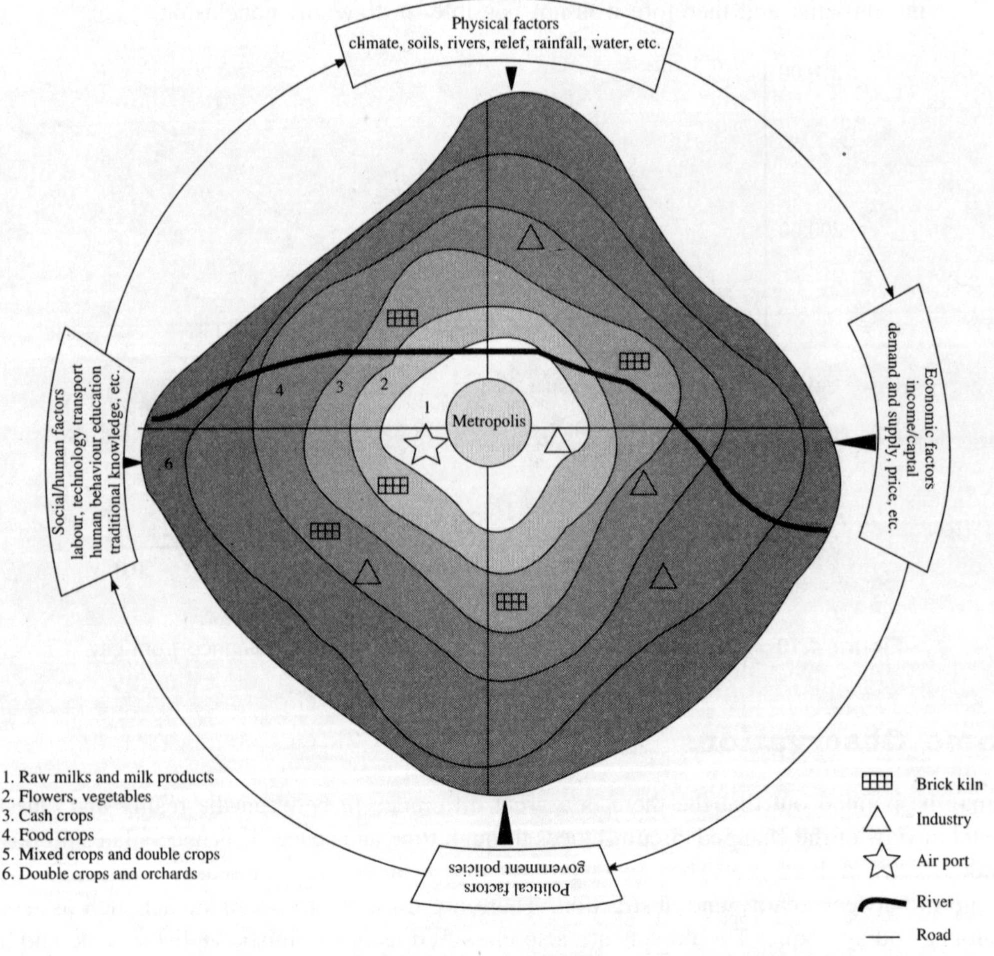

Figure 4.11 Modified version of classical land use model.

use pattern. The public policies issued by government from time to time do influence the human behaviour and land use pattern. Green revolution is a clear cut example of public policy. Similar such programmes such as white revolution, yellow revolution and gold revolution are making dent in the behavioural pattern of farmers.

The Second Part attempts to present a modified version of the classical model keeping in view the trend and pattern of land use found around the city of Allahabad which is based on field observations and data derived from 12 sample villages located at different distances from the city of Allahabad.

This star shaped model identifies six zones which are as follows:

1. First zone: This is the closest area to the city rather the city itself where milk and milk products are produced.
2. Second zone: The second subsequent area is devoted to flowers and vegetables.
3. Third zone is devoted to production of cash crops.
4. Fourth zone is represented by food crops such as wheat, paddy, oil seeds, pulses etc.
5. The fifth zone is characterized by double and mixed cropping pattern.
6. The orchards such as banana, guava, aunla and mango etc. are produced in the most distant zone from the city i.e. the sixth zone.

There are several specific locations among these zones where brick kilns, small industrial outlets, warehouses, cold storages, and petrol pumps etc. are interspersed. This model is based on the land use pattern around the city of Allahabad and may hold true in similar such situations elsewhere also. The proposed model does not in any sense decry the utility and importance of the Von Thunen's Model, Rather, it plays critical role in measuring the departures between theoretical and empirical observations.

Conclusion

The land use analysis of twelve selected villages clearly indicates that Von Thunen's classical model is not fully applicable in the present day context. There are whole range of factors which impinge upon the land use pattern. The family compulsions, social commitment, economic circumstances, geographical factors and political decisions have great impact on the processes and patterns of land use. The technological innovations also play critical role in influencing the pattern. In addition to this, the irrigation technology and traditional knowledge have great bearing on land use changes. This, therefore, necessitates a revisit to the classical land use model proposed by Von Thunen. In this paper, an effort has been made to present a modified version of the classical land use model by identifying the current contextual developments obtaining in the field of agriculture in India. Accordingly a model of land use has been proposed. It is expected that a more sophisticated version of model may come in due course.

References

Birch, J.W. (1963), Rural land use and location theory: A review, *Economic Geography*, **39**, 273–276.

Chisolm, M. (1962), *Rural Settlements and Land Use*, Hutchinson, London.

Dunn, E.S. (1955), *The Location of Agricultural Production*, University of Florida Press, Gainesville, 115.

Garrison, W.L. and D.F. Marble (1957), The spatial structure of agricultural activities, *Annals of the Association of American Geographers*, **47**, 133–144.

Haggett, P. (1975), *Geography: A Modern Synthesis*, Harper&Row, New York.

Hoover, E.M. (1937), *Location Theory and the Shoe and Leather Industries*, Harvard University Press, Cambridge, MA.

Isard, W. (1951), Distance inputs and the space economy, Part I: The conceptual framework, *Quarterly Journal of Economics*, **62**, 182–198.

Losch, A. (1954), *The Economics of Location*, Yale University Press, New Haven.

Peet, J.R. (1969), The spatial structure of commercial agriculture in the nineteenth century: A Von Thunen interpretation, *Economic Geography*, **45**(4), 283–301.

Thünen, Von J.H. (1826), *Der Isolierte Staat in Beziehung auf Landschaft und Nationalökonomie*, Trans. By C.M. Wartenberg, 1966, Von Thünen's Isolated State, Pergamon Press, Oxford.

5

Water as Foe, Water as Friend
Lessons from Bengal's Millennium Flood

Graham P. Chapman and Kalyan Rudra

Abstract: In September 2000, at the end of a good monsoon and during a tropical cyclonic storm, Bengal suffered a particularly severe flood, in which more than one and a half thousand people died. In West Bengal, more than 20 million people, and in Bangladesh more than 3 million, lost their homes and virtually all of their possessions. This chapter explores different experiences of the disaster, and many differing explanations of its causes, both physical and social. It proposes the idea that the specific form of development that has taken place in Bengal since the mid 19th century, the 'standard' road–rail and urban–industrial model, has been transplanted into an inappropriate geographical setting. The result is that the urban sector has externalized its costs onto the rural poor. In this context, it is suggested that the new 'open policy' on floods, also advocated elsewhere in the world, be seriously considered as more appropriate and sustainable for Bengal.

Keywords: THED, Land-Slip, Upstream Catchment, Third World Cities, Alluvial Cone, Land Sinking, Beels, Oxbow Lakes, Dangas, Khals, Borrow Pits

Introduction

This article results from the study of a major flood in Bengal in September 2000, known locally as the Millennium Flood. The official death toll, almost certainly an underestimate, was about 1500. The impact of the flood was, however, much broader than this figure suggests. The flood destroyed most of the assets of approximately 20 million poor, rural people in West Bengal (India) and 3 million in an adjacent part of Bangladesh, effectively wiping out the small gains in development that have occurred in recent decades.

In disasters such as this, there is usually an 'extreme' natural event, such as a tropical storm; but how that event impacts on society depends on local patterns of development, both of a physical kind (e.g., the construction of protective barriers) and of an institutional kind (the provision of warnings, emergency evacuation plans, etc.). In the case of the Ganga–Brahmaputra delta, shared between India and Bangladesh, there has been an extensive literature suggesting that the frequency of damaging flood is the result of environmentally damaging 'development' in the mountains. This thesis, known as the Thesis of Himalayan Environmental Degradation (THED) is strongly established. In a recent reformulation of this theory Kasperson et al. (1999), and Kasperson and Kasperson (2001) suggest that in Nepal population pressure and remoteness lead to over-exploitation of fragile ecosystems, increasing the frequency of landslips and erosion. Consequently, it is suggested, there are enhanced rates of downstream sedimentation and an increased incidence of flood on the plains. The original thesis has been criticized by Ives and Messerli (1989) and Chapman and Thompson (1995), who provide evidence that farming may stabilize some slopes, that forest cover is increasing in places, and that where increased erosion does take place, much of the material is redeposited within upstream catchments. Mirza et al. (2001) conclude that over the last few decades there is no statistical evidence for an increased frequency of flood events, defined hydrologically, in the Ganga, the Brahmaputra and the Meghna basins, although they leave open the possibility of increasing flood damage because of changing settlement patterns. In reviewing THED, Blaikie and Muldavin (2004) suggest that indeed there are multiple environmental 'truths', and that different stake holders will use different truths for their own purposes.

It seems, then, that claims to environmental 'truth' are inherently political. Thus, if the problem of flooding in the delta 'is caused' by accelerated erosion in the mountains, then there is no need to change the pattern of development locally. An investigation into flooding in the plains may then be framed by this view, and start by finding evidence of road building in the hills, or other development associated with an incidence of increase. The framing of problems is examined in the field of political ecology (Stott and Sullivan, 2000; Forsyth, 2003; Zimmerer and Bassett, 2003) where nuanced case studies unravel the connections between the framing of environmental knowledge and the evolution of policy.

In disasters in the developing world, it seems an empirical truth that the people who suffer most are the poor. They are the most 'vulnerable' in society (Wisner et al., 2003). For example, it is the poor of Third World cities who put their shanty towns on the flood-prone land shunned by the wealthy classes, or on steep hill slopes liable to landslips. This leads Wisner et al. to propose a 'pressure' model, in which the root causes for the pressures that place people at risk are to be found in political structures that may originate far away. An example would be the trade discrimination against agriculture in developing countries that is partly responsible for perpetuating rural poverty in the developing world. In turn, this leads to high rates of migration to urban areas, and the occupation of such risky sites.

When the Millennium flood happened a range of interest groups each claimed their own environmental 'truth'. For some, it was purely a 'natural' event, for others the result of the mismanagement of dams and barrages, for yet others the fault of brick yards that blocked drainage channels. In this article, we move through the initial confusion of the disaster, to point out what we believe to be the most important 'truths'. We then identify the most important root causes, and recommend a complete rethinking concerning patterns of development in Bengal. We begin, however, by setting this analysis in the context of the physical and human geography of the delta.

Physical Geography and Settlement in Bengal

The delta of the Ganga–Brahmaputra–Meghna (popularly known in the literature as GBM) is the largest and most dynamic on earth. By comparison with other major world rivers, only the Ganga and the Brahmaputra combine extreme total discharge, extreme discharge per unit area, extreme ratio of peak to average discharge, and very high sediment loads (Subba, 2001). These characteristics follow from the conjunction of the heaviest monsoon on earth with the highest mountains on earth (the latter being implicated in the former). The alluvial cone (subaquatic delta) extends 2000 nautical miles from the delta out into the Bay of Bengal on the ocean floor—meaning that in many ways the current delta is just like an ice-berg – that small fraction of the depositional zone which is above sea-level (Figure 5.1).

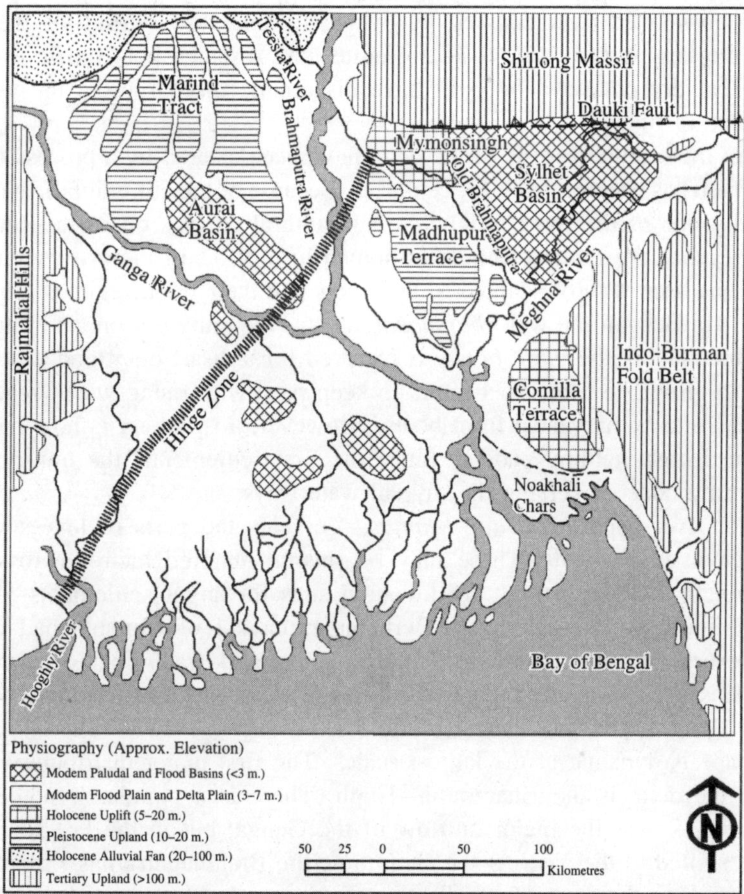

Figure 5.1 Physiography of West Bengal.

Structural Physiography of Bengal

The major rivers are liable to shift their courses significantly. This may occur because they raise their own beds by sedimentation. They then avulse—in effect sliding sideways to form a new channel in a less blocked region or to re-occupy an older channel. They may shift because of the land sinking (by compression of sediment or by tectonic activity) or because of uplift. Aerial survey clearly shows how the rivers have braided, split, diverted, captured, over-flowed, re-invigorated different channels—but such is the confusion of traces of former water channels, it is not possible to say what was the definite major pattern of drainage at any one time in the past—and, even in the present, rivers can flow in different directions at different times according to sources of inflow and the heights of water in different outflows. In all parts of deltaic Bengal there are *bil*s (sometimes spelt *beel*s), otherwise called **backswamps**. These are lakes of water that stay long into the dry season, and may not dry up at all. Some are disconnected ox-bow lakes. Others are very long linear features, which are extensive lengths of substantially abandoned river courses, but which fill and flow during the wet season, and in the case of the largest, may still maintain quite long distance boat traffic even in the dry season. Those that dry out most but still have discernible discharges in the wet season are often called **nulas** or **nalas**.

Nearly all of the original forests of the delta have been cleared by a process of agricultural colonization, which has been ongoing for centuries. Because of the silt, rainfall, and temperature, this is potentially one of the most productive agricultural regions on earth. Rural population densities have reached the highest known in human history. Until the last century and a half, the technology has been wholly adapted to the rivers and their flood regimes. This is reflected in the language—in Bengali the word *barshakal* denotes the rainy season, and implies expected and beneficial inundation: the word *bonya* is reserved for a disastrous flood. Local deep water rice varieties can grow one foot in 24 hours to keep pace with rising water, reach a height in excess of 12 feet, and be harvested from boats. (However, this variety is now mostly replaced by short stemmed high-yielding paddy). Since the first settlements, the transport of cargoes has mostly been by boats traversing the myriad waterways.

Along major river banks there are *'dangas'*—or elevated parts of levées which usually remain dry even in high floods. These may be several hundred metres across, and several kilometres in length. Naturally these are favoured sites for larger settlements—Kolkata is on one—hence its linear north-south form. Berhampur, capital of Murshidabad district, is on another. The levées are not continuous features—the flood water that over tops them and forms them drains back in to the main river through *khals*—natural channels which occur at periodic points along the line of levies (Figure 5.2).

The landscape is dynamic at the largest scales. The first major distributary of the Ganga at the head of the delta is the Bhagirathi—Hugli. There is a popular hypothesis that prior to the 16th century it was the major outflow of the Ganga; but in the last few centuries the major flow has shifted to the east. At the same time the Brahmaputra has shifted from east of the Madhupur tract, to the west of it. The two rivers which once entered the Bay of Bengal separately now have a confluence inland. In Mukherjee's (1938) book *The Changing Face of Bengal: A Study in Riverine Economy*, there is a detailed discussion of how the shifts in the rivers affect hydrology, agriculture, malaria—just about all aspects of life—and how settlement adjusts in consequence. Eaton (1993) in his account of Islam and the Bengal Frontier notes how these changes affected towns, trade and settlement. Towns abandoned by rivers were themselves abandoned by inhabitants, who moved to found new towns by the new courses of rivers.

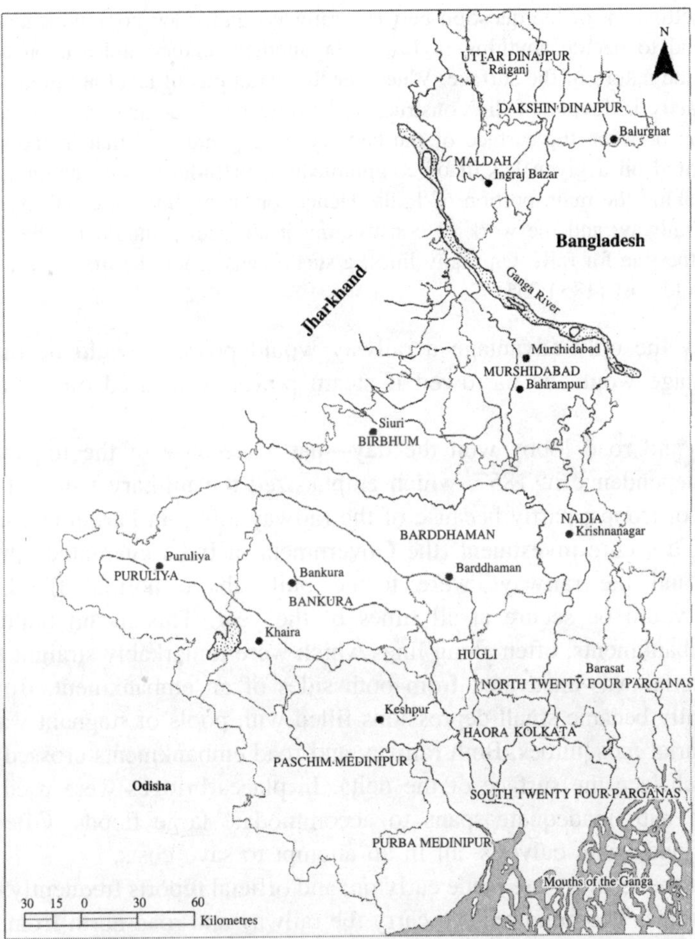

Figure 5.2 Administrative units of West Bengal.

The Colonial Impact and Development Models

The British East India Company took control of Bengal in the mid 18th century, at the time that Britain itself was in the throes of the industrial revolution. In England, the use of coke to smelt iron was accompanied by the development of inland canals from the 1770s. But cheap iron, then steel, led to the development of steam-power, and the railway revolution took off from the 1830s. Both in India and in Britain there were debates about 'development' using these new technologies, and about Bengal in particular there was a fierce debate on the relative merits of canals or railways.

One of the protagonists for the canals was Sir Arthur Cotton, a military engineer who had restored large irrigation schemes in South India. He proposed that Bengal should be provided with canals:

> Further, the settlement of the question between railways and water communications in England would not tend to decide anything in India, for another century at least, on account of the difference in the nature of the surface. Wherever the variations of level are great, the advantage is proportionately in favour of the construction of railways as compared with canals. There is no comparison between the surface of the country in England, and that in India. The amount of work required on a given length of communication in India is not one-tenth of what it is in England, taking the main portion of India. Hence, on many lines, a canal may be almost as straight as a railway, and the work of constructing it altogether should not be more than that of preparing the line for rails. On many lines, a steam canal could be made for a tenth of what a railway would cost (1854;251).

In Cotton's view the only advantage a railway would possess would be that of speed, and even that advantage would be narrowed if steam power were used on the canals instead of hauling animals.

But the rail and road lobby won the day—partly because of the impact of the Mutiny/ First War of Independence in 1857, which emphasized the military value of railways for the fast deployment of troops; partly because of the railway lobby in Parliament in London, which sensed a large and secure investment (the Government in India guaranteed the rate of return).

The roads and the railways were to be built above normal flood levels—so that communication would be secure at all times of the year. This meant building hundreds of miles of new embankments, often along lines which were remarkably straight across the plains. Usually the material was excavated from both sides of an embankment, from 'borrow pits', which subsequently became small depressions filled with pools of stagnant water and breeding grounds for malarial mosquitoes. Both railway and road embankments crossed the myriad lines of drainage which lace the surface of the delta. In places bridges were used over significant rivers, but often with inadequate spans to accommodate large floods. Often there were no bridges, or else inadequate culverts, all in an attempt to save costs.

Criticisms of the results were made early on, and official reports frequently recorded damage to the new structures. The bund built to carry the railway and road north from Berhampur, also acting as a flood protection bund for the town, broke at Kalukhali in 1871 and 1874.

> ... As in 1871, the bridge at Kalukhali has been destroyed, and a breach of over 200 feet made in the road. It is an important and much frequented thoroughfare, connecting the Bhagirathi with the Ganga during the rainy season; and the Committee regret that they are unable, in justice to the other numerous roads under their charge, to allot as much money to this road as would be necessary to keep it in first-class order (Hunter, 1876:142).

The bund (embankment) had filled in the entry point to an old (distributary) course of the Bhagirathi, now a nala, the Gobra Nala. The breach re-opened the old course for the excess discharge. Because of such breaches, the aim, of achieving secure communication at all times of the year and in all years, was not, and has never, been achieved.

The problems were general. Willcocks (1930) cited the *Indian Mirror* of 1907:

> 66. I now give some quotations from the December 21, 1907, number of the *Indian Mirror*. 'The East Indian Railway was constructed in 1853–54 and opened in 1855. The line begins in Howrah and runs through the district of Hughli, after the Bally station, almost parallel with and close to the Hughli river. The river bank being higher, the natural drainage was to the fields

behind or westward, returning immediately to the river through 'Khals', natural drains. When the railway line was constructed with an insufficient and inadequate number of waterways for the sake of economy, on the west of the towns and villages on the river bank, the natural drainage of the Province was interfered with and obstructed.'

67. 'To protect the E.I. railroad from Burdwan onwards, a high embankment was constructed on the east bank of the Damodar to stop the floods. The P.W.D. extended their operations to other rivers like the Rupnarain, the Selye, the Cossye and other rivers in Midnapore and Orissa. Wherever embankments were thrown up, tanks and artificial lakes were choked with weeds and the crops suffered for want of fertilizing silt. Scarcity and famines have become more frequent and severe, and ague and fever are caused.'

In the 1920s, Professor M.N. Saha (Chatterjee, 1987:46–47) condemned the railway line connecting Howrah and Burdwan for increasing the frequency and magnitude of floods on their western side, and increasing malaria. Ray (1935:236) also blamed the Railway Authority for devastating flood in North Bengal in 1922. He opined...

'the Government was wilfully and criminally responsible for the great havoc...unless the narrow culverts were replaced by bridges of long span they would always be liable to the calamity of flood. And this is what exactly happened. The fact is that railway lines are always constructed with an eye to the interest of foreign shareholder. The less the cost, greater the expectation of dividend'.

In 1938, Mukherjee considered the continuing development of roads and railways in East Bengal.

A systematic policy of road and railway construction in the eastern districts of Bengal would be a repetition of the mistakes, which have contributed in no small measure to the economic decline of Central and Western Bengal. More attention should be diverted to the policy of the improvement of waterways and inland navigation, the making of new waterways by means of cuts, where none exists at present, the easing of bad bends of rivers and the clearance of aquatic weeds in the waterways. The German policy of *railways and waterways* rather than of *railways versus waterways* is nowhere so indispensable as in Eastern Bengal, where the water borne traffic is still one of the largest in the world (1938:69).

Reversing Hydrological Change: The Ganga Barrage at Farakka

The decay of the Bhagirathi and resultant threat to the port–industrial economy has been a matter of deep concern to the port authority of Kolkata since its inception. There were many reports and enquiries into the changing condition of the rivers, such as the Stevenson-Moore Committee's (1919) *Report on the Hooghly River and its headwater*. Nearly all of them shied away from major interference with the rivers because of considerations of cost, but also because of the recognition that the rivers were probably not tameable in the long run anyway. An exception was Willcocks (1930:50) who proposed that serious consideration be given to a barrage on the Ganga to divert water down the Mathabhanga, another distributary connecting the Ganga (here in Bangladesh named Padma) with the Bhagirathi. It was a speculation not supported by the government of the day.

After the transfer of power from Britain to South Asia in 1947, the circumstances can be summarized:

1. The navigation channel from Calcutta (Kolkata) was silting up;
2. There were diminishing fresh water supplies down the Bhagirathi;
3. There was no longer a rail or road bridge to the northern part of West Bengal, because the Hardinge Bridge was now in East Pakistan (East Bengal);
4. The down-stream province was part of a hostile state with which India had frozen its relations.

A complex scheme was initiated, which involved building a barrage-cum-road-rail-bridge across the Ganga at Farakka. The barrage would raise the Ganga 7 m during the low (lean) season. On the right bank (south and west) a 38 km long feeder canal would lead across country to the Bhagirathi at Jangipur. The idea was and is that during the low season the canal would divert 40,000 cusecs of water, turning the Bhagirathi into a perennial river leading downstream to Kolkata.

Significantly, the canal cuts across the drainage outlets of four small rivers coming from the hills of Chotanagpur in adjacent Jharkhand state—the Trimohoni, Kanloi, Bagmari and Madhabjani. Before the canal was built, these drained into the Ganga just upstream of its first distributary, the Bhagirathi. After the canal was built, they drained into it, thence into the Bhagirathi. In ordinary seasons, their small contribution to discharge would be welcome, but there is no alternative escape for major influxes. Thus the huge discharges from Jharkhand down these rivers in late September 2000 were ducted straight into the Bhagirathi. The blockage of the line of drainage has also turned much of the land on the west side of the canal into unusable swamp-land.

Downstream of the confluence of the feeder canal with the Bhagirathi there are other west bank tributaries draining from Jharkhand. It is thought that one of these, the Damodar, until the 18th century used to drain into the Bhagirathi north of Kolkata. Now it makes a bend south and joins the Hugli lower downstream. It was known at Independence to be one of India's 'rivers of sorrow', because of its high frequency of flooding. One of Prime Minister Nehru's first commitments after Independence in 1947 was to a combined power, flood control, and irrigation scheme on the Damodar, including two large dams, the Maithon and the Panchet, in its upper reaches. These are managed by the Damodar Valley Corporation, modelled on the Tennessee Valley Authority of the USA. Another of the right bank rivers, the Mayurakshi, also has a dam at Massanjore—but in this case for irrigation only, with no designed flood storage.

The Millennium Flood

Experiencing the Flood

After the event, the flood becomes tagged as a single event—a single disaster with an associated death toll, costed losses of possessions, estimated reconstruction costs, etc., and it is even given a single number (2000–061) and entry in such records as the Dartmouth Flood Observatory's Global Register of Extreme Flood Events (http://www.dartmouth.edu). This is the source for Figures 5.3 and 5.4, which show the dıamatic change between early and late September 2000.

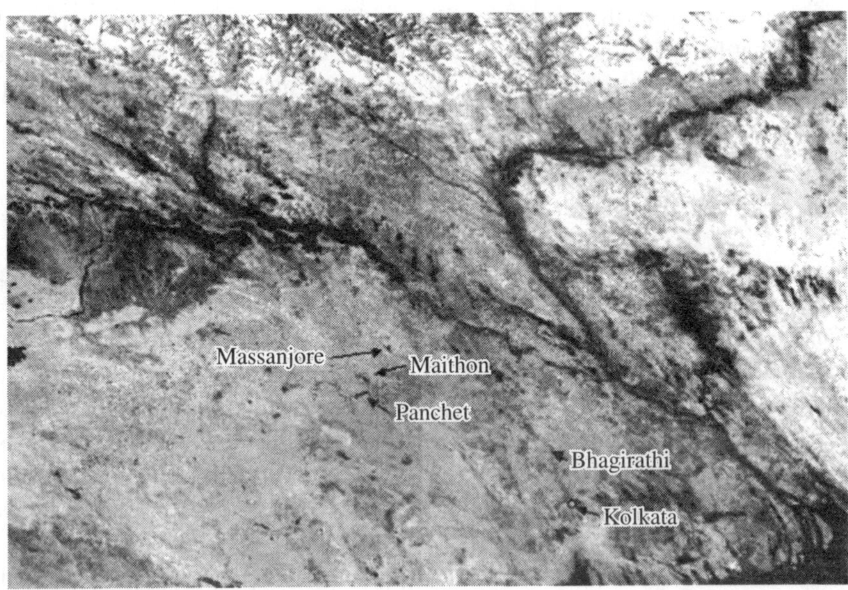

Figure 5.3 Satellite image of Bihar and Bengal, 5th September, 2000.

Source: Darthmouth Flood Observatory note the Sylhet depression East of the Brahmputra is already 'normally' flooded.

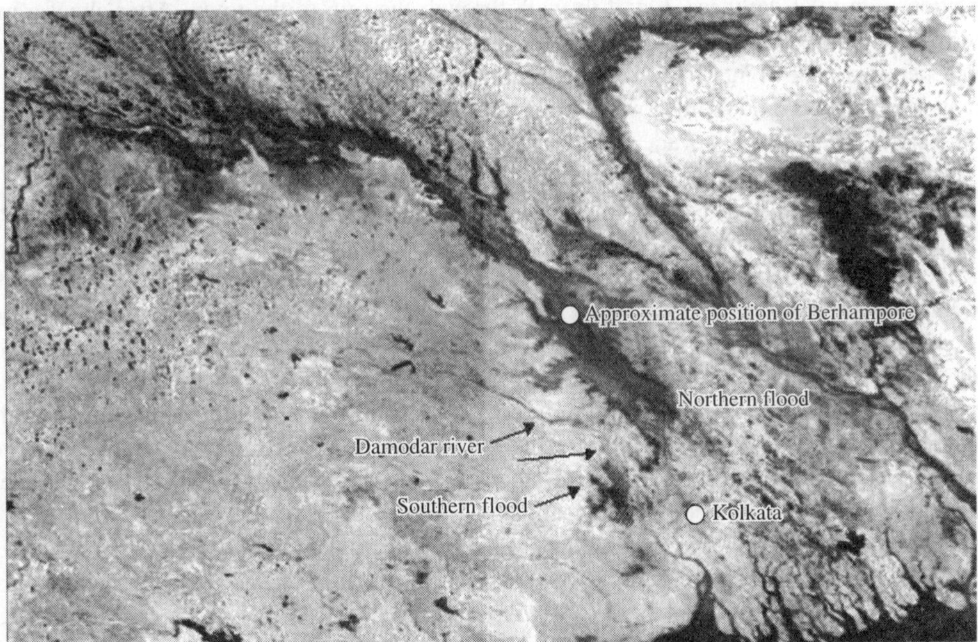

Figure 5.4 Satellite image of flooded area, 22–28th September, 2000.

Source: Darthmouth Flood Obseratory.

But for those caught up in it, there are 20 million different experiences, of what was expected, happened first, what happened next, how they survived, what they lost and how they recovered. We will start with an account at a personal level, written in Murshidabad District at the time by one of us.

Rising Waters: September 18–21st 2000

'On the morning of Monday 18th September 2000, I left Kolkata by train for Berhampur, the administrative centre of Murshidabad District. I see that some of the rice crop has been harvested, and there are some stacks of straw for fodder. I notice most of the rice is short-strawed, presumably high yielding varieties. There are many fish ponds, all with their water levels just at ground height—because everywhere the drainage systems are only just taking off the water. The jute harvest has started, and in many waterways the cut jute floats on rafts weighed down by the trunks of banana trees or clods of earth. It is being retted, to loosen the fibre from the central wooden stick-like stalk. There are banana groves, and orchards of other trees, little vegetable gardens, and stands of sugar cane. There are small linear shades woven out of bamboo and palm leaves that cover nursery plants, rather like cloches. It is a landscape of painstaking care. In one or two places, I notice some of the kutcha (mud, adobe) houses, mostly the smaller hovels of the poor, have puddles precariously close to the mud plinth on which they are built.

'It is 6 O'clock in the evening when we reach Berhampur, it is raining very heavily, and the station is in total darkness. I start to walk through the rain to the town. After about a mile, some of the buildings are lit up; these, of course, are far the more important buildings, which have generators. The lights from one of them shine down on water flowing across the road, through which a bus is coming towards me with water half-way up its wheels. Before I have found a hotel I have had to wade through flood waters almost waist deep'.

'Next day, with the wind howling and the rain torrential, the few rickshaw wallahs on the streets are wearing large plastic bags, which they put on first by tying to a top knot of their hair, and then by strings around their backs, which pass under their armpits and across their chests, and then usually by another string around their waists as well. From behind they look like red or blue terrapins. One of them takes me to the station, where my suspicions are confirmed. No trains are running, the tracks have been flooded. And so I begin to wait, either to find some other way out of town, or to do nothing until the floods have abated. I take a small walk around town and I move off to a little road parallel to the main road. It is still above water, but on each side are the kutcha dwellings of the poor people who work in town. It is quite obvious that many of them are the rickshaw wallahs'. I see a scene of devastation. The water has come up around the walls of each of these houses, and they are slowly, agonisingly crumbling, and sinking from the bottom. A kind of architectural necrotizing fascicles has taken grip, as the walls twist, sink, and ultimately dissolve, so the bamboo poles above them supporting the roof begin to twist, and the big *pukka* (fired brick-earth) tiles, in which the rickshaw wallahs have invested, slide to the ground, and the few belongings inside their house are exposed to the ceaseless rain. Some of the rickshaws have been staked to the back-road, which is still above water, to become one end of a new plastic tent where the family may seek shelter. Further along the road I see a woman washing cut pieces of fish by the hand pump, which is still above flood water and offers cleaner water from a shallow aquifer. There is a bus stand here at the corner, in which the buses look like they will stay standing for a long time, because the water is halfway up their radiators and has reached floor level inside. The people trying to pass on the road are chest deep in water. I am astonished, because this is the first firm datum that I have that says that the flood level has come up more than 3 ft in just over 24 hours. In Bangladesh, there are native deepwater rice varieties that can grow 12 in. in 24 hours to keep pace with rising water, and they grow to more than 12 ft, and can be harvested from boats. Not even they would have kept pace with this flood. Since this town is on a little ridge a few feet high in the middle of one of the flattest plains on Earth, and we are a long way away from any little hills that may push flash-flood water this way, it seems inconceivable to me that the rainfall we have just received can alone account for this flood and, above all, of the rapidity of its onset.

'A couple from Darjeeling, who are also stranded, ask a taxi to attempt the drive south on the main road and I manage to get a seat with them. As we leave town and clear the buildings, either side of the road embankment there is nothing to see but rippled water, with only the tops of some sugar cane and the tops of trees showing. There is no rice crop, no stacks of straw for fodder, no fish ponds nestling between green fields, and in this part I cannot even see floating jute retting in the water. I cannot even see tops of buildings. Everything has turned into a *Sagar* (an ocean), with little archipelagos of islands covered in dark green shrubs—actually the tops of the orchard trees and the trees around the *bagan*s (the kitchen garden around the homesteads).

'A few of the trees along the road side have been blown over, and their roots pulled up. One or two of them that have fallen across the road have been cut, less I suspect to allow traffic to pass than for the value of their wood and fodder. To begin with there are not so many people by the road, but then we come across a group of stringy, agitated men, who are waving sickles and machetes in the air. Most are wearing nothing but a short cotton lungi which clings in the rain to their thin limbs. A few have umbrellas; many have plastic bags on their heads, some have sodden cloth turbans. It seems to me they are menacing, but at the moment they are not threatening us directly. But then I am not sure that I am properly interpreting what is going on. Quite a few of them are scrabbling with logs and branches to dam a culvert under the road, to stop the water flowing from West to East. Since the water on the east side is only marginally lower than the water on the west, and the view on the east is just as much an ocean as the view on the west, I'm not sure that there is much point in this. But then I, like them, keep seeking to do something, because doing nothing means giving up all hope.

'Apparently the road ahead is impassable. The driver stops the car, turns it around, and then blowing his horn, he runs again through the gauntlet of the angry men. My companions are very quiet. When we get back to the edge of town the gentleman from Darjeeling turns to me and says that the people have been looting the buses. So far no passenger has been hurt, but they have lost all their valuables. He adds that the labourers and farmers have lost everything, that they have no money, no food, no shelter, nothing. And I note that there were remarkably few cattle or goats on the causeway. Something else puzzles me too: given that the landscape as far as the eye can see has turned into an ocean, there were not so many people on the embankment leading into Berhampur. Where were the others? And what would it be like to find shelter on an island, which was then later submerged?

'Outside the hotel there is a bridge which is conducting the on-rush of muddy flood water under the road. A lot of people are gathered there, and there is something of a party atmosphere. This is because scrawny men in lungis are putting fishing nets across the culvert, and managing to pull out some pretty big carp along with smaller fry. Inside the hotel one of the guests blames the Farakka barrage. This barrage-cum-railway bridge has been built across the Ganga, north of Murshidabad, to divert water down the Bhagirathi–Hugli on which the town stands, but during the low season. In the wet season, the off-take to the Bhagirathi should be shut, and the main channel gates should be open. But such has been the flow of the river this week, that there were fears the structure would be damaged, and the railway line lost. So the guests think that the engineers opened the Bhagirathi gates as an escape for extra water. This would certainly account for the suddenness of the flood. A Mr. Mazumdar, then adds something I have forgotten about and overlooked. The water is muddy, which means it is river water. Rain water is clear. Rain water floods look black from space, because you can see through the water to the ground. The river floods make milky trails. However, the distinction between a rain water and river water flood is not always easy to make, because a rising river may be what stops rain water from draining in the first place. Mr. Mazumdar is an anti-dam man. He says they just make everything worse. After I get back to Kolkata, I hear people saying that it is the dams of the Damodar Valley which are even more to blame than Farakka (These ideas are analyzed below).

'Next day a taxi agrees to try a road to the East, which is rumoured still to be open. We drive down it slowly because the road develops new holes, which are clearly not just potholes, but produced by subsidence. The embankments are melting. The road is as full of people and animals as the summer-evening air is full of insects. This is the great refuge of all the undrowned of Murshidabad district. There are meandering cattle, and calves straying slowly after them, then there are hens and geese and ducks; and through all of these weave bicycles, motor scooters, ox carts, bullock carts, and rickshaws, using either side of the road to go in either direction, according to taste.

'We have left Murshidabad district and we are now in Nadia. Here, new 'villages' are being constructed along the road embankment. Men are cutting the bamboo for building frames, and they and their womenfolk are binding them together with jute cord. Even little markets have sprung up within the 'villages' and new fishing nets are hanging for sale. Some cattle have already been parked under plastic awnings in improvised byres. It rains harder and then softer, but always it rains. People are lopping branches, both for poles and for the fodder. Here, men are cutting a dyke to let water go from left to right. There they are trying to stem a breach to stop water going from right to left. Here, the water on the right is higher, and it is clear rain water, falling over the embankment to the lower muddy water on the left. Here, it is muddy water, flowing into clean water on the right. Mostly, though, it is just muddy water.

'Eventually, after many diversions and deviations, late at night we reach Kolkata.'

The View from Kolkata: September 22–28th, 2000

In Kolkata, the news next day is that the floods are getting worse, and covering more districts. It is 24 hours since there has been any response from Berhampur or Murshidabad, which are now completely cut-off, and nothing is moving north of Krishnanagar.

The national press (i.e., Delhi-based) has a paragraph on inside pages saying something about floods in Bengal and Bihar, but that is all. The Kolkata major broadsheets do print flood stories about West Bengal on the front pages, and they make grim reading. Bihar hardly gets a mention. Bangladesh is not mentioned at all, except very briefly on one day on an inside page. The growing scale of the problem is reported, with a peak of 17 million stated as homeless in West Bengal, and a death toll reportedly about 600 or so. (Both final figures are higher.)

The stories in the papers include arguments between the political parties about the state government's performance in planning for disaster and in providing relief, the fact that country boatmen are hiding their boats because they have not been paid for last year's relief operations yet, that Eastern Railways are trying to evict villagers who have taken refuge in stranded railway carriages, that the army has sent three columns, or seven columns, to the stricken areas, and that three helicopters are dropping food. In two separate places, people are reported killed by sacks of food aid falling from the sky. The police have had to open fire on people looting relief trucks, and in Nadia district a grain trader has been shot dead. The government attacks the meteorological office for not having predicted the week-long downpour. A tourist officer says all the palaces and mosques of Murshidabad and Lalbag are inundated, and they will not have a good tourist season. Cases of snakebite have increased very greatly, and antivenum is not available. There are reported outbreaks of diarrhoea. Everyone blames the Damodar Valley Corporation for letting too much water out of their dams, and engineers at Farakka for opening the gates to the Bhagirathi. In one area on the banks of the Ajoy river, the archaeologists proclaimed that the total removal of all top soil for more than 1 km^2 had revealed a site of the ancient Ajoy civilization (early Hindu).

The floods creep south. Haora, Hugli, Midnapore and 24-Parganas are added to the list of districts. Now Kolkata is threatened. It is built mostly on a high *danga* (levee), but many areas are under threat, particularly as a spring tide is due. Water has entered a power station already, it may have to shut down, and the water pumping station is threatened. The mayor blames the irrigation department for their failure to mend gates on a canal running round south Kolkata, while the irrigation department believes it is the corporation's responsibility. Sandbags are rushed to build a barricade, which, when tested for real, fails in full media spotlight. Milk is in short supply, and the price of food is rising steadily. The flood warnings in Kolkata are timely and effective. 20,000 people mainly living in shanty towns are evacuated, efficiently. Conveniently, the house of opposition politician Mamata Bannerjee in Kalighat, South Kolkata, is flooded, for the first time in 40 years she says. It certainly enhances her credibility and the righteousness of her indignation.

The flood water moved on into Jessore and Khulna districts of Bangladesh, causing further extensive damage. In India, this impact was virtually totally ignored: in Bangladesh it became the reason to castigate India as the source of the floods.

A Macro-view of the Flood through Hydrological Data

The many different claims about what had happened and who was to blame, such as those in the press, just mentioned above, created a climate of apprehension in which it was difficult to get frank discussion with officials about the disaster, to get access to data, and to think through the lessons to be learnt. One intriguing reflexivity has been that the acquisition of some data has affected the availability of other data. Taking the satellite imagery (Figures 5.3 and 5.4) into the field on a laptop in December 2001 proved a very powerful device for attracting the attention of officials who were otherwise inclined to be indifferent. One look at Figure 5.4 provoked the response "So that is what happened!" relieved officials of a sense of blame and failure, and opened the way for more open discussion.

The Weather Event

The figures of how much rain fell, where and when, what the discharges were down rivers and from dams, are in dispute—because of failures of equipment, because they are simply not known accurately, and perhaps even because of the fear of blame. However, there is enough agreement to say that an exceptionally heavy four-day rainfall event happened at the end of the monsoon when the ground was already saturated, so that run-off was rapid.

Table 5.1 shows that major inundations all occur in the period late August to early October, and most are in September. If these figures are correct, five districts in West Bengal had more than 20 per cent of their annual rainfall in just a few days at the end of the monsoon in 2000 when the ground was already wet. Table 5.4 column 3 shows that there was equally heavy rainfall in the upstream catchments of tributaries to the Bhagirathi. The rainfall figures for September 2000 are apparently worse if one takes the Irrigation Department figures, shown in Table 5.2, for some river basins. These are so much at variance with the Meteorological Office that many observers have been inclined to dismiss them as manufactured excuses. The more it rained, the less the responsibility that lay on the managers of the barrages and dams in the face of insuperable problems. The Flood Damage Report by the District Magistrate in Berhampur published astonishingly quickly on 10th October 2000 stated that 1300 mm had fallen in 6 days.

Table 5.1 Depressions which have given high rainfall (total in mm for days noted)

Districts	1956	1959	1959	1978	1978	1995	2000	*Annual* (mm)	*Millennium Flood as per cent annual*
	23–27 Sept.	8–12 Sept.	30–03 (Sept.–Oct.)	31–03 (Aug.–Sept.)	27–01 (Sept.–Oct.)	26–28 Sept.	18–21 Sept.		
Murshidabad	256	141	370			276	470	1338	35.1
Birbhum	321	121	206	102	636	347	800	1234	64.8
Nadia	296	203	331	87	349		311	1401	22.2
Bardhaman		229	231	76	162		369	1271	29.0
Hugli	276	291	274				352	1516	23.2
Haora	331		254				122	1676	7.3
Purulia		142	168	345	208		169	1307	12.9
Bankura		201	202	281	417		50	1271	3.9
Medinipur	133	193	192	351	248		90		
24 Parganas (N and S)	284	276	298	154	646	151	160	1428	11.2

Source: Collected by from published records of the Irrigation and Waterways Department of the Govt. of West Bengal, and unpublished records of the Indian Meteorological Department, Calcutta.

Table 5.2 Conflicting rainfall data recorded by irrigation department and Indian meteorological department, September 2000

Basin/Station Sept. 18–21	*Irrigation department data* (mm)	*Indian meteorological department data* (mm)
Mayurakshi	1015	224
Ajoy	796	272
Berhampur (Murshidabad)	1207	470
Damodar	359	371

Discharge

There are two ways we have estimated discharge figures. The first is very simple: to measure the area flooded from satellite imagery and used an estimated average depth, to give us a total volume of impounded water. The second way is to use rainfall and catchment area figures, plus official river discharge figures.

By the first method, we have estimated the area of the northern flood on the satellite image, as approximately 7500 km^2. Table 5.3 gives the depth of the flood at different places in Murshidabad District. The simple arithmetic average of these depths is 3.0 m. If, conservatively, we assume an average depth of 2 m over 7500 km^2, then the volume of excess water in the landscape was 15000 million m^3. (Ray 2001, calculates a figure of 127.29 lakh (1 lakh = 100,000) acre/ft, which is also 15000 million m^3).

Table 5.3 Depth of inundation in Murshidabad

Block	*Depth* (m)	
	From	*To*
Burdwan	1.8	2.4
Khargram	1.5	4.6
Kandi	3.0	6.1
Bharatpur	2.1	4.3
Kandi Municipal	0.9	3.0

Source: Flood Damage Report, District Magistrate's Office, Berhampur, 10.10.2000.

Using the second method, in Table 5.4 an attempt has been made to account for the river flows by river catchment and rainfall over the four-day period of the depression, using rainfall data and discharge data. For each basin, the area is divided into 'controlled' (upstream of a dam, if there is one) and 'uncontrolled' (downstream of a dam). The discharge data is from the Irrigation Department. For rainfall, the estimates of Meteorological Department are taken, and it is assumed that 80 per cent of the rain is 'effective', i.e., becomes discharge. (The rest is taken up by ground water and evapo-transpiration).

Table 5.4 Areas and discharges of rivers, west bank rivers, 18–21 September 2000

Region	*Basin area* (km^2)	*Controlled*	*Uncontrolled*	*Rainfall depth* (mm)		*Components of discharge* (million m^3)					*Resultant discharge* (millions m^3)	
				Total	*80%*	*Flood storage*	*Dam/ barrage release*	*Generated from controlled area*	*Net release*	*Generated from uncontrolled area*	*Total flow*	*Net release as per cent of total flow*
Northern Flood												
Farakka Feeder canal												
Pagla Bansloi			2200	635	508		387		387		387	4
Mayurakshi		1860	6695	635	508					1118	1118	
Ajoy			306	5694	584		1253	945	308	3401	4654	3
Murshidabd (half district)	2663	470	450		467					2659	2659	
										1198	1198	
						Totals	1640	945	695	8376	10016	7
Southern Flood												
Damodar			17260	4755	220							
Rupnarayan		8530	164	131	176	1270	763	3038	–2275	837	1600	–64
Kkansai-Haldi		3626	8220	129	104					1117	1117	0

Source: Data from Irrigation Department and Meteorological Department, with further calculation.

The effective rainfall figure is multiplied by the controlled area to give discharge from upstream of any dam. This figure is what would have come downstream without interception by a dam. If the discharge from a dam equals this figure, then the dam had no net impact. If it is less than this figure, then water was stored. If it is more than this figure, then there was a net release.

Discharge: The Northern Flood

As the satellite photo shows, there were two separated flooded areas in West Bengal—a larger northern area straddling the Bhagirathi, and a smaller southern area in the lower Damodar Valley. Data for these are shown separately in Table 5.4.

The figures in Table 5.4 reflect only discharges from west of the Bhagirathi, plus what was released from Farakka. To these totals we should therefore add the amounts of rain that fell east of Murshidabad, and what over spilled from the Ganga down the Jalangi and Matabanga–Churni–Icchamati. Of the latter, there is no known record.

The last column shows the net release (the release of stored water) as a per cent of the total volume. The Farakka Barrage and the Massanjore dam contributed in a direct sense at most 7.0 per cent to the flood–hardly enough to indict them as the principal causes of the disaster. Usually there is no release from Farakka down the feeder canal in the wet season. However, on this occasion the discharge of the Ganga over the main barrage was so high that there were fears for the safety of the structure, so water was 'escaped' into the feeder canal.

However, even if the *barrage* contributed proportionately only a small amount to the flood, the Farakka *Project* did cause significant damage. The feeder canal leading from the Ganga to the Bhagirathi intercepted drainage from Jharkhand (Figure 5.5). The four 'minor' tributaries—Trimohoni, Kanloi, Bagmari and Madhabjani—emptied their flood flows into it.

The Farakka Barrage authority was powerless to do anything about this. (Except that, if the bays of the Jangipur Barrage had been opened, a substantial proportion of the discharge would have flowed back to the Ganga, reducing the peak discharge of the Bhagirathi at Jangipur (Figure 5.6). The Farakka management did not do this). Figure 5.7 shows the peak in the discharge of the Bhagirathi at Jangipur, down stream of the feeder canal. The Pagla-Bansloi, the first right hand tributary, also directly discharged into the Bhagirathi. In the summer of 2006, the land to the west of the feeder canal again flooded as badly as in 2000. This can be seen on a recent flood-map from the Dartmouth Flood Observatory (2006).

Discharge: The Southern Flood

The key question about the Southern Flood is whether the two dams, the Maithon and Panchet, mitigated or deepened the hazard. The Damodar Valley Corporation (DVC) data shown in Table 5.5 indicates that they stored 359 and 339 million m^3, or a total of about 700 m^3 of

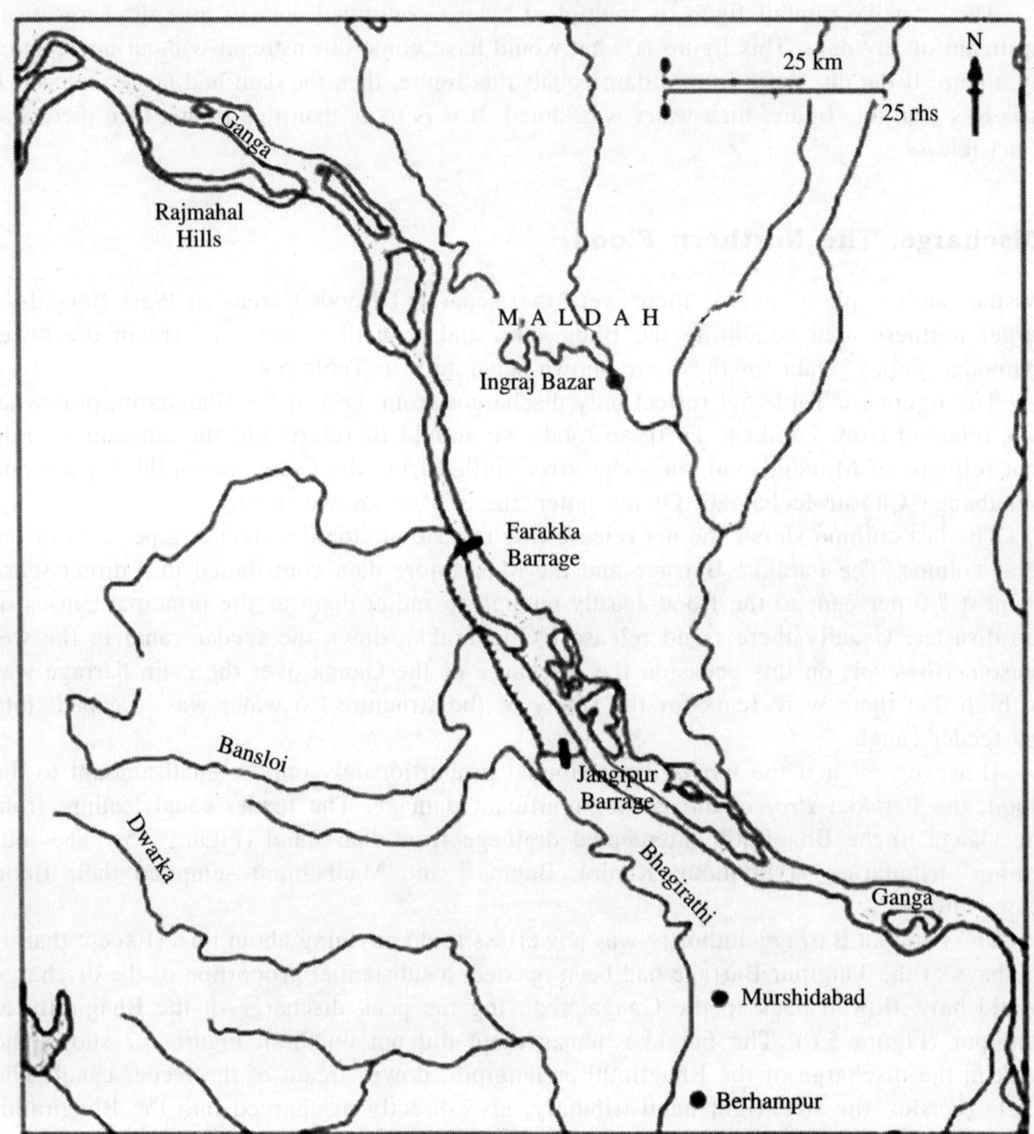

Figure 5.5 Farakka barrage, the feeder canal and the Jangipur Barrage.

water. This is actually less than we have calculated in Table 5.4. The explanation for such a difference could be found in innumerable sources—but the point remains that on either calculation the dams did store flood water.

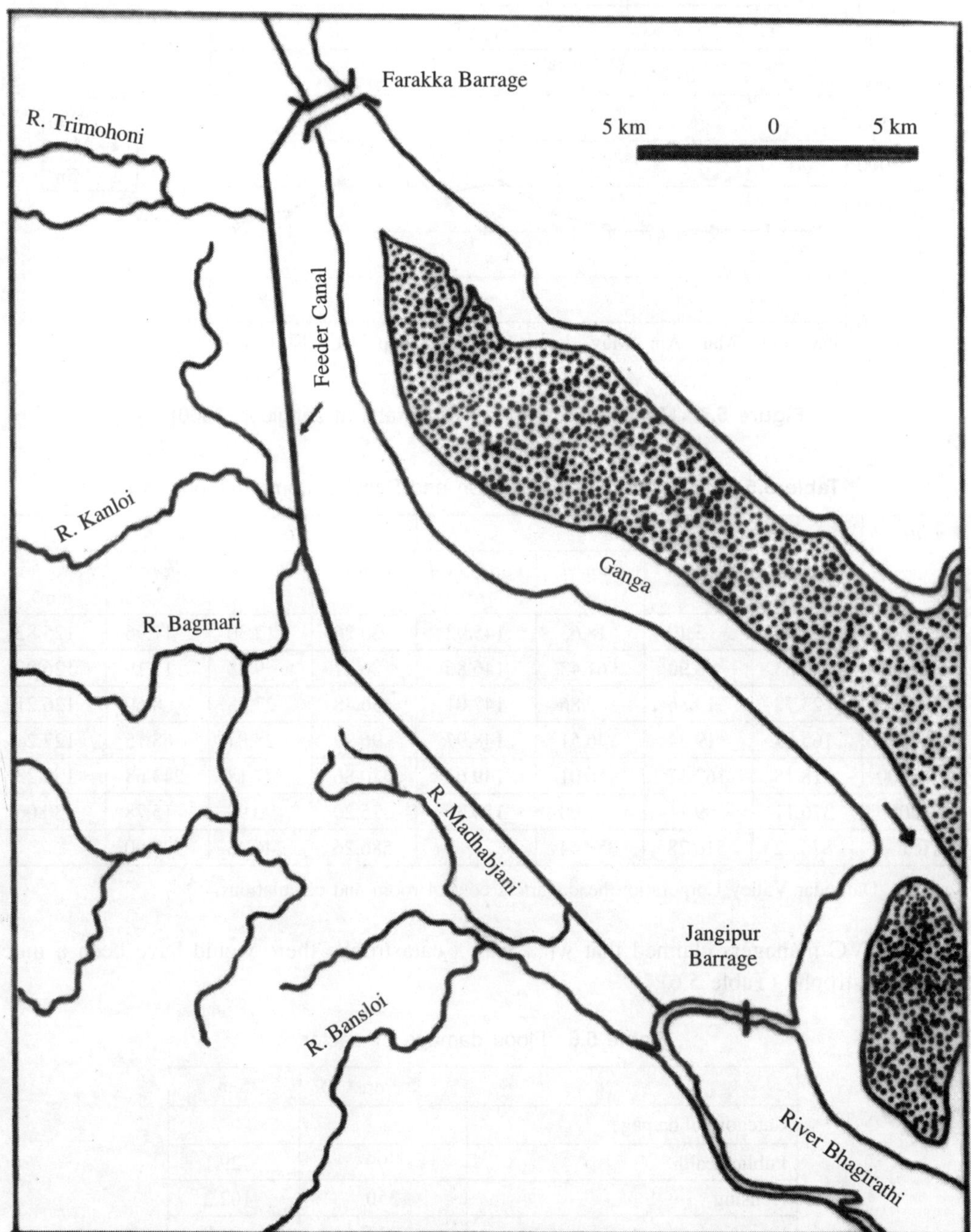

Figure 5.6 Discharge locations of the river Bhagirathi.

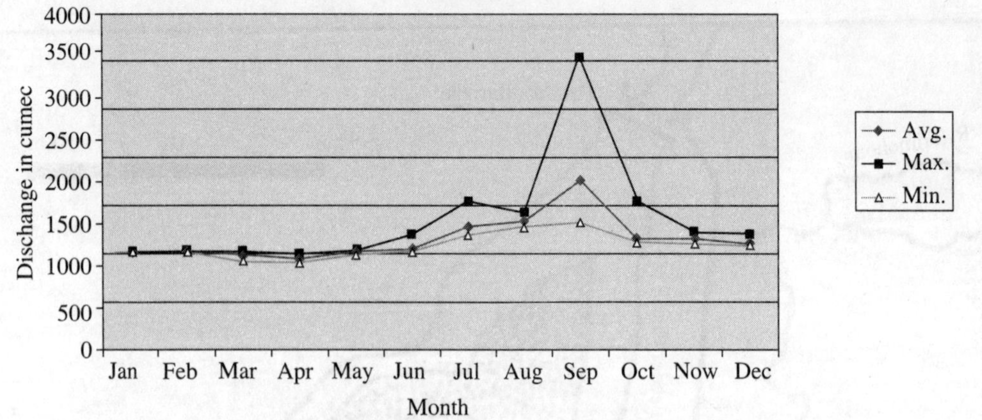

Figure 5.7 Monthly discharge of Bhagirathi at Jangipur (2000).

Table 5.5 Inflow and outflow Maithon and Panchet dams (millions m^3)

Date	*Maithon*				*Panchet*			
	Inflow	*Outflow*	*Stored*	*Pond level* (m)	*Inflow*	*Outflow*	*Stored*	*Pond level* (m)
17.9.2000	22.03	3.40	18.63	145.92	30.26	12.30	17.96	125.82
18.9.2000	70.33	8.90	61.43	146.86	26.47	9.28	17.19	126.07
19.9.2000	23.72	13.86	9.86	147.01	36.48	27.88	8.60	126.21
20.9.2000	165.85	19.34	146.51	148.97	96.99	28.84	68.15	127.24
21.9.2000	218.18	162.17	56.01	149.62	320.86	77.18	243.68	130.23
22.9.2000	376.11	309.11	67.00	150.36	75.20	90.98	–15.78	130.06
Total	876.22	516.78	359.44		586.26	246.46	339.80	

Source: Damodar Valley Corporation headquarters control room and calculations.

The DVC managers claimed that what was a catastrophe there would have been a much bigger catastrophe (Table 5.6).

Table 5.6 Flood damage by sector

	₹ crore*	$ m
Category of damage		
Public health	99	29.1
Housing	350	102.2
Irrigation and waterways	314	91.8
Drinking water	56	16.3
Municipal and panchayat property	150	43.9
Agriculture	3866	1130.1
Animal Husbandry	187	54.5

(*Contd.*)

Table 5.6 Flood damage by sector (*Contd.*)

	₹ crore*	$ m
PWD Roads	329	96.1
Fishing	18	5.3
Small Scale Industries	67	19.6
Food processing	10	2.9
Forest	1	0.2
Power/Electricity	50	14.6
Education	135	39.5
Transport	5	1.3
Small Irrigation	9	2.5
Others	14	4.2
	5660	1654.9

*Note: 1 crore = 10,000,000.

Source: Finance Minister, W. Bengal Govt. (Ganashakti): 3.11.2000.

It is still possible, nevertheless, that people who live very close to the river have a different experience: the suddenness of discharges from the dams means that locally there may indeed have been more flood than would otherwise be the case.

The Hydrological Impact on Rural Settlement

In September 2001 and September 2002, we conducted small group-interviews in 15 villages in Murshidabad distict, randomly selected on both sides of the Bhagirathi. The interviews were semi-structred—to find out how much notice the villages had, how they had survived, what losses they had suffered, and how rehabiltation had proceeded. In all of these areas some degree of flooding in some of the lower land would be considered normal and would be expected in most years. Though details varied, the stories told had some very consistent themes.

Their first point was that there was no warning—although the suggestions varied about how warnings could be given. The second point was that the onset of the flood was extremely rapid and from unexpected directions. Whereas the villagers might have expected a local river to rise, often the flood had come across fields rushing *towards* their local river. In nearly all cases the flood had achieved its maximum depth—be it two or even seven metres, within 12 hours of the first onset. In some unfortunate cases near major breaches in bunds, flooding to such depths was instantaneous as a wall of water burst over a tract of land. The onset occurred in some areas at night, in other areas during daylight hours. This variation was noticeable at a local level, with adjacent villages having distinctly different timings.

The most spectacular evidence of the power of the water is given by the breach of the road and rail bunds of the left-bank embankment of the Bhagirathi at Kalu Khali, just north of Murshidabad. This was a repeat of the events of 1871 and 1874 noted above. Where once there were fields and a village, there is now a lake scoured out to a depth said to be more than 20 m, and half a kilometre long. There was a rumour (unsubstantiated as far as we know) that the Border Security Guards had detonated the bunds to relieve a threat to their barracks.

The timing and sequence of flooding was essentially completely unpredictable. Because there are inadequate culverts and bridges for allowing the passage of major floods, the countryside is a network of unintended polders. The flood passed from one to another as embankments collapsed at unpredictable places. These places were unpredictable because no-one could know in advance the relative height of water and embankment as the flood progressed; because of the scour of currents; because of random weakness; and because of random action by villagers and others to break bunds to let water out of affected areas. The data in Table 5.7 list 1366 kms. of damaged railway-track, with 236 breaches, and a requirement of 800,000 man-days for repairs. For roads it is given as 2763 kms and 4 million man-days. The number of breaches is not given and we do not know the official figure. On the extremely conservative assumption that a road breach takes as much time on average to repair as a rail breach, then there were *at least* 1200 breaches.

Table 5.7 Road and rail damage

	Railway		*Road*
Length of damaged sections	1366 km		2763 km
Man-days to repair	800,000		4,000,000
Breaches	236	Cost of temporary repair	$9.0 m
Bridges washed away	9	Cost of permanent (?) repair	$12.25 m
Revenue lost	$2.3 m (₹ 110 m)	State buses lost revenue	$0.35 m

Most of what happened next was the result of the unexpected nature and rapidity of onset of the flood. There was no time to save personal possessions—either domestic ones like clothing or cooking pots, or farm implements, or farm animals. The animals that were least likely lost were the cows which were tethered in byres near houses. Goats, sheep, chickens and ducks which are usually fairly free ranging had to take care of themselves. People, often with nothing but what they stood up in, had to seek shelter, however, and wherever they could. In some instances the only options were to go up trees. In many villages there was at least one pukka (brick) building, usually belonging to one of the wealthier farmers, with a flat roof and/or first floor. In a few villages there are brick-built schools. The brick buildings often harboured such large numbers of people, it is difficult to understand why they in turn did not collapse. Three hundred people on a single house were not unusual. Although there was some loss of pukka buildings, most survived, together with the people on them.

Other people made their way to high points on road and rail embankments, joining what were sometimes very large groups of people. So the embankments that were implicated in the disaster also become refuges from the disaster. There are official flood shelters in Murshidabad—but there are only twelve built in areas of risk identified some decades ago (Dangroup, 1990). We presume (we do not know) that these were useful and used, but obviously they cannot serve the population of the whole district. The Additional District Magistrate in Murshidabad had heard about them, but did not know where they were.

Over a period of day's boatmen worked to move people from trees to better places—if they agreed. Some preferred to stay near their own homes, to maximize their chances of rescuing some of their belongings. Some constructed *machans* (bamboo platforms) for the purpose. Boatmen saw goats, jackals, foxes, dogs, ducks, hens and even snakes co-habiting on isolated roof-tops.

The water level was slow to subside. A comment, the only one we have come across in recent literature which names a village in Murshidabad, says: "Nazipur village is surrounded by embankments which are used as village roads. Hence, floodwater remains for a long time in the village". (Manual for Community Based Flood Management in India, 2004, p. 148). The average period of being stranded was somewhere between ten days and three weeks. In this period, although government aid began to reach people slowly, the majority survived by sharing whatever they had, and by going hungry. The vast majority had no access to clean water, and when kerosene fuel for boiling water ran out (or was not available from the start) there was no option but to drink the flood water, despite the bloated carcasses it contained. There was obviously an increased incidence of fevers of different kinds, and an increase in dysentery. But the number of deaths from these diseases was small. In a few cases tube wells on high ground provided access to clean water, and in even fewer cases there were tube wells installed on the first floor of a pukka building which were of inestimable value for refugees.

As the flood receded people tried to go back to their homesteads. Since these were mostly destroyed and covered in an offensively smelling mud, the initial forays would be short-term, to try and re-establish some sort of shelter— from rescued tin sheeting, from plastic sheeting handed out as relief, from rescued tiles, from plant material. There then followed a period in which dependent women and children were sent to distant relatives wherever possible, to leave the men folk to start the reconstruction. This obviously reduced the immediate local food needs as well.

What is clear from these accounts is that nearly all the people survived the worst period of the tragedy by their own unaided resourcefulness. The District Magistrate of Murshidabad (who was not the post-holder at the time of the flood) in December 2001 paid them that compliment too, in commenting on the flood. In several places it was noted that youth wings of local NGOs had been prominent in organising refugees, and in assisting those left in trees, etc., to get boats to safety. As more aid and organizations arrived, there was a 'sharing' of the work—often on a political basis. In one locality, Congress looked after one side of the road, and the CPM (Communist Party Marxist) the other side. Charities such as Bharat Sevashram Sangha were prominent in helping.

The landscape, looked at casually in December 2001, appeared to be fairly 'normal'. The impact of the flood was and is not apparent until the landscape is looked at more closely. The vernacular architecture of established households is of two- (or two-and-a-half) storied *kutcha* houses (adobe) with either tin (corrugated galvanised iron) or tiled roof. These houses used to have substantial door and window furniture. In widespread areas these houses collapsed, sometimes trapping animals within them, usually entombing agricultural implements such as ploughs along with clothing, utensils and items such as radios. The loss of the cut jute crop was nearly universal, as was the loss of fodder. G*olas* (grain stores) were washed away everywhere, and in December 2001 there were not many yet to be seen as replacements. Late-harvesting rice was also lost in fields. Again the official figures do not seem to reflect this scale of loss.

Official damage records were collated very quickly. They were assembled from District Magistrates, The Railways Board, the Highways Board, the Irrigation Department, and other sectoral bodies such as the State Electricity Board. The following tables give the figures for household and business losses, and for losses to infrastructure.

To make the data in Table 5.8 more meaningful, we have taken the official damage figures, and scaled them by number of households.

Table 5.8 District damage scaled by number of households

	Birbhum	*Murshidabad*	*Nadia*	N 24 *Parganas*	*Hugli*	*Bardhaman*	*Malda*	*Medinipur*	*Haora*
Population 2001	30,12,546	58,63,717	46,03,756	89,30,295	50,40,047	69,19,698	32,90,160	50,40,047	42,74,010
Person per house 1991	5.39	5.70	5.50	5.46	5.45	5.39	5.47	5.90	5.56
Estimated houses 2001	558962	1028733	836879	1634168	924702	1284877	601267	854052	768570
Area affected km^2	282.5	524.1	390.0	210.4	290.0	359.8	39.7	180.6	120.0
per cent population affected	109.5	75.0	86.0	20.3	68.8	48.1	3.1	19.8	10.5
Crop area affected hectares	0.0505	0.0509	0.0466	0.0129	0.0314	0.0280	0.0066	0.0211	0.0156
Persons dead and missing	0.0004	0.0007	0.0004	0.0000	0.0000	0.0001	0.0000	0.0000	0.0000
Houses damaged	0.8193	0.4766	0.6655	0.1068	0.2325	0.1679	0.0008	0.0850	0.0155
Affected cattle and buffalo	0.3483	0.9478	0.0626	0.0472	0.0873	0.5681	0.0000	0.1772	0.0000
Affected sheep and goat	0.1827	0.4812	0.0868	0.0290	0.0890	0.8522	0.0000	0.1716	0.0000
Affected poultry	0.3686	1.1684	0.1060	0.0000	0.1089	2.2064	0.0000	0.2024	0.0000

Source: Rudra (2001) Based on Govt. of West Bengal and UNICEF, Situation Report.

At the time of the collation of the damage data, the 2001 census results were not known. On our calculations the number of people affected in Birbhum in September 2000 is 110 per cent of the population recorded in the census of 2001, which at first thought seems nonsensical. However, it may be the case that many evacuees had yet to return to the district by the time of the 2001 census, and the number of affected people is actually correct. The number of houses broken or damaged is consistent with the visual sampling and satellite imagery—in Murshidabad it is over 47 per cent and in Birbhum 82 per cent and Nadia 67 per cent.[1]

[1]The 1991 Census makes available total population; and the number of houses and households by district. The latter two are almost exactly the same, as could be expected of a predominantly rural area. So far the 2001 Census has released only the population figures. To estimate the number of houses in 2001, Table 5.8 applies the 1991 ratio houses/people to the population of 2001. The number of houses is then used to standardize the damage figures.

Conclusions

In the case of the Millennium Flood in West Bengal, and we imagine in nearly all other similar cases which are closely observed and analyzed, different stake holders propose different 'truths' for their own purpose. Many poor farmers in this case believed that the Farakka Barrage was The Cause; the Irrigation Department clearly believed excessive late-season rainfall was The Cause; we believe that inappropriate road and rail embankments were a major Cause accentuating the impact of the disaster: and so it goes on. The blame game can continue indefinitely, with fingers pointing in all directions.

The initiative of local people was the most important part of recovery. They largely invented their own recovery process. Larger NGOs played their biggest role in the mid-term 3 weeks–3 month period, helping with food and building materials. Local consumption was reduced by sending family members to distant relatives, and agriculture restarted with extensive loaning and swapping of seeds and equipment. Helping communities help themselves is clearly one key to a better future. The embrace of Community Based Disaster Preparedness Schemes by INGOs and NGOs is to be welcomed.

Most importantly, we think now is the time to re-open the debate in Bengal, both in West Bengal and Bangladesh, about what constitutes appropriate and sustainable development. There are alternatives to the paradigm of engineering defences and control. Perhaps urban areas do need some flood defence, but for the vast majority of the country, a reversion to 'normal' flooding could be beneficial. Existing road and protection embankments could be breached at chosen sites at fairly frequent intervals, the breaches being faced with stone or concrete. These are known as "Irishman's bridges." As floods rise, so water enters new territories in an observable fashion from selected points. The problems of lack of warning, rapidity, and unpredictability are eliminated. The benefits of flooding (silt and groundwater recharge) can be then be reaped. In short, there should be serious reconsideration of the sustainable policy of open flooding.

References

Blaikie, P.M. and J.S.S. Muldavin (2004), Upstream, Downstream, China, India: The politics of environment in the Himalayan region, *Annals of the Association of American Geographers*, **94**(3), 520–548.

Chapman, G.P. and M. Thompson (Eds.) (1995), *Water and the Quest for Sustainable Development in the The Ganga Valley,* Mansell, London.

Chatterjee, S. (Ed.) (1987), *Collected Works of Meghnad Saha*. Orient Longman, Bombay, Kolkata.

Cotton, Sir Arthur (1854), *Public Works in India: their Importance with Suggestions for their Extension and Improvement*, Wm. H. Allen, London.

Dangroup (1990), *EEC-Assisted Projects in India: Anti-disaster Shelters*, Commission of the European Communities. EC Ref. No. CC/ALA/930/A/2/89/87.

Eaton, R.M. (1993), *The Rise of Islam and the Bengal Frontier,* 1204–1760, University of California Press, Berkeley.

Forsyth, T. (2003) *Critical Political Ecology: The Politics of Environmental Science*, Routledge, London.

Hunter, W.W. (1876), *The Statistical Account of Bengal: Volume IX Districts of Murshidabad and Pabna*, Trubner and Co., London.

Ives, J. and B. Messerli (1989), *The Himalayan Dilemma: Reconciling Development and Conservation*, John Wiley and Sons, London.

Kasperson, J.X. and R.E. Kasperson (Eds.) (2001), *Global Environmental Risk,* United nations University Press, Tokyo.

Kasperson, R.E., J.X. Kasperson and B.L. Turner (1999), Risk and criticality: trajectories of regional environmental degradation, *Ambio* **28**(6), 562–569.

Manual for Community Based Flood Management in India (2004), *Asia Pacific Journal on Environment and Development*, **11**, 99–226.

Mirza, M.M.Q., R.A. Warrick, N.J. Ericksen and G.J. Kenny (2001), Are floods getting worse in the Ganga, Brahmaputra, Meghna Basins? *Environmental Hazards*, **3**, 37–48.

Mukerjee, R. (1938), *The Changing face of Bengal: a Study in Riverine Economy,* University of Calcutta, Calcutta.

Ray, P.C. (1935), *Life and Experiences of a Bengali Chemist, Part II,* Chatterjee & Co. Ltd., Calcutta.

Rudra, K. (2001), *The Flood of September 2000*, Jayasree Press, Kolkata.

Stevenson-Moore, C.J. (1919), *Report on the River Hooghly River and its Headwaters*, Calcutta: the Bengal Secretariat Book Depot, reprinted in: K.R. Biswas (2002), *Rivers of Bengal: A Compilation*, by Govt. of West Bengal, Kolkata.

Stott, P. and S. Sullivan (Eds.) (2000), *Political Ecology: Science, Myth and Power*, Arnold, London.

Subba, B. (2001), *Himalayan Waters: Promise and Potential: Problems and Politics*, Panos South Asia, Kathmandu.

Willcocks, W. (1930), *Ancient System of Irrigation in Bengal,* University of Kolkata, Kolkata.

Wisner, B., P. Blaikie, T. Cannon and I. Davis (2004), *At Risk: Natural hazards, people's vulnerability and disasters.* Routledge, London.

Zimmerer, K.S. and T.J. Bassett (Eds.) (2003), *Political Ecology: an Integrative Approach to Geography and Environment-Development Studies*, Guildford Press, New York.

6

Resources in the Indian Ocean and National Security

Harvir Sharma

Abstract: This chapter focuses on different types of resources which oceans possess and which could be fruitfully used, especially in the backdrop of resources getting scarce. The oceans provide rich alternative and, therefore, need to be properly managed. The role of the coast guards in protecting the exclusive economic zone, offshore assets, maritime environment and collection of scientific data, etc. has also been highlighted.

Keywords: Energy Resources, Exclusive Economic Zone, Sea Bed Mining, Aquaculture, Artificial Island, Offshore Asset, Maritime Environment

Introduction

The oceans have played a major part in the shaping of this planet and its civilizational evolution. With the continuous rise in the world's population, there has been an associated rise in living standards in almost all societies. This has led to a simultaneous rise in the demand for raw materials generated by industrial and post-industrial technology, creating growing pressure on natural resources of all types and kinds. As resources become increasingly scarce, man's attention is turning to the oceans for his further development, and, in fact, for his very survival. The year 1998 was, therefore, declared the International Year of the Ocean by the United Nations, to focus the attention of the world on the vast water bodies that surround us. It did manage to highlight, and bring into general focus, the extreme importance of the oceanic domain in the daily lives of common people, be it for carriage of commerce, energy or for dependence on living or mineral resources.

More than half of the world's population lives within about 100 km from the sea coast. Large sections of our own population depend on the sea for their livelihood. As the seas become the future hope for a resource-depleted world, it is imperative that we pay attention to the management of these resources. Scarcity of resources and the intense competition to acquire them inevitably give rise to conflict among nations. The management of these resources is, therefore, an important part of the national security perspective of those countries fortunate enough to possess marine wealth in all its forms.

This paper attempts to discuss a broad overview of India's ocean resources, the management of the resources, the security implications involved in the process, and the role of the Indian Coast Guard in this context (Figure 6.1).

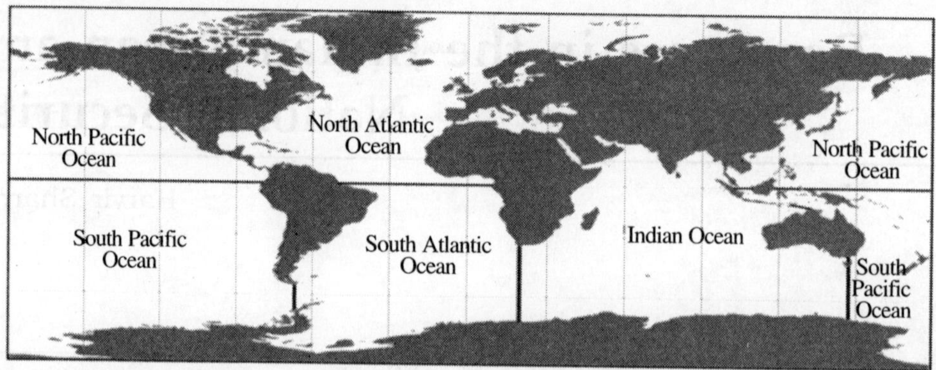

Figure 6.1 Expanse of oceans on earth.

Resources in the Ocean

Almost 71 per cent of the earth's surface is covered by the oceans, which hold about 97 per cent of the earth's water. Indian Ocean is the third largest encompassing about 20 per cent surface water of world. Each year, about 75 million tons of fish are harvested from the sea. The oceans produce over 50 per cent of the earth's oxygen. All major weather phenomena—the monsoons which are so critical for the agricultural economy, disasters like cyclones, tidal waves, cloud formations, water distribution over the earth's surface, and global temperature variations—are attributable to the vast water bodies that cover this planet that is paradoxically called earth. Let us take a quick look at the important resources that the oceans hold for us.

Food Resources

As mentioned earlier, each year, 75 million tons of fish are harvested from the sea. The global production of fish exceeds that of eggs, poultry or meat. This is a vital food resource that can easily be destroyed by mismanagement. In fact, every year, over 15 million sq. miles of fishing grounds are rendered unusable because of pollution and indiscriminate and wasteful fishing methods. For example, every year, over a million sharks are killed. The Thai fishermen catch sharks in their nets, cut-off their fins, which fetch huge profits, and throw the huge fish back into the water to die.

There is growing exploitation of the potential for seabed farming of vegetable products, which are highly nutritious and rich in iodine. While this awareness is yet to reach India, other countries are producing thousands of tons of edible seaweed and marine vegetables for human as well as animal consumption.

Mineral Resources

The seabed is rich in many minerals such as silver, iron ore and cobalt. However, in most cases, the technology currently available to carry out mining on a commercial scale is sadly lacking. In this context, amongst the most important discoveries of the last few decades has been the location of manganese nodules on the seabed. These nodules range in size from a few grams to tens of kilograms, and what is remarkable is the high concentration of the metal present in these nodules. This makes the process of refinement economically viable. The problem, of course, is that of recovering the nodules from the ocean depths. This is an engineering feat that is certain to be mastered in the near future.

The recovery of gems from the seabed has been practiced for a very long time, since mythological days. In practice, the harvesting and culturing of pearls and shells is a major industry that has acquired prominence with the advance of biotechnology.

Energy Resources: Oil and Gas

The ocean is a vast energy resource. Today, the production of oil and gas from the seabed nearly exceeds that produced from the land. As technology develops, it is becoming possible to go further and deeper in search of this precious mineral that is so often referred to as 'liquid gold'. Oil is used not only for energy production, but also in the production of pharmaceuticals, aromatics, fertilizers, plastics and synthetic materials.

The potential for harnessing tidal and wave energy has long engaged the attention of scientists and engineers. There are hopes that their efforts will be successful and that the limitless energy of the waves and tides will be available for exploitation.

Drugs and Pharmaceuticals

Marine products have shown great promise as a source of drugs to combat a range of diseases, from cancer to AIDS. As the disease-carrying bacteria develop resistance to land and plant-based medicines, sea-based cures offer great potential. A variety of marine organisms such as sponges are currently being researched to find cures for afflictions that have so far defeated the efforts of medical science.

Communication Arteries

Those who live and work on land commonly misperceive the seas as separating countries and people. Sailors, on the other hand, know that the oceans, in fact, join countries. They are the global highways which even in this age of supersonic jet travel, offer the fastest, most economical, and convenient means of mass transportation of goods and commodities. The seas, thus, represent a vital communication artery and must be kept open to permit free flow of commerce.

India's Marine Wealth and Exclusive Economic Zone

Seeing the growing importance of the sea as a source of food and energy, the world community rightly foresaw the potential for conflict between nations over their rights over marine resources. Here, India played a leading part in safeguarding the interest of the developing world when the United Nations Convention on the Law of the Sea (UNCLOS) (1982) declared that the oceans are the common heritage of mankind. Further, the UN defined the limits within which all maritime states would have exclusive rights of exploitation of all marine resources, whether living, fossil-based, or vegetable. The total extent of this area, which is known as the exclusive economic zone (EEZ), extends to 200 nautical miles or 360 km from the coast. India, because of her peninsular shape, has a relatively large EEZ of over two million sq. km.

Fisheries

India has considerable potential to develop her fisheries, but this is sadly underdeveloped. There is an estimated potential for over two million tons of fish catch annually; only about 40 per cent of this potential wealth is currently harvested. Owing to outdated methods, India has perforce allowed foreign companies to fish in her waters. They make huge profits considering that a single 30 day voyage by a small to a medium-sized trawler can fetch about ₹ 90 lakh in current dollar terms. The Andaman and Nicobar region and the Lakshadweep area abound in tuna, which commands high prices in the international market.

Oil and Gas Reserves

'Indian Ocean Rising states have more than 58 per cent of the world's proven reserves and more than 46 per cent of gas reserves' (Herbert-Burns, 2012). Presently, India's annual oil production is around 33 million tons, and that of gas is about 31.7 billion cubic metres (bcm). In contrast, her estimated reserves are about 423 million tons of crude and 377 bcm of gas. In other words, at current rates of production, India has about 20 years of estimated reserves of oil. As is probably well known, domestic production accounts for about 35–40 per cent of the country's annual consumption.

Seabed Mining

There are promising results of manganese nodule fields on the seabed within India's EEZ. At present, however, the technology available for recovery of these deposits is still too costly to allow this to be a viable proposition. There is little doubt that this will soon become an important source for mineral resources.

Aquaculture and Gems

The collection of gems from the ocean deeps is a romantic notion that has existed in Indian mythology for centuries. In reality, pearls which were once abundantly available in the Palk Bay and the southern coastal region have now virtually disappeared because of indiscriminate and unregulated exploitation. Recently, pearl culture has been receiving some attention in the southern states, and modern biotechnology has been applied. It will, however, be a long while before India can hope to establish a pearl industry to match that of, say, Japan.

Implications for National Security

Having seen what the oceans hold for India and her vast EEZ, we can now turn to some of the questions of security that automatically arise when possessions and territories have to be guarded. It is a fact that if even one sq. km of desert land is illegally occupied by a foreign power, it will raise a furore in India. However, despite thousands of sq. km of ocean territories being vulnerable to illegal exploitation by other countries, this does not generate the same degree of alarm, because it happens far away, out of sight and in an environment foreign to most of India besieged by a continental outlook. The fact remains, however, that possession of such large tracts of oceanic area teeming with wealth, imposes a security burden on the possessor. This is analogous to the possession of a fruit orchard, which would impose on the owner the onerous task of watching over his land lest someone rob him of his rightful harvest of fruit.

The security implications and problems associated with the management of India's ocean resources can be grouped into military, energy, economic and environmental security.

Military Security

This is perhaps the first aspect that comes to mind when we talk of security. In its rawest and most elemental form, military security implies the application of force to retain or gain an objective. With the ocean resources becoming attractive, the possibility of inimical powers using force to attain their ends cannot be entirely' ruled out. In turn, this would imply that India has to study various options in such a scenario, and depending on the availability of the means at her command, then devise a strategy to deal with the situation. Specific aspects that affect military security would be, e.g., the vulnerability of offshore oil platforms and shipping in times of hostilities.

Energy Security

Energy is a vital resource and one of its most important components is oil. Uninterrupted flow of energy is closely linked to the developmental indices of any state dependent on energy imports. In case imports and production were to be reduced, India would grind to a total halt— stoppage of transportation, breakdown of power, no movement of commodities, etc.—in a short period of time. Thus, it is incumbent that the energy flow is always safe and continuous.

This gives rise to two aspects of energy security in the maritime context: (i) supply chain security; and (ii) production security. While the first involves ensuring the security of the supply chain, i.e., the sea lines of communication (SLOG) and transfer of energy by the seas; the second revolves around providing physical security to the country's offshore platforms. Consequently, it is necessary that a well defined policy be in place to ensure the security management of India's offshore oil resources and the security of her energy transport life lines coming through the seas.

Economic Security

The management of the ocean and its resources has a direct bearing on the economic well-being of India. Every aspect of the exploitation of the ocean resources that we have talked about is ultimately related to economic prosperity. Two activities have the most direct impact on the economy: fisheries and energy production. This is because both these activities involve production of resources which are directly translated to the economy. India's economic security, therefore, demands that the management of the ocean resources take into account world trends in pricing and production. Also, the system should be capable of forecasting shortages and scarcities so that the exploitation of domestic reserves can be regulated accordingly.

Environmental Security

Environmental security is a relatively new concept which has crept in with the realisation that environmental disasters can affect the free flow of maritime traffic and, additionally, affect marine life that has its linkage to the related economic activity like fishing, etc. Thus, the degradation of the marine environment would undoubtedly have a deleterious effect on fish production. It would also affect tourism, aqua-farms, salt production enterprises, as well as the lives of thousands of people who live near the coast. Hence, in such a scenario, security of the environment assumes prime importance not only for the free flow of maritime traffic, but also for the millions of people connected to such oceanic enterprises.

Role of the Coast Guard in India

The Indian Coast Guard is the maritime enforcement organization equipped to carry out constabulary duties on the national coastline while at the same time being responsible for disaster management and prevention of environmental degradation of the oceans surrounding the country. In this context, we can broadly examine the roles of the coast guard in assisting in management of the maritime resources.

Protection of National Maritime Interest in India's EEZ

This is an over-arching and broad directive given to the coast guard in the Coast Guard Act which enables it to do a variety of tasks, and gives the service a certain amount of freedom of action. Thus, it is tasked to protect India's mineral and living resources from being poached upon or being over-exploited.

Protection of Artificial Island and Offshore Assets

Whereas the protection of all vital installations against a direct enemy threat will be the role of the navy during war-time, the coast guard's responsibility in peace-time is to coordinate offshore security among all the various agencies that are involved with it.

Control Fishing Activity and Assist in Distress

Each year, the coast guard responds to a large number calls for assistance from fisher-men in distress. On an average, more than 100 lives are saved at sea each year in normal times.

Protect and Preserve the Maritime Environment

The role of the coast guard is to prevent pollution of the marine environment, to enforce anti-pollution laws in India's EEZ, and to apprehend those who break the law. It is the national nodal agency for the coordination of oil spill response operations, and has promulgated a National Oil Spill Disaster Contingency Plan.

Assist the Customs in Anti-Smuggling Operations

The coast guard works in close coordination with the Department of Revenue Intelligence to prevent smuggling and to arrest offenders.

Enforce Safety of Life and Property at Sea

The coast guard works in coordination with the director general of shipping to enforce safety standards and to apprehend law-breakers in this aspect.

Assist in Collection of Scientific Oceanic Data

The coast guard also works in cooperation with the Department of Ocean Development in gathering and collection of scientific data, and monitoring of special offshore scientific equipment.

Its war-time roles can be very briefly summarized as working under the overall operational control of the Indian Navy to supplement naval efforts and to take on some of the routine but vital security tasks like providing local defence of Indian ports, controlling the shipping and examination service, defending offshore installations and supplementing Indian naval resources.

It must be mentioned that the Indian Navy is the primary organization which is entrusted with the security of the sea of communication (SLOG) and offshore energy installations. A dedicated group under the supervision of a flag officer, called the Offshore Defence Advisory Group, acts as the nodal agency overseeing the security of offshore installations.

Conclusion

India is a maritime nation which needs to realise the extreme importance of proper management of her marine resources. The security implications of resource management are large and are linked to national security. The ability to use the resources of the seas optimally to enhance commerce and national security are the primary interlinked objectives. The Indian Coast Guard is the national maritime agency entrusted to ensure the security of India's maritime zones with a view to protect the maritime and other national interests in such zones.

Unless mankind is able to harness the bounty of the maritime domain carefully and in a controlled fashion, the world population will be starved for these resources and there will be nowhere to turn, since the resources on land would have exhausted by then.

References

United Nations Convention on Law of the Sea (UNCLOS), (1982).

Herbert-Burns, R. (2012), Energy in the Indian Ocean Region: Vital Features and New Frontiers, In: David, M. and Russell, S. (Eds.), *Indian Ocean Rising: Maritime Security and Policy Challenges*, Stimson, Washington, DC.

PART II

Land Resources

7

Population Resource and Development The Contemporary Situation in Madhya Pradesh

S.K. Sharma

Abstract: Man is the pivot of resource creation and development. The degree of exploitation of the development potentials depends heavily upon human, socio-political and economic-technological characteristics of the society. The present chapter discusses the conceptual background of the resource and focuses on the resource situation of Madhya Pradesh with particular emphasis on land resources and its different aspects such as population pressure and land use, spatial pattern of man–land ratio, nutritional density of population and contemporary situation of land resource development such as social determinants of agricultural land development and land use changes besides carrying capacity and population pressure.

Keywords: Neutral stuff, Transferable and non-transferable resources, Poverty in plenty, Core–periphery paradigm, Resource creator, Dependent–dominant relationship, Arithmetic Density, Nutritional Density, Survival algorithm.

Introduction

The socio-economic structure of the society hinges heavily on resources. Man has been developing his capacity and utilizing the entire natural environment for the fulfillment of his needs and aspirations. As a result a cultural environment is created, which is accepted as an index of his development. But initially he was simply collector of the resources because of limited demand ensuing from the small size and slow growth of population and also from rudimentary technology. Gradually he developed and improved science and technology and institutions, etc., which facilitated the exploitation of natural resources enormously. As such the pivot of the resource creation and development is man and the degree of exploitation of the development potentials depends heavily upon human, socio-political and economic-technological characteristics of the society. The objective of the present chapter is to illustrate this cyclic relationship with special reference to land resources, citing examples of Madhya Pradesh.

Man and Resource Creation

Resources are the aspects of the biophysical environment. These substances existed in the environment since geological times but they could function as resources only when man perceived their utility and developed technology for their exploitation. Attributes of nature are simply 'neutral stuff' unless man is able to perceive their significance, to recognize their capacity to satisfy human wants and to invent means to utilize them. With the advancement in science and technology, man's capacity of appraising his environment has increased enormously and so the concept of resource has changed in meaning. Therefore, resource is accepted, as a functional relationship that exists between man's wants, his abilities and his appraisal of his environment. Man is both resource creator and its beneficiary. He himself is most dynamic resource; capital and natural resources are passive factors of production. Further, man accumulates capital, exploits resources and builds technology and institutions, which facilitate development. The relationship between man, culture and nature as depicted by Zimmermann (1959) is reproduced below (Figure 7.1).

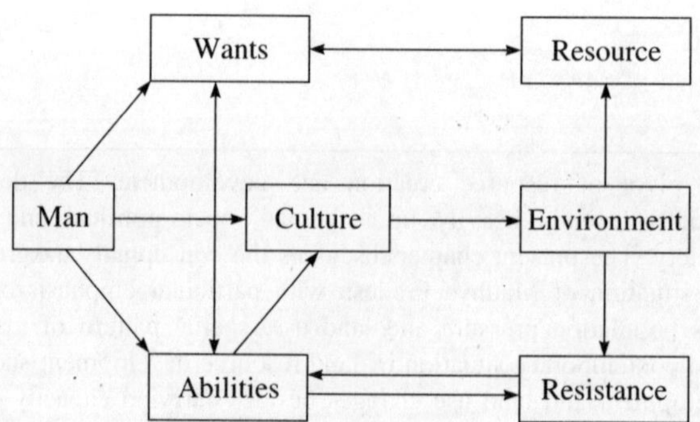

Figure 7.1 Interrelationship between man, culture and nature.

Resources expand and contract in response to human wants and abilities. These wants and capabilities are influenced by the culture. Culture is the sum total of all the devices produced by man to assist him in the attainment of his objectives (Zimmermann, 1951:96). The availability, renewability and exploitability of natural resources, all depend, to a great extent, on technological inventions. The relationship of natural resources with the technology are elaborated by Zobler (1962:191), who illustrated how the conditions of abundance and scarcity, both relative and absolute, are the consequence of human culture.

There is close relationship between resource utilization and level of development. It may be said that economic activities begin with the exploitation of resources. Though in the initial stage of development, availability of natural resources matters to a great extent; however, it is not prerequisite. In reality, exploitation of resources and their utilization for economic development are two distinct economic activities and their locational factors are also different to a great extent. Exploitation of resources has to be carried out in the localities of their occurrences but the processing units based on them are located in areas which have some initial advantages of production, such as availability of capital, market and linkages with other developed areas. With such advancement in the economic activities in these areas supply of local resources appears to be inadequate to support them and this inadequacy of resources is met with the interregional transfer of resources. On the other hand, there are certain regions, which for some reasons could not increase their efficiency of resource use, and therefore, their resource bases appear larger in relation to their level of development. This creates one-way channel of transfer of resources from surplus areas to the deficit areas. These two types of areas present dependent–dominant relationship (Sharma, 1993:129–130), explained by the core–periphery paradigm.

It may be observed that resources are essential for development but merely their presence does not guarantee development. Second, rich regions and countries are capable of importing resources from outside. In this context, resources can be classified into two classes, viz., transferable and non-transferable. Among them, only non-transferable resources, such as land and soil, are in the share of the regions of their occurrences and can be utilized for the development of these regions. Contrary to it, transferable resources, such as minerals and fuels, etc., are extracted and siphoned to dominant regions for their industrial processing. Madhya Pradesh provides good example of this phenomenon.

Resource Situation in Madhya Pradesh

The state economy is still highly dependent on primary sector. More than one-fourth (28.5 per cent) of total value of net domestic products is contributed by the extraction activities at current prices in 2010–11. Agriculture stands at the top. Mineral and power resources and forests and forestry follow agriculture. Madhya Pradesh presents a very good example of the dichotomy of 'poverty in plenty'. The eastern part of the state is very rich in natural resources but the western part is far ahead in development (Sharma, 1993; 2000). Production of natural resources increased by leaps and bounds but most of them are exported to other parts of the state or other parts of the country, leaving these areas lagging far behind in development. It would be clear from the analysis of the development of land resources.

Land Resources

Land is the basic resource because it yields benefits to the local people and is non-transferable resource. The nature of terrain and characteristics of soils are the principal determinants of the land capability. These elements along with some climatic characteristics determine the suitability of land for general use. Land must be used in accordance with its capability to avoid its deterioration and to adopt appropriate conservation measures. But the state is endowed with limited good agricultural land. Agricultural suitability of most of the surface area is reduced by the typical plateau characteristics, high local relief and low fertile soils. Owing to unsuitable physical conditions, major portion of the Baghelkhand plateau, Satpura range, Vindhyan range and Madhya Bharat plateau is not cultivable (Figure 7.2). However, there are some pockets of level land between hills and dissected areas in these regions. Contrary to it, land classed as suitable for cultivation are confined to the Narmada valley, Rewa plateau, Malwa plateau and on part of the Bundelkhand upland.

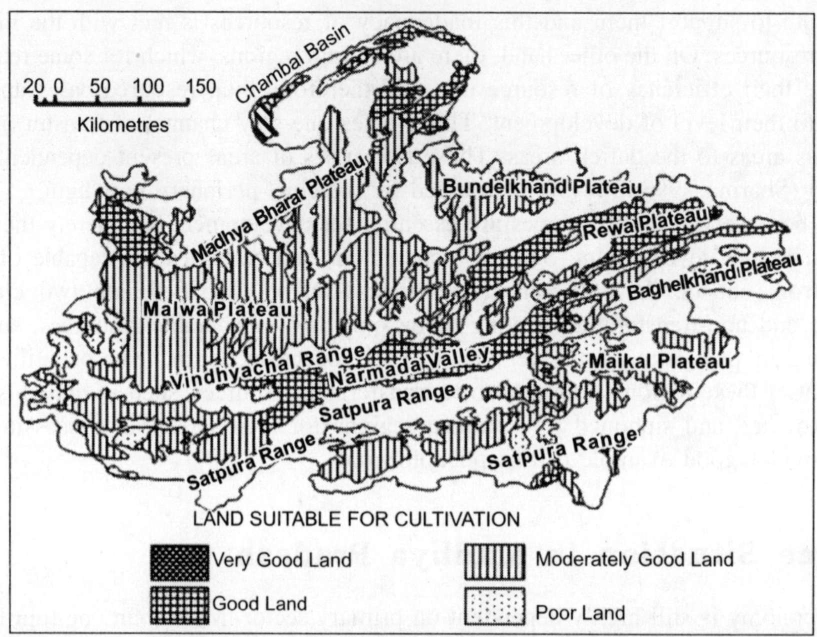

Figure 7.2 Land capability of Madhya Pradesh.

Population Pressure and Land Use

Population pressure is a very potent and dynamic force affecting land use. In fact, land is the only true resource for common man, because, being non-transportable, it must be used for the development of the area of its occurrence. All other natural resources including water are transportable and need not to be used for the development of the region of their occurrences. Normally there should be balance between the distribution of population, especially rural population and the carrying capacity of the area. A number of studies have shown that population growth compels agricultural communities to change their methods and land uses (Clark, 1967; Brookfield, 1972; Boserup, 1965, Grigg, 1967; Turner et al., 1977). Under the given standard of living, carrying capacity of land has to be enhanced with the increasing pressure of population.

Along with the physical character of land, demographic attributes of the region also go long way in influencing the development of land resources. The physical environment provides potentialities of and puts limitations to the land development. Among this group of factors only pressure of rural population is selected for the present purpose. Since population data are for 2011, data for agricultural land use for 2009–10 have been utilized. It is more meaningful to assess the net sown area in relation with the rural population. It can be done by analyzing the density of rural population on net sown area, known as the **nutritional density**.

Pressure of Population

Total population of Madhya Pradesh is 72,597 thousand in 2011 (6.0 per cent of total population of the country), which is distributed over 3,08,245 sq. km (9.38 per cent of total area of the country), yielding average arithmetic density of 236 persons per sq. km. It is very low in comparison to the national average of 382 persons per sq. km. However, rapid growth (473 per cent during 1901–2011) of population has been increasing pressure on land simultaneously. Arithmetic density was only 41 persons per sq. km in 1901 in the state, which reached to 60 persons in 1951 and 236 in 2011. It means pressure of population increased nearly four times during last 60 years. Similarly, pressure of rural population on net sown area also increased three times during the same period. In 1951, rural population was 15.85 million and net sown area was 100.85 thousand sq. km, resulting 119 rural people per sq. km. In 2011, rural population rose to 52.54 million but net sown area reached to 152.23 thousand sq. km only, which works to 349 rural persons per sq. km of net sown area. Further, nearly three-fourths (72.4 per cent) of the total population live in rural areas, and traditionally depend on land resources. In absence of other economic pursuits, about three-fourths of total workers are engaged in cultivation as cultivators and agricultural labourers. It means land resource determines the fate of the majority of the people of this state. In this perspective, relationship of population distribution and land use has been analyzed here.

Spatial Pattern of Man–Land Ratio

Distribution of population, expressed in terms of man–land ratio, is very uneven in this state also. One-fourth (25 per cent) of the total population is concentrated on one-tenth (12.4 per cent) of total area. Contrary to it, half of the area (49.8 per cent) supports one-third (35.5 per cent) of total population. This variation is evident from the range of arithmetic density of population, which varies from only 48 persons in Karahal tehsil of Sheopur district and 56 in Kusumi Tehsil of Sidhi district to 1632 in Huzur Tehsil of Bhopal and 2337 persons in Indore Tehsil of Indore district. On district level, it varies from only 94 persons per sq. km in Dindori district to 854 persons in Bhopal district. Ratio between highest and lowest Tehsil-wise density figures, 1:49, is indicative of very uneven distribution of population in the state as is evident from the Figure 7.2 depicting the spatial pattern of the arithmetic density of population.

There are certain densely populated tracts in the state. Among them, lower Chambal basin, Narmada valley, Rewa plateau and the Wainganga valley are important. There are 17 out of 50 districts with population density more than 250 persons per sq. km. These districts are distributed in certain tracts. Major tracts are: (i) Lashkar plain in the Chambal valley, (ii) the Satna-Rewa high plain, (iii) western Bundelkhand plateau, (iv) Indore Dewas–Ujjain tract, (v) Bhopal–Sehore–Rajgarh tract, (vi) Nimar plain, (vii) Dhar–Jhabua–Ratlam tract, (viii) Wainganga basin, and (ix) Anuppur–Sohagpur belt (Figure 7.3).

Contrary to them, sparsely populated tracts extend over the Baghelkhand plateau, Maikal plateau and ranges, Satpura and Vindhyachal ranges, Panna–Bijawar hills, western margin of the Malwa plateau, Guna plateau and the Bundelkhand uplands. In these sparsely populated tracts there are certain tracts, which can be said as blank areas. Such blank areas are Maikal and associated ranges and Paraswara plateau on Maikal area; Asirgarh hills in western Gawilgarh, Kalibhit, Mahadeo and Gondwana hills in Central Satpura; entire Vindhyachal range and Bijawar–Panna hills of the Bundelkhand uplands. On the other hand, even in these sparsely populated tracts, there are small pockets of concentration of population. For instance, in the

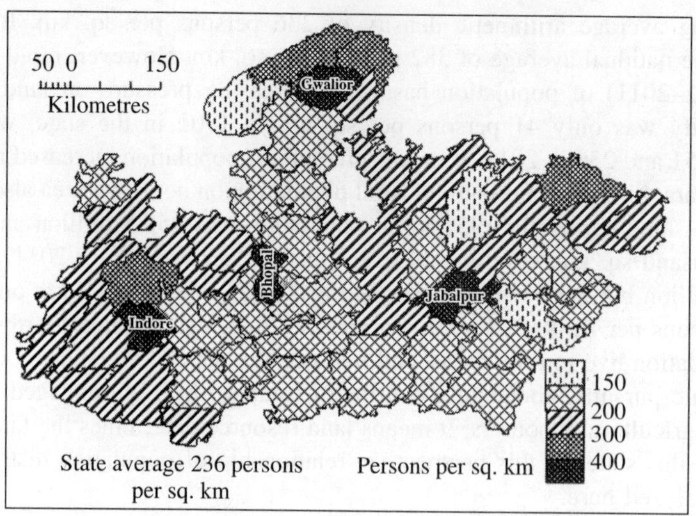

Figure 7.3 Density of population in Madhya Pradesh (2011).

Baghelkhand plateau, which happens to be sparsely settled region, most of the population is concentrated in the Sohagpur basin, containing coal-belt of the region and in the Son valley and the Singrauli basin.

Spatial distribution of population is the manifestation of the carrying capacity of the area. This carrying capacity depends on the nature of economic activities carried out there. Since more than three–fourths of the people of this state live in rural areas and nearly three-fourths of the working population is also engaged in cultivation, the basic pattern of the distribution of population is determined by the cultivability of the land. Nature of terrain, degree of slope, characteristics of soils including their water holding capacity, amount of rainfall and provision of irrigation are important factors affecting cultivation. The basic pattern established by these factors is variegated by other factors such as the development of mineral resources, urbanization and industrialization. Active mineral zones have attracted large number of migrants and sustain more density than the supporting capacity of land in those areas. In the coal-mining tracts of Singrauli, Shahdol–Anuppur and Chhindwara, new townships have come up, recording phenomenal increase of population and high density. Industrialization and urbanization are almost twin phenomena. Industries possess very high supporting capacity concentrated at a point, and induce the genesis of towns. Towns can develop otherwise also and industries are added later on to them. Bases of all towns are secondary and tertiary economic activities. Because of economic reasons such activities, unlike agriculture, develop at points not in areas. Consequently, density of population of areas containing these points (i.e., towns) becomes very high. Peaks of density can be seen at large industrial and urban centres on the map (Figure 7.3) of the arithmetic density. This distribution pattern is highly influenced by the degree of urbanization, besides agricultural productivity. It is evident from high coefficient of correlation ($r = +0.864$) between proportion of urban population and arithmetic density. Arithmetic density also shows significant relationship ($r = +0.366$) with the proportion of net sown area.

Nearly half (22) of the districts have low and very low density (below 200 persons per sq. km). These districts are concentrated in: (i) the Baghelkhand plateau extending over hilly tracts of Sidhi, Shahdol and Umaria districts, (ii) Sheopur–Shivpuri–Guna plateau, (iii) Bijawar–Panna hills of Chhatarpur and Panna districts, (iv) Dhar uplands and northern part of the middle Satpura region, (v) Vindhyachal range extending over southern Sagar, Damoh and northern Raisen districts, and (vi) Baihar Tehsil of Balaghat. These are very rugged hilly, dissected plateau and stony areas. Consequently, carrying capacity of these areas is very limited. These are poor not only in agricultural resources but lack mineral resources also.

Relationship between Rural Population and Land Development

Nutritional density is more realistic expression of pressure of rural population on cultivated land. It is ratio between rural population and net sown area. There are, on average, 349 rural persons per sq. km of net sown area of the state in 2011. On district level, it ranges from only 211 persons in Vidisha district to 569 persons in Morena district (Figure 7.4). Total 21 districts have higher nutritional density than the state average (349 persons).

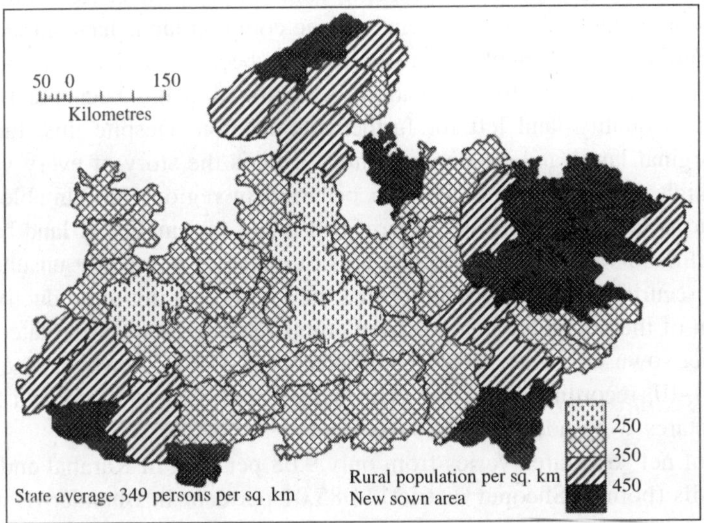

Figure 7.4 Nutritional density of Madhya Predesh (2011).

Concentration of districts with high nutritional density is in: (i) the Chambal region, (ii) Bundelkhand uplands, (iii) Baghelkhand plateau, (iv) Bhander upland, (v) Jhabua upland–Nimar plain–western Satpura, (vi) northern Betul–Chhindwara plateau, and (vii) Wainganga basin–Baihar plateau–Dindori plateau. Contrary to them, pressure of rural population on net sown area is usually low and very low in the Malwa plateau, Madhya Bharat plateau and the Narmada valley.

This pattern of distribution of nutritional density (Figure 7.4) is quite different from that of arithmetic density (Figure 7.3). Nutritional density is the interplay of the extent of net sown area and size of the rural population. It presents inverse relationship with the proportion of net sown area (r = –0.462) at tehsil level. Two-fifths (40.8 per cent) of the high nutritional density Tehsils have comparatively lower proportion (below 50 per cent) of net sown area to total area. But most of the low nutritional density Tehsils (74.1 per cent) have higher proportion of net sown area. A total of 152 Tehsils have proportion of net sown area more than 50 per cent of the total area and two-thirds (103 or 67.76 per cent) of them have nutritional densities below 350 persons per sq. km. On the other hand, 107 Tehsils have proportion of net sown below 50 per cent and two-thirds (71 or 66.4 per cent) of them have nutritional density higher than 300. It can be summed up that the large size of rural population in relation to the net sown area is responsible for high pressure of rural population on land resources.

Contemporary Situation of Land Resource Development

Agriculture is not only major contributor to the net domestic products but also a major means of livelihood of the people. Nearly three-fourths of workers are engaged in farming. Excessive dependency on agriculture led to the excessive exploitation of agricultural resources, particularly of land. There is keen competition for grabbing land among people, rich and poor alike, and virtually all cultivable lands, fallow lands and village common lands have already been brought under plough. Further, large extent of forests has also been cleared for the purpose. Most of them are physically unsuitable for cultivation. As cultivation has been practiced since long, there was no good quality land left for further colonization. Despite this, farming has been extended on marginal lands and on slopes of hills. This is the story of every village. As such, high and very high growth in net sown area occurred in regions not suitable for large-scale cultivation as far as land capability is concerned. It is not the quality of land but the necessity to get some livelihood which compelled peasants to cultivate physically unsuitable land. With the objective of security not the profitability that they moved to dig unproductive hazard-prone areas. Expansion of the net sown area has been comparatively rapid in the later half of the last century. Total net sown area was 100.85 lakh hectares in 1950–51, which rose to 152.23 lakh hectares in 2009–10, recording 50.95 per cent increase between 1950–51 and 2009–10. Thus, 5.14 million hectares were added to net sown area.

Proportion of net sown area varies from only 9.08 per cent in Karahal and 12.13 per cent in Bijeypur tehsils (both in Sheopur district) to 85.01 per cent in Bhander (Datia district) and 85.53 per cent in Sawer tehsil (Indore district) with state average of 49.5 per cent. Slightly less than half (155 tehsils or 59.84 per cent) of tehsils have lower proportion of net sown area than the state average and only two-fifths (40.16 per cent) are above this average. Proportion is very low (i.e., below 20 per cent) in eight tehsils and low (i.e., between 20 and 40 per cent) in 54 tehsils. On the other extreme, it is more than 80 per cent in 13 tehsils. District-wise proportion of net sown area is presented in Figure 7.5 which shows resemblance to the cultivability of land shown in Figure 7.1. In most cases, capability of land has been over-used. Very good, good and moderately good lands are widely cultivated. Even non-cultivable lands are cropped ignoring their suitability. Nowhere land suitable for cultivation is under-used. However, on micro scale it is not only the quality of land but also socio-economic status of the farmers which go long way to determine the way and extent of the utilization of land resources.

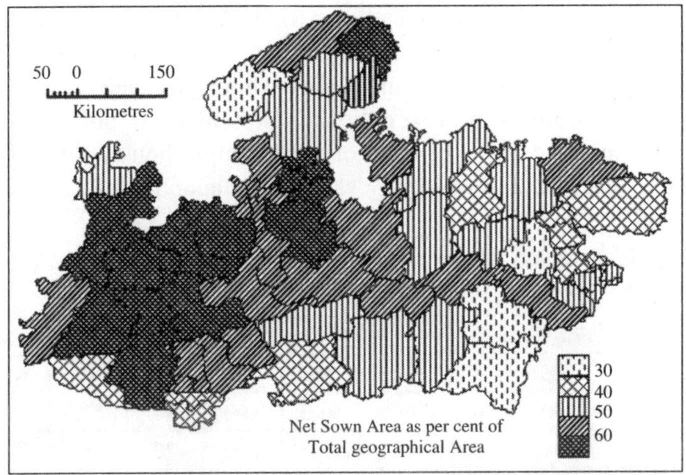

Figure 7.5 Net sown area of Madhya Pradesh (2009–10).

Social Determinants of Agricultural Land Development

Within the framework of the physical conditions, use of land in general and of agricultural land in particular depends on the socio-economic status as well as characteristics of farmers. Social structure is the third dimension of the reality along with the spatial and temporal dimensions. Access to land is the pivot of the social structure determining the nature of the land development. Adoption of modern methods, techniques and inputs varies not only spatially and temporally but it also varies from community to community and from person to person. In fact, the capacity of adoption hinges, with other things, upon the size of holding of the farmer and his social status donated by caste. Even these two characteristics of farmers have resulted in unequal accessibility of farmers to the new scientific knowledge and technology. It has manifested in differential level of the utilization of land resources.

This situation is corroborated by the distribution of the size of operational holdings. Proportion of marginal (less than 1 ha) and small (1–2 ha) holdings ranges from 29.7 per cent of all holdings in Harda district in the west to 83.3 per cent in Balaghat district in the southeast in 2000–10. Spatial pattern clearly shows that more than 60 per cent of the operational holdings in the eastern part are marginal and small in size while on major portion of Malwa and Narmada valley these holdings constitute less than 50 per cent of the total holdings. Such distribution pattern of the per capita net sown area as well as size of the holdings has bearings on adoption of agricultural innovations and also on agricultural productivity.

Adoption of modern agricultural inputs has proved panacea for raising production. Being capital intensive and scientific in nature, the use of modern inputs depends on the capacity and capability of the farmers. The capacity of the farmer, on the other hand, depends mainly on the size of holdings. In fact, size of holdings is necessary qualification for most of the opportunities including the access to the institutions and organizations involved in the process of diffusion of innovations and to the entire infrastructure. Therefore, the size of holding creates disparity in level of adoption. It has been seen on meso–(Sharma, 1988) and household–

level (Sharma, 1999). Further, adoption and size of holdings have direct relation with the productivity (Sharma, 2003). Surveys conducted in this connection on household level in the Betul–Chhindwara plateau, Raisen district and Tons basin of this state reveal this fact. Situation of adoption of certain innovations in these regions is presented in Table 7.1 in which adopters of each variable are converted as percentage of total sample households to the size class. It presents spatial, inter society and intra-society variation in adoption of agricultural innovations.

Table 7.1 Variation in adoption of agricultural innovations by size of holdings (Adopters as percentage of total households of size-class)

Innovations	*Chhindwara–Betul*				*Raisen district*				*Tons basin*			
	Ma	Me	L	All	Ma	Me	L	All	Ma	Me	L	All
Irrigation	38.7	82.5	100	63	68.5	91.3	100	84	59.3	88.5	100	82
HYVs*	80.6	80	81.3	80	15.7	64.5	100	72	56	77	78.1	66
Fertilizers	57.4	63.6	63.3	62	71.4	95.6	100	84	62.6	98.4	100	85

*High yielding variety of seeds.

Farmers have perceived the significance of irrigation and are trying their best to irrigate their fields. It is evident from the above table that more than half of the households of the Chhattisgarh basin, two-thirds of the Betul–Chhindwara plateau and more than three-fourths of the Tons basin practice irrigation. This proportion varies with the size of holdings. As a rule, proportion of irrigating households is lower in case of marginal and small holdings than their averages and much lower than the proportion of medium and large holdings. This proportion also varies with the community (Table 7.2). Scheduled castes (SC) are at bottom while other castes are at top followed by backward communities in this respect.

Table 7.2 Variation in adoption of agricultural innovations by communities (Users as per cent of total household of the community)

Innovations	*Chhindwara–Betul*				*Raisen district*				*Tons Basin*			
	ST	SC	BC	OC	ST	SC	BC	OC	ST	SC	BC	OC
Irrigation	49.7	44.4	73.9	83	63.9	75.6	90.7	98	39.1	83.3	75.3	87
HYVs	60.8	66	93.6	100	8.2	36.9	51.4	79	47.8	54.2	56.5	72
Fertilizers	33.4	39.3	79.3	83	67.2	71.1	93	95	39.1	66.7	87.1	90
Land treatment	2.3	6.7	23.4	23	0	0.9	2.9	3.6	4.3	4.2	2.4	4.1
Seed treatment	4.1	8.9	28	42	0	0	2.3	6.7	4.3	8.3	3.5	10
Pesticides	10.5	15.6	30.3	54	27.8	66.6	59	9.3	0	0	2.4	7.2

Under the scientific management of farming certain measures have been used to maintain and enhance the soil fertility. With the advent of green revolution, use of chemical fertilizers is popularized and they are widely used in regions under consideration. There is clear cut influence of size of holding and social status of the farmers on use of fertilizers. Marginal farmers and scheduled population are trailing far behind in use of fertilizers.

Along with the yield-raising technology, certain protection measures also have been propagated. These protection measures include land and seed treatments, rat control, etc. The use of these practices is also positively related with the size of holdings and community. These practices are usually limited to semi-medium, medium and large holdings. Further, it seems that these practices are exogenous to scheduled tribes and, to some extent, to scheduled castes also. They are incapable of accepting these methods readily.

Mechanization is also associated with the socio-economic capacity of farmers. Example can be cited of the thresher, use of which is size-specific and caste-specific. It can, therefore, be inferred that the size of the operational holdings is the kingpin of the entire socio-economic structure and manifests itself in the use of agricultural development measures. At the same time, place of farmer in social arena goes long way in influencing the adoption.

Changes in Land Uses during 1955–2010

Increasing pressure of population increases the demand of food and raw materials, fuel and fodder and land for non-agricultural establishments. Therefore land use is bound to change with the increasing pressure of population. For raising production of agricultural produces net sown area as well as double cropped area have been increased. Net sown rose to 152.23 thousand sq. km in 2009–10 from 100.08 thousand in 1955–56; and area sown more than once increased from 9.77 thousand sq. km to 69.25 thousand sq. km during the same period (Table 7.3).

Table 7.3 Madhya Pradesh: Changes in land uses during 1955–56 and 2009–10 (000 ha)

	Land use	1955–56	2009–10	*Change*		*Per cent share in total area*		
		Area	*Area*	'000 ha	*Percentage*	1955–56	2009–10	*Point change*
	Total area	30756	30756	0	0.0	100	100	0.0
1	Forests	7445	8697	1252	16.8	24.21	28.3	4.1
2	Non–agricultural uses	1413	2089	676	47.8	4.59	6.8	2.2
3	Barren lands	2510	1365	–1145	–45.6	8.16	4.4	–3.7
4	Pastures etc.	2128	1328	–800	–37.6	6.92	4.3	–2.6
5	Misc. tree crops	131	28	–103	–78.6	0.43	0.1	–0.3
6	Cultivable wastes	3699	1088	–2611	–70.6	12.03	3.5	–8.5
7	Fallow lands	2378	1072	–1306	–54.9	7.73	3.5	–4.2
8	Net sown area	11708	15223	3515	30.0	38.07	49.5	11.4
	Double cropped area	977	6926	5949	608.9	8.3	45.5	37.2
	Gross cropped area	12685	22149	9464	74.6	108.3	145.5	37.2

Unlike the net sown area, absolute as well as share of area put to other categories of uses declined sharply. In fact, cropped area, forested area and area under other human occupancy increased at the cost of these classes (Table 7.3). Major portion of the cultivable wastelands has been annexed to cropland. Even barren and uncultivable lands have been brought under cultivation, though they are physically unsuitable for this purpose. More than one-third of the permanent pastures and other grazing lands have shifted to other uses. It is fatal to the rural agrarian economy because of negligible area (5.8 thousand sq. km in 2004–05) under fodder crops for sustaining 33,988 thousand animals. Natural grazing lands and fallows provide them shelter. Area under orchards and other tree crops has almost banished. Further, population pressure has compelled people not to leave cropped area as fallow for longer period to recoup natural soil fertility. And as such proportion of fallow lands also declined sharply.

Such changes in uses of land are closely associated with the changes in density during this period. For example, close relationship between growth in density and increase in net sown area results in very high coefficient of correlation between them ($r = +0.753$). Similarly, correlation with other classes of land uses is negative indicating that with the increasing pressure land under them is shrinking. Growth in irrigated area presents positive relation though not much significant with the increasing pressure; however, it has significantly high correlation with the growth of net sown area ($r = 0.47$). Insignificant relation between growing pressure of population and growth in double-cropped area is strange.

Growth of Net Sown Area

As a consequence of increasing pressure of population on land agriculture expanded on all possible lands. Consequently, net sown area increased by 51 per cent, from 100.08 thousand sq. km in 1950–51 to 152.23 thousand sq. km in 2009–10. Total 52.2 thousand sq. km was added to net cropped area during this period. It is pertinent to mention that population of the state increased by 290 per cent during last 60 (1951–2011) years. Expansion of net sown is, thus, negligible in comparison to this. Thus, there is a decline in per capita net sown area. Per rural person net area sown was 0.841 ha in 1950–51 but only 0.210 ha in 2009–10. High and very high growth in net sown area has been witnessed in the northeastern Malwa, Madhya Bharat Plateau, Bundelkhand uplands and Baghelkhand plateau owing to extensive reclamation of cultivable wastelands and fallow lands.

Changes in Area Sown More than Once

Since proportion of cultivable land is limited, the second possibility of increasing food production is by multiple cropping. It has been observed by Boserup (1965) that farmers are likely to intensify their land use—crop the land more frequently—if there is some urgent need as an increase in population. In Madhya Pradesh, the area cropped more than once increased from 7.07 thousand sq. km in 1950–51 to 69.26 thousand sq. km in 2009–10, recording growth of 608.9 per cent. This increase is much higher than that of net sown area (51.0 per cent) during the same period. Growth rate of area sown more than once ranges from –29.2 per cent in Balaghat and 40.3 per cent in Shahdol district to 8251.8 per cent in Hoshangabad district. Exceptionally high increase in double cropped area (DCA) occurred in western half of the state. But it does not coincide with the area of high growth of density. Consequently, coefficient of correlation between them is insignificant ($r = -0.09$). Thus Boserup's postulation is not true in this case.

Changes in Irrigated Area

Irrigation helps in mitigating the scarcity of agricultural land by helping intensification of farming and more by increasing productivity. As such, growth of irrigation facilities has been one of the major objectives of agricultural development programmes, with the event of green revolution. Total irrigated area in the state increased from 469.5 thousand hectares in 1950–2051 [4.48 per cent of gross cropped area (GCA)] to 7161 thousand ha (33.5 per cent of GCA) in 2009–10. Thus growth has been more than fifteen times (1425 per cent) during 1950–2010. Growth in gross irrigated area ranges from 65.2 per cent in Balaghat to 45,787 per cent in Vidisha district. Spatial pattern of the growth in irrigated area is dissimilar to that of the growth of the density pattern, resulting in very low positive coefficient of correlation (r = +0.151) between them.

Aggregate Changes in Land Uses

If all changes in proportion of area under major land use classes are summed, ignoring their signs, it arrives at 35.45 points. It means more than one-third of the total area of the state has been involved in changes during last 50 years. Spatial pattern of net changes in land uses is also interesting (Figure 7.6). It ranges from only 12.17 per cent points in Shahdol district and 15.78 per cent points in Balaghat district to 92.48 per cent points in Sehore district. Districts where more than 50 per cent area is involved in changes are distributed north of the Narmada–Son line with exception of Khargone, Chhindwara and Sidhi.

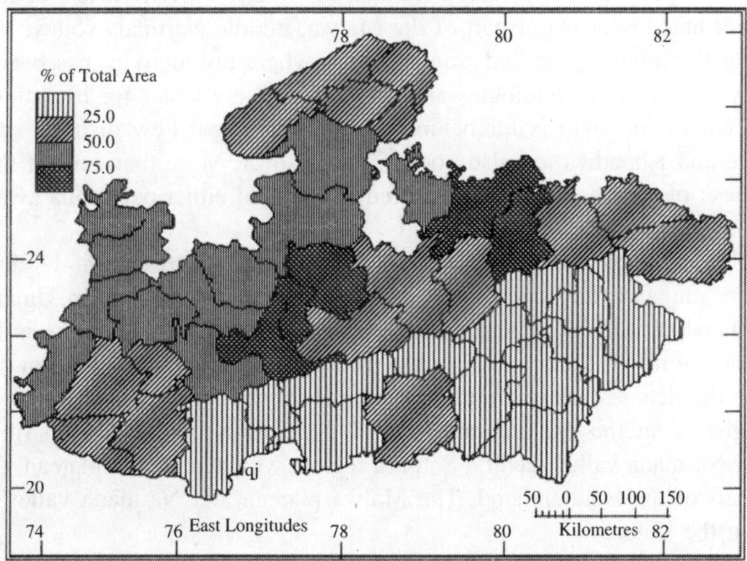

Figure 7.6 Aggregate change of land use in Madhya Pradesh (1955–56 to 2003–04).

When this pattern is viewed in terms of population pressure, it is seen that arithmetic density has no relation with this pattern of distribution, with very insignificant coefficient of correlation (r = 0.063). But density of total population on net cropped area shows inverse low relationship

(r = –0.210). Further, density of rural people on net cropped area, called **nutritional density**, shows moderate negative relationship (r = –0.313). It is indicative that scope of changing land use is more in areas where population pressure is low. Second, changes in land uses are not solely due to the expansion of agricultural land. Of course, major share of area withdrawn from other uses was annexed to net cropped area, addition to forested land and land put to non-agricultural uses also caused reduction in their shares in area.

Thus, population has caused changes in land uses in this state. As such growth of population presents positive and significant relationship with changes in land uses. Growth rates of three different periods were correlated with the aggregate changes in uses of land. Population growth during 1991–2001 has highest impact, with coefficient of correlation at +0.45; followed by growth during 1951–2001 (r = + 0.40) and during 1901–2001 (r = + 0.26).

Carrying Capacity and Population Pressure

Ultimate goal of changing land use is the increasing supporting capacity of land. It is a measure for assessing the supporting capacity of the cropped area particularly of area under food grains. Production of foodgrains per unit of area is assessed in terms of calories, after making allowance of about 16.8 per cent, which is not available for consumption due to several reasons. Taking account of annual need of average person, per unit caloric production is converted into human unit, which is called **carrying capacity**. In Madhya Pradesh, average carrying capacity is 363 persons per sq. km. It ranges from only 148 persons in Mandla district to 771 persons in Morena and 773 persons in Hoshangabad districts in 2000–01. Districts of higher carrying capacity are distributed over major part of the Malwa, middle Narmada valley, Madhya Bharat Pathar including Chambal region and Bundelkhand, where productivity has been enhanced by using modern yield-raising technologies and providing timely water for irrigation. Contrary to them, eastern half of the state is far behind the state average. Few districts such as Jhabua, Dhar, Khargone and Khandwa are also poor in this respect. More than half of the districts are insecure in respect of food availability measured in terms of either per capita available quantity or caloric output (Sharma, 2007:81–93).

Pressure of rural population is in excess of the carrying capacity in 17 districts. Deficit in these districts ranges from 208 persons in Mandla and 206 persons in Umaria districts to 27 persons in Jabalpur and 21 in Khargone district. In all, existing pressure is higher by 100 and more persons in ten districts and less than 100 persons in remaining seven districts. These are problematic districts as far as agricultural productivity is concerned. Contrary to it, carrying capacity is higher than the existing pressure of population in districts distributed over the Malwa plateau, Narmada valley, central Satpura region, Madhya Bharat plateau, Chambal basin and irrigated part of the Bundelkhand. The Malwa plateau and Narmada valley are important surplus areas in the state.

Conclusion

It can be concluded that though the arithmetic density is quite low in the state, pressure of population particularly of rural population on agricultural land is quite high. This high pressure has necessitated the expansion and intensification of cropped area. Consequently, net sown area increased at faster rate resulting in significantly high correlation. Area sown more than once also increased very rapidly. Land under other categories of use lost significance and absolute area simultaneously. Carrying capacity of cropped area has been enhanced by intensification and by increasing use of yield raising inputs. Irrigation has been instrumental in increasing intensification and adoption of yield raising technologies. It has ushered the increase in net sown area also. Because of increasing irrigation facilities use of fertilizers and high yielding variety of seeds have also expanded rapidly. As such these inputs have come up to meet the scarcity of land.

Despite slower growth of net sown area than that of population, productivity of agricultural land has increased substantially. Productivity measured in terms of supporting capacity, called carrying capacity, is higher than the pressure of rural population. Situation is not promising at state level in this respect and state has reached at the critical stage. Therefore, use of land particularly of agricultural land has to be optimized soon. Low land productivity and larger number of agricultural workers result in low productivity per worker. This situation nullifies the general conclusion derived by several studies that the density of rural population is directly related to the productivity of land (Nityanand, 1966; Ayyar and Dube, 1968; Mehta, 1973). Even in eighties of last century similar situation existed (Sharma, 1980). In the poverty-ridden society the survival algorithm is operative rather than the principle of productivity. People still live in suppressing poverty in low productivity areas. Large number of ruralites constantly moves in search of profitable jobs.

The contemporary land resource development is incapable of improving the fate of the people unless it is integrated with the development (not exploitation) of other resources within the regions of the state.

References

Ayyar, N.P. and R.S. Dube (1968), Some aspects of rural population of Madhya Pradesh, *Geographical Outlook,* **5**, 53.

Boserup, E. (1965), *The Conditions of Agricultural Growth*, Allen & Unwin, London.

Brookfield, H.C. (1972), Intensification and dis-intensification in Pacific agriculture, *Pacific Viewpoint*, **13**, 30–48.

Clark, C. (1967), *Population Growth and Land use,* Macmillan, London.

Grigg, D.B. (1967), Population pressure and agricultural change, in: Christopher Board et al. (Eds.), *Progress in Geography.* **8**, Edward Arnold, London, 135–167.

Mehta, B.C. (1973), Spatial distribution of population in Rajasthan, *National Geographical Journal of India*, **19**, Parts 3–4, 149–157.

Nityanand (1966), Distribution and spatial arrangement of rural population in East Rajasthan, India, *Ann. Asso. Am. Geogrs.* **56**, 205.

Sharma, S.K. (1980), Agricultural productivity and density of rural population in Madhya Pradesh—A correlation, *Geographical Review of India,* **42**(1), 21–30.

Sharma, S.K. (1988), Adoption of agricultural development measures in relation to Size and tenancy of operational holdings in Madhya Pradesh, *Journal of Indian Regional Science*, **20**(2), 27–39.

Sharma, S.K. (1993), Resource Utilization and Development-Perspective Study of Madhya Pradesh. Northern Book Centre, New Delhi.

Sharma, S.K. (1999), Social Structure and adoption of Agricultural Innovations in Madhya Pradesh, *Geographical Review of India,* **61**(2), 16–164.

Sharma, S.K. (2000), *Spatial Framework and Economic Development. Perspective Study of Madhya Pradesh*, Northern Book Centre, New Delhi.

Sharma, S.K. (2003), Agricultural Innovations and their impact on Agricultural Productivity in Madhya Pradesh, *The Deccan Geographer*, **41**(2), 49–64.

Sharma, S.K. (2007), Status of Food Security in Madhya Pradesh. *The Geographer*, **54**(1), 81–93.

Zimmermann, E.W. (1951, 1959), *World Resources and Industries*, Harper & Row, New York.

Zobler, L. (1962), An Economical Historical View on Natural Resource Use and Conservation, *Economic Geography*, **38**, 191.

8

Land and Land Use Planning in Indian Context

Arun Chaturvedi and A.K. Maji

Abstract: Land is the basic resource base which provides the sustenance to the people. The chapter presents the physiographic, climatic and agro-ecological regions of India along with the land resources in different parts. The land use classification, land use policy and guiding principles of land use policy have also been discussed. Finally, this chapter focuses on land use planning and national land use policy of the country and states.

Keywords: Land Use Policy, Watershed, Special Economic Zone, Peneplain, Agro-Ecological Zones, Physiography, National Land Use Policy

Introduction

Land use planning is the process of evaluating land and alternative patterns of land use and other physical, social and economic conditions for the purposes of selecting and adopting the kinds of land use and courses of action best calculated to achieve specified objectives. Land use planning may be at national, regional, state, district, watershed or village and also at farm level. The process involves the participation of the land users. It entails systematically evaluating land and alternative pattern of land use, choosing that use which meets specified goals, and the drawing up of policies and programmes for the use of the land (Gautam, 2002). Land utilization manifests the man-environment relationship at any given time and place.

In the present Indian scenario, area under non-agricultural use has been increasing, area under forests has been increasing, area under wastelands is decreasing and net sown area is increasing (Anonymous, 2005). On the other hand, the increase in population is creating problems of land use especially in the issues of land use conflicts. The controversy about Special Economic Zones, the pressure of tribal to resettle them in forest lands and the threat to good agricultural land from various other utilizations are matters which have revived the need for proper land use planning.

Land Resources of India

India, with a total geographical area of 329 m.ha, has the seventh largest land area (occupying 2.4 per cent of the earth's surface) in the world, with second largest population (population density—382 persons per sq. km). It is located between 8°4' N – 37°6' N latitudes and 68°7' E – 97°25' E longitudes. It spans 3214 km from north to south, and 2,933 km from east to west. The coastline stretches for over 7516.6 km. It is endowed with a variety of physiographic, edaphic, climatic and biological attributes ranging from the glacial undulating terrain to high rainfall level plains. Nearly 265 m.ha of the land has potential for biological production.

With more than 183 m.ha, categorized as cultivable lands and a population above a billion, India has less than 0.183125 ha. of cultivable land per person. This makes land use planning a very crucial aspect for food security of the country. Assessment of soil and land resources is the first step in any land related planning process. The various land units based on physiography in India are presented in Table 8.1.

Table 8.1 Physiographic regions and sub-regions of India

Physiographic region/sub-region	*Area* (m.ha)	*Per cent area*	*Physiographic region/sub-region*	*Area* (m.ha)	*Per cent area*
Indo-Gangetic Alluvial Plain	37.94	11.54	Hill ranges (Ghats)	25.43	7.73
Bengal basin	7.85	2.39	Islands	0.83	0.25
Central Highlands	41.05	12.49	Himalayas and other Mountain ranges	34.15	10.39
Deccan Plateau	62.90	19.13	North Eastern Ranges, Eastern Himalayas and Brahmaputra valley	25.51	7.76
Eastern Plateau	33.23	10.11	Coastal plain	23.96	7.29
Gujarat coastal plain	16.36	4.98	Western plains	19.52	5.94

Source: Soils of India (2002).

The most productive landforms in the country, in continuity, can be summarized as: Indo Gangetic plains (37.94 m.ha, 11.54 per cent), Bengal basin (7.85 m.ha, 2.39 per cent), Coastal plains (23.96 m.ha, 7.29 per cent) and Brahmaputra valley (3.01 m.ha, <1 per cent), respectively of the total area reported in Table 8.1.

These landforms having all the basic contributory factors towards sustainable agricultural requirement like fertile alluvium, available perennial source of irrigation, easily manageable soil quality and agriculturally suitable terrain parameters had also been the vital sites for the initiation of early civilizations since time immemorial. One of the most basic factors for better agricultural developments at these sites had been the process of soil enrichment by periodic replacement of soil cover by the adjoining perennial river systems. Some of these areas are now affected by accelerated nutrient depletion because of intensive use through a long period of time.

Physiographic Setting

The Indo-gangetic plain is an aggradational plain formed by the rivers Ganga and Brahmaputra. The plain extends from extremely arid and semi-arid environment of Rajasthan in the west to humid and perihumid Brahmaputra valley in the east. The elevation is up to 300 m above MSL with low gradient. It includes the Indus plain, the Rajasthan plain, Ganga plain and valleys of Brahmaputra. The coastal plains dominate along the Arabian Sea and Bay of Bengal. The east coastal plain is widely curving and comprises of Utkal, Andhra and Tamil Nadu plains. The western coastal plain comprises of Kerala, Karnataka, Konkan, Gujarat and Kathiawar peninsula.

The central high land comprises of Malwa plateau, Aravalli ranges, Madhya Bharat Pathar, Rajasthan uplands, Bundelkhand uplands and Narmada valley. The Deccan plateau consists of Satpura ranges, Karnataka and Telangana plateau. The north Deccan plateau is derived from lava (basalt). The Eastern plateau is represented by Baghelkhand, Chhotanagpur, Garhjat hills and Mahanadi basin. The landscape exhibits a peneplain surface with diverse topography including escarpment, rounded hills and rolling plateaus. The ghats (hill ranges) comprise of Western and Eastern Ghats consisting of the Sahyadri, the Nilgiri, etc. The plateaus of Eastern ghats are Machkund and Koraput, the escarps are of Madugula Kondas and the gneissic piedmont plateau of Malakangiri are the important features. The islands are in two groups, i.e., Lakshadweep in the Arabian sea and the Andaman and Nicobar island in the Bay of Bengal with hill escarpments and small plateaus.

Climatic Regions

Climate is an important factor of soil formation and also influences its further use. India is bestowed with a climatic variety ranging from Arid Cold Deserts in the North to Humid and Perihumid areas in the North East. The climatic regions in India with the length of growing period have been summarized in Table 8.2.

Table 8.2 Agro-ecological regions

Sl. No.	*Region*	*LGP* (days)	*Area* (per cent of TGA)	*AER*
1.	Arid	<90	16.0	1, 2, 3
2.	Semi-arid	90–150	36.0	4, 5, 6, 7, 8
3.	Sub-humid	>150	32.0	9, 10, 11, 12, 13, 14
4.	Humid/peri humid	>270	10.0	15, 16, 17
5.	Coastal	varying	6.5	18, 19

More than 50 per cent of the country has semi-arid to arid climate and needs to be irrigated for agricultural production. Nearly 42 per cent of the country has Length of Growing Period (LGP) above 150 days in a year and makes it possible to cultivate with the help of available soil moisture. These areas need to be provided with some supplemental irrigation at the time of crop stress.

Land Use

Till 1949–50, the land area in India was classified into five categories known as the five-fold land utilization classification. These categories were: (i) forests, (ii) area not available for cultivation, (iii) other uncultivated land, excluding the current fallows, (iv) fallow land, and (v) the net area sown. This five-fold classification was, however, a very broad outline of land-use in the country and was not found adequate enough to meet the needs of agricultural planning in the country. The states were also finding it difficult to present comparable data according to this classification owing to the lack of uniformity in the definitions and scope of classification covered by these five broad categories. To remove the non-comparability and to break up the broad categories into smaller constituents for better comprehension, the Technical Committee on Co-ordination of Agricultural Statistics, set up in 1948 by the Ministry of Food and Agriculture, recommended a nine-fold land-use classification replacing the old five-fold classification, and also recommended standard concepts and definitions for all the states to follow. The statement below gives the nine-fold classification and its relationship with the old five-fold classification (Table 8.3). A generalized land use map of the country has been shown in Figure 8.1. This map shows 6 categories of land use, which are arable, forest, non-agricultural, plantation, scrub and grass and unproductive or waste land.

Table 8.3 Classification adopted for land-utilization statistics

Sl. No.	*Old classification*	*New classification*
1.	Forests	Forests
2.	Area not available for cultivation	Land put to non-agricultural uses
3.	Other cultivated land, excluding current fallows	Barren and unculturable land
4.	Fallow lands	Permanent pastures and other grazing lands
5.	Net area sown	Miscellaneous tree crops and groves, not included in the net area sown
6.		Culturable waste
7.		Fallow land, other than current fallows
8.		current fallows
9.		Net area sown

Land Use Planning

As speculated by David Dent (1990), a very broad spectrum of people is involved in planning and making decisions about land use. They operate in ground, in villages and on farms and at all levels between and include all personals from every discipline. They bring a wide range of skills and experience to bear on land use planning but few are specialist land use planners, opportunities for formal training being limited. The land use planning has been learnt by doing. Any guide lines cannot be a prescription for land use planning; it should be flexible involving local or national procedures that can be modified by the people on the spot. The land planning

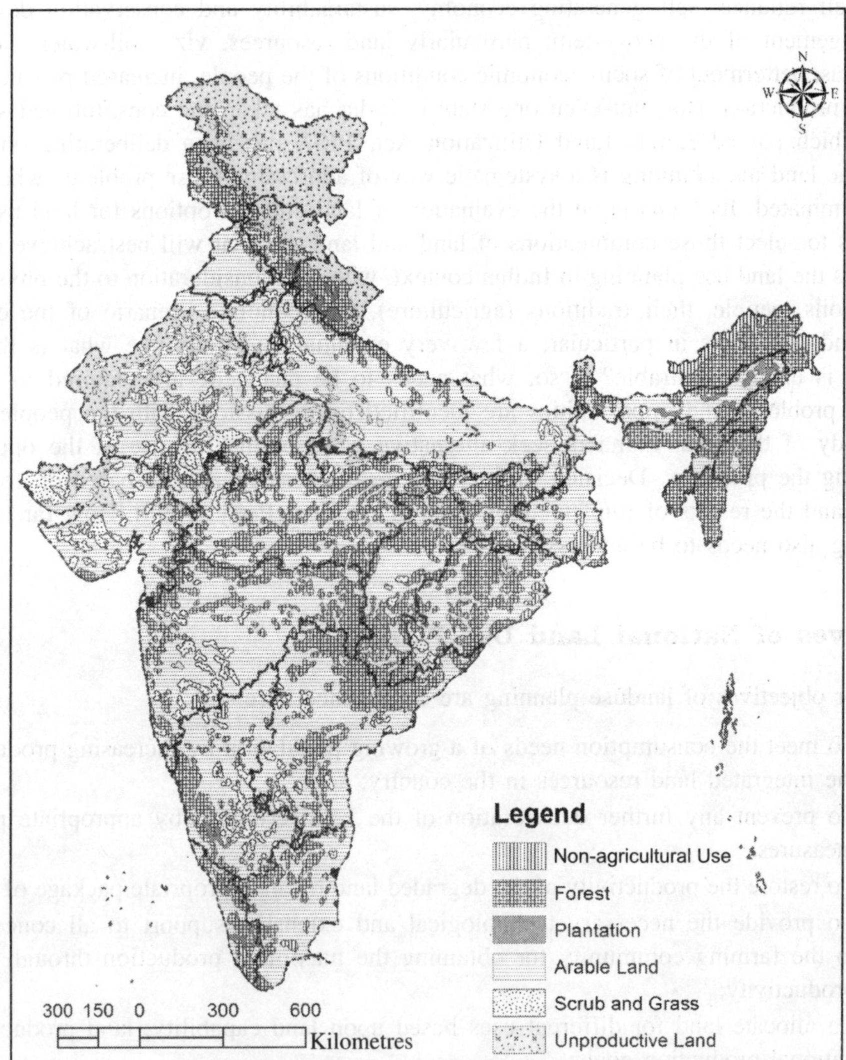

Figure 8.1 Land use pattern in India.

should encompass wide range of situations in which it can be applied. The techniques and even the strategy of land use planning can be very different at national level, village level and at any level in between. Chamla and Mortiss (1990) draw attention to '10 painful years' of planning effort needed to arrive at the degree of participation now achieved in Western Australia.

Guiding Principles of Land Use Policy

The land use policy has to be formulated in accordance with the geographical, climatic and soil conditions (agro-ecological regions) in a state. Through land use planning, the state must achieve self reliance, self generating economy, sustainability and conservation development and management of the ecosystem, particularly land resources, viz., soil-water-plant-animal sub-systems, betterment of socio-economic conditions of the people, increased productivity and enhanced production. But, not even one state in India has taken the constitutional step. Only Kerala, which passed Kerala Land Utilization Act, 1967, has been deliberating on the state policy. The land use planning is a systematic way of addressing these problems where misuse can be eliminated. Its focus is on the evaluation of land and the options for land use, and its purpose is to select those combinations of land and land use that will best achieve our goals. To address the land use planning in Indian context, with due consideration to the physiography, climate, soils, people, their traditions (agriculture), the economic scenario of the country in general and occupants in particular, a few very essential questions like what is the present situation? is change desirable? if so, what needs to be changed? are required to be asked. Land use problems and opportunities are identified by discussions with the people involved and a study of the area. Planners seek alternative ways of making use of the opportunities and solving the problems. Decision makers choose the best alternative based on forecasts of the costs and the results of implementing each alternative (Petry, 1990). How far is the plan succeeding also needs to be addressed.

Objectives of National Land Use Planning

The major objectives of landuse planning are enumerated here:

1. To meet the consumption needs of a growing population by increasing productivity of the integrated land resources in the country;
2. To prevent any further deterioration of the land resources by appropriate preventive measures;
3. To restore the productivity of the degraded land by an appropriate package of practices;
4. To provide the necessary technological and extension support to all concerned and to the farming community for obtaining the maximum production through increased productivity;
5. To allocate land for different uses based upon land capability, land productivity and national production goals;
6. To install efficient and effective administrative structure for prescribing and regulating land use by all concerned, including the Government Departments and to revitalize the land use boards in this behalf;
7. To involve the community for adoption of appropriate land use for increased productivity by ensuring that the land use policy provides adequately for the consumption and energy needs and generally improves their income levels and provides them a better quality of life;
8. To create greater awareness of the advantages of national land use policies at all levels through appropriate educational, extension and training programmes;
9. To restructure the livestock production programmes in such a manner that the livestock population is gradually limited to economically productive stock and to prevent degradation of grassland;

10. To provide for optimum use of land which is under agriculture by promoting the concept of mixed-farming system in which the production programme will include the production of fodder and tree crops also on the marginal and sub-marginal land of farmers;
11. To motivate farmers by organizing input supplies and marketing support for encouraging them to cultivate the appropriate crop or fodder or trees in conformity with land use policy;
12. To take up on priority basis the completion of land and soil surveys and the inventory of land resources on the basis of the prescribed land use classification so that resource allocation can be based on a reliable data base;
13. To examine the legal support available for enforcement of land use policy in the form of existing State and Central laws and to consider the need for comprehensive legislation to provide some teeth to any machinery entrusted with implementation of national land use policy;
14. To coordinate the formulation and implementation of water resource management policies, forest management policies and urban planning within the overall resource allocation needs dictated by a comprehensive national land use policy; and
15. To prepare a plan of action at all levels covering a time frame relevant to all the objectives specified above and to continuously monitor action taken thereon in an effective fashion;

Land resources in India are limited. Measured in terms of acreage of land available for productive use per capita, the availability of the resources is, in fact, declining. The availability of cultivable land is even worse. The demand for arable land, grazing, vegetation, mining, wildlife and urban development are greater than the land resources available. The surveys indicate at least some areas in which the land is either wrongly used or degraded and is not contributing as fully as it should to the nation's well being.

The following two points must be met if planning is to be successful:

(a) The need for changes in land use, or actions to prevent some unwanted changes must be accepted by the people involved. Then a land use plan can identify the most desirable pattern of land use and ways of achieving it.

(b) There must be the political will and ability to put the plan into effect.

It is not successful when these conditions are not met. When there is no political will, there will be no enforced statutory provision, no money will be forthcoming and or support from decision-makers or collaboration between implementing agencies will also be not possible. Wilkinson (1985), rightly points out the role of legislation in landuse planning especially in developing countries.

National Land Use Policy

The National Land Use Policy guideline and action points were prepared by the Government of India, Ministry of Agriculture after intensive deliberations. In the said policy, framing of suitable legislation and its sincere enforcement were stressed by imposing penalties for violation thereof. The said policy guidelines were placed before the 'National Land Use and Waste Land Development Council' under the chairmanship of the Prime Minister and its first meeting was held on 6th February, 1986. The Council agreed to the adoption of policy and circulated the same throughout the country for adoption after suitable considerations at the state level. Of the 19 points, some of the most important ones are:

1. Land Use Boards at the State level should be revitalized.
2. Land Use Policy must be evolved by all users of land within Government jointly and must be enforced on the basis of both legislation for enforcing land use as well as their promotional and preserving methods.
3. Urban Policy must be restructured so as to ensure that highly productive land is not taken away. Town planning should also provide for green belts.
4. A national campaign should be launched for educating the farmers and Government Departments about the need to conform to an integrated land use policy.
5. Cropping pattern should be reviewed specially in the drought prone/desert areas so that maximum advantage is taken of improved soil and water management practices.
6. Land and soil surveys should be completed and inventory of land resources should be prepared in each state so that resource allocation is based on a reliable data base.
7. Heavy penalties should be imposed against those who interfere with land resources and its productivity. It must be recognized that environmental protection cannot succeed unless this is done.
8. The problems of water logging, salinity and alkalinity must be brought under control by the use of appropriate technologies and by the adoption of proper water management practices.
9. The management of Command Areas should be reviewed, restructured and revitalized within a specified time limit so that water is used efficiently. Necessary investments for treating the catchments must be met to prevent the collapse of irrigation system due to premature siltation.
10. Technologies relating to dry farming, land shaping and water harvesting must be propagated and adopted in the interest of moisture conservation and optimal use.
11. Land Use Planning should be integrated with rural employment programmes in such a manner that loans and subsidies are given only for those productive activities which represent efficient land use.
12. Rights of tribals and poorer sections on common land should be protected through legal and administrative structures.
13. Stall feeding should be popularized, especially in such areas where grazing land is already degraded.
14. Special Fodder Development Programme in select blocks should be launched together with a Livestock Development Programme. The aim should be to limit the livestock population to economically productive stock.
15. Plantations for meeting commercial and industrial needs should preferably be located far away from the habitat.

16. The policy of supplying forest raw materials on subsidized basis to users other than the rural poor should be reviewed so that raw material is supplied at the prevailing market price, with a view to induce such users to go in for massive afforestation programmes, as also to motivate small and marginal farmers to grow forest based raw material for industry at remunerative prices.
17. The use of alternative packaging material such as corrugated card boards, etc. instead of wooden packaging must be explored and encouraged.

The policy was finally adopted in 1988 but has not really been able to move things. It has been circulated to all concerned for adoption and implementation through enactment of suitable legislation. The policy, however, did not make the desired impact mainly due to the fragmented handling of different components of agriculture like land and soil. However, a Land Resource Management Policy and Approach is now being finalised in consultation with FAO, the Lal Bahadur Shastri National Academy of Administration and the National Institute of Rural Development (NIRD). The policy is intended to have dynamic conservation, sustainable development and equitable access to the benefits of intervention as its thrust. Land being a state subject, many states have enacted legislation on land.

State Land Use Board

Land being a state subject, no meaningful discussion on the subject of land use can take place without discussions on the State Land Use Boards. The Centrally Sponsored Scheme on strengthening of State Land Use Board (SLUB) was launched in 1983. From November, 2000 onwards, this scheme is being implemented in the states through Macro Management of Agriculture (MMA). The objectives of the SLUB are:

1. To provide policy directive for sustainable development of land resources,
2. To ensure close coordination among various land user departments, and
3. To initiate necessary steps for integrated planning for optimal use of available land resources.

All the states and Union Territories have constituted SLUB under the chairmanship of Chief Minister/Chief Secretaries as an apex body except in three newly created states, namely, Chhattisgarh, Jharkhand and Uttarakhand and Union Territory of Chandigarh.

The main achievements of the programme are:

Perspective Plan: Six states, namely, Andhra Pradesh, Haryana, Karnataka, Kerala, Punjab, Tamil Nadu, and Union Territory of Dadra & Nagar Haveli have prepared perspective plans. Five States, namely, Assam, Gujarat, Maharashtra, Himachal Pradesh, Tripura and Union Territory of Pondicherry have initiated preparation of plan.

Land Use Policy: Draft Land Use Policy has been formulated by five states, namely, Bihar, Kerala, Tamil Nadu, Punjab and Uttar Pradesh and policy outline has been prepared by State Government of Andhra Pradesh. Eight States, namely, Arunachal Pradesh, Assam, Gujarat, Haryana, Jammu & Kashmir, Maharashtra, Mizoram and Rajasthan have initiated formulation of land use policy.

Laws/Acts: The State Governments of Arunachal Pradesh, Himachal Pradesh, Karnataka, Kerala, Maharashtra, Tripura, Goa and Union Territory of Dadra & Nagar Haveli and Pondicherry have Laws/Acts for checking diversion of agricultural land for non-agricultural purposes.

The State Governments of Uttar Pradesh, Rajasthan and Assam have issued rules/executive orders to check the diversion of good agricultural land for non-agricultural purposes.

States/Union Territories of Uttar Pradesh, Mizoram, Orissa, Punjab, Andhra Pradesh, Arunachal Pradesh, Bihar, Haryana, Jammu & Kashmir, Nagaland, Punjab, Rajasthan, Tamil Nadu, West Bengal, Andaman & Nicobar Islands, Daman & Diu, Chandigarh and Lakshadweep have initiated action for revision/formulation of the Act.

Conclusion

The general perception in India is that we have no shortage of land. There are people who make claims that urban population of India can be settled in 2.5–3 per cent of total area of the country. There are also those who feel that Indian agriculture can never be the base for total livelihood and economic development and give example of Japan which has the lowest area under cultivation but is self sufficient in essential commodities. This is not true and the Government woke up to this reality in 2004–05 when they realized that the growth of Indian economy is not reflecting in ground realities and there is disparity between agricultural growth and overall growth. The agricultural growth has been 1.5 per cent in the last 5 years and national growth has been 6–7 per cent in the same period. With 65 per cent of its 110 million population having farming as way of life and means of livelihood, agriculture has to be the mainstay of Indian economic growth. Nearly 42 per cent of total geographical area being under agriculture makes it the largest land utilization category in the country. The irony is that agriculture contributes only 21 per cent to the GDP. The highest growth rate is only 2.5 per cent (in U.P.) in spite of our best efforts.

Each parcel of land has inherent biological properties favourable or otherwise for each crop/land use. Soil and, thus, land is an ecological entity. Any agrarian economy is highly natural resource dependent. The status of natural resources determines the productive capacity of soils and land, in spite of all the claims of Hi-Fi technology in the field of genetic engineering. According to government statistics, only 1,56,030 thousand ha. is under cultivation out of 1,83,125 thousand ha. (55 per cent of TGA) cultivable land.

Poverty alleviation and livelihood security have become the two major tools of economic development in the quest for Bharat Nirman as outlined by the government. Land, labour and capital are the three important resources, as between them they constitute all the factors of production. Scientific land use planning based on soil and land characteristics directed towards long term ecological and economic security is the need of the hour.

References

Anonymous (2005), *Agriculture Statistics at a Glance*, Ministry of Agriculture, Govt. of India, New Delhi.

Chamla, S. and P.D. Mortiss (1990), *Working together for land care*, Australian Academic Press, Brisbane.

Dent, David (1990), *Land use applications*, Proceedings of the FAQ Expert Consultation, 1990, Rome, Italy, 10–14, December, Food and Agriculture Organization of the United Nations.

Gautam, N.C. (2002), *Methodology for Land Use Planning*, Center for Land Use Management (CLUMA), Hyderabad.

Soils of India (2002), *NBSS& LUP Publication 94*, National Bureau of Soil Survey and Land Use Planning, Nagpur, India, 134.

Petry, F. (1 990), *Multi-criteria decision-making and rural development*, Agricultural Systems, Special Issue.

Wilkinson, G.K. (1985), The role of legislation in land use planning for developing countries, *Legislative studies*, 31, FAO, Rome.

9

Land Resource Management Key to Sustainable Agricultural Development

Mridula Singh

Abstract: In spite of the fact that the state of Uttar Pradesh is situated in the fertile Gangetic plain and characterized by fertile soils, it has been facing great economic stress due to ill management of land resources. This chapter focuses on key issues which need to be addressed in order to maintain the eco-balance and meet the needs and aspirations of a vast majority of farmers who have been suffering due to small land holdings, poor technology and low productivity.

Keywords: State Agriculture Price Commission, Beej Vikas Nigam, Genetic Upgradation, Degraded Land, Conjunctive use of surface and ground water, Geographical Information System.

Introduction

Natural resources play very important role in the process of economic growth and development. There are natural resources which are exhaustible while some are renewable. In achieving economic growth and development, their utilization pattern and rate of regeneration plays a very important role. The optimal pattern of utilization, conservation and preservation can well be determined if there are necessary and suitable institutions. The institutional set up comprises the political processes, policies, rules and regulations, etc.

It is indeed a very serious issue whether in future the natural resource base, particularly land, would be able to support the likely increase in population and provide better standard of living to people. Land, which includes soil, water and associated plants and animals, is a complex and dynamic combination of factors like geology, topography, hydrology, soil, micro climates and community of plants and animals that are continuously interacting under the influence of climate and people's activity. The use, to which land is put, is determined by owners, farmers, government institutions, etc. Such decisions are influenced by factors like-soil and climate, technology and socio-economic aspirations and compulsions of the community and families (Misra, 2002).

The relevance of land use planning assumes significance in this scenario where population is rapidly increasing and land is constant. The purpose of land use planning is to regulate uses on scientific–ecological basis to curb misuse or abuse of land. The management of plants, animals, land and water as an integrated system is very important. To achieve equitable distribution of income, social parity as well as self reliance for all regions of country as well as all sections of society, it is imperative to improve the living conditions of people especially in rural India. The land use policy should aim at optimizing returns on long term basis rather than meeting short term requirement on adhoc basis.

It is well established now that 80 per cent of the world's population lives in countries where agriculture and land are primary sources of earning and livelihood. The rising trend of land degradation is a distinct feature here. And this indeed, is a concern for all in terms of food security and sustainable development (Swaminathan, 2002; Sehgal et al., 1994).

In addition to the natural resource base, the infrastructural development is also one of the major factors explaining regional variations in economic growth and agricultural productivity. The shift for such a regional-specific approach to infrastructural development lies in the fact that all regions do not require all components at the same time. For instance, the additional benefits from irrigation are far higher in dry land regions than in an already irrigated area. Similarly, improved and high grade land and efficient marketing system yield higher benefits in regions with an already higher agricultural productivity than elsewhere. In this way, a regional-specific policy will help in advancing an optimal use of the resource and infrastructural investment consistent with the regional growth potential and development requirements (Tiwari, 2000).

Status of Land Resources

Land is not only the solid part of earth but also a solid complex of soil, mineral, water and forests. It is also a basic natural resource. Over the span of human history, man has drawn most of his sustenance and much of his fuel, clothing and shelter from the land. While relentless increase in human and live stock population has been putting mounting pressure on the limited resources, the conservation and management of land resources have been neglected by the Indian planners. The sad consequence has been deteriorating soil health and overall ecological imbalance. According to an estimate, in the developing world, one billion hectare of arable land is moderately and severely degraded and nine million hectares is beyond ameliorative measure. This indeed is a matter of great concern.

Among the developing countries, India ranks very high in respect of both, the extent and severity of land degradation. In India 53.2 per cent of total area is affected by different kinds of degradation whereas in China it's only 20 per cent, Pakistan 26 per cent, 0.7 per cent in Bangladesh and 10 per cent in Sri Lanka. The continued degradation of productive land is a serious threat to the survival of human race. The per capita availability of arable land has decreased from 0.32 to 0.14 hectare over a period of five decades.

India has nearly 2.4 per cent of world's land on which 16 per cent of world's population and over 18 per cent of world's livestock depend. The land surface of the country is approximately

329 million hectares, which includes inaccessible and snow bound area of 24 million hectares. Human population has increased from 36.11 crores in 1951 to 112 million in 2011. Total land availability, per capita, decreased from 0.89 hectares in 1950 to 0.33 hectare in 2000. It has further declined in 2011. Land per animal unit also shrank from 0.37 hectare in 1950 to 0.10 hectare in 2000.

Uttar Pradesh: A Case Study

In Uttar Pradesh, about 65 per cent of work force earns its livelihood from agriculture. The Ganga Plain, one of the most fertile tracts of the world, covers half of Uttar Pradesh, and this is agricultural heartland. It has plenty of rich alluvial soil and abundant ground and surface water. The state has nine distinct agro-climatic zones which have variation in productivity of various types of food crops (Figure 9.1). The nine agro-climatic zones are; Terai, Western Plain, Central Western Plain, South Western Semi-Arid Plain, Central Plain, Bundelkhand, North Eastern Plain, Eastern Plain and Vindhyan.

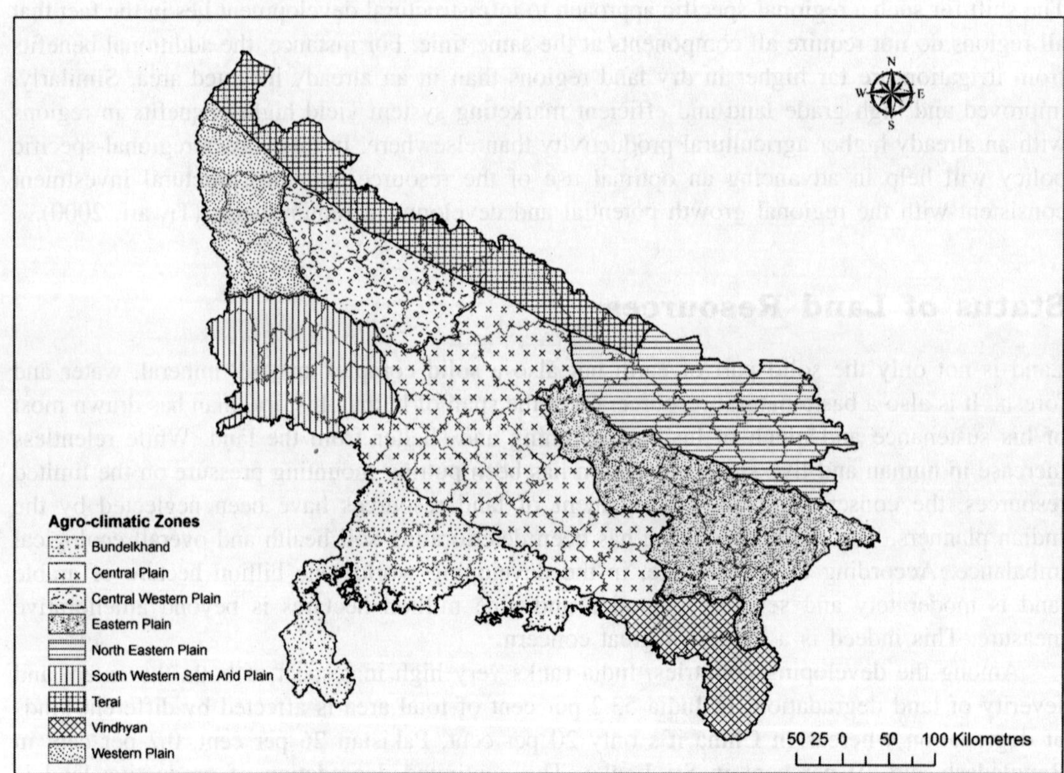

Figure 9.1 Agro-climatic zones of Uttar Pradesh.

The state has 253 lakh hectares, which is 13 per cent of the country's total cropped area. The food grain production is 50 million tones, contributing 19.5 per cent to the nation. The net cultivated area of the State is 168 lakh hectares, which is 12 per cent of country's net cultivated area. The productivity of food grains is 23.86 quintals per hectare whereas country's productivity is 6.63 quintals per hectare (2010–2011). The pressure of population on land is a matter of great concern in the development planning of land resources. The density of population in Uttar Pradesh according to census 2001 was 689 persons per sq. km, which was higher than most of the other states except West Bengal, Bihar and Kerala. The population was 16.6 million in 2001. According to 2011 census, the population of the state is 19.9 million and the density has gone up to 828 persons per sq. km. It is, therefore, imperative that an integrated approach of management, conservation and development of land resources for optimal use is ensured.

The concept of optimal land use is basic to land use planning which aims at balancing the competitive demands of land resource in a scientific manner for sustainable development of economy as well as society. A rational land use plan has to take into account the sustainability and capacity of land in such a way that superior quality of land is not put for a purpose, which can be fulfilled through inferior quality land and vice-versa.

Land Management in Uttar Pradesh

Uttar Pradesh is one of the richest states in India in terms of availability of natural resources, i.e., land, water, forests, soil capability, etc. It, thus, occupies a unique position in the country. However, nearly one-fifth of India lives here, while the state has less than one-thirteenth of the country's land. Nearly four-fifths of the population lives in about 97,000 villages. Land use in Uttar Pradesh is largely oriented to crop cultivation. Other uses include forests, pastures and grazing lands. Growing demands of land required for urbanization, industries, roads, parks, government buildings, housing, educational institutions, business centers, etc., are also necessary to be met. The diversion of agricultural land for non-agricultural uses is also an area of concern in the state. According to a rough estimate almost 35,000 hectares of agricultural land is being diverted to some other uses every year.

Relevance of Land Management

The purpose of land use planning is to regulate its use on scientific and ecological basis. FAO has aptly defined land as "an area of earth surface, the characteristics of which embraces all reasonably stable or periodically cyclical attributes of biosphere vertically above or below. The attributes exert a significant influence on present and future use of land". The aim of land use policy is to provide supportive technological and institutional structures to enable the rural communities to manage the resources in optimum manner. Uttar Pradesh, which has predominantly an agrarian economy and where agriculture sector commands highest share of 42 per cent in the state income and sustains about 80 per cent of population for livelihood, neither can achieve a higher sustainable growth in economy nor can any significant reduction take place in poverty and unemployment unless appropriate measures are taken to manage these resources. In this perspective, relevance of land resource management in the state is quite obvious.

Land utilization pattern of the state indicates that net sown area, which has been almost constant at about 58 per cent of the reported area, has gone up in 2001 (67.5 per cent) as well as in 2007 (69.6 per cent). About 7.0 per cent of land is lying fallow (Table 9.1).

Table 9.1 Land use statistics of U.P. (in Lakh Hectares)

Item	1950–51	1961–62	1970–71	1980–81	1990–91	2000–01	2006–07
Reporting area	292.58 (100)	293.98 (100)	298.06 (100)	297.39 (100)	242.45 (100)	242.01 (100)	241.7 (100)
Forest	31.94 (10.92)	37.10 (12.62)	49.53 (16.62)	51.28 (17.24)	16.98 (7.04)	16.98 (6.98)	16.57 (6.86)
Barren and unculturable land	28.87 (9.87)	25.74 (8.76)	14.18 (4.76)	11.40 (3.83)	7.20 (2.96)	6.17 (2.55)	5.07 (2.10)
Area put to non-agricultural uses	18.35 (6.27)	19.30 (6.57)	20.34 (6.82)	22.80 (7.67)	23.23 (9.58)	24.36 (10.06)	27.29 (11.29)
Culturable wasteland	2.16 (0.74)	16.09 (5.47)	13.44 (4.51)	11.48 (3.86)	7.02 (2.92)	5.35 (2.21)	4.39 (1.82)
Permanent pasture and other grazing land	21.11 (7.21)	0.48 (0.16)	0.77 (0.25)	2.96 (0.99)	0.74 (0.30)	0.70 (0.29)	0.64 (0.26)
Land under misc. trees and groves	14.15 (4.85)	8.55 (2.90)	12.60 (4.23)	6.39 (2.15)	3.30 (1.36)	3.40 (1.40)	3.73 (1.54)
Current fallow	10.78 (3.68)	1.54 (0.52)	8.70 (2.92)	11.70 (3.93)	11.52 (4.75)	10.48 (4.33)	12.85 (5.32)
Other fallow	2.91 (0.99)	12.31 (4.19)	5.46 (1.83)	7.16 (2.41)	8.05 (3.37)	6.41 (2.65)	5.42 (2.24)
Net area sown	162.31 (55.47)	172.90 (58.81)	173.04 (58.06)	172.22 (57.92)	164.30 (67.76)	168.25 (69.52)	165.73 (65.57)

(Figures in bracket indicate percentage)

Source: Agriculture Census 2001, DLDWR, Government of U.P., 2009.

The forest area has declined and so is the case with permanent pasture and grazing land. Even culturable wasteland has also declined. But the area put to non-agricultural uses has continuously increased from 7.67 per cent in 1980-81 to 11.26 per cent in 2006–07. The fragmentation of the land holdings has been taking place at a very large scale. This is evident from the increase in the number of marginal holdings. The small, semi-medium, medium and large holdings are declining (Table 9.2). The area under each category of holdings has also decreased. This change has great bearing on cropping pattern and land utilization.

Land use changes are transforming land cover at a steady and even accelerating pace. The changes in the terrestrial eco-system also have an impact on the quantum and components of our natural capital—climate, soil, vegetation, water resources and bio-diversity. It is now recognized by the scientists, experts and other knowledgeable people that the human kind has totally ignored the natural limit in the utilization of natural resources. While this can be attributed to ever increasing population pressure and family fragmentation, it is greed more than need that has impelled humans to go beyond the law of nature.

Table 9.2 Land holding distribution pattern in Uttar Pradesh

Holding size	*Number in '000*		*Area in '000 ha.*		*Per cent variation*	
	2005	2011	2005	2011	*Number*	*Area*
Marginal	17507	18167	6972	6711	3.77	–3.74
Small	3103	3014	4341	4200	–2.89	–3.24
Semi-medium	1392	1327	3796	3605	–4.67	–5.02
Medium	428	397	2374	2191	–7.29	–7.71
Large	28	25	424	382	–8.76	–9.87
All size class	3845	4019	1943	1968	4.52	1.32

Source: Agriculture Census 2010–11, Agriculture Census Division, DAC, Ministry of Agriculture, Government of India.

The neglect of land management and improper land use are bound to jeopardize the process of sustainable growth which is reflected in:

1. standard of living;
2. material flows (production equaling consumption);
3. bio-diversity.

Unfortunately, a large share of the proposed public investment in agriculture is gulped by the mammoth subsidies on irrigation, fertilizer, power, seed and credit. These subsidies have posed more deleterious impact in terms of reduced public investment in agriculture on account of erosion of intestable resources. In some cases these subsidies also encouraged wasteful application of resources like water and power, and adversely affected the sustainability of natural resources in the state. The foremost priority of the government should be to mobilize resources for investment in those areas that attract private sector participation and promote agricultural growth

Agricultural Scenario in Uttar Pradesh

The economy of the state is predominantly based on agriculture and its allied sector having around 24 per cent contribution in the state's gross domestic product as against 14.1 per cent contribution of this sector in the country (2010–11). In fact, U.P. is called the agricultural heartland of the country and is rich in alluvial soils, huge reserve of ground and surface water with one of the most fertile tracts in the world. Admittedly, this has resulted in about 21 per cent contribution of the state in food grain production. The state is leading in production of wheat (32.26 per cent), sugarcane (36.02 per cent), potato (40 per cent) and barley. It has second place in the production of rice, sugar, pulses and millets. In vegetable, fruits and milk production also the state is ahead of other states. In the national perspective, U.P. stands at number one in terms of net and gross cropped area, net and gross irrigated area having the cropping intensity of around 150 per cent against 135 per cent of the country. All the above facts indicate that the state is leading in major fronts of agriculture. However, at the productivity front, it lags behind many states, i.e., Punjab, Haryana, and Tamil Nadu, etc. The formulation of the Twelfth Plan provides an opportunity to restructure polices to achieve a new vision for the path of rapid growth. This obviously has to be broad based and inclusive of all the aspects of development. There are several issues which need immediate attention.

Major Issues and Recommendations

The areas which are important from the point of view of the growth rate of agriculture and demands restructuring of the system are listed below:

Extension Services

These services have a vital role to play in achieving the goals of production. There are farmers in each district who have achieved the average yield of food production at 60–75 quintal/h whereas the average yield in the State is about one third of this. This clearly indicates that if peasantry is provided with well researched knowledge/technology, the production can be doubled in the State. Therefore, the extension services should be suitably strengthened with the development of private extension services. Agriculture graduates can be registered as private extension managers and extension training centers can be set-up at three agriculture universities, KVK's and agriculture colleges functioning in the state. There should be registered agriculture extension societies in every district, with regular training programmes for private extension services. Agriculture Extension Services should be linked with ATMA (Agricultural Technology Management Agency) at district level. Computer based agriculture technology also needs to be strengthened so that village farmers could take full advantage.

Soil Testing

The declining soil health is also a matter of great concern for which soil testing is necessary and important. Based on soil health, suitable cropping pattern/crop rotation can be adopted to remove the backwardness in agriculture. The balanced use of organic and inorganic fertilizers and bio-fertilizers also needs to be promoted at massive scale.

Certified High Yielding Varieties of Seeds

In the area of agricultural production, the availability of high yielding variety seeds (HYVS) and a healthy seed replacement rate is the need of the day. The seed replacement rate has been 13.5 per cent in 2001–02 which rose to the level of 20.13 per cent during 2005–06. For Eleventh Five Year Plan a rate of 35 per cent was targeted but it could not be achieved. The *Beej Vikas Nigam* has to take appropriate action with active participation of the private sector to apprise the farmers about the HYV seeds. Keeping in the view the small size of holdings in the state, the diversification of agriculture is another potential area to be tapped. Through proper arrangements for research and development hybrid/high yielding varieties have to be developed for each agro-climatic zone during the twelfth Five Year Plan. Genetic upgradation has to be continuously made a part of the whole strategy.

Restoration of Degraded Lands

It has been estimated that about 62.01 lakh hectares of land is problematic because it cannot be used due to its degraded nature. A strategy to bring it under the plough/production/vegetative cover with the use of suitable watershed management is the need of the hour. The lack of appropriate data is yet another major problem. The timely availability of reliable statistics regarding land utilization and its use in the planning process has to be ensured.

Conjunctive Use of Surface and Ground Water

In the state only 77.41 per cent net area sown has been irrigated with irrigation intensity at 138.48 per cent. Out of net irrigated area about 20 per cent has been irrigated by canals and about 72 per cent by tube-wells (68 per cent by private tube wells). Hence, there is a need for conjunctive use of surface and ground water, keeping in view the rising prices of fuel. The energization of private tube-wells is an important area for twelfth Five Year Plan strategy.

Balanced Use of Agricultural Land for Non-agricultural Purposes

The diversion of prime agricultural land for non-agricultural purposes is also a matter of grave concern. To check this diversion suitable legal framework should be evolved. A proper land use mapping of the state is essential. The Geographic Information System may be used to prepare the soil and land use maps.

Appropriate/Suitable Prices of Agricultural Produce

To sustain peasantry, it is necessary to make arrangement for suitable and remunerative prices of agricultural produce. Therefore, there is a need to set-up *State Agriculture Price Commission*. This commission should make suitable recommendations to the Central Agriculture Price Commission for fixing the support prices of agricultural produce.

These and other related issues need to be addressed clearly and categorically for effective and sustainable development of agriculture and allied sectors in the country in general and the state of Uttar Pradesh in particular.

Conclusion

Although there is no significant change in the net sown area, yet the area under forests and pasture and grazing land has been continuously declining .This is a matter of grave concern as there is a clear message for ecological crisis. All possible measures should be taken to prevent this uncalled for situation. There are several key areas which need to be immediately taken care off. These are extension services, soil testing, HYV seeds, restoration of degraded land, conjunctive use of surface and ground water and balanced use of agricultural land for non-agricultural purposes, besides suitable measures to fix the support prices of agricultural produce. These may partially help in alleviating the problems. But for effective and sustainable development of agriculture and allied sectors long-term land management with the built in strategies is really the need of hour especially in states like Uttar Pradesh, where land is major natural resource base and agriculture is main source of sustenance for increasing population.

References

Misra, H.N. (2002), Landuse/cover change in Middle Ganga valley, In: Y.P. Abrol (Ed.), *Landuse—Historical Perspectives: Focus on Indo-Gangetic Plains*, Allied Publishers, New Delhi.

Sehgal, J. and Abrol, I.P. (1994), *Soil Degradation in India: Status and Impact*, National Bureau of Soil Survey & Land Use Planning, Nagpur.

Swaminathan, M.S. (2002), The century of hope, In: Lal, R. et al., (Eds.), *Food Security and Environmental Quality in the Developing World,* CRC Press, Florida.

Tiwari, P.C. (2000), Land-use changes in Himalayas and their impact on the plains ecosystem: Need for sustainable land use, *Land Use Policy*, **17**(2), 101–111.

10

Wasteland Mapping Analysis and Management of the Rushikulya Basin

Damodar Panda

Abstract: Wastelands which are generally culturable and unculturable types, have great potential as land resource. They can play as shock absorber of the pressure created by man on land. It is, therefore, essential that they should be properly identified, mapped and reclaimed. The present chapter uses GIS and Remote Sensing techniques to map different types and subtypes of wastelands and suggests the methods for their reclamation in Rishikulya Basin of Orissa.

Keywords: Podu, Ravine land, Gully Erosion, Wasteland reclamation, Denuded, Canopy, Plantation crops, Sand Dunes, Rock Outcrop, Cultivable and Unculturable Wasteland.

Introduction

The burgeoning population growth has resulted into increasing demand for more land for agriculture and non-agricultural activities. This has resulted in the over exploitation of existing land and reclamation of land which has been turned unproductive due to various reasons. Hence, for sustainable development, it is necessary to generate timely and accurate information about the location and extent of the wastelands. Wasteland may be defined as that land which has been previously used but which has been abandoned and for which no further use has been found. Wasteland Survey and Reclamation Committee, Ministry of Food and Agriculture, has defined wasteland as those land, which are either not available for cultivation or left out without being cultivated like fallows and cultivable waste (l964). Wasteland is described as that land which is presently lying unused or which is not being used to its optimum potential due to some constraints (NRSA, 1985). As the land available for cultivation is very much limited, the only solution to the problem is the prevention of further degradation of the existing wastelands by adopting several reclamation measures. The wastelands are gullied ravine land, upland with or without scrub, waterlogged and marshy land, land affected by salinity/alkalinity coastal/inland, shifting cultivation area, sands, mining/industrial wasteland, underutilized/degraded notified forest land, degraded land under plantation crops, barren rocky/stony waste/sheet rock area, steep sloping area, snow covered or glacial area.

Study Area

The Rushikulya Basin is a medium order river basin of 8402 sq. km area located on the eastern coast of India in southern Orissa adjacent to the south of the Chilka Lake. The basin is flanked by the Eastern Ghats in a semi circular manner and open to the Bay of Bengal. The basin is located between 19°3'17" N and 20°17'17" N latitudes and between 84° E and 85°1'17" E longitudes. The basin spreads over the administrative districts of Ganjam, Khurda, Nayagarh and Phulbani (Figure 10.1).

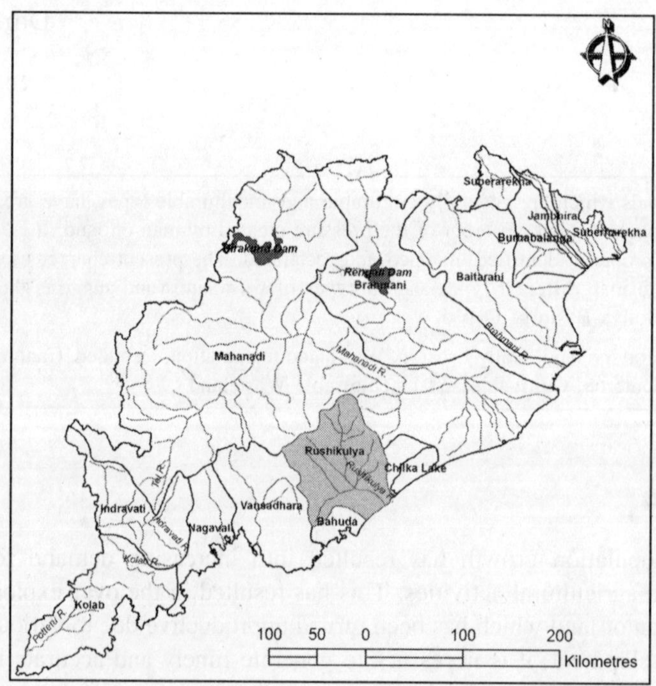

Figure 10.1 Location map of Rushikulya basin.

It is industrially backward; there are a few agro-based industries and major industrial minerals are missing. The dominating economy of the basin is agriculture. With increasing population coupled with environmental degradation due to large scale deforestation and prevalence of wastelands, large scale migration is taking place every year.

Database and Methodology

The wasteland mapping of the basin has been done using Remote Sensing Technique, SOI toposheets, limited ground checks and reference of limited literature. The multidate satellite imagery, Landsat (TM), FCC and SOI toposheets of scale 1:50,000 are used for the extraction of the spatial distribution of wastelands. The methodology is based on the visual interpretation of the satellite imagery using interpretation key of the NRSA (1991). The multidate satellite data of both *Kharif* and *Rabi* seasons are used. After necessary ground verification of the doubtful areas, the wastelands are mapped. The SOI toposheets are used for the preparation of the base map. The forest boundaries are transferred to the base map. The final wasteland map is prepared, area estimated and analysed (Panda, 1999). The methodology for analysis of wasteland has been shown in the flow chart (Figure 10.2).

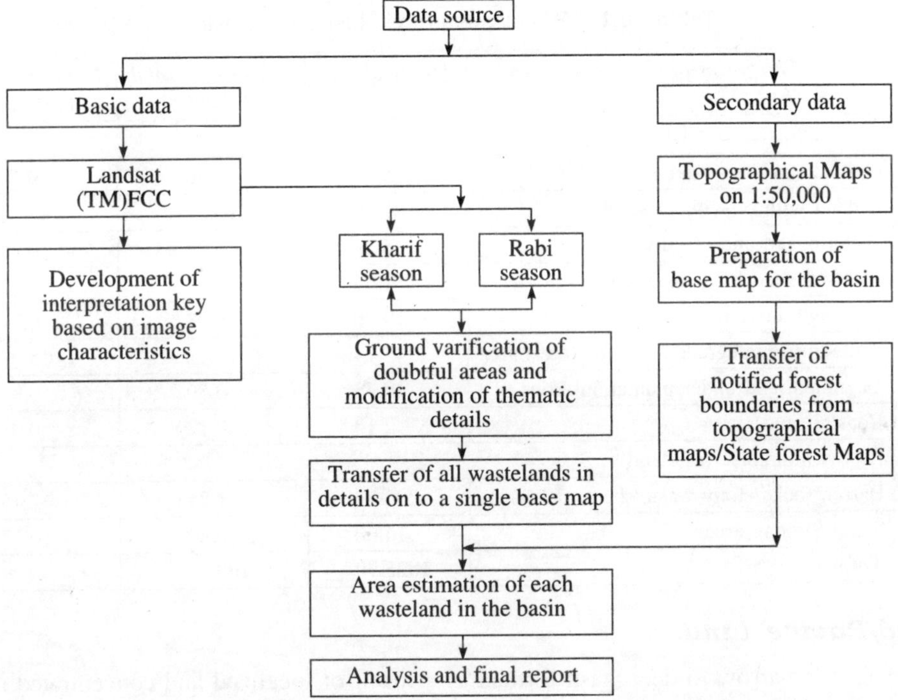

Figure 10.2 Flow chart of methodology of wasteland analysis.

Type of Wasteland

The wasteland of the basin is 1835.90 sq. km which is about 21.85 per cent of the basin area. The wastelands of the basin are classified in two categories, i.e., (a) culturable and (b) unculturable wasteland.

Culturable Wastelands

The National Remote Sensing Agency (NRSA, 1985) has defined **culturable wasteland** as those lands which are capable or have the potential for the development of agriculture, pasture and afforestation but are not being used to their optimum due to certain constraints like salinity and alkalinity, erosion, water logging, absence of vegetation cover, occurrence of abundant deposits of sands, unfavourable physiographic positions and by and large due to human negligence. The Technical Task Group on Wasteland Planning Mission, New Delhi (National Wasteland Development Board, 1986) has defined it as the land which is capable or has the potential for the development of vegetation cover and is not being used due to different constraints of varying degrees. The culturable wasteland spread over an area of 1618.53 sq. km which is about 88 per cent of the wastelands of the basin (Table 10.1) (Figures 10.3 and 10.4). The culturable wastelands of the study area may be divided into several categories, which are as under:

Table 10.1 Wastelands in the Rushikulya basin

Sl. No.	*Categories of wastelands*	*Area* (sq. km)	*Per cent to total wasteland area*	*Per cent to total basin area*
	A. Culturable wasteland			
1.	Gullied/Ravinous land	45.14	2.46	0.54
2.	Upland with or without scrub	187.60	10.21	2.23
3.	Waterlogged and marshy land	5.31	0.29	0.06
4.	Land affected by salinity coastal	1.56	0.08	0.02
5.	Shifting cultivation area	19.90	1.08	0.24
6.	Underutilized/degraded notified forest area	1343.14	73.16	15.99
7.	Degraded land under plantation crops	10.75	0.59	0.3
8.	Coastal sand	2.13	0.12	0.03
	B. Unculturable wasteland			
9.	Barren rocky/stony waste/sheet rock area	205.77	11.21	2.45
10.	Steep Sloping area	14.60	0.80	0.17
	Total	**1835.90**	**100**	

Gullied/Ravine land

Gully refers to a narrow to deep gash formed as a result of localized and concentrated run-off by running water especially on loosely deposited sediments. Gullies with steep sides and which are very deep (more than 9 m.) and wide are known as **ravines**. The gullies are formed as a result of localized surface run-off affecting the friable unconsolidated material resulting in the formation of steep slopes and undulating terrain having a maximum depth of 3 m. The gullies are the first stage of land dissection followed by their networking which leads to the development of ravinous land. These are formed generally in deep alluvium and entering a nearby river following much lower than the surrounding table lands. In the imagery, gullies or ravinous land appear light yellow to bluish green in tone, vary in size and depth (gullies are shallow and ravines are deep) with irregular and broken shapes, very coarse to coarse in texture, dendrite to subdendriatic in pattern. They occur along rivers and streams and other drainage on sloping grounds associated with severe to very severely eroded area made of loose and unconsolidated sediments, area under good rainfall and surface run-off. The gullies can be distinctly identified in the imagery from January to March. In the basin the gullied land is 45.14 sq. km which is about 2.46 per cent of the total wasteland of the basin and 0.54 per cent of the total basin area. The fertile agricultural land is severely affected due to the gully.

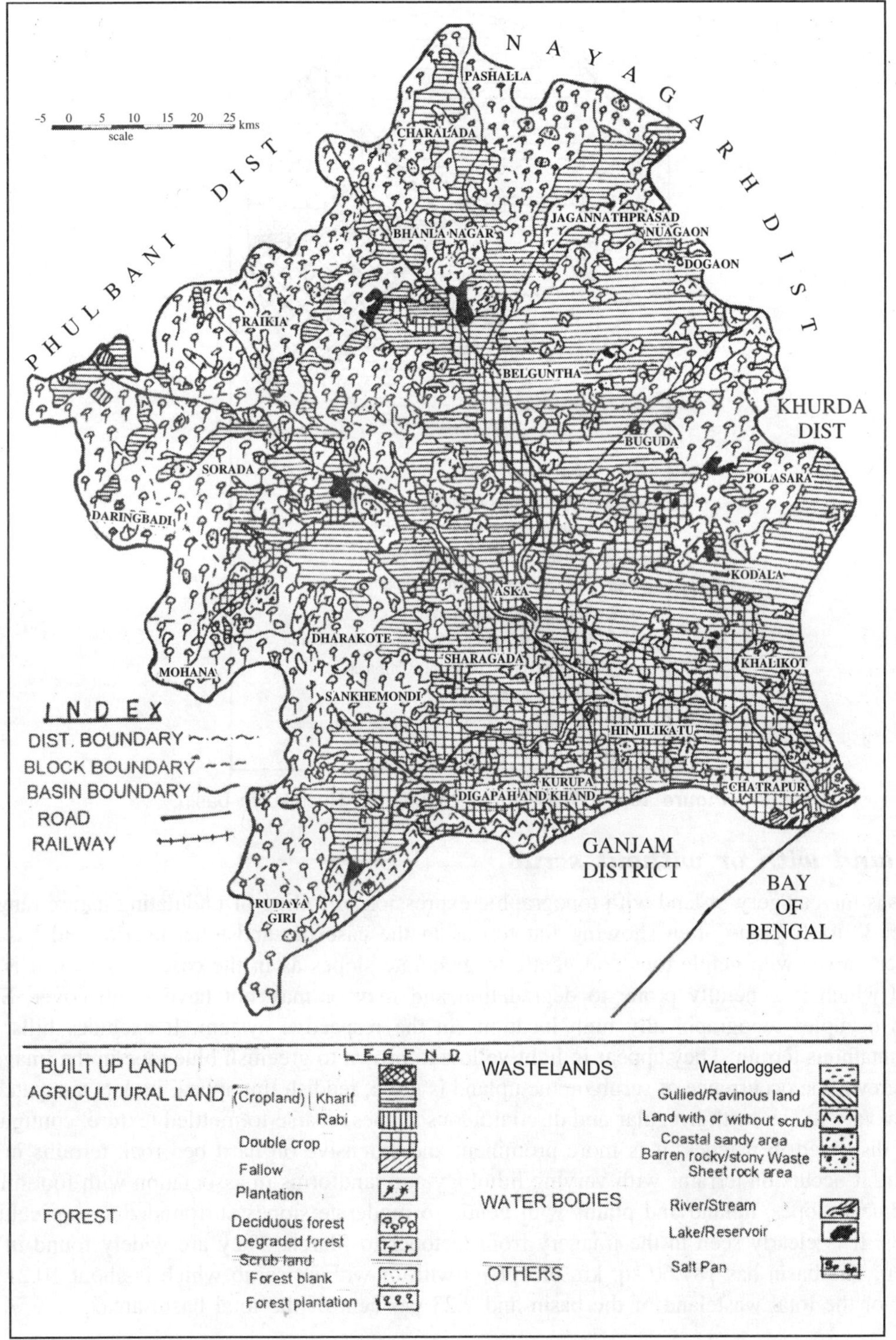

Figure 10.3 Wasteland map of Rushikulya basin.

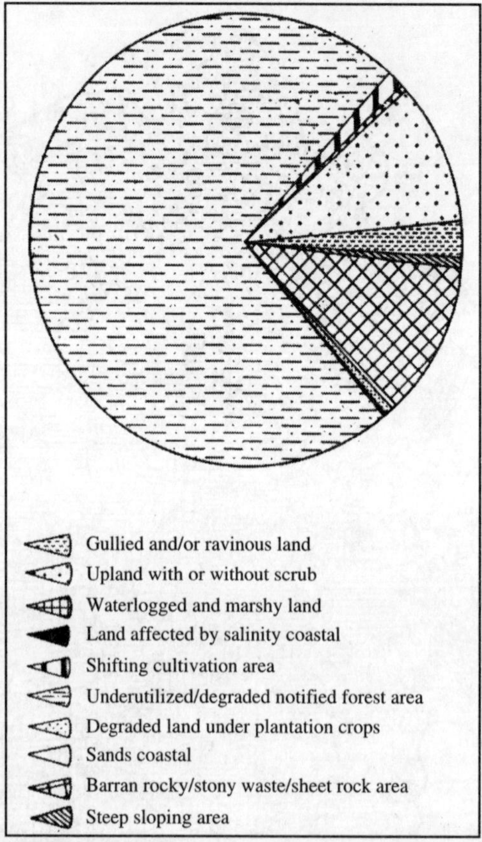

Figure 10.4 Wasteland categories of Rushikulya basin.

Upland with or without scrub

This is the category of land with topographic expression of rolling or undulating nature ranging from 3° to 1° slope often showing flat top as in the case of sandstone, laterite and basaltic plateau areas with gentle tops and gentle to moderate slopes as in the case of others. It is the land which is generally prone to degradation and may or may not have scrub cover. Such land occupies topographically high locations in the respective system. It excludes hills and mountainous terrain. They appear in light yellow to brown to greenish blue tone in the imagery. Wherever the occurrence of scrub on the upland is more, reddish tint appear in dots and patches. They vary in size with irregular and discontinuous shapes, coarse to mottled texture, contiguous and dispersed in patches. It is more prominent and extensive on hard bed rock terrains in the basin. It occurs on terrains with varying lithology and landforms in association with foot hill or pediment slopes, upland and plains with gentle to moderate slopes surrounded by agricultural lands. It is clearly seen in the imagery from October to March. They are widely found in the basin. The basin has 187.60 sq. km of upland with or without scrub which is about 10.21 per cent of the total wasteland of the basin and 2.23 per cent of the total basin area.

Waterlogged and marshy land

Waterlogged land is the land with soil pores within the root zones of the crops getting saturated with water. Surface waterlogged land is that land where the water is at/or near the surface and water stands for most of the year. Marsh is a land which is permanently or periodically inundated by water and is characterized by vegetation which includes grasses and weeds (*Planning Commission, 1986*). In the imagery the waterlogged lands are seen in light to dark blue tone, varying in size with irregular and discontinuous shapes, smooth to mottled texture due to the presence of the aquatic vegetation. It occurs in river plains, coastal lowlands along canals in association with and proximity to flood plains, coastal marshes/swamps, and tidal flat grounds near canal with water seepages, etc. It can be identified on the imagery from December to March. In the basin the waterlogged/marshy lands are found towards the coast and adjacent to the railway track and roads and cover an area of 5.31 sq. km which is about 0.29 per cent of the basin area. The marshy land found in the basin are categorized as fresh water and brackish water.

Land affected by salinity

The salt affected land is generally characterized as the land that has the adverse effects on the growth of plants due to the action or presence of excess soluble or excess exchangeable sodium. The salt affected land in the basin is located close to the coast due to the tidal action. The salt affected land in the basin (1.56 sq. km) is about 0.08 per cent of the total wasteland and 0.02 per cent of the basin area The salt affected land or salt pan is the important source of salt in the basin. The salt affected land in the imagery appears in white light blue tone. They vary from small to medium in size with irregular and discontinuous shape, smooth to mottled texture dispersed. They can be identified in the imagery from January to March.

Shifting cultivation area

Shifting cultivation is a cyclic process by which forests are slashed and burned to enable the cleared lands for cultivation by the tribes (Chakrapani, 1993). In the imagery, shifting cultivation (**Podu**) areas appear light yellow to brown in tone. The presence of vegetation gives spots of red tone amidst such openings. They occur in small patches with irregular shapes, coarse to mottle in texture, non-contiguous and dispersed in pattern. They occur amidst forests in hill slopes and hill tops in association with forest areas essentially cleared for cultivation. In the basin total land under shifting cultivation is 19.90 sq. km which is about 1.08 per cent of the total wasteland and 0.24 per cent the basin area. Shifting cultivation areas are mostly found in the western and southern part the basin in the mountainous tracts inhabited by tribal population.

Underutilized/degraded notified forest area

The land notified under the forest act and those lands with various types of forest cover in which denudation of vegetation is less than 20 per cent of the canopy cover are classified as degraded land. In the basin, the degraded land accounts for largest area (343.14 sq. km). This is about 73.16 per cent of the total wasteland and 15.99 per cent of the basin area. Extensive areas of degraded land are found in the notified forest areas.

Degraded land under plantation crops

The land outside the notified forest areas subjected to degradation under plantation crops are mostly along the coast and on the foothills which provide fuel and fodder. Area under plantation crops is 10.75 sq. km which is about 0.59 per cent of the total wasteland and 0.13 per cent of the basin area.

Coastal sand

These appear in light white to yellow with bluish to medium tone, vary in size with regular to irregular shapes smooth to mottled texture, contiguous and linear in pattern. It occurs in river beds, coastal onshore plain in association with shifting sand dunes, coastal beach sands, sand dunes and natural levees. It appears better in the imagery from October to March. Total coastal sandy area in the basin is 2.13 sq. km which is about 0.12 per cent of the total wasteland and 0.03 per cent of the basin area. It is found in the form of narrow sandy strip along the coast and in the form of coastal sand dunes.

Unculturable Wasteland

Unculturable wasteland is defined as all barren and unculturable land like mountains and deserts, etc., which can neither be brought under cultivation nor be utilized for agriculture or forest purposes because of snow covered glacial area; barren or rocky outcrop comes under this category.

Barren rocky/Stony waste/Sheet rock

These are rock exposures of varying lithology often barren and devoid of soil cover and vegetation. They occur amidst hill-forests as openings or scattered as isolated exposures on plateau and plains. In the imagery, it appears in greenish blue to brownish tone, vary in size with irregular and discontinuous shape, very coarse to coarse to medium texture, linear to contiguous dispersed in pattern. It occurs on steep hill slopes, crest, isolated hillocks, plateau and eroded plains in association with barren and exposed rocks/stony waste, laterite caps, boulders and quarried sites. This category appears clearly in the imagery from January to March. This category of wasteland in the basin is 205.77 sq. km, which is about 11.21 per cent of the total wasteland and 2.45 per cent of the basin area. These are mostly found towards the central part of the basin.

Steep sloping area

It is the steep land which is normally not culturable. In the imagery, the steep sloping area is seen as elongated patches of reddish dark in colour. The land is very often devoid of major vegetative cover. It covers 14.60 sq. km area which is about 0.80 per cent of the wasteland and 0.17 per cent of the basin area. It is found in the upper part of the basin.

Wasteland Reclaimation

The demand for land is increasing at such a fast rate that any attempt made in this direction of reclaiming unused, denuded and less productive areas for useful purposes is worth of time and money spent for it (Gautam and Narayanan, 1988; Mathur et al., 1989). The reclamation of the wasteland in India is now possible through modern scientific technology. The wasteland reclamation and development programme aims at achieving the following objectives:

1. The physio-chemical characteristics of the soil should be periodically monitored to enable modification, if any, of the reclamation methods.
2. Pilot operational research project on watershed basis to be taken up to assess economic feasibility of developing wasteland.
3. Standard soil survey should be carried out to delineate different land capability classes suitable either for cultivation of crops or grasses or forest plantation.
4. Using available technology, salt resistant coastal plantation of casuarinas, eucalyptus, coconut, etc. should be taken up extensively for profitable land use. About half of the coastal area is purely saline.
5. Stony and gravel lands lying extensively as wasteland should be prohibited from grazing for a few years to establish good vegetation cover before controlled grazing is permitted. Rocky, stony and hilly areas with skeletal soil not considered suitable for agriculture may be developed for recreation purposes. The forest department should initiate research in this direction.
6. The extensive wastelands should be reached by planting suitable trees to meet the growing demand for fuel, fodder, small timber and soft wood for pulp.
7. Reclamation of extensive areas lying unutilized or underutilized along the railway line, national highways, canals, etc.
8. Ravine and gully lands need to be controlled by adopting anti erosion measures like control of run-off by diversion, contour bunding, closure to grazing and cultivation of crops.
9. The impact of wind erosion at the coast can be reduced by coastal plantation, reduction of biotic interference, sowing of grasses, transplanting of trees and shrub species.
10. Suitable practices should be evolved to manage sandy areas, flooded and waterlogged land and saline land apart from evolving suitable crop and forage production technology. The waterlogged area should be brought under suitable crops avoiding flood periods in addition to improvement of surface drainage and prevention of seepage from the canal exploitation of ground water to lower water table. The marshy, swampy and waterlogged areas represent rich biodiversity, hence steps should be taken to preserve and promote tourism, aquatic research and source of water during scarcity.
11. Afforestation of wastelands with fast growing species to convert large areas for fodder, fuel and small timber for meeting the needs of expanding rural and semi-urban population.
12. The rehabilitation of tribal people may be tried by providing them alternative livelihood in order to prevent them from shifting cultivation.
13. Biotechnology has great potential for improving productivity and profitability of wasteland through biological, nitrogen fixation and large scale and rapid production of stress tolerant/elite/hybrid and new varieties of plants suitable for cultivation.

Conclusion

The wastelands may be classified as culturable and unculturable wastelands. The wastelands are of different types such as gullied and ravine land, upland with or without scrub, waterlogged and marshy land, etc. Likewise unculturable wastelands are also of two types—barren or rocky and steep sloping. All of these need surface treatment for their reclamation. While there is a need for proper monitoring of their march, it is important that grazing should be stopped temporarily and large scale afforestation should be done in addition to preventing erosion by contouring and crop rotation. Obviously biotechnology has great scope in treating this kind of land to make it productive.

References

Chakrapani, C. (1993), Shifting cultivation and deforestation: A socio-economic nexus, *Journal of Human Ecology*, Delhi School of Economics, New Delhi.

Gautam, N.C. and L.R.A. Narayanan (1988), *Wastelands in India*, Pink Publishing House.

Mathur, K.A. and P.N. Pandev (1989), *Wasteland Management in India*, Ashish Publishing House, New Delhi.

Ministry of Food and Agriculture, Govt. of India (1964), *Wasteland Survey and Reclamation*, Committee Report on location and utilization of wastelands in India, New Delhi.

National Remote Sensing Agency (1985), *Summary Report on Mapping of Wastelands in India from Satellite Imagery*, Hyderabad.

National Remote Sensing Agency (1991), *Guidelines to use wastelands maps*, Hyderabad.

National Wasteland Development Board (1986), Wastelands definition and classification, Technical Task Group Report, New Delhi, 1–12.

Panda, D. (1999), Environmental characteristics of the Rushikulya basin with special reference to Bioclimatic and Terrain components, *Unpublished Ph.D. thesis*, Utkal University, Bhubaneswar.

Planning Commission (1963), *Study of wastelands including saline, alkaline and waterlogged lands and their reclamation measures*, New Delhi.

11

Geomorphic Features in Land Resource Management

S.P. Mishra and Kavita Mishra

Abstract: Geomorphic features amongst all the geotechnical elements of Visual Image Processing (VIP) provide very significant clues for extracting information from satellite imagery regarding the spatial extent, nature and characteristics of natural resources including land resources. Recent development in geospatial technology especially in remote sensing, has added more values in mapping and analysis of these features with quite precision and enumerable differences. This chapter attempts to associate geomorphologic features in defining nature of land resources utilization in Chakia Tahsil, Chandauli district, Uttar Pradesh, India using satellite imagery.

Keywords: Remote Sensing, Visual Image Processing (VIP), Ground Truth Information, Flood Plain, Plateau Features, Land Resource Management, Social Fencing

Introduction

Geomorphic features by virtue of their genesis, surface coverage and other characteristics provide basic platforms for all sorts of human activities. These features, being the gift of nature, are accompanied with various natural resources such as natural vegetation (forest), water, soil (land), minerals, etc. of various dimensions. Because of these facts, the study of applied geomorphology has been focused to explain the man–land relationship, especially during last few decades. The geomorphological maps are now being considered as very useful assets for those scholars who are associated with the geo-related specific fields like resource evaluation, geo-hydrology, terrain evaluation, environmental hazards monitoring and management, etc. Recent changes in geospatial information technologies especially remote sensing and geographic information science have put forward a new dimension and interactive approaches in geomorphological mapping. The remote sensing technology with selective fieldworks provides an edge to characterize the geomorphologic aspects (Rao, 2002). During the last three decades, the availability of remotely sensed data with improved spatial and spectral resolutions along with temporal and multi-scale explanations have generated more momentum in the study of landform features (Mishra, 2006). As such, the modern techniques of remote sensing have facilitated for time/effort/cost effective observations, mapping and analysis procedures even for the remote areas. Because of such facts, the investigators have the better opportunity for 'direct' evaluation of landforms and to establish a proper relationship with the associated surface elements including soil, land use/land cover. There exists a close linkage between the landform features and other terrain features including land use/land covers in the spatial distribution pattern. For example, a strong correlation is noticed in Indo-Gangetic plain where point bars/ natural levees/back swamps pattern of fluvial landscape have been occupied by typical land uses. The levees, being higher in elevation are invariably occupied by settlements whereas the back swamps are associated with agriculture/aquatic vegetation.

The concepts and approaches of applied geomorphology are discussed by numerous scholars both at international and national platforms. In this reference, mention may be made of the works of Thornbury (1954), Gourou (1961), Tricart (1965), Coates (1973), Thomas (1974), Craig and Craft (1982), Faniran and Jeje (1983), Chorley et al. (1984), Allison (2002) and Huggett (2002), Sharma (1979, 1991), Dayal (1990), Sharma and Mishra (1993), Kalwar et al. (2005). Studies pertaining to remote sensing and its applications in geologic/geomorphologic investigations have been put forward by Verstappen et al. (1969), Verstappen (1963, 1966, 1977, 1983), Barrett and Curtis (1976), Way (1978), Townshend (1981), Curran (1985), Sabins (1987), Lillesand and Kiefer (1987, 2004), Campbell (1997), Renez (1999), Jenson (2005), Nag and Kudrat (1998), Misra and Singh (1998), Mishra (1997, 2003, 2006, 2009, 2010), Mishra and Chaube (1999) Joseph (2005), Mishra and Kumra (2007), and several others. The present paper attempts to illustrate the efficacy of remote sensing in geomorphological mapping and its role in managing the land resources of Chakia Tahsil (24°4' N to 25°3' N and 83°3' E to 83°24' E, area 1206.50 km^2) of southern Chandauli district of Eastern Uttar Pradesh (Figure 11.1).

To illustrate the clear vision of the issues, attempt has also been made for large scale mapping and analysis of Lower Chandraprabha Basin which covers western part of Chakia Tahsil and some portion of Mirzapur District (Figure 11.2).

Physiographically, about one-fifth of area under study in the north comes under the Middle Ganga plain and remaining major portion in the south (approximately bounded by 100 m contours) constitutes the Vindhyan upland. Geologically, the area consists of (i) Gangetic alluvium and (ii) Vindhyan formation (Upper Vindhyan Sub-group). Gangetic flood plains were formed during the Quaternary period whereas the southern part was defined by the development of Vindhyan plateau during Pre-Cambrian to Recent periods. The Gangetic alluvium has been mainly observed in northern part of Chakia and Shahabganj blocks while the Vindhyan formation are noticed in southern part of Chakia and Naugarh blocks. The rock out-crops mainly belong to Kaimur Dhandhraul quartzite (Vindhyan Super Group) and are found exposed as extensive mesas and isolated hillocks. Rocks are more or less horizontally bedded and are generally overlaid by lateritic pebbles on the hillocks situated in the northern rim of Vindhyan plateau. The drainage and lineaments are the most peculiar elements in shaping the landform features of the area under study which is drained by the river Karmnasa and its tributaries like the Chandraprabha, the Gurwat and the Garai rivers.

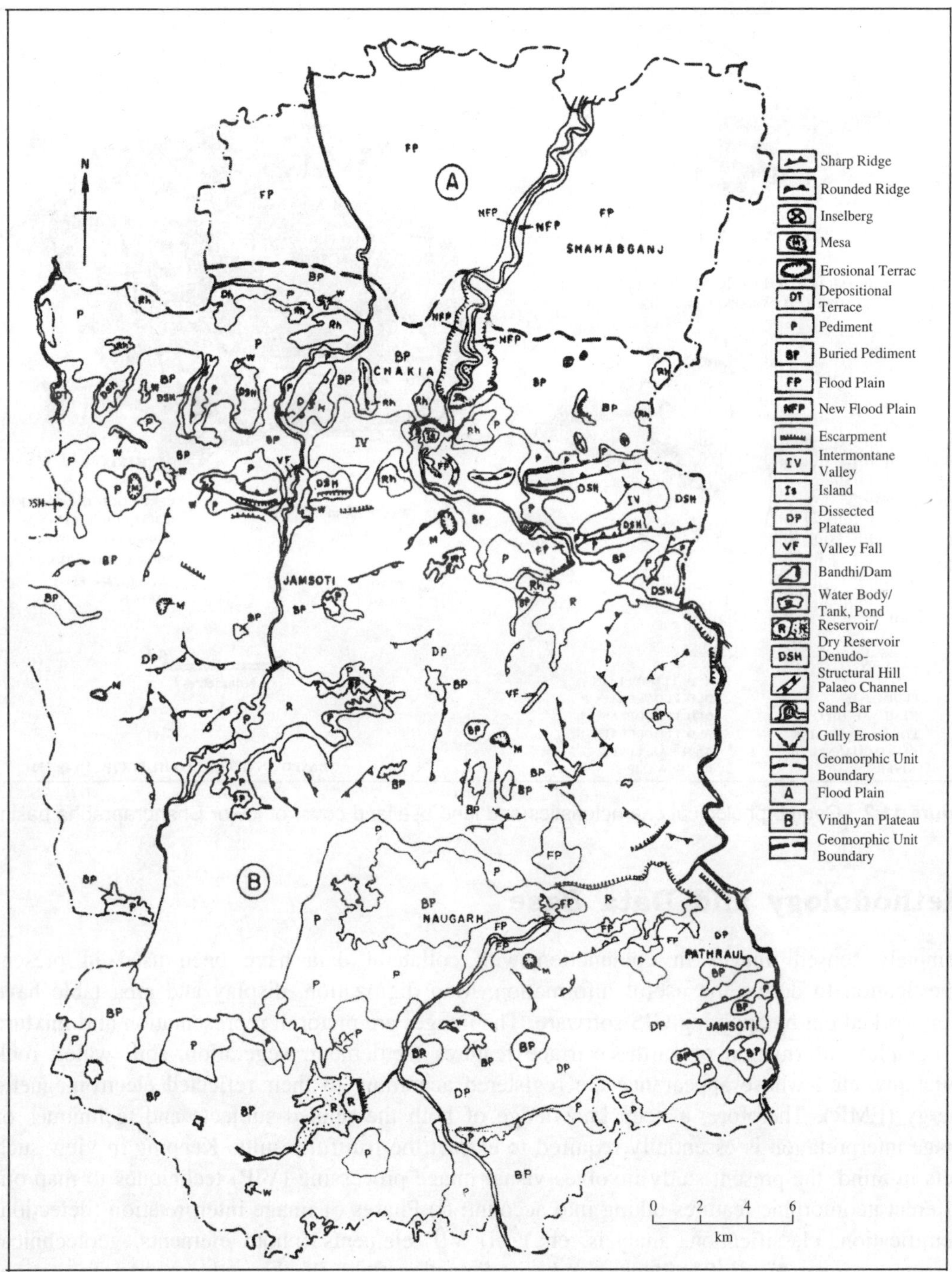

Figure 11.1 Geomorphological map of Chakia tehsil.

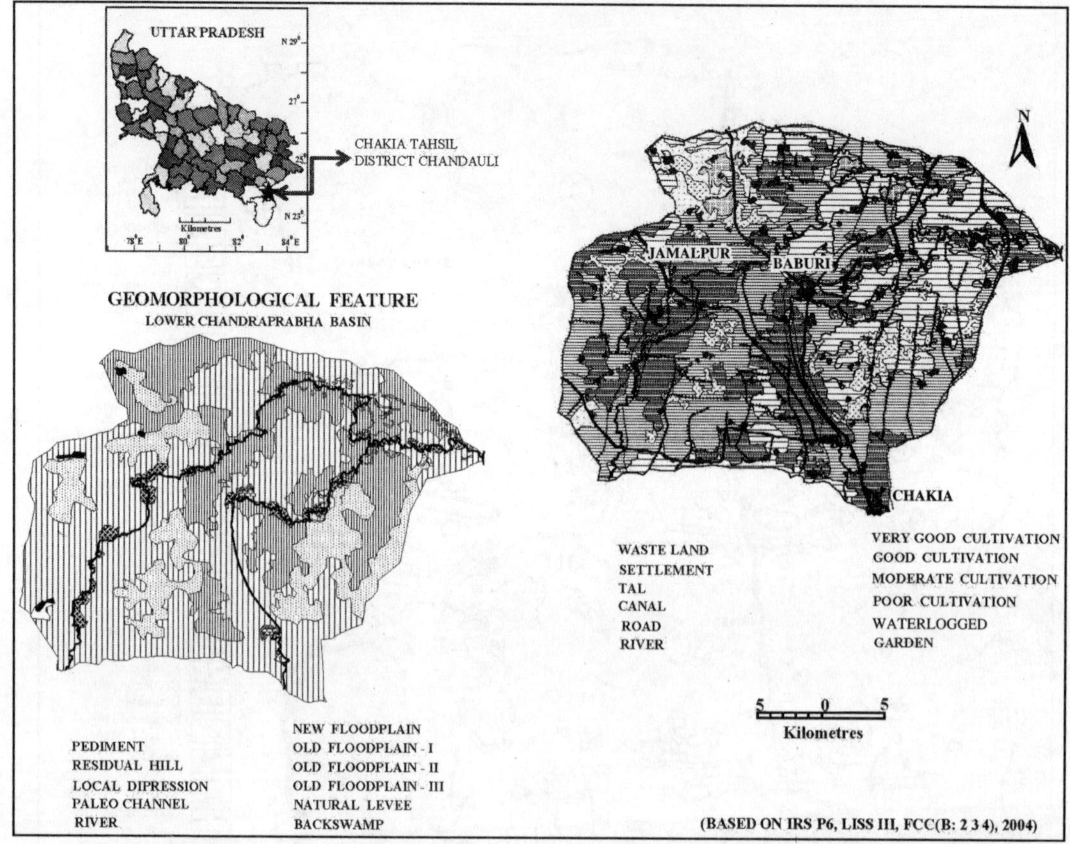

Figure 11.2 Geomorphological characteristics and land use/land cover of lower Chandraprabha basin.

Methodology and Data Base

Remotely sensed images in conjunction with collateral data have been used in present investigation to derive the useful information. Map digitization, display and area table have been worked out by applying GIS software. The images are pictorial representation and mixture of complex information of earth's surface features (settlement, vegetation, soil, water, rock structures, etc.) whose appearance are registered according to their reflected electromagnetic energy (EMR). Therefore, a deep knowledge of both the related subjects and techniques of image interpretation is essentially required to extract the fruitful results. Keeping in view such facts in mind, the present study involves visual image processing (VIP) techniques to map out different geomorphic features taking into account: (i) Phases of image interpretation (detection, identification, classification, analysis, etc.) (ii) VIP elements (photo elements, geotechnical elements, convergence of evidence) and (iii) Selective field checks and ground information. Different steps have been followed in extracting the information during investigation such as: (i) Preparation of base map from Survey of India (SOI) topographical sheet Nos. 630/4,

0/8, 63P/1, P/2, P/5 and P/6 at scale 1:50,000, (ii) Pre-field satellite image interpretation for identification, demarcation and mapping of geomorphologic features and land use/land cover, (iii) Transfer of detailed image interpreted information on base map by selecting numerous control points, (iv) Selective field checks to assess the validity of pre-field image interpretation and to make necessary corrections and (v) Finalization of image based map and analysis. The study is largely based on remotely sensed data such as: (i) IRS-1B, LISS-I, FCC (B-2, 3, 4), covering Path 23 and Row 50 at scale 1:250,000 for regional view, (ii) Hard copy and soft copy (digital data) of IRS-P6, LISS-III, FCC at a scale of 1:50,000 for large scale observation, (iii) Black and white panchromatic vertical aerial photographs at scale 1:60,000 (approx) for stereo-viewing, (iv) ground truth information and (v) the images available through internet/ Webs (Google Earth, Wikimapia).

Geomorphological Features and Land Utilization Pattern

The relations between landforms and land use are diversified. In some cases, the relations may be direct but more frequently land utilization is affected by a specific environmental parameter (or a combination of such parameters) or by certain geomorphological processes (Verstappen, 1983:112). Geomorphological features play a vital role in the mapping and analysis of land use/land cover and because of such fact, they are interchangeably considered as basic tools of geotechnical elements in image interpretation. The mapping and analysis of these two may significantly be accounted in deciding the nature of human activities especially related to the availability and utilization of natural resources including land. In the area under study, the complex structure of old geologic formation (Vindhyan Super-group) consisting of stratified un-metamorphosed rocks like sandstone, shale, quartzite and limestone effects the process of denudation and denotes structural imprints in the form of alluvial plain in the northern part and high relief variations in the southern part (plateau region). The land use/land cover patterns in the area are largely governed and adjusted to the surface materials (soil), topography, slope, moisture and climate. Changes in profiles of vegetation cover indicate that the morphology including micromorphology has strong control on the regional ecological variations. The geomorphic units/features identified in Chakia Tehsil can broadly be divided in two units: (A) Flood plain features and (B) Vindhyan Upland; and three sub-units such as (A.1) Fluvial units—flood plain, sand-bar, river terraces, palaeo-channel, (B.1) Denudational units—dissected plateau, residual hill/ridges, rock-outcrop, and (B.2) Denudo-Fluvial units—pediment, buried pediment, valley fill, intermontanne valley, escarpment, waterfalls (Tables 11.1 and 11.2).

Food Plains are formed by the Karamnasa river and its tributaries, the Chandraprabha and the Garai and characterized with relatively smooth and nearly flat low land, consisting of unconsolidated materials like clay, sand gravel and silt. On the imagery, they are represented by dark to light red and smooth to coarse textures indicating variations in soil moisture from well-drained to poorly drained areas. The flood plains may be categorized as (i) Old flood plain types—I, II, III and (ii) New flood plain. The old flood plain is characterized with uniform flat topography sloping towards north and marked in the north-east of the Karamnasa river of Shahabganj block (Sarangpur to Illia and Rasulpur to Kushaha villages), Karamnasa-Chandraprabha interfluves and from Jalapur to Karnail and Sikatia to Utrait villages of Chakia

Table 11.1 Categories of land uses/land covers and geomorphic features in lower Chandraprabha basin

Land use/Land cover		*Geomorphic features*	*Photo elements*			
Level-I	*Level-II*		*Tone*	*Texture*	*Shape*	*Size*
1. Forest	(i) Dense forest	Deeply dissected plateau, Denudational hills, gorge, valley fill	Dark to medium gray	Smooth to medium	Indefinite	Large
	(ii) Open forest	Less dissected plateau, structural hills	Light gray	Coarse	Indefinite	Large
	(iii) Scrubs/bushes	Pediment, structural hills	Light gray	Coarse	Indefinite	Small
	(iv) Plantation	Less dissected plateau, pediment	Dark gray	Smooth	Indefinite	Small
2. Cultivated land	(i) Very good	New flood plain, Paleo channel, old flood plain-I, Back swamp, deeply buried pediment	Very dark Red	Smooth	Indefinite	Medium
	(ii) Good	Old flood plain-II, Paleo channel, Intermontane valley, deeply buried pediment	Red mixed with gray	Coarse	Indefinite	Large
	(iii) Moderate	Old flood plain-II, old flood plain-III, intermontane valley, shallow buried pediment	Light red to gray	Coarse	Indefinite	Large
	(iv) Poor	Old flood plain-III, shallow buried pediment	White mixed red	Coarse	Indefinite	Medium
	(v) Waterlogged	Old flood plain-III	Dark gray	Medium	Indefinite	Small
3. Land not suitable for cultivation	(i) Stony waste	Pediment	White	Medium	Indefinite	Small
	(ii) Other waste	Old flood plain-III	Mixed white	Coarse	Indefinite	Small
4. Land not available for cultivation	(i) Settlement	Densely in flood plain, sparsely in buried pediment	Light gray	Medium	Indefinite	Small
	(ii) Road	Flood plain, buried pediment,	Light gray	Medium	Linear	–
	(iii) Canal	Flood plain, buried pediment,	Blue/black	Medium	Linear	–
	(iv) Water bodies	Old flood plain, dissected plateau	Dark blue	Smooth	Indefinite	Small

Source: Based on Image Interpretation by Authors.

Table 11.2 Percentage share of various land uses/land covers and geomorphic features in lower Chandraprabha basin

Land use/Land cover	*Total area (%)*	*Geomorphic features*	*Total area (%)*
Very good cultivation	23.66	Old flood plain-I	46.05
Good cultivation	38.67	Old flood plain-II	32.96
Moderate cultivation	22.63	Old flood plain-III	17.48
Poor cultivation	1.87	**Total old flood plain**	**96.49**
Waterlogged area	4.97	**New flood plain**	**2.91**
Total cultivated area	**91.80**	**Local depression**	**0.33**
Wasteland	**3.10**	**Pediment**	**0.19**
Others*	**5.10**	**Hills**	**0.08**
Total	**100**	**Total**	**100**

Source: Visual Image Processing (VIP) and GIS based analysis by Authors.

block. Flood-plain features are largely associated with crop land of varying natures. The new flood plain areas are dominated by very good to good cultivation mainly of paddy in *Kharif* and wheat in *Rabi* seasons. Very good cultivation areas are associated with new flood plain, paleo-channel, old flood plain-I, back swamp while some patches of old flood plain-I along with old flood plain-II are denoted by good to very good cultivation. Due to certain topographic and cultural limitations, the old flood plain-II and old flood plain-III are marked with moderate to poor cultivation whereas old flood plain-III associated with inferior land quality, waterlogged areas and saline patches are registered under poor cultivation. Due to flat topography and poor drainage, waterlogging problems are common in lower areas that generally submerged during heavy rains and are marked with poor cultivation or marshy/saline (*Usar*) lands. Old flood plain zones are marked with good to very good cultivation (*Rabi* and *Kharif*) because of the fertile soils and very good canal networks.

Sand bar, Palaeochannel and Island are the other landforms of flood plain zones with smaller areal extent and confined in certain pockets. The underlying materials can be observed as sand, gravel and silt. These features are characterized with either poor crop lands or marshy lands. Palaeochannels are the earlier routes of streams which are generally inundated during flood hence they are marked with poor cultivation during *Kharif* but very good cultivation of wheat with higher productivity at lower cost during *Rabi* season. Channel bars located in the stream course are perhaps the most characteristic features of braided channels although by no means they are restricted to them whereas point bars or meander bars are found on the convex side of meanders and grow by individual increments outward into the meander curve (Thornbury, 1954:165). These features are identified by light tone on the imagery. Sand-bars are traced out near Deobal Mangral and Sopahi villages (Chakia block). **Island** refers to a piece of land lying in the river channel formed by accumulation of sediments. This feature is marked near Latifshah in the Karamnasa river which is created by accumulation of alluvium on bared bed rock.

River terraces are topographic surfaces which mark the former levels of valley-floors, consisting of gravel, sand and fine alluvium (Thornbury, 1954:156). There are two types of river terraces marked in the area under study through the satellite image interpretation as (i) depositional terraces and (ii) erosional terraces. The depositional terraces are associated with successive flood level of rivers, therefore, they are generally characterized with good to moderate cultivation depending on the nature of deposits and availability of irrigation. The erosional terraces can be marked in the east of Chakia town where the river Karamnasa has created a long belt of this feature by erosional activities performed on buried pediment zone. The southern extent of this feature is restricted by the nearby residual hills located in both sides of river.

Dissected Plateau, Escarpment, Hills and Valleys occupy major portion of the Vindhyan Upland. which is largely dissected by the rivers Chandraprabha, the Karamnasa and the Gurwat. This unit is divided into three sub-categories as (i) north-west, (ii) north-east, and (iii) southern plateau, depending on its spatial location and nature of dissection. North-west portion of the dissected plateau lies in the north-west of the Chandraprabha river with relative relief varying from 192 to 332 m. while north-east dissected plateau located between the Chandraprabha and the Karamnasa rivers shows a very rugged topographic expression where relative relief varies from 220 to 384 m. The south-east portion of the dissected plateau lies in Karamnasa-Gurwat interfluves with relative relief of 250–375 m and is characterized with highly dissected and undulating terrain with steeper slopes especially facing toward the eastern margin along the river Gurwat that also makes the eastern boundary of the study area. On the imagery, dissected plateaus are identified by their grey to dark grey tones with coarse texture and irregular shape. Escarpments are prominent in the northern ribs of plateau region where rivers descend from the Vindhyan upland. These features are formed due to lithologic variations where weathering of softer rocks creates the front lower surfaces and the hard sando-quartz form the escarpments. These features are easily detected by very dark grey tones with linear pattern on imagery due to dense forest cover.

Residual hills are isolated hills formed by more resistant rocks (sando-quartz) in the zones of pediment and buried pediment features. These hills are generally enclosed with barren land or rocky surfaces partly buried by debris. A number of such hillocks can be observed in the northern vicinity of the Vindhyan plateau like Kashiba (259 m), Batwar Mafi (225 m), Hathin (224 m), Dantarbir (224 m), Dubebar Mafi (214 m), Latbetai (210 m), Kalaini (200 m) and Kata (188 m), etc. These residual hills are the denuded fragments of former continuous plateau surface. The Vindhyan escarpment marks the southern boundary of the region where several tributaries of the Chandraprabha and the Karamnasa rivers descending down the plateau front, have developed deep gullies giving rise to ravine lands with fine drainage texture. The dissected plateau zone and residual hills are covered with natural vegetations (forest) although their mode of concentration, quality, variety and utilization are deeply controlled by the nature of dissection or depth of soil covers. The hill slopes with promising depth of soil laden with moisture content are covered with dense forests. The dissected plateaus in the central, northern and south eastern parts have also been marked with dense forest. These areas actually consist of numerous tributaries of rivers whose valleys present some short of better vegetation coverage due to the availability of soil and moisture. On the other hand, the dissected plateau in its outskirts shows poor vegetation (open forest) and sparse trees/ bushes due to poor depth of soil and flat topography with rock out crops where possibility of ground water is very poor.

Rock-outcrops are the vestiges of residual hills of earlier period where shale and sando-quartz were deposited one after another in succession. Shale being the most easily erodible rock occupies a subdued or lowland position in the topography (Way, 1978:90). Sando-quartz on the other hand is more hard and massive than shale, hence they are found in the form of rock out-crops. These features are prominently marked near Sonbarasa and Marahua villages in Chakia block and near Ballalpur, Golabad, Majhgain, etc. in Naugarh block. On the imagery such features have been identified by typical light to very light tones. Rock-Outcrop surfaces show a very poor to negligible vegetation cover or scattered bushes.

Pediments are gently sloping (less than 7°), rock floored or bed-rock surfaces found at the base of a mountain mass or cliff in arid/semi-arid regions. The pediments in the area under study have been identified in two varying spatial locations. First type of pediments can be marked on the tabular part of plateau region (in central and southern parts) in small patches of bare rocks with gentle sloping, surrounded by the buried pediment zones. Second types of pediments are marked in the northern bland of plateau region having escarpments/residual hills such as around Sirthapur, Gaighat, Pipar Kharia, Lamia Uchartha Shikarganj, Firozpur, Taktapur, Niwajganj, Ghaina calan, Dhamapur and Ghurahupur Kata villages. Pediments with thin soil cover have shown scanty vegetation at places while some of them have no vegetation due to lack of soil veneers. Pediments are mostly the wastelands covered with rock fragments and are well defined on the imagery by their association with hills, lower relative relief, fine to coarse texture, light to light grey tones.

Buried Pediment features have probably drawn more attention of scholars than any other type of polymorphic features because of their economic significance. Buried pediments in the area under study are detected in three sub groups such as shallow buried (SBP), moderately buried (MBP) and deeply buried pediments (DBP) depending on the variations and nature of deposited materials over them. The shallow buried pediments are generally characterized with a very thin soil covers and exposed patterns of rocks. They are marked by light red to mixed white tones on imagery which denote the presence of rocky terrain. The moderately buried pediment constitutes somewhat more depth of soil cover than SBP. Deeply buried pediments (DBP) denoted by thick soil cover are observed near Sandsot, Gahia, Parhauti, Chiki, Kesan, Nunwat, Deori Kalan, Baluhwa, Pandang, Dakahi, Jamsoti, Dhusria, Kalani Kalan, Maruttitpur Surya, Mairahwa villages and in extreme south-west of Naugarh block. They are well defined on the imagery by dark red tone with smooth texture due to better vegetative growth (crops/trees), higher depth of soil cover and better soil moisture content. Buried pediment and intermontanne valleys in the northern flanks of plateau region near Chakia Town and north east part are marked with intensive paddy cultivation along with numerous varieties of garden and groves due to availability of fertile soils, rich ground water prospect and canal irrigation facility. On the other hand, buried pediments marked in the south and south west are denoted by moderate cultivation because of lower depth of soil cover with poor water holding capacity and moderate ground water prospects.

Valley Fill is the fundamental landform produced by lateral erosion associated with bed-rock erosion surfaces which remains unidentified due to commonly veneered alluvium. In the beginning, a valley fill may accentuate the impression of a flood-plain because of covered alluvium. It may be noted that along many such valleys, the flood-plains are a veneer of alluvium over bed-rock floor cut by lateral erosion (Thornbury, 1969:48). The valley-fills in the area under study have been identified at and around villages of Lowari Kalan and Lowari Khurd (along Kusmaha Nala), Chamer (Chandraprabha River), Burhan (along tributary of the Garai), Puranadih (along the Chandraprabha river), Shahpur, Jamsoti and Pathraul villages, Baluhwa and Lehra villages along the Barghat Nala. Such landforms are identified on imagery by their dark red tone, smooth texture, and low relief. Valley fills are marked with moderate to good cultivation and at some places are covered with dense natural vegetation.

Intermontane Valleys are mostly confined in the northern flank of plateau region near Premapur and Raghunathpur villages (Chakia blocks), southern part of Shahabganj block and east of the Chandraprabha river (Naugarh block). The underlying materials in these features are silt, clay, sand and alluviums where good aquifers (in sand strata) for hand pump have been reported at 101–105 m depth. The intermontane valleys are characterized with intensive cultivation along with varying nature of garden and groves due to fertile soils and better ground water prospects.

Waterfalls have been formed due to lineaments and lithological factors such as horizontally bedded sando-quartz of Kaimur plateau in Naugarh block. Such waterfalls may be observed as Rajdari fall (43 m), and Deodari fall-I (15 m) (Chandraprabha river), Dewdari fall-II (58 m) and

Talruhawa Nala fall (42 m) (Karamnasa river), and Naktidari fall (45 m) (Jharwania Nala). On the imagery, waterfalls are not clearly traced out due to their smaller sizes and merging with other images. However, they have been detected by visualizing the minor level differences in the river courses. Waterfalls are the good picnic places although, except Rajdari and Deodari falls, others are not maintained.

Land Resource Management

Land is a fundamental base of production and its utilization pattern reflects the nature of human activities and economic growth pertaining to agriculture, industry, forestry, energy production, settlement, recreation, water storage, etc. The unplanned and indiscriminate use of land may create tremendous loss in associated natural resources and may disturb the regional ecological balance. Therefore, the proper management for rational use of this valuable natural resource is of utmost significance to fulfill the growing demand of the people of area. For sustainable utilization of the land resources, it is essential to know the exact spatial location and extent, geomorphic control on land quality and productivity, and limitations related to various uses of land. The relations between land utilization and physical environment including geomorphic parameters should properly be analyzed to improve the existing conditions and to get maximum return. In fact, the land use is a product of interactions between socio-cultural, techno-economic factors and needs of the people concerned on the one hand, and natural consequences and potential of land on the other. Therefore, management of land resources requires a detailed knowledge of the determinants which ultimately decide the quality of land as well as the geo-environmental conditions that force anthropogenic activities to decide the nature of utilization.

As outlined in the earlier discussion, there exists a close relation between geomorphic features and land use/land covers in Chakia Tahsil which has a much diversified terrain conditions. The geomorphic features of the area serve as 'basic clues' in deciding the quality of land and its counter effect on land use/land covers. The geomorphological processes and landforms largely help to explore the availability and coordination of direct or indirect factors which influence and support land suitability assessment for different kinds of land use/land covers like underlying (surface) materials (soil/rock characteristics), depth of soil cover, bed rocks, hydrogeomorphological properties including ground water potentiality, topographic relief, drainage morphometry (density, frequency, dissection, etc.), erosion-gully analysis and such other phenomena (Mishra, 2009). Taking into account such facts in mind, some suggestions for land resources development in the area under study are suggested here:

(i) Flood plains are the most valuable land for agriculture in the northern part of study area but due to leveled topography with minor local variations, quality of land is hindered by flood during heavy rain when the water is spread over larger areas (especially in lower areas) and stay for a longer period. This creates problems of waterlogging and salinity in soil that affect the crop-productivity and cropping intensity. By improving the condition, existing areas under moderate cultivation and waterlogging may be converted into most productive areas. The problems of waterlogging (4.97 per cent area) and its counter effect as poor and moderate cropped land may be controlled by renovating existing ponds, drains and channels to activate quick runoff process. Three actions in this reference may be suggested such as: (a) The dredging and desilting of the Chandraprabha and the Garai rivers may be taken up to contain the flood, (b) The traditional drains which used to take away excess water are now chocked with sediments. The labourers under MNREGA may be fruitfully used to dig the channels. (c) The natural *Tals*/ponds may be renovated to reduce the problem of waterlogging and encroachments. The conversion of such features into agricultural land should be prohibited by imposing the land development laws.

(ii) The flood plain areas excell in production of paddy and wheat. The agro-industries based on these products may be encouraged. The road connectivity among Varanasi, Mughalsarai and Chandauli may be of great help in promoting commercial agriculture.

(iii) In the plateau region (southern part), both the agricultural and forest covers should be given due emphasis depending on the nature of terrain, land capability and agro-ecology of the region. Thus, buried pediment and intermontane valleys having thick soil cover are recommended for intensive cultivation by creating better techno-economic environments. The existing areas under moderate to poor cultivation may be provided better irrigational facilities for transforming the traditional practices of agriculture.

(iv) Management of land under forest has to be given top priority in plateau region for maintaining regional ecological balance. The area under dense forests may be expanded on the bare hill slopes and valleys while the open forests may be preserved from ill-impacts of anthropogenic activities.

(v) The existing areal extent of scrub/bushes in pediment and shallow buried pediment zones must be reduced by increasing plantation.

(vi) To make the forest more productive, proper care has to be taken for the collection and commercialization of products like honey, flowers and seeds of *Mahua, Piar*, *etc*, and leaves of *Tendu* and *Palas*, etc. The major hurdle in proper management of forest resources is the increasing impact of *Naxal* movement. To mitigate this problem, there is an urgent need of politico-administrative willingness to improve socio-economic conditions of the local people.

(vii) Social fencing is the important method of forest conservation under which villagers should be facilitated with alternative arrangement for their livelihood. The area under dense forest should be protected from further damage caused by the anti-social elements. The attached marginal zones between pediments and dissected plateau can be utilized for plantation by adopting appropriate forestry measures.

(viii) There is need for encouraging the peoples` participation in order to derive the benefit of their experiences and knowledge regarding the local problems associated with land resource management.

Conclusion

The results of the study establish the fact that the geomorphic features enable us towards appreciating better land resource using modern techniques of remote sensing. In Chakia Tahsil, a significant and distinct correlation exists between geomorphic features and distributional pattern of agricultural and other land uses. In fact, landforms act as a vehicle for detecting the various categories of land use/land covers during extraction of information through image interpretation. The network of roads and canals, settlements and other socio-economic facilities are largely attracted by flood plain zones while dissected plateau region is devoid of such facilities due to unfavourable terrain condition. Hill-slopes and valleys are supported by dense natural vegetations while pediment features are mostly covered with scrubs/bushes/open forest or rocky wastes depending on the nature and depth of surface deposits consisting of bolder mixed soil. Intensive paddy and wheat cultivations are often associated with flood plain, intermontenne valley and deeply buried pediment features. The large scale analysis of area under study covering Lower Chandraprabha Basin clearly indicates towards a deep relationship between geomorphic features and land use/land cover categories in flood plain zones. For example, very good to good crop-lands are associated with features like back swamp, paleochannel, new flood plain, old flood plain-I and II. Due to certain topographic and cultural limitations, old flood plain-III is marked with moderate to poor cultivation, waterlogged areas and saline patches. Significant potentiality of the area under study could be observed in its scenic beauty and historic-cultural treasure. Provision should be made for the development of some such spots for tourist attraction like Rajdari and Deodari-I falls on the Chandraprabha river, Deodari fall-II and Talruhawa fall on Karamnasa river, and Naktidari fall on the Jharwania Nala. The main constraint that has emerged in plateau region during last few years is the Naxal-impact which hinders the proper utilization and management of forest and other resources and prompting illicit cutting of trees. This could be controlled through politico-administrative and information-based socio-economic development. The results of the research may prove essential and precious documents for government authorities, development planners and others who are directly or indirectly engaged in the development of area under study.

References

Allison, R.J. (2002), *Applied Geomorphology: Theory and Practice*, John Wiley & Sons, West Sussex, UK.

Barrett, E.C. and L.F. Curtis (1976), *Introduction to Environmental Remote Sensing,* Chapman and Hall, London

Campbell, J.B. (1997), *Introduction to Remote Sensing*, Guilford Press, New York.

Chorley, R.J., S.A Schumm and E.D. Sugden (1984), *Geomorphology,* Methuen, London.

Coates, D.R. (Ed.) (1973), *Environmental Geomorphology and Landscape Conservation,* Stroudsbur, PA, Dowaen, Hutchinson Ross, **1**.

Craig, R.G. and J.L. Crafteds (1982), *Applied Geomorphology,* Allen and Unwin, London.

Curran, P.J. (1985), *Principles of Remote Sensing,* Longman, London.

Dayal, P. (1990), *A Textbook of Geomorphology,* Shukla Book, Patna.

Faniran, A. and Jeje (1983), *Humid Tropical Geomorphology,* Longman, Haslow, England.

Gourou, F. (1961), *The Tropical World*, Longman, London.

Huggett, R.J. (2002), *Fundamentals of Geomorphology*, Taylor & Francis, Ind.

Jensen, J.R. (2005), *Remote Sensing of the Environment: An Earth Resource Perspective*, Pearson Education, Singapore, Indian Branch, Delhi, 3rd Reprint.

Joseph, George (2005), *Fundamentals of Remote Sensing*, Universities Press Pvt. Ltd., Hyderabad.

Kalwar, S.C. et al. (Eds.) (2005), Geomorphology *and Environmental Sustainability*, Concept Pub. Co., New Delhi.

Lillesand, T.M. and R.W. Kiefer (2004), *Remote Sensing and Image Interpretation* (5th ed.), John Wiley & Sons, Inc. New York.

Mishra, Kavita (2009), *Hydrogeomorphological Investigation and Watershed Management of Chandraprabha Basin using Remote Sensing and GIS*, approved Ph.D thesis in Geography, Banaras Hindu University, Varanasi.

Mishra, Kavita (2010), Remote Sensing and GIS in mapping and analysis of spatial variations in hydrogeomorphic features: A case study. *Indian Journal of Landscape Systems and Ecological Studies,* **33**(2), 771–782.

Mishra, Kavita and V.K. Kumra (2007), Hydrogeomorphological approach in water resource management in part of Chandraprabha basin, Vindhyan Upland, Eastern UP. *National Geographical Journal of India*, **53**, 1–2, 61–72.

Mishra, S.P. (1997), Landform evaluation through integrated remote sensing, *Indian Journal of Landscape Systems and Ecological Studies*, **20**(1), 136–141.

Mishra, S.P. (2003), Hydrogeomorphological characteristics of Karmanasha basin, Eastern Uttar Pradesh, *Indian Geographical Journal*, **78**(1), 13–26.

Mishra, S.P. (2006), Regional geomorphic features and their significance in Ground Water Resources Inventory Using Remote Sensing, *National Geographical Journal of India*, 52, 1–2.

Mishra, S.P. and S.K. Chaube (1999), Geomorphic features and their relation with agricultural land quality: A case study of Chahania Block, Chandauli District, *Transactions: Institute of Indian Geographers*, **21**(2), 23–34.

Misra, H.N. and V.P. Singh (Eds.) (1998), *Research Methodology in Geography* , Rawat Pub., Jaipur.

Nag, P. and M. Kudrat (1998), *Digital Image Processing*, Concept Pub. Co., New Delhi.

Rao, D.P. (1975), Applied geomorphological mapping for erosion surveys: The example of the Oliva basin, Calabria, *ITC Journal*, 3, 341–350.

Rao, D.P. (2002), Remote sensing application in geomorphology, *Tropical Ecology,* **43**(1), 49–59.

Renez, A. (Ed.) (1999), *Manual of Remote Sensing: Geosciences*, John Wiley & Sons, New York.

Sabins, Flyd, F. Jr. (1987), *Remote Sensing: Principles and Interpretation*, W.H. Freeman & Co., San Francisco, USA, Revised Edition.

Sharma, H.S. (1979), *Physiography of the Lower Chambal Valley and its Agricultural Development*, Concept Pub. Co., New Delhi.

Sharma, H.S. (Ed.) (1991), *Indian Geomorphology,* Concept Pub. Co., New Delhi.

Sharma, P.R. and S.P. Mishra (Eds.) (1993), *Applied Geomorphology in the Tropics,* Rishi, Pub., Varanasi.

Thomas, Michael, F. (1974), *Tropical Geomorphology: A Study of Weathering and Landform Development in Warm Climates,* Macmillan, London.

Thornbury, W.D. (1954, 1969), *Principles of Geomorphology,* John Wiley & Sons.

Townshend, J.R.G. (1981), Image analysis and interpretation for land resources survey, Chapter 4 in: *Terrain Analysis and Remote Sensing,* J.R.G. Townshend (Ed.), George Allen & Unwin Ltd., London.

Tricart, J. (1965), *Geomorphogie Applicable,* Masson Cie, Paris, 1–167.

Verstappen, H.T. (1963), The Role of Aerial Survey in Applied Geomorphology, *Rev. Geom. Dyn.* **10**, 237–252.

Verstappen, H.T. (1966), Landforms, water and land use in west of the Indus plain, *Nature & Resources,* **2**, 6–8.

Verstappen, H.T. et al. (1969), *Landforms and Resources in Cental Rajasthan,* ITC Pub. B. 51.

Verstappen, H.T. (1977), *Remote Sensing in Geomorphology, Elsevier Scientific Pub. Co.*, Amsterdam.

Verstappen. H.T. (1983), *Applied Geomorphology: Geomorphological Surveys for Environmental Development,* Elsevier, Amsterdam.

Way, Douglas S. (1978), *Terrain Analysis: A Guide to Site Selection Using Aerial Photographic Interpretation* (2nd ed.), McGraw-Hill Co., New York.

12

Morphometric Analysis of Watershed A Case of Thirot in Himachal Pradesh

Ashwani Kumar and D.D. Sharma

Abstract: Morphometric analysis refers to quantitative explanation of different surface features, and watershed represents a homogenous region where land and water, the two components of land use, play critical role in development process. The present chapter focuses on the morphometric aspects of watershed, i.e., relief, slope, stream ordering, stream frequency, bifurcation ratio, elongation ratio, etc. which can be of great significance in land use management and sustainable development of Himalayan region in general and cold desert areas in particular.

Keywords: Watershed Management, Morphometry, Slope, Relief, Stream Frequency, Stream Ordering, Bifurcation Ratio, Elongation Ratio

Introduction

The Himalayas are considered as one of the most fragile ecosystems of the world. Increasing interference of the people due to various economic activities has disturbed its ecological equilibrium. Deforestation, unplanned construction works and unscientific grazing practices, etc. have largely affected the physical environment of the region. To combat these environmental problems, the Government of India has initiated various area specific programmes. Watershed Management Programme is one of them. It adopts a multi-disciplinary approach with the primary aim of land-water management along with sustainable development of other socio-economic and human resources.

The watershed is a purely geographic entity. But today, this aspect is grossly ignored by the planners. For the preparation of an effective watershed management plan and its execution, geographical analysis of a watershed such as relief, drainage, climate, slope, aspect and some other morphometric parameters is very important. Drainage characteristics determines the stage of landform development. The distribution pattern of the land forms, texture of the surface material and availability of water resources have great bearing on agriculture, horticulture and forestry development. Quantitative analysis of drainage characteristics of a given river catchment is helpful in understanding the physical and hydrological conditions of the catchment area. The morphometric analysis of river basin catchment area is very useful in formulating the effective management plan to overcome the problem of severe environmental degradation. The dictionary meaning of watershed is a water divide line which separates the drainage area of one stream/lake/depression from the other one. It is a ridge line which delineates the catchment area. But today, especially in the American geographical literature, a catchment area is known as **watershed**. A watershed is a geo-hydrological entity wherein all the surface runoff drains into a common exit.

Study Area

The state of Himachal Pradesh is mainly drained by six rivers. They are: the Jhelum, the Ravi, the Chenab, the Beas, the Satluj and the Yamuna. Accordingly it is divided into several major and minor watersheds.

The Thirot watershed, as delineated by All India Soil and Land Use Survey (AIS & LUS, 1990) is a mini watershed which has been selected for the morphometric analysis and landuse planning. It is codified as IDID8 which is a part of the Chenab river basin of the Indus water resource region. It entirely lies in the tribal district of Lahaul and Spiti of Himanchal Pradesh. It is situated in the Greater Himalayas and, therefore, characterized by very high altitude and rugged terrain. The drainage pattern of the watershed is dendritic. The Chenab and the Thirot nala are the major streams. Thirot watershed extends from 32°30'34" N to 32°49'30 N latitudes and 76°37'22' E to 77°0' E longitudes covering a total geographical area of 7000 hectares. Altitude of the watershed ranges from 2700 to 6000 m above sea level. The climate of the watershed is mid-latitude cold desert type, but in winters it is semi-arctic type. Owing to very low temperature and precipitation and rugged mountainous relief, climate of the area is very harsh and people live a very hard life (Figure 12.1).

Morphometric Analysis and Watershed Management

Morphometry is defined as the measurement and mathematical analysis of the configuration of the earth's surface and of the shape and dimensions of its landforms (Cole et. al., 1968, Goudie 1990, Strahler et al., 2007). It incorporates quantitative study of the area, altitude, volume, shape, profiles of the land and drainage basin characteristics of the area concerned. Watershed management is an amalgam of various socio-economic and engineering works. For the effective operation of watershed management programmes, it is very necessary to have general understanding of different physical parameters. Morphometric analysis is equally important to prepare a proper management plan in order to harness the available resources more effectively and judiciously.

Following data have been used in the present study:

1. Survey of India topographical sheets no. 52D/10, 52D/13 and 52D/14 on 1:50000 scale.
2. Watershed Atlas of India prepared by All India Soil and Land Use Survey (AIS and LUS) on 1:1,000,000 scale.

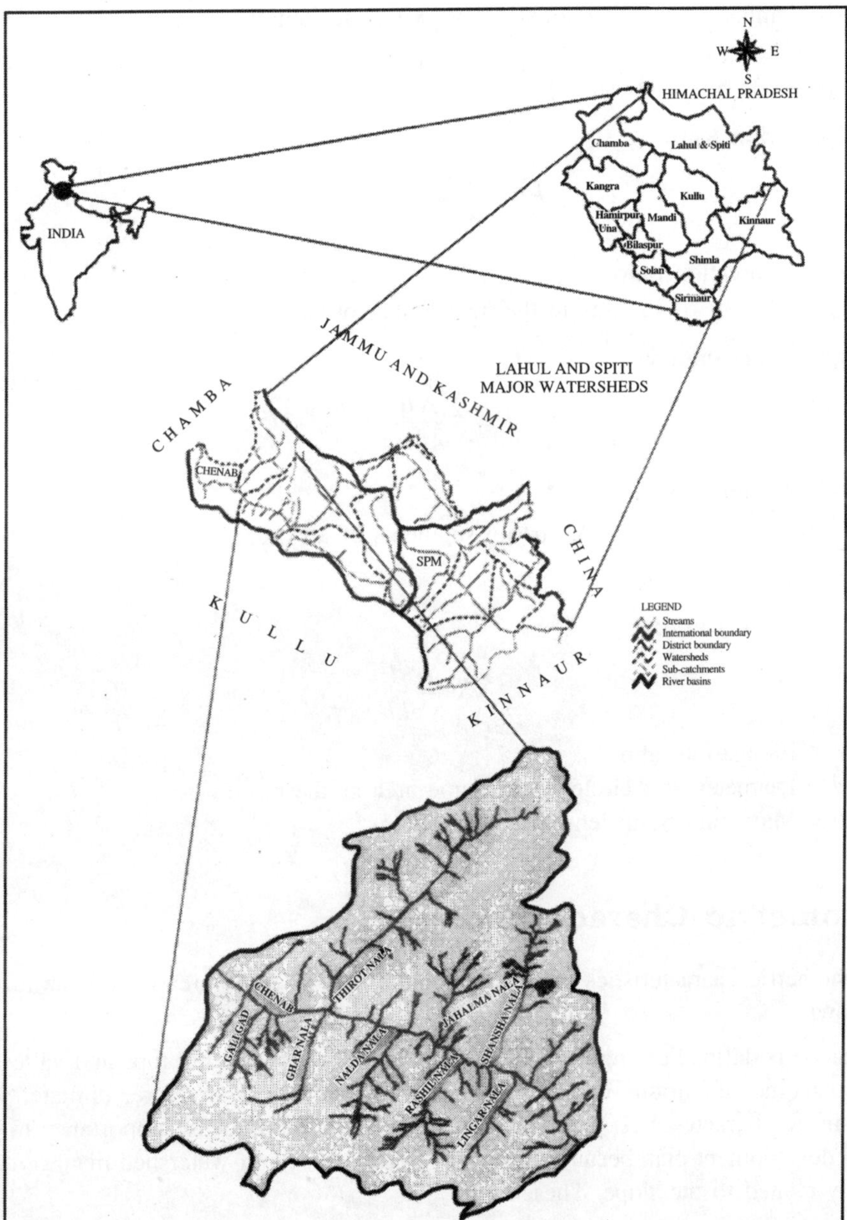

Figure 12.1 Location map of Thirot watershed.

The methodology of morphometric analysis is based on some formulae. These formulae have been expressed as under:

(a) Wentworth's Average Slope Method:

$$\text{Slope angle } (\tan\theta) = \frac{N \times I}{636.6}$$

N = Number of contours crossing per kilometer length
I = Contour interval
(where 636.6 is a constant.)

(b) Bifurcation Ratio:

$$Rb = \frac{N_\mu}{N_\mu + 1}$$

Rb = Bifurcation ratio
N_μ = Number of streams in the next higher order

(c) Stream Frequency:

$$F = \frac{\sum N\mu}{A\mu}$$

F = Frequency
$\sum N\mu$ = Total number of stream segments of all order
$A\mu$ = Areal unit

(d) Elongation Ratio:

$$Re = \frac{d}{Lb}$$

Re = Elongation ratio
d = Diameter of a circle of the same area as the basin
Lb = Maximum basin length

Morphometric Characteristics

The morphometric characteristics of surface features of the study area have been discussed as given below:

Slope: Slope is defined as angular inclination of terrain between hill tops and valley bottoms. It is the outcome of various causative factors, i.e. geological structure, climate, vegetation cover, drainage characteristics, etc. The slope analysis is of immense importance to prepare a watershed development plan because there are several aspects of watershed management which are directly related to the slope. These are;

1. Identification of erosion prone areas
2. Estimation of surface run off
3. Estimation of water infiltration rates
4. Land use pattern and,
5. Identification of appropriate sites for the construction of water harvesting structures—check dams, water channels and other engineering works.

Based on Wentworth's average slope method, the entire watershed has been classified into four slope categories, i.e., gentle (<20°), moderate (20°–40°), steep (40°–60° and very steep (>60°). It is apparent that approximately 95 per cent of the watershed area comes under steep and very steep slope category (Figure 12.2) and, therefore, this cannot be used for any productive purposes. Any interference in these areas is likely to result in land slide or some other disasters.

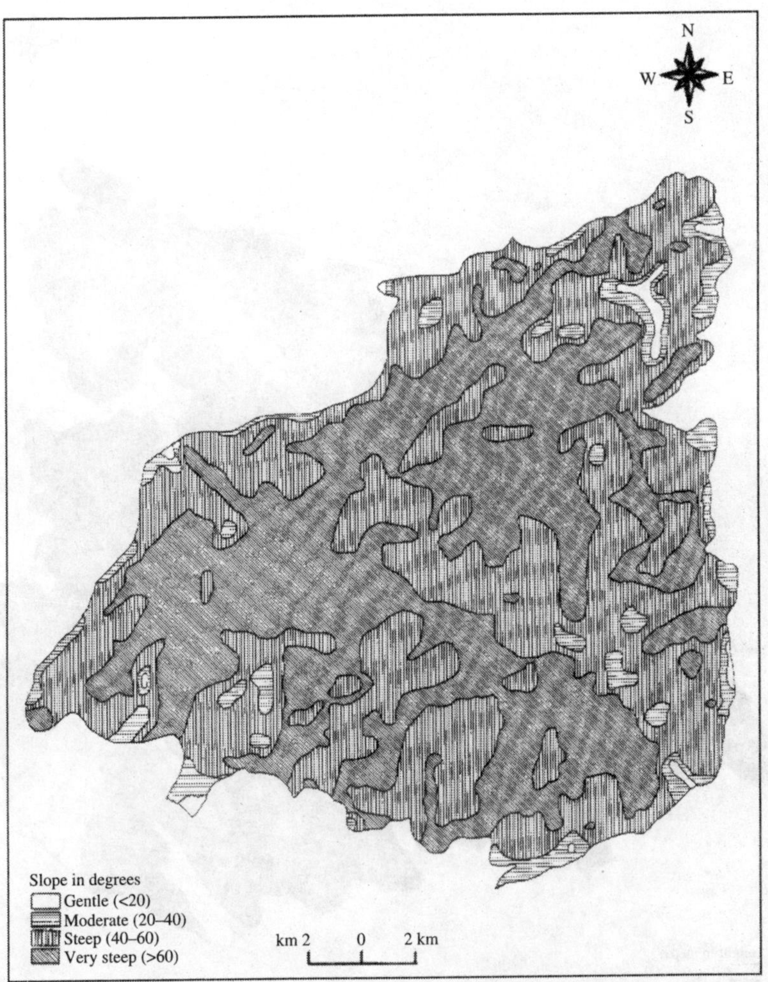

Figure 12.2 Slope map of Thirot watershed.

Relief: Relief refers to the altitudinal variation of a given landmass. It is also an outcome of the interplay of various climatic, geological, geomorphological, endogenetic and exogenetic processes. Relief analysis is useful when watershed area is hilly or mountainous because in plains altitudinal variation are not very much pronounced. It is quite imperative to know the general characteristics of watershed area at different elevations. Based on relief, the watershed can be divided into six categories varying between 3000–5400 m. Broadly, three types of lands may be identified. These are uplands, midlands and lowlands.

Generally uplands are characterized by snow cover, rocky outcrops and forests. In snowbound areas availability of water is restricted by seasonal melting of snow, hence this factor determines the cropping season and cropping pattern of the area. The midlands are mostly grazing lands or wastelands with sign of soil erosion. All the drained water tends to converge in the lowlands which are characterized by fertile tracts for agricultural pursuits (Figure 12.3).

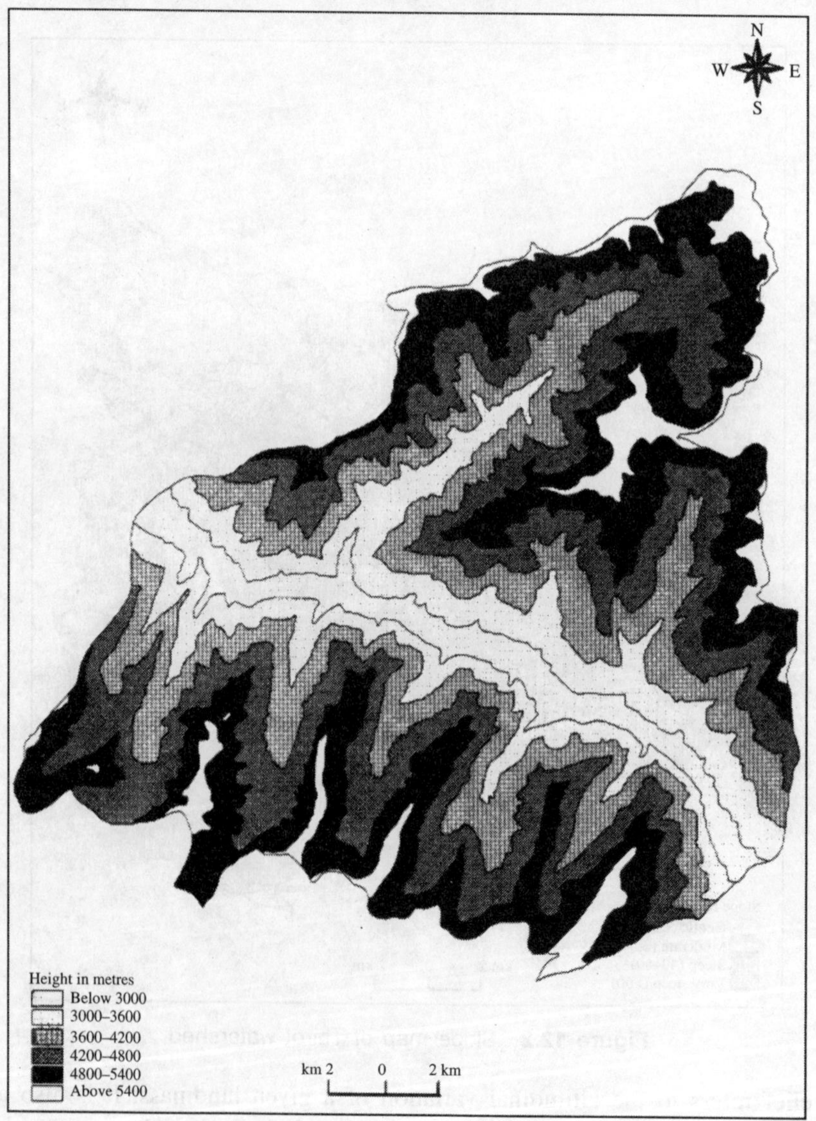

Figure 12.3 Relief map of Thirot watershed.

Stream frequency: This refers to number of streams per unit area. The stream frequency analysis is imperative in order to identify erosion prone areas, because greater the number of streams greater will be the surface run off and soil erosion. This also determines the permeability of soil. The higher stream frequency is the resultant of weak or impermeable sub-surface material, sparse vegetation and mountainous relief, while lower stream frequency is the result of highly resistant or permeable sub-soil material, dense vegetation and low relief. From Figure 12.4, it appears that most of the watershed area comes under poor and moderate stream frequency. Higher stream frequency area is very small and found only in the form of small patches.

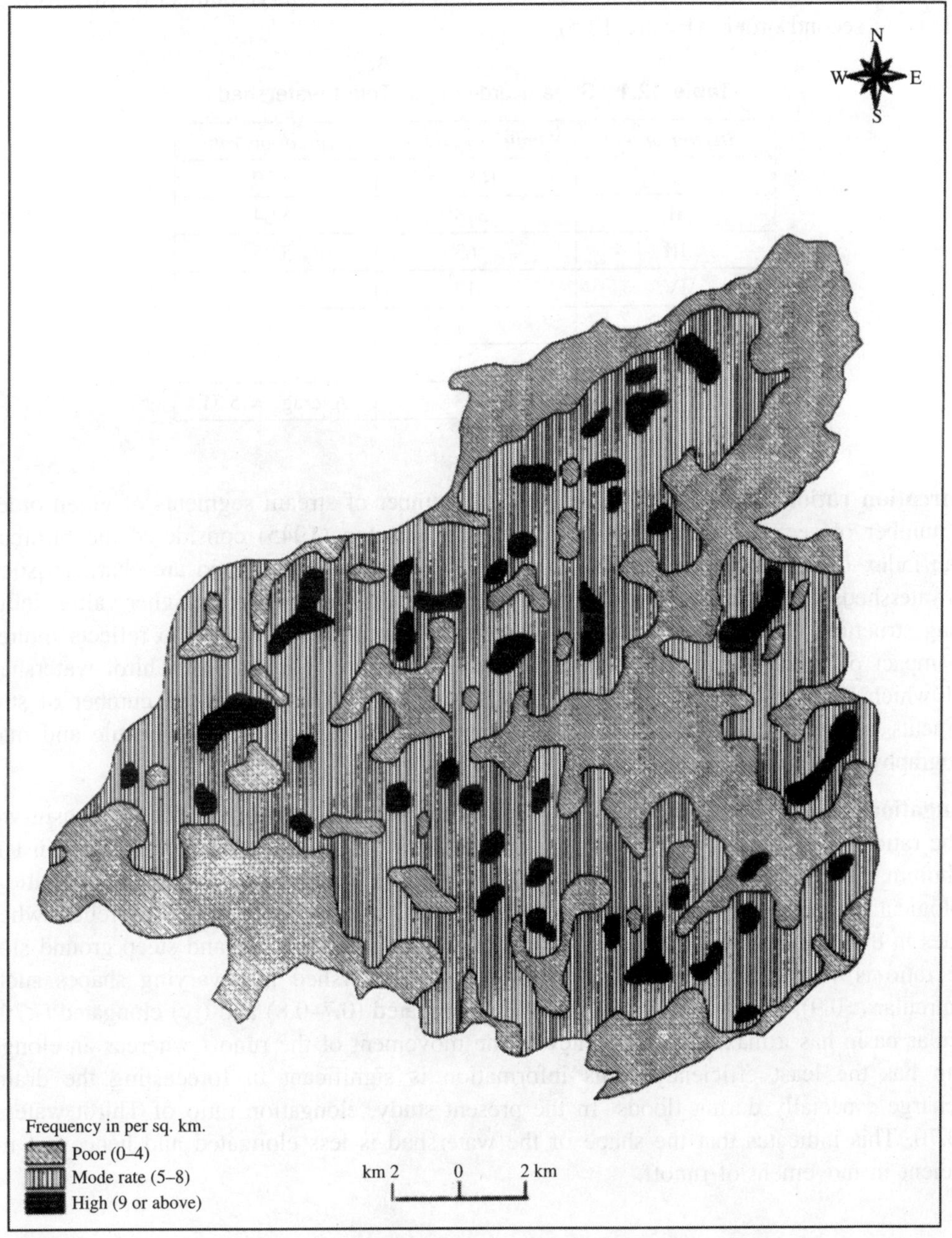

Figure 12.4 Stream frequency map of Thirot watershed.

Stream ordering: The stream ordering refers to the determination of hierarchical position of a stream within a drainage basin. A river basin consists of several branches (tributaries) in which some are seasonal, some are perennial and some are mere channels. Stream ordering is useful along with stream frequency to locate various seasonal and perennial streams according to their order. This is helpful to utilize the water resource potentials of the area. Table 12.1 shows the stream ordering of Thirot watershed. It is clear that a large number of streams belong to first and second orders (Figure 12.5).

Table 12.1 Stream ordering in Thirot watershed

Stream order	*Number of streams*	*Bifurcation ratio*
I	1688	5.30
II	318	5.04
III	63	5.25
IV	12	12
V	1	1
Consequent stream	1	–
	2083	Average = 5.71

Source: Computed.

Bifurcation ratio: It refers to the ratio of the number of stream segments of given order to the number of segments of the next higher order. Horton (1945) considered the bifurcation as an index of relief and dissections. Lower values of bifurcation ratio are characteristics of the watersheds which have suffered less structural disturbances whereas higher values indicate strong structural control on the drainage pattern. The bifurcation ratio also reflects indirectly the impact of lithology on watersheds. The average bifurcation ratio of Thirot watershed is 5.71 which is quite high (Table 12.1). It is due to large variations in the number of stream segments of lower and higher orders indicating occurrence of relatively juvenile and mature topography side by side.

Elongation ratio: The elongation ratio reveals the shape or form of a drainage basin which is the ratio of diameter of a circle of the same area as the basin to the maximum basin length (Schumm, 1977). This ratio runs between 0.6 and 1.0 over a wide variety of climatic and geological characteristics. Values near 1.0 are typical of regions of very low relief, whereas values in the range 0.6–0.8 are generally associated with strong relief and steep ground slopes. The ratio is very meaningful index for classifying watershed into varying shapes such as (i) circular (>0.9), (ii) Oval (0.8–0.9), (iii) less elongated (0.7–0.8) and (iv) elongated (<70). A circular basin has a maximum efficiency in the movement of the runoff whereas an elongated basin has the least efficiency. This information is significant in forecasting the drainage discharge especially during floods. In the present study, elongation ratio of Thirot watershed is 0.70. This indicates that the shape of the watershed is less elongated and hence not much efficient in movement of runoff.

Figure 12.5 Stream ordering map of Thirot watershed.

Conclusion

The area under study presents the case of a watershed which is part of mountainous terrain. Most of the area of this watershed is characterised by very steep slope. The relief features vary between 3000–5400 m. The area under upland is larger as compared to the area under low land. The low land is confined to some narrow patches. The lower stream frequency values of the area indicate that it is underlain by resistant permeable rocks. The mean bifurcation ratio is 5.71 which represents the juvenile stage of the watershed. The shape of the watershed is much less elongated and therefore surface runoff is not very efficient. The human habitation is confined only in the areas having altitude ranging between 2700–3400 m.

In a terrain like this, the planning of land and water cannot be done successfully unless and until the aforesaid parameters are taken into account. Based on the morphometric analysis, the priority areas may be identified and accordingly land and water management may be suggested. This is needless to say that in a sensitive environment like this, the conservation of water and utilization of land needs to be done very carefully or else the basic objective of sustainable management may be set at naught.

References

AIS & LUS (1990), *Watershed Atlas of India*, Department of Agriculture, IARI, New Delhi.

Cole, John P. and C.A.M. King (1968), *Quantitative Geography: Techniques and Theories in Geography*, John Wiley, London

Goudie, A.S. (Ed.) (1990), *Geomorphological Techniques*, Allen and Unwin, London.

Horton, R.E. (1945), Erosional development of streams and their drainage basins: Hydrological approach to quantitative geomorphology, *Bulletin of Geological Society of America*, **56**, 275–370.

Schumm, S.A. (1977), *The Fluvial Systems*, John Wiley, New York.

Strahler, Alan and Strahler, Arthur (2007), *Physical Geography*, John Wiley, London.

13

Spatial Pattern of Agricultural Development in J&K

G.B. Singh and Sandeep Kaur

Abstract: Land is an important economic resource base. Its utilization depends on several factors such as social, economic and political. However, in a hilly terrain and mountainous topography, physical factors especially relief features play critical role. The present chapter underlines this by studying the levels of agricultural development in Jammu region. Based on the agricultural development index, the study area has been divided into four categories and the characteristics of each one of them has been discussed here.

Keywords: Kuhls, Rabi, Kharif, Composite Index, Net Sown Area, Gross Cropped Area

Introduction

Agriculture is the only economic activity on the face of earth which varies immensely both over time and space. The agricultural production is the result of the combination of two sets of forces, viz., physical and social. Even if these two sets of forces in a broader sense may be similar over two different areas, yet one cannot expect similar agricultural production. It is because a very small variation in any one of these factors may result into the big change in the production. The variation in agricultural production can be seen from one village to other, from one holding to another and even from one field to another. It sometimes so happens that the production varies within a field itself. In such a situation it becomes the responsibility of geographers to find out the casual relationship between the variation in the agricultural production in any area both over time and space. It is important because on the agricultural production, the level of economic development of any region depends. It is the enhanced agricultural production which creates surplus for the investment in the industrial sector. And the development of industry decides the level of development of any area. Thus, the roots of development lie in the development of agriculture and agricultural production. The major task of geographer is to find out the variations in agricultural production and to identify the reasons for such variations. In doing so he will be identifying agriculturally rich and poor areas to enable planners to plan the future course both for agricultural and economic development (Lal, R. et al., 2002; Shafi, 1960; Tiwari, 2000).

Taking above factors into consideration an attempt in the present paper is being made to identify the levels of agricultural development in the Jammu region of Jammu and Kashmir State. The region enjoys a huge variation in physiography with corresponding variation in the climatic conditions. Physiographically region extends from outer plains to Siwalik Hills and then to mighty Himalayan ranges known popularly as the middle Himalayas. Corresponding to these physiographic variations climate also varies from sub-tropical to temperate and even to alpine conditions. These physiographic and climatic variations are accompanied by different soil conditions. Similarly social and human conditions in such situations cannot be expected to be similar. Under all these dissimilarities the agricultural development has to be variable. The present paper attempts to identify such variations. Thus, the major objective of this chapter is to identify areas of Jammu region which are agriculturally least developed and the areas which are comparatively better developed so that planning for future development may be suggested.

Study Area

The Jammu region stretches from 32°17' N to 34°12' N latitudes and from73°28' E to 76°47' E longitudes. Nestled against the back drop of the snow capped Pir Panjal Mountains, the Jammu region constitutes the southernmost unit of the state of Jammu and Kashmir. It forms part of the transition between the Himalayan range in the north and the dusty plains of Punjab in the south. Between these two extremities lie a series of scrub-covered hills, forested mountain ranges and river valleys, encompassing several micro-climatic regions that extend from Kishtwar in the north-east to Akhnoor in the south-west and the historic town of Poonch in the north-west to the borders of Kangra (H.P.) in the south-east. The Shivalik hills cut across the area from the east to the west while the river Ravi, the Tawi and the Chenab cut their ways through the region. This region covers an area of 26,293 sq. km which is 1/8th of total area of the state of Jammu and Kashmir. Administratively, Jammu region is divided into six districts, viz., Jammu, Kathua, Udhampur, Doda, Rajouri and Poonch which are further subdivided into 30 tehsils, 57 blocks and 3617 villages.

The region, occupies a strategic location since it lies in the south western part of the state sharing its border with Pakistan in the west and south-west. In the north, it touches the beautiful valley of Kashmir. Altitudinally the region extends from 300 m above mean sea level in the outer plains to over 5000 m in the middle Himalayas.

Data Source and Methodology

The data has been collected from the secondary sources for the *Kharif and Rabi* crops for the year 2000–2001 for each Tehsil, while the population data has been collected from the census of India. The 10 selected variables are as under:

X_1 = Net sown area as percentage to reporting area.

X_2 = Net sown area as percentage to gross cropped area.

X_3 = Irrigated area as percentage to net sown area.
X_4 = Area under Maize as percentage of net sown area.
X_5 = Area under Wheat as percentage of net sown area.
X_6 = Area under Paddy as percentage of net sown area.
X_7 = Literate population as percentage to total population.
X_8 = Percentage of workers to total population.
X_9 = Cultivators as percentage of working population.
X_{10} = Agricultural labourers as percentage of total workers.

The levels of development have been determined by the composite index. The formula for computing the index is as given below:

$$\text{C.I.} = \sum_{j=1}^{n} \frac{X_{ij}}{X_j} C$$

Here, X_{ij} = value of jth variate for ith tehsil
n = number of variables or indicators.

The value of the composite index shows the level of development. Higher the value of composite index, higher will be the development. The value of the composite scores was made scale free by dividing the values of each indicator by their respective (X_{ij}) mean for the indicators. Then, those scale free values were added to obtain composite index for each tehsil. The value of each column represents the relative position of different tehsils in the relative aspects. These values of index obtained for 30 tehsils were grouped into four categories:

1. More Developed or Very High (>15)
2. Moderately Developed or High (10–15)
3. Less Developed or Medium (5–10)
4. Least Developed or Low (<5)

Based on the above methodology, the study region has been divided into four categories based on the development of agriculture (Table 13.1 and Figure 13.1).

Table 13.1 Levels of agricultural development

Category	*Name of the tehsil*	*No. of tehsils*	*Rank*
(>15) More Developed Regions	R.S. Pura, Akhnoor, Hiranagar, Surankote	4	1st
(10–15) Moderately Developed	Bishnah, Ramban, Banihal, Thathri, Billawar, Kathua, Poonch, Mendhar	8	IInd
(5–10) Low Developed	Jammu, Samba, Ramnagar, Udhampur, Reasi, Goolgulabgarh, Chenani, Kishtwar, Bhalaessa, Budhal, Kalakote, Nowshera, Rajouri, Sunderbani, Thanamandi, Basohli	16	IIIrd
(<5) Least Developed	Bhaderwah, Doda	2	IVth
Total		**30**	

Source: Computed.

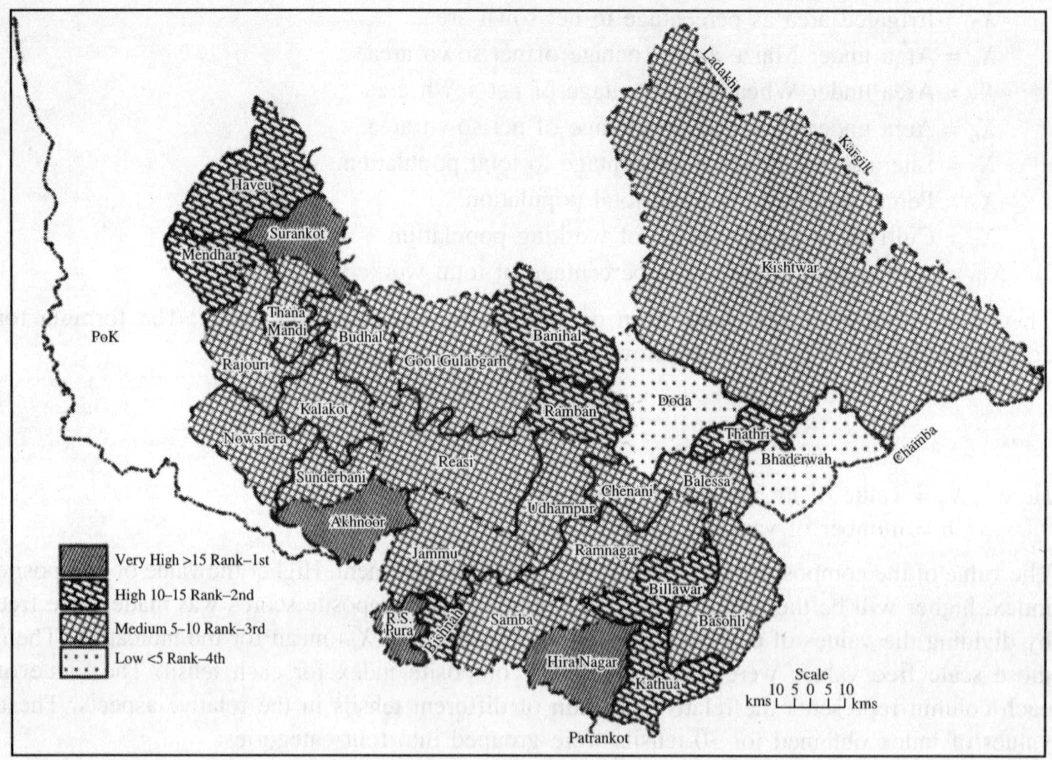

Figure 13.1 Levels of agricultural development in J&K.

This is to be noted that the territorial units do not form a contiguous area of a given region but these have been considered to form a category based on the agricultural productivity. Each region has been briefly examined in the discussion.

Results and Discussions

More Developed Region

All those territorial units having composite index value above 15 have been included in this group. Evidently, these units, are agriculturally better developed as compared to other regions. But only four (13.2 per cent) out of the thirty tehsils fall in this category. These four tehsils are R.S. Pura, Akhnoor, Hiranagar and Surankote. Except for Surankote, all the other three tehsils lie in outer plain region of the study region. The Surankote tehsil, no doubt, lies in the hilly region surrounding Pir Panjal range. But most of the area available for cultivation lies in the vicinity of the Suran valley and as such it can be termed as agriculturally rich area. The other three tehsils, i.e., R.S. Pura, Hiranagar and Akhnoor are highly irrigated and possess fertile, alluvial/clayey soils with agro-climatic conditions permitting agricultural operations throughout the year. All these tehsils have high proportion of their net sown area under rice and wheat in rotation. Both these crops are economically profitable and yield good economic returns because these areas have a very high proportion of irrigated area. Other corresponding technological inputs further make the region agriculturally more developed. Thus, the use of tractors, threshers, HYV seeds, chemical fertilizers, etc. further help these tehsils to move ahead of other territorial units in respect of agricultural development. It can, thus, be concluded that Hiranagar tehsil of Kathua district, R.S. Pura and Akhnoor tehsils of Jammu district and Surankote tehsil of Poonch district form an area where agricultural development is reasonably high as compared to other territorial units of the study region.

Moderately Developed Region

The areas having composite index values between 10 and 15 are classed as a region where agricultural development is not very high but can be termed as moderate considering the status of agriculture in the state of Jammu and Kashmir in general and area of the study in particular. There are eight (26.4 per cent) tehsils falling in this category. These are Bishnah (Jammu district), Kathua, Billawar (Kathua district), Thathri (Doda District), Mendhar, Poonch (Poonch District), Ramban and Banihal (Ramban District). Except the Bishnah and Kathua tehsils which lie in outer plain region, all other tehsils are located in the mountainous region. Though proportion of net sown area to the total reported area in all these tehsils is limited, yet the fertile soil on the terraced fields is rrigated to produce valuable crops like rice, maize, wheat and pulses. The use of chemical fertilizers and high yielding varieties of seeds further adds to agricultural production.

Less Developed Region

By far the largest number of tehsils form part of this region. There are 16 (52.8 per cent) tehsils of the total of 30 of the study area which form part of this region. These 16 tehsils are Jammu, Samba, Ramnagar, Udhampur, Reasi, Goolgulabgarh, Chenani, Kishtwar, Bhalaessa, Budhal, Kalakote, Nowshera, Rajouri, Sunderbani, Thanamandi and Basohli. The composite index value of each of these sixteen tehsils lies between 5 and 10. Except for Jammu and Samba tehsils of Jammu district, which partially lie in the outer plains and partially in outer siwaliks, all other tehsils are located in the middle mountains. However, some portions of Basohli tehsil of Kathua district fall in the Siwaliks. Irrigation in almost all these areas, except for some portions of Jammu and Samba tehsils, is a difficult proposition. Although difficult, yet some farmers manage irrigation through Kuhls. Since environmental conditions are not very favourably disposed for agriculture, the development in general and agriculture in particular is less developed.

Least Developed Region

Only two tehsils—Doda and Bhaderwah of the Doda district fall in this category. The region seems to be agriculturally weak as the composite index value of the ten selected parameters falls below 5. Both these tehsils are physiographically highly dissected, rugged and rough where agricultural operations are difficult. The agro-climatic conditions are such that cultivation of *Rabi* crops in most of the area of these tehsils is not possible. It is only during summers that cultivation of paddy in irrigated areas and maize and pulses in unirrigated areas is possible. High altitudes of these tehsils further reduce the possibility of agriculture. Thus this represents the least or very poorly developed agriculture region.

Conclusion

To conclude it may be said that agriculture occupies the major share as far as the land utilization is concerned. This is so because this happens to be the major source of sustenance of people. Nevertheless, geographical factors such as relief, soil, rainfall and other climatic conditions play significant role in the spatial variation of production and productivity. Irrigation, technology and other innovations in the field of agriculture further add to variations in the spatial pattern. Based on the spatial variations of agricultural production as many as four categories of areas—more developed, moderately developed, less developed and least developed may be identified. This division may help in formulating the strategies for development of less and least developed areas. Significantly, less and least developed areas command the major portion of Jammu region. The physio-cultural milieu of these areas requires sustained planning effort to accelerate the process of development in general and agriculture in particular in a hilly terrain like the one under study.

References

Lal, R. et al. (Eds.) (2002), *Food Security and Environmental Quality in the Developing World*, CRC Press, Florida.

Shafi, M. (1960), Measurement of agricultural efficiency in Uttar Pradesh, *Economic Geography*, **36**(4), 296–305.

Tiwari, P.C. (2000), Land-use changes in Himalaya and their impact on the plains ecosystem: Need for sustainable land use, *Land Use Policy*, **17**(2), 101–111.

PART III

Water Resources

14

Perennials in Peril
A Case of the Yamuna River Basin

H.N. Misra and Ashutosh Mishra

Abstract: There are 14 major, 44 medium and 53 minor river basins which account for 91 per cent of the total drainage of the country. The Yamuna, together with the Ganga, constitutes the largest river basin. The drainage basin of the Yamuna river spreads over an area of 345,848 sq. km which is 42.5 per cent of the entire Ganga basin and 10.7 per cent of the total geographical landmass of the country. This chapter highlights the case of the Yamuna river, which has been facing the crisis of being almost non-existent in not too distant a future, if not protected in time.

Keywords: Landmass, Materialistic, Renewable, Basin, Tributaries, Organic Matter, Territorial Limits, Environment enriching, Desilting, Greening, Bio-degradable

Introduction

The metaphor that water is liquid gold is a very materialistic view. In fact water is invaluable renewable resource without which any form of life is inconceivable. The very existence of biosphere is because of water. It is, therefore, rightly said that water is life and life is water. More than 71 per cent of the globe is covered by water but the drinkable water is just 3 per cent. India's position is definitely better in this context. It is one of the wettest countries of the world as it records an average rainfall of 1170 mm which is reasonably very high. But this rainfall is confined to 120 days from July to September. Besides, it is characterized by extremes such as Mausimram in Cherrapunji (Meghalaya) with 11,000 mm of rainfall at one end and Jaisalmer (Rajasthan) with 200 mm of annual rainfall on the other. In view of this rivers play the role of life line by providing irrigation to a very vast expanse of agriculture which has been the major source of sustenance to a large majority of human population. There are 14 major, 44 medium and 53 minor rivers basins which account for 91 per cent of the country's total drainage. The Ganga together with the Yamuna constitutes the largest river basin.

The present chapter attempts to highlight the case of the Yamuna river[1] which has been facing the crisis of being non-existent (Rai, et al., 2010; CSE, 2009; CPCB, 2006), if not protected in time.

Geographical Profile

The Yamuna river finds its origin from the Yamunotri glacier (Saptarishi Kund) near Bander Punch peak (38°59' N and 78°27' E) at an elevation of 6320 m. from the mean sea level in the Mussoorie range of Uttarkashi district in the state of Uttarakhand. Travelling a distance of 1376 km through the states of Uttarakhand, Himachal Pradesh, Haryana, Delhi and Uttar Pradesh it finally meets with the Ganga at Triveni Sangam (Allahabad) popularly known as Tirtha Raj Prayag (Figure 14.1) The drainage basin of the river spreads over an area of 345,848 km^2 which is 42.5 per cent of the entire Ganga basin and 10.7 per cent of the total geographical landmass of the country.

The catchment of the river is spread in different states which can be gauged from the Figure 14.2 and Table 14.1. From this table, it may be seen that the major part of its catchment area lies in Madhya Pradesh (40.54 per cent) followed by Rajasthan (29.75 per cent), Uttar Pradesh (20.37 per cent), Haryana (6.15 per cent), Himachal Pradesh (1.68 per cent) and Uttarakhand (1.10 per cent).

The upper valley of the river is characterized by the presence of morranic deposits, interlocking spurs, rock benches and terraces. The tributaries which mainly enrich the river in this part are the Tons (the largest and longest), the Giri, the Rishi Ganga, the Kunta, the Hanuman Ganga and the Bata. While descending in the plain it is joined by the Chambal, the Hindon, the Betwa, the Sindh and the Ken. There are some evidences that the Yamuna river was originally the tributary of the Ghagghar river (also known as the Vedic Saraswati river). Owing to some tectonic events it changed its course to become the tributary of the Ganga. The Tons has been the principal contributor in the mountainous region whereas in the plain the Chambal river has been mainly responsible for augmenting the water of the Yamuna. About 80 per cent of the total annual water flow is carried during monsoon period. The water flow reduces significantly during non-monsoon period. The reduction of the flow is further accentuated due to diversion of its water for irrigation and drinking purposes. The rate of fall of the river is shown in the Table 14.2.

---

[1]**The** Yamuna river finds mention in Rig-Veda and Atharva-Veda which are the ancient most scriptures of the world. It is said that Yamuna was born from Sun, the father and Sanjana, the mother as twins? Originally known as Yami, her brother Yama is the god of death. Because of her closeness to her brother she is popularly known as endowed with unique ability of granting freedom from death.

Figure 14.1 Location map of the Yamuna basin.

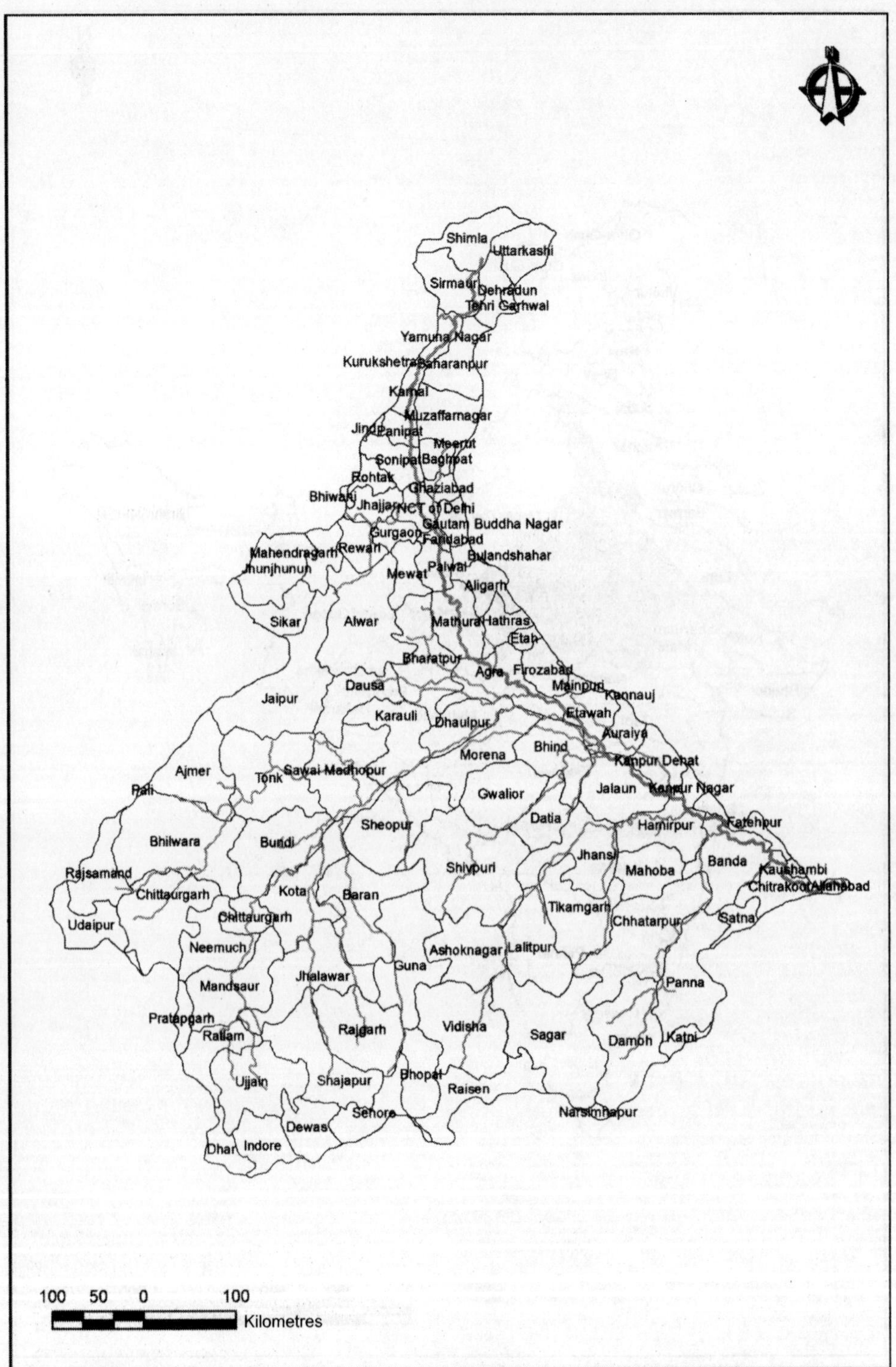

Figure 14.2 Catchment area of the Yamuna basin.

Table 14.1 Catchment area of the Yamuna river

State/territory	*Total area in the Yamuna river catchment* (km^2)	*Area in the major sub-basin* (km^2)					
		River Hindon	*River Chambal*	*River Sind*	*River Betwa*	*River Ken*	*Other sub basin*
Uttarakhand	3,771 (1.10 per cent)	–	–	–	–	–	3,771
Uttar Pradesh	70,437 (20.37 per cent)	7,083	452	748	14,438	3,336	44,380
Himachal Pradesh	5,799 (1.68 per cent)	–	–	–	–	–	5799
Haryana	21,265 (6.15 per cent)	–	–	–	–	–	21,265
Rajasthan	102,883 (29.75 per cent)	–	79,495	–	–	–	23,388
Madhya Pradesh	140,208 (40.54 per cent)	–	59,838	25,131	33,502	21,090	647
NCT–Delhi	1,485 (0.43 per cent)	–	–	–	–	–	1,485
Total	345,848 (100 per cent)	7,083 (2.0 per cent)	139,785 (40.5 per cent)	25,879 (7.5 per cent)	47,940 (13.9 per cent)	24,426 (7.1 per cent)	100,735 (29.1 per cent)

Source: National River Conservation Directorate, Ministry of Environment and Forests.

Table 14.2 Rate of fall in the Yamuna river stretches

Stretch	*Length of stretch* (km)	*Rate of fall* (m/km)
Upper Himalaya Stretch	25	59.0
Himalaya Stretch	152	19.1
Total Plain Stretch	1224	0.2
Lower Plain Stretch	768	0.08

The maximum rate of fall (59.0 m/km) is in the first upper stretch of 25 km from its origin and it comes down to 0.08 m/km starting from Agra. The ground elevation ranges from 6320 m above mean sea level near Yamunotri glacier to about 100 m above mean sea level near the confluence of this river with the Ganga at Allahabad. Topographically the basin of this river may be classified in three categories: (a) Hilly terrain—600 m and above (11,700 km^2/3.38 per cent), (b) Foot hills and plateau—300 m to 600 m (172,917 km^2/49.99 per cent) and (c) Plain terrain—300 m to 100 m (161,231 km^2/49.62 per cent).

The river may be divided into four segments based on the characteristics of the water flow: (i) First segment extends for 157 km. between Yamunotri and Hathnikund/Tajewala barrage. The melting glaciers form the source of water. The water flow in this segment terminates into Western Yamuna Canal (WYC). (ii) The second segment is of 224 km between Hathnikund/Tajewala barrage and Wazirabad barrage. The ground water accrual is the major source of water. The Wazirabad reservoir is after treatment used to meet the requirement of drinking water in the capital city of Delhi. (iii) The next segment of 22 km is between Wazirabad and Okhla barrage. More than 17 sewage drains of Delhi meet in this segment and accelerate the pollution of the river water. (iv) The fourth segment is the largest downstream between Okhla barrage and the confluence at Allahabad for 973 km. The water in this segment is augmented by several rivers such as the Hindon, the Chambal, the Sindh, the Ken and the Betwa in addition to drains of Mathura, Agra and Etawah.

The Yamuna river basin is characterized mainly by alluvial soil which constitutes about 42 per cent of the total basin. The calcareous seirozemic soil has minimal share of only about 0.5 per cent. As many as eight types of soils are found in the basin (Table 14.3).

Table 14.3 Soil types in the Yamuna basin

Types of soil	*Per cent of total basin area covered*	*Locations*
Red Sandy	2.5	Along UP–MP border in districts of Jhansi, Hamirpur, Chhattarpur, etc.
Red and Yellow	5.0	Parts of Jaipur, Alwar, SawaiMadhopur, Banda, Panna districts and along western boundary of basin in Rajasthan
Calcareous Seirozemic	0.5	Parts of Mohindergarh and Bhiwani districts in Haryana
Deep Black	5.5	On the southern boundary of the basin in Sehore, Bhopal, Raisen, Vidisha, Sagar & Damoh districts
Medium Black	25.5	Most of the basin in MP and strips north of river Chambal in Rajasthan
Mixed Red and Black	15.0	Chittaurgarh, Bhilwara, Banda, Mandasaur, Shivpur, Lalitpur, Tikamgarh, Panna and Chattarpur districts
Brown Hill	4.0	Hills and foot hills in the north
Alluvial	42.0	Plains and valleys

Source: National River Conservation Directorate, Ministry of Environment and Forests.

A perusal of the land use pattern reveals that 60 per cent land is cultivable which clearly speaks the agricultural potential of the basin (Table 14.4).

Table 14.4 State-wise land use pattern in the Yamuna river catchment

State	*Area* (per cent of total catchment)	*Land use pattern*			*Land actually cultivated* (%)	*Land under habitational use* (%)
		Non-arable land (%)	*Forest land* (%)	*Cultivable land* (%)		
Himachal Pradesh	1.6	25.0	59.4	15.6	14.2	1.5
Haryana	6.1	18.1	2.4	79.5	59.9	3.6
NCT of Delhi	0.4	51.0	1.0	48.0	46.5	43.7
Uttaranchal	1.1	5.0	22.0	23.0	14.3	1.6
Uttar Pradesh	20.4	14.5	3.9	81.1	68.0	5.1
Rajasthan	29.8	40.8	8.8	50.4	43.9	2.2
Madhya Pradesh	40.6	26.0	18.0	56.0	50.7	1.8
Total	100.0	27.5	12.5	60.0	51.9	2.9

Source: National River Conservation Directorate, Ministry of Environment and Forests.

The forest land is just 12.5 per cent and this is evident that there has been large scale deforestation. This is mainly confined in Uttarakhand, Uttar Pradesh and Himachal Pradesh.

Socio-economic Characteristics

The Yamuna basin covers 2 districts in Himachal Pradesh, 3 in Uttarakhand, 15 in Haryana, 21 in Rajasthan, 29 in Madhya Pradesh and 29 in Uttar Pradesh besides Delhi. According 2011 census population of the basin is 200,383,131 which is 16.56 per cent of the total population of the country. The share of the states in the population is presented in the Table 14.5.

Table 14.5 Population share of states in the Yamuna basin

State	*Population*	*Per cent population share of the entire basin*
Himachal Pradesh	1,343,548	0.67
Uttarakhand	2,644,655	1.32
Haryana	18,605,095	9.28
NCT of Delhi	16,753,235	8.36
Uttar Pradesh	71,280,992	35.57
Rajasthan	44,137,113	22.02
Madhya Pradesh	45,618,493	22.77
Total (*Yamuna basin*)	200,383,131 (16.56 per cent of India's population)	

Source: Census, 2011.

The states which make larger contribution in the population are U.P. (35.57 per cent), Rajasthan (22.02 per cent), Madhya Pradesh (22.77 per cent), Uttarakhand (1.32 per cent) and Delhi (8.36 per cent). A detailed socio-economic characteristics of the basin based on 2001 census has been presented in the Table 14.6.

Table 14.6 Socio-economic statistics of the states of the Yamuna river basin

Indicator	*Uttarakhand*	*Himachal Pradesh*	*Haryana*	*Delhi*	*Uttar Pradesh*	*Rajasthan*	*Madhya Pradesh*
Per cent Drainage Area	1.48	1.67	9.19	0.40	19.19	29.82	38.25
Per cent Share of Population	1.0	1.0	11.0	11.0	33.0	19.0	24.0
Per cent Share of Urban Population	1.01	0.40	8.91	26.85	27.51	15.5	19.83
Per cent Share of Rural Population	0.69	1.15	13.15	1.22	36.49	21.09	26.21
Population Density (/ km^2)	300.5	128.67	506.1	9412	844.2	220.1	254.4
Sex Ratio	938	883	864	821	863	925	899
Population Growth Rate (1991–2001)	22.47	18.47	26.85	46.31	25.17	25.95	25.83
Per cent Migration	37.72	37.21	34.73	43.42	25.72	28.92	30.39

(*Contd.*)

Table 14.6 Socio-economic statistics of the states of the Yamuna river basin (*Contd.*)

Indicator	*Uttarakhand*	*Himachal Pradesh*	*Haryana*	*Delhi*	*Uttar Pradesh*	*Rajasthan*	*Madhya Pradesh*
Literacy Rate	71.62	76.48	67.91	81.67	56.27	60.41	63.74
Per cent Workers	37.54	54.16	39.85	32.82	33.34	42.84	46.67
Per cent Cultivators	0.61	2.1	11.68	0.20	27.51	29.10	28.90
Birth Rate	21.0	18.8	23.9	18.4	30.1	28.3	29.1
Death Rate	6.7	6.8	6.5	4.7	8.6	6.9	8.9
Infant Mortality Rate	43.0	50.0	57	37	71	67	74
Life	60.0	65.9	65.2	70.0	59.1	61.1	56.9
BPL per cent	–	7.63	8.74	8.23	31.15	15.28	37.43
HDI	0.38	0.48	0.50	0.68	0.38	0.42	0.39

Source: National River Conservation Directorate, Ministry of Environment and Forests.

The Human Development Index varies between 0.38 and 0.68. Obviously Delhi ranks on top and Uttarakhand and Uttar Pradesh rank at the bottom. Delhi recorded highest growth of population (46.31 per cent) during 1991–2001. The socio-economic characteristics of the basin is very heavily influenced by the location of some of the major cities such as Karnal, Panipat, Sonepat, Delhi, Gurgaon, Vrindavan, Mathura, Agra, Etawah and Allahabad through the course of the river. Table 14.7 displays the major cities and their population according to 2001–2011 census.

Table 14.7 Major cities along the Yamuna river and their population

City	*Year*		*Population growth (%) (2001–11)*
	2001	2011	
Karnal	221,236	303,425	37
Panipat	354,148	442,277	25
Sonipat	225,074	292,339	30
Delhi	12,877,470	16,314,838	27
Mathura	323,315	454,937	41
Agra	1,331,339	1,746,467	31
Etawah	210,453	256,790	22
Allahabad	1,042,229	1,216,719	17

Source: Census, 2001 and 2011.

Their decadal growth is indicative of urban population pressure being exerted by these cities. These are infact the major sources of domestic and industrial pollution of the Yamuna river. These cities use the water and discharge the filth through drains and sewage originating from them.

The pressure of population is cleanly discernible by the fact that 3 per cent area is occupied by the settlements. The cultivated land is about 52 per cent and forest cover is just 12.5 per cent of the total basin area. About 92 per cent of the water is used for irrigation purposes. The major canals are the Western Yamuna Canal and Eastern Yamuna Canal.

Perils of the Perennial

The future of the river of this magnitude has been endangered for a variety of reasons. Some of the factors which contribute in endangering the Yamuna river are mentioned as under:

1. ***Decreasing water flow:*** The river maintains its flow during monsoon period but during the non-monsoon season, it turns into a dry channel for a distance of about 800 km between Panipat and Etawah. The fact of the matter is that the water of this river in Mathura and Vrindavan, which have tremendous religious value, turns out to be the water of drains and sewage coming all the way from Delhi and Agra. There are several reasons for this state of affair. The use of water by Eastern and Western Yamuna canals for irrigational purposes and hydroelectric power production severely affect the flow. The drains and sewage emanating from cities located along the bank of the river have been continuously polluting the river water.
2. ***Increasing pollution:*** There are different types of pollutions such as domestic, agricultural, and industrial which have been regularly and continuously contributing organic and inorganic matter in the water. The location of towns and cities along the bank augments the process of pollution in the river because of the bio-degradable and non-bio-degradable wastes. Interestingly, the level of pollution is especially very high close to towns and cities (Figure 14.3). The dissolved oxygen content is either very low or conspicuous by its absence. Continuous flow of sewage waste, dumping of caracas and use of water for bathing of cattle contribute significantly in loading of pathogens in the river, making it unsuitable for drinking purposes. The organic, inorganic and toxic pollutants, which are generated from agriculture and industrial sources, get accumulated especially during dry season adversely affecting the aquatic life.

   The load of organic matter between Delhi and Etawah stretch is so high that it consumes the entire dissolved oxygen present in the river water. There are some sewage treatment plants especially in big cities but often they become dysfunctional due to power shortage and, thus, this adds to the problem of pollution in a most concentrated manner.
3. ***Deteriorating ecosystem:*** There has been very large scale deforestation in the catchment area of the Yamuna river. As a result, the process of soil erosion has increased and the mixing of high amount of silt and mud has enhanced the turbidity. The domestic and industrial waste water have accelerated the turbidity. This has not gone well with the biotic life of aquatic ecosystem. It has played a negative role in maintaining the ecosystem and thereby the different species of flora and fauna which enrich the ecosystem. This has been causing a very serious situation as the sustainability of life support system has been adversely affected. The rich ecosystem

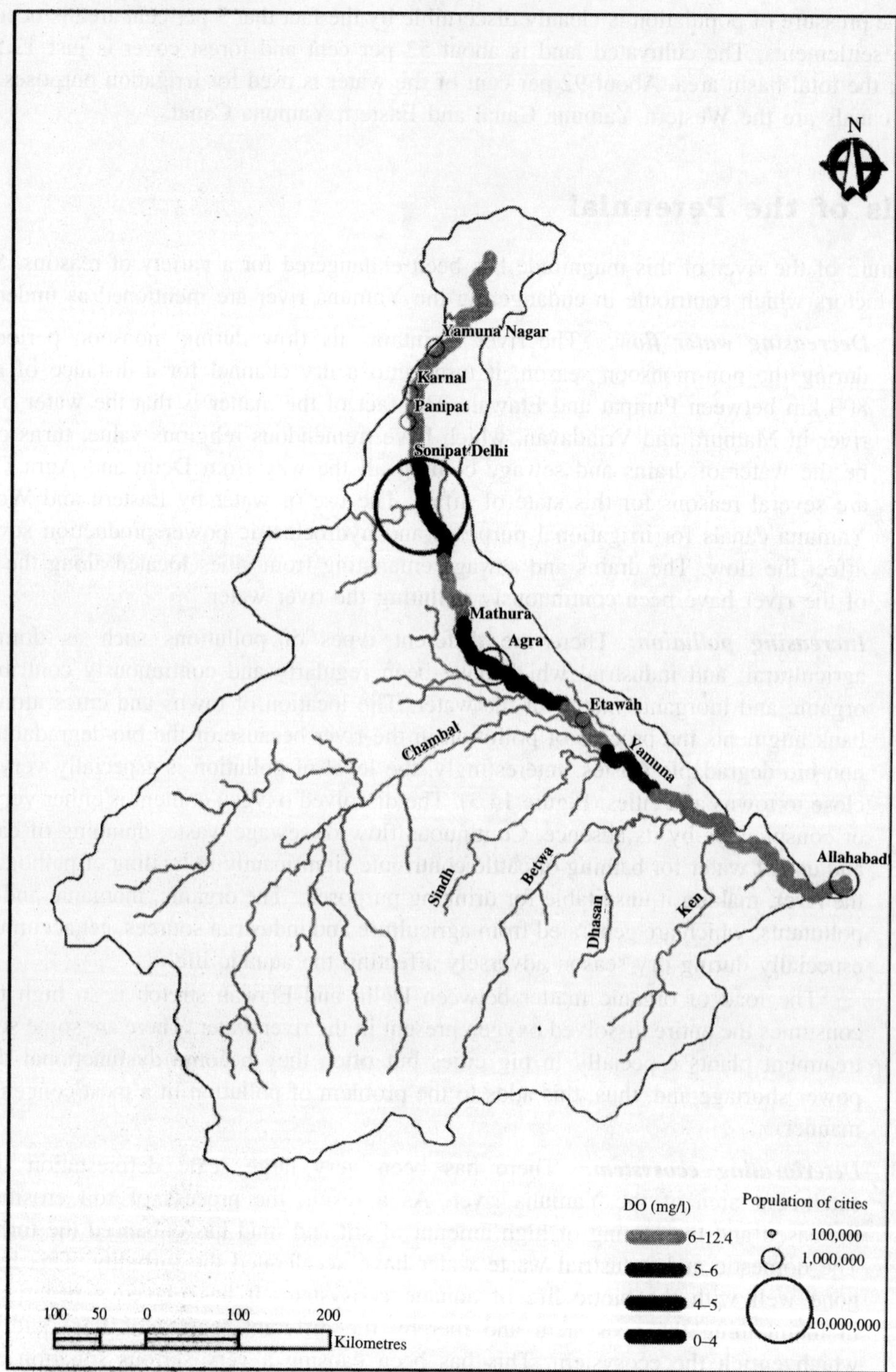

Figure 14.3 Water quality status of the Yamuna river based on dissolved oxygen.

which should have been a great natural wealth has been missing. Several developed countries in the world have been able to protect the river ecosystem which adds charm and fascination to tourists. It could be a rich source of variety of fishes and birds, but the turbidity of water has forced them not to flourish because the quality of water is highly contaminated.

4. ***Increasing encroachment of land:*** This is a very common phenomenon. There is a very large scale grabbing and encroachment of land near the river bank. This has enhanced the process of soil erosion as well as the agricultural pollution. The bank of the rivers is not natural any more. There are several anthropogenic activities which have disturbed the ecological setting of the river. The river bank served as common property resource (CPR). It does not merely promote, it also helps in maintaining the ecological balance but this CPR has vanished due to accelerated pace of encroachment especially due to expanding built up areas of the urban settlements.

Some Conflict Resolutions

There is too much talk on water harvesting but we are not able to save this natural wealth which is available in our perennial rivers. Our ancestors were forward looking people who could foresee problems of future. The Yamuna river, which has been considered so very pious since ages is in danger of disappearing. There is immediate and urgent need to take following measures to save this river:

1. ***Desilting the bed:*** Over the period of years, on account of large scale erosion due to deforestation, the width of river has increased but the depth has declined. This has often culminated into flood. There is a need for a large scale dredging and desilting of the river throughout the course especially the stretch which extends in plain. The desilting will prevent not only the flood but also allow the continuous flow of water in its channel. In fact, all the rivers of northern India need desilting at a very large scale in order to conserve the water from going waste. This is the need of the hour in view of shortage of water in foreseeable future.
2. ***Arresting pollution:*** This is one of the major problems especially in this river. This river like the Ganga is considered to be of great religious significance but the water is highly polluted and this causes several problems such as different type of water born diseases. The cause of pollution has already been enumerated. However, some of the steps which may be taken to overcome the problem of pollution are: (a) Construction of underground drains from each city which does not mix with the river water instead terminates in agricultural fields, (b) the treatment of solid and liquid waste emanating from industries, (c) prevention of immersion of idols and caracas of dead bodies in the river water by law and its strict implementation, (d) containing the brackishness and turbidity of the water by taking frequent samples.
3. ***Enriching ecosystem:*** The cleanliness of the water and afforestation along the bank of the river are only ways by which the ecosystem can be enriched. There are several hot spots along the Yamuna river where endangered species of flora and fauna can be

preserved. The biosphere reserves and wild life sanctuaries can be easily developed near the confluence points of the Chambal, the Betwa, the Sindh, the Ken and the Hindon tributaries. The large scale afforestation along the river bank will not only prevent the soil erosion, it will also help in reducing the organic and inorganic pollution and maintaining the eco balance. Several varieties of fish can be introduced to make the water cleaner and richer in terms of quality.

4. ***Defining the territorial limits:*** Defining the territorial limits of the Yamuna river is imperative. In fact this is important in case of all the major rivers in order to protect them from being encroached. This is a very serious menace which our rivers have been encountering owing to accelerated pace of urbanization and this has also resulted into large scale damage of different kinds of species. The delimitation of territorial limit of the Yamuna river like any other Indian river should be done at the earliest in order to prevent any further damage to the ecology of the river. This may be done by appointing experts having specialization in spatial sciences. Nothing should be allowed to be done within the territorial limit of the river. This step will automatically take care of the acute problems of water flow shortage, ecology and pollution which pose serious challenges to the survival of the Yamuna river.
5. ***Implementing watershed planning:*** The river needs integrated treatment for its sustainability and this is possible only through scrupulous management of water and land which are the two major ingredients of a watershed. There is an urgent need to identify mini, meso and macro watersheds along both the banks of the river. These watersheds may be planned both in terms of structural and non-structural elements. The structural elements may be related to infrastructural developments such as social, economic and cultural institutions, check dams, roads, power and communication whereas the non-structural elements may be related to development policies and their implementing committees or bodies. The monitoring and feedback mechanism has got to be built into this process of development. This will help promote the development of pisciculture, animal husbandry, crop diversification and cottage and small scale agro-based industries which are urgently needed in order to retain the exodus of people from rural to urban areas.

Conclusion

Rivers serve as lifeline in the regional development process. The mythology attached with the Yamuna river clearly indicates that this has been a very important lifeline of northern India insofar as the development of agriculture and economy is concerned. However, from the aforesaid discussion, it is evident that the Yamuna river has been experiencing pollution for a variety of reasons; the water flow has been decreasing and the entire river ecosystem has been endangered mainly on account of uncalled for anthropogenic activities. It is being increasingly realized that the situation has come to a pause mainly on account of increasing pressure of human population. The time has come that we should immediately try to free these rivers much before they are chocked. There are several measures which may help solve the problems and these are: dredging the river bed, controlling pollution, enriching ecosystem besides implementing the watershed planning for integrated and sustainable development of the Yamuna basin.

References

Rai, R.K., R.C. Trivedi, Alka Upadhyay, P.E. Kadam (2010), *Integrated Water Resources Management and Water Quality Modeling of River Yamuna Basin*, National River Conservation Directorate, Ministry of Environment and Forests.

CSE (2009), *State of Pollution in Yamuna*, Centre for Science and Environment, Delhi, India.

CPCB (2006), *Water Quality Status of Yamuna River* (1999–2005), Central Pollution Control Board, Ministry of Environment and Forests, Assessment and Development of River Basin Series: ADSORBS/41/2006–07.

15

Water Resource Management of the Brahmaputra Basin

S.C. Mukhopadhyay

Abstract: The Ganga–Brahmaputra basin is the most densely populated river basin of the world. It has, therefore, great implications in terms of water resources management. The Brahmaputra basin alone spreads over seven broad geomorphic divisions with different landforms and land use types. This chapter analyzes the applied hydro-geomorphic characteristics of the Brahmaputra basin besides focusing on the problems of cooperation between two smaller upstream countries (Bhutan and Nepal) and the larger downstream country (India). This chapter also throws light on integrated water resource management and the global water partnership besides focusing on the importance of the availability of potable water and traditional wisdom in water harvesting and resource management.

Keywords: Decentralized, IWRM, Global World Water, Seismotectonics, Traditional Wisdom, WCD, Global Water Partnership

Introduction

We know that water is a resource which is regenerated in a highly decentralized manner on the surface of the earth. Contemporary challenges in water resource management including new programmes like *Integrated Water Resource Management* (IWRM) have to be understood at all levels, from the local or the micro, to the macro. Large river basins like the Ganga and the Brahmaputra, etc. as considered in the present paper are well-identified geographical areas for developing these understandings mainly at macro levels (Mukhopadhyay, 1982, 2000, 2004). In view of the profound hydro-geomorphological as well as geo-political importance of the large river basins, this author has put much weightage on the Brahmaputra Basin as a case study too. In an applied hydro-geomorphological sense, the IWRM, etc. relate to focus the significance of the recent remarkable development programmes on water resources use and management that have a wider scope than the prevailing methods (the conventional technical focus of water resource education, etc). Virtually, these incorporate concerns of—(a) ecological sustainability, (b) equity and (c) poverty of the developing countries. It also involves gender relations and democratic governance into professional water education (Bandyopadhyay, 2006, Mollinga, et al., 2006).

Objectives and Methods

The major objective of this paper is to study the principal aspects of hydro-geomorphology of the Brahmaputra Basin including recent programmes of water resources management (such as IWRM and others) both qualitatively and quantitatively. In an applied sense, it includes primarily (a) a detailed analysis of water resource development and management, geohazards like floods and landslides and current status of natural environment of the Ganga–Brahmaputra Basin (GBB) in general and the Brahmaputra Basin in particular. It extends from Uttarakhand in the north and to the border of Bangladesh (in the south) via Tsangpo–Gorge downstreams. Besides, (b) an attempt has also been made to evaluate the effects of fluvial dynamics and neo-tectonics being manifested in the tectonically unstable terrain under consideration. All the fluvial and neo-tectonic features are developed as the results of the interactions of natural and anthropogenic parameters against the back drop of the environmental changes in the Eastern Himalaya and surrounding terrain establishing the cause and effect relationship both in space and time.

The methods adopted relate broadly to the three major stages—(a) Pre-field, (b) Field work, and (c) Post-field methods with an application of advanced techniques of measurement and analysis. The current data, information and evidences have been procured from fieldwork as the primary source primarily by the author in terms of intensive field survey in the constituent geographic divisions. In regard to the modern methods and techniques—the related IRS-ID LISS (III and IV) satellite data of different seasons (Winter, Pre Monsoon, S.W. Monsoon and the Post monsoon, etc.) 2004–2005 covering major parts of the Lower Brahmaputra Basin have also been procured (Mukhopadhyay, 1982). Frequent field checks have also been conducted in various sites particularly in the lower geomorphic divisions with great applied hydrogeomorphological interests. In addition, an intensive fieldwork was carried out to have the data and information of the socio-economic variables.

Locational Characteristics

Covering an area of about 580,000.00 sq. km, the Brahmaputra Basin spreads over seven broad geomorphic divisions with different landforms and land use types within four countries (India, China, Bhutan and Bangladesh) and six border states in India. The study area is bounded by the latitudes 25°00' N to 28°10' N and longitudes 88°0' E to 98°30' E approximately mainly in India. The Brahmaputra is considered to be the mightiest dynamic river in the world flowing through a series of seismotectonically active zone of very complex tectonic framework (Figure 15.1). The diametrically opposite drainage pattern has imparted a universal uniqueness to the Brahmaputra valley. In view of the limitations of conventional study of neo-tectonic activities, remote sensing technique serves as a very useful tool to draw a meaningful correlation between neotectonism and resulting land instability and flood hazards also (Acharyya, 2005; Mukhopadhyay, 2004, 1982; Vaidyanadhan, 2002; Nandy, 2001; Goswami, 1985).

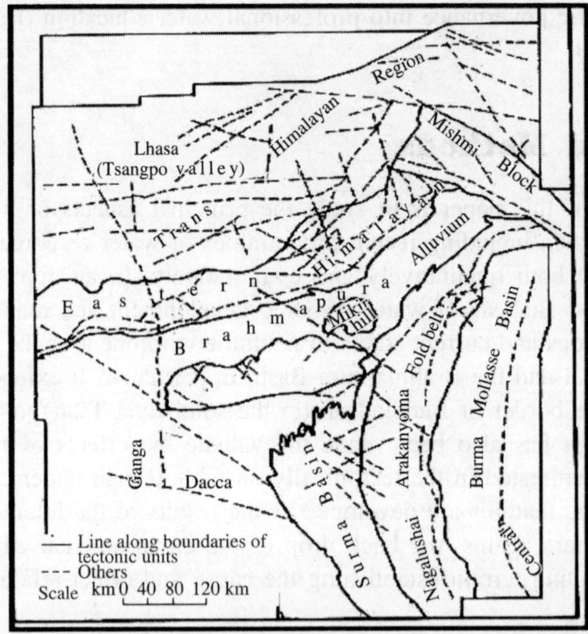

Figure 15.1 Geomorphological divisions of the Brahmaputra basin.

The weather pattern in the basin is dominated by the summer monsoon, under the influence of which there is a wide variation in the level of precipitation in the various parts of the year as well as the basin (Tables 15.1 and 15.2). The spatial and temporal inequity presents the main challenges in water management in the basin. About 80 per cent of the annual precipitation occurs within a span of 2.5 summer months from July to September. More precisely, about half of the total rainfall occurs in storms spread over a total period of about 100 hours. Thus, a large part of the annual run-off flows out during the monsoon months.

Table 15.1 Mean annual peak discharges recorded on the Ganga–Brahmaputra rivers in India

Sites (Stations)	*Highest discharge on record* ($m^3\ s^{-1}$)	*Mean peak discharge* ($m^3\ s^{-1}$)	*Ratio (highest & mean discharge)*
Ganga at Farakka	72,915	55,776	1.31
Brahmaputra at Pandu	72,794	51,156	1.42

Table 15.2 Mean annual run-off in the Ganga–Brahmaputra river basin of India

Rivers	*Catchment area* (km^2)	*Annual Run-off* (in $10^6 m^3\ y^{-1}$)
Ganga	750,000	493,000
Brahmaputra	580,000	510,000

The basin suffers from water scarcity of varying degrees during the rest of the year, especially in the pre-monsoon months of April to June. Additional complexities to the problems already posed by nature are contributed by the fact that the GBM is an international basin, and regional cooperation is needed for making more holistic water management strategies. The availability of this great volume of monsoon run-off has been seen by many as a vital resource base for poverty alleviation and economic advancement in the basin. There is no doubt that wise management of this volume of water and utilization of the hydropower potential latent in them, constitute a good tool for economic advancement of the region. In terms of the volume of the run-off, the GBM basin stands third highest at the global level, next only to that of the Amazon and the Congo. However, in terms of the number of people residing in a basin and depending on its waters, with a population of about 700 millions, the GBM basin comes at the top. What is more important is that about a third of this population lives below the poverty line. Thus, in the GBM basin the world's largest number of the poor people co-exists with the world's third largest river run-off. About 75 per cent of this large population is located in the Ganga sub basins, which has extensive areas under intensive agriculture and has an appreciable industrial activity. This has put an enormous pressure on the quality as well as quantity of the water resources in the Ganga sub basin. The rest of this population lives in the Brahmaputra and Meghna sub-basins, which has a much larger annual run-off but much lower level of economic activity.

It is important to note that over the last one decade, in particular after the two successive years of widespread flooding of Bangladesh (1987 and 1988), the problems of water resource management in the Ganga–Brahmaputra Basin (GBB) has gathered worldwide attention. The idea of the Flood Action Plan has emerged as a dominant feature in the context of Bangladesh. A number of independent papers have also been published, though many of them represent local or national contexts and situations. In those cases in which the totality of the river basin is considered, there is often a lack of a uniform identification of the basin boundary (Table 15.3). In order to have comparative understanding and to proceed towards ecologically appropriate suggestions for water management, it will be necessary to follow a uniform boundary of the Ganga–Brahmaputra basin identified through accurate hydrological considerations independent of political boundaries.

Table 15.3 Area of the Ganga–Brahmaputra basin by countries and geographical regions

Countries	*Basin area in different regions* (m.ha)				
	Mountain	*Hills*	*Plains*	*Southern fringe*	*Total*
Bangladesh	–	–	12.90		12.90
Bhutan	4.50	–	–		4.50
India	14.94	5.72	54.47	34.71	109.84
Nepal	11.89	2.11	–	–	14.00
Tibet	33.30	–	–	–	33.30
Total	64.63	5.72	69.48		174.54

Source: Based on Mukhopadhyay (1986) and Bandyopadhyay (2006).

It has already been hinted that the GBB is one of the most densely populated river basins in the world and its population is predominantly concentrated in the fertile and industrialized Ganga basin (Bandyopadhyay, 2006). In addition, the GBB is characterized by some unique ecological and socio-political diversities and complexities, which give the basin a number of typical advantages as well as difficulties in the utilization of its water resources.

Water Utilization Pattern in the Ganga–Brahmaputra Basin

India is among the foremost countries in the world in exploiting its river water resources. Remarkable achievement has been made in conserving the water resources for irrigation, generation of hydropower and domestic water supply during the five decades of planned development of independent India. The International Food Policy Research Institute opines that India's water demand in the next 25 years will increase from over 600 BCM to 900 BCM. The per capita availability will fall to 1700 cubic meters from today's 2200 cubic meters, which is about one third less than the global average. In less than a decade, underground water tables have dropped from three meters to 20 m in Nagaland, Mizoram, Assam, Bengal, and Tripura, etc. (Nandy, 2001; Vaidyanadhan, 2002).

The current stage of utilization of surface and groundwater resources is about 70 per cent and 30 per cent, respectively. Protection of valley and flood plain environment is one of the major priorities. The wet land is a major source of bio-diversity covering an area of 17,000 sq. km (5.18 per cent) against the total area of 3.28 million sq. km. Major wetlands comprise 14,308 sq. km of natural and 252 sq. km of man-made wetlands distributed in 93 sites of which 85 wetlands are considered to be of international importance. The Ministry of Environment and Forest estimates only 28 per cent area under total protection and 45 per cent are subject to moderate to high threat. India is fast moving towards water stress zone. In most parts of our country, water is present at a depth of 0–50 m–37 per cent has water at depth of 3–10 m, and 58 per cent areas have depth below 40 m. Vast stretches of the Ganga and the Brahmaputra rivers continue to remain most polluted. Coliform bacteria are present at the rates of 7000–7 million in each mm of water. A survey undertaken by CPCB of 241 class II cities (population between 50,000–100,000) indicates that on average 90 per cent water supplied is polluted. Only 1.6 per cent of the waste water is treated before discharge. According to TERI, with the rise in the demand of water for irrigation, industry and for domestic purposes, it is estimated that the demand would outstrip availability by the year 2025. In India 30 per cent of agricultural land has been converted to urban and Industrial uses. Topsoil in many states (within the Ganga–Brahmaputra Basin) is polluted by nickel, chromium, zinc or lead. 6000 million tonnes of soil is washed off the surface every year and 248 kg potassium gets depleted from one hectare of soil. Indiscriminate use of chemical fertilizers (in tea gardens in particular) has adversely affected the health of the soil and underground water. From 1951 to 2001 use of chemical fertilizers and pesticides has increased by 15,000 per cent. TERI has estimated that the area affected by soil erosion will increase from 1660 lakh hectares in 1997 to 2000 lakh hectares in 2047, and the area under waterlogged soils will increase from 130 lakh ha in 2001 to 396 lakh ha in 2047. Areas where the soil is affected by salinity are likely to increase from 112 lakh ha in 2001 to 220 lakh ha in 2047. According to TERI estimates, the industrial wood requirement is likely to increase nearly four-fold from 350 lakh tonnes in 2001 to 1420 lakh tonnes in 2047. In the long-term perspective, forestry management will have to deal with the growing demand for industrial wood and fuel wood.

The pattern of water utilization in the Ganga–Brahmaputra Basin and adjacent areas are shown in the Figure 15.2.

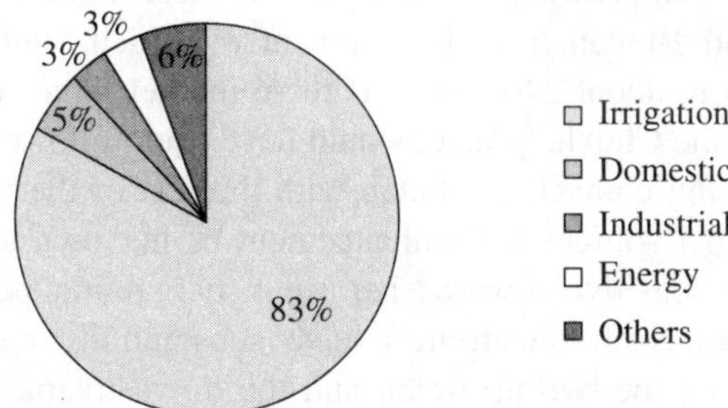

Figure 15.2 Water utilization pattern in Ganga–Brahmaputra basin and adjacent areas.

About 83 per cent (501 BCM) is devoted to irrigation followed by domestic (30 BCM), industrial (20 BCM), energy (20 BCM) and others (34 BCM). Apparently irrigation happens to be the major activity where utilization is maximum. However, there are several physical and cultural constraints in the optimum utilization of water resource. The removal of these constraints requires a level of political wisdom and leadership in the region that, unfortunately, has been conspicuous by its absence in the recent past. Addressing these constraints in an innovative and dispassionate manner and opening up of the path for widely acceptable regional cooperation appears to be one of the most important challenges facing the South East Asian region in the 21st century. Otherwise, with demand in the lean period outstripping the supply, the region runs the risk of emergence of further water conflicts in the coming years. In order to understand the related problems and the nature of the conflicts to the resolution of the emerging conflicts, the main elements of the complexities and sensitivities associated with the process of collaboration on the Himalayan rivers may be reviewed. First, the nature of the problems in cooperation between the two smaller upstream countries, Bhutan and Nepal, and the larger downstream country, India, may be thoroughly reviewed.

Water Utilization and Joint Ventures

In the Eastern section, the independent mountain kingdom of Bhutan receives ample monsoonal precipitation which is drained by several major perennial rivers like the Amochu (Torsa), the Wangchu (Raidak), the Mouchu (Sankosh) and the Dangmechu (Manas). These rivers flow mainly from the north to the south direction and it is estimated that the total hydro-potential of Bhutan at 30 p.c. load factor is 20,000 MW. This is a potential resource of significance for the kingdom. Though the domestic market for electricity in Bhutan is limited, there is a very large demand for peak power from the urban industrial areas of India across the border in the south, for which hydro power is an excellent source. This led Bhutan–India accord in 1974 for the construction of the 336 MW Chukha Hydel power project on the river Wangchu. This plant was designed, financed, and constructed through a grant and loan agreement between Bhutan and India. The project was constructed by an autonomous Indo-Bhutan Chukha Project Authority chaired by Bhutan and managed by an Indian engineer. According to Rao (1994), the Indian engineer managing the Chukha project, it stands as a testimony of Indo-Bhutan friendship and co-operation. The availability of power from this project increased electricity consumption in Bhutan and encouraged some industrial growth. According to Verghese and there are several collaborative projects between India and Bhutan, full development of which, within a decade, could raise Bhutan's installed capacity to about 2400 MW. If mere market forces of supply and demand for peak-power were decisive, the Chukha project would have been followed up by the several others.

More recently, increasing contact of Bhutan with the rest of the world, easy availability of international aid from global sources and enhancement of her own technical competence, has made Bhutan much more sensitive towards her weak bargaining position in the agreements between the two countries. Such sensitivities have substantially reduced early prospects of further co-operation between the two upstream and the downstream countries. The difficulties in reaching a simple sales agreement for Chukha electricity between the governments of Bhutan and India is a good indicator of the degree of the difficulty associated with developing new collaborations on joint water development projects.

The problems between Nepal and India have also grown along similar lines. It becomes evident on the consideration of topography, drainage, climate, etc. that nature of the upstream–downstream ecological linkage of both Bhutan and Nepal with India is largely similar. Actually, co-operative development of water resource in the case of India and Nepal has a longer history and a larger dimension. Here, the very first formal agreement for co-operation between India (then under British rule) and Nepal (then under Rana rule) was made as far back in 1927, for the construction of a barrage near Tanakpur across the river Sharda (Mahakali) which forms the western border between the two countries. The two countries have deep cultural ties, friendly links and the boundary of the nation–states are much more recent in comparison to people to people interaction in the region. Nepal's immense hydro-potential of 45,825 MW cannot be economically utilized within the country and the growing industrial economy of India will surely be willing to buy the peak power produced in Nepal.

Joint venture on the water projects to harness the water resources and control floods are in the interest of both the countries. In the case of Nepal–India collaboration, both hydropower and irrigation have received significant importance, while flood control is also expected to be important element in future big dam projects. However, the problems associated with collaboration between a technically superior and economically stronger India, as was noted earlier in the case of Bhutan, is also present in the case of Nepal. An impression has been created in Nepal, and Indian interest in joint water projects is guided by an agenda of 'independent development'.

Dam Building in the Basin

From less than 300 large dams existing at the beginning of planned development, the number of dams constructed has gone up to about 4300. As a result of this the total live storage capacity of dams and reservoirs completed in the country has augmented upto about 177 BCM since independence. Besides, dams to create an additional live storage capacity of 75 BCM are under various stages of construction. Further, dams under planning will provide an additional live storage of 132 BCM. Present net ground draft is about 115 BCM.

A series of large dams have been planned on the Himalayan rivers, particularly in the Ganga–Brahmaputra-Meghna (GBM) river basin in Asia. Figures 15.3 and 15.4 show the

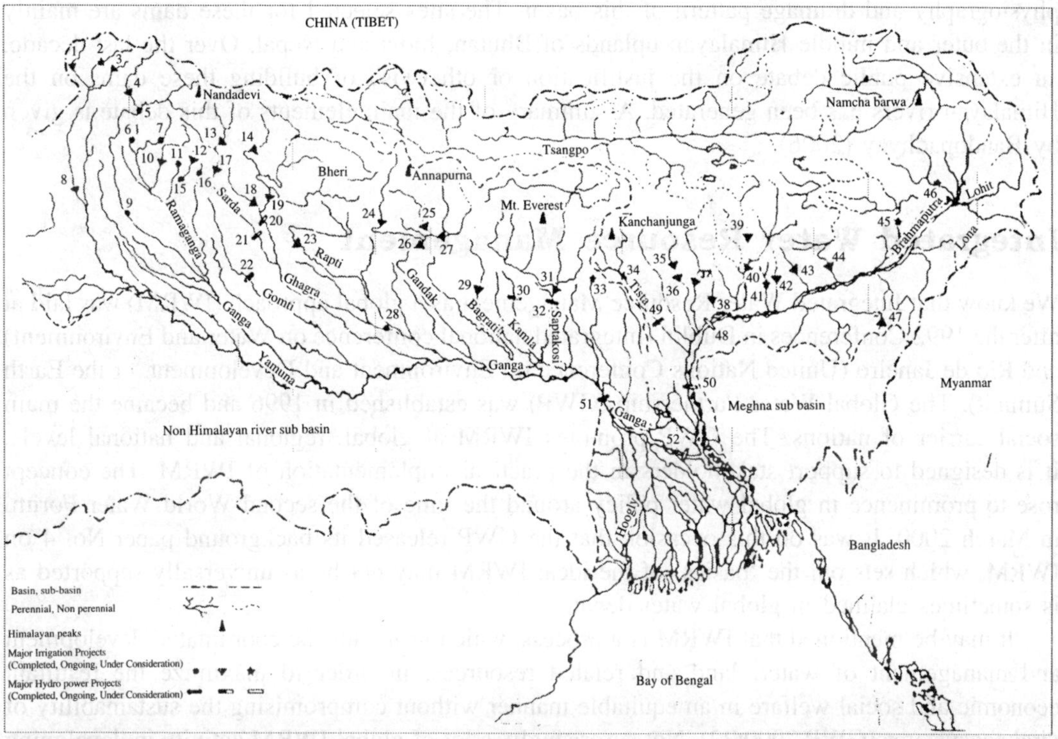

Figure 15.3 Hydroelectric power plant locations in the Ganga–Brahmaputra basin.

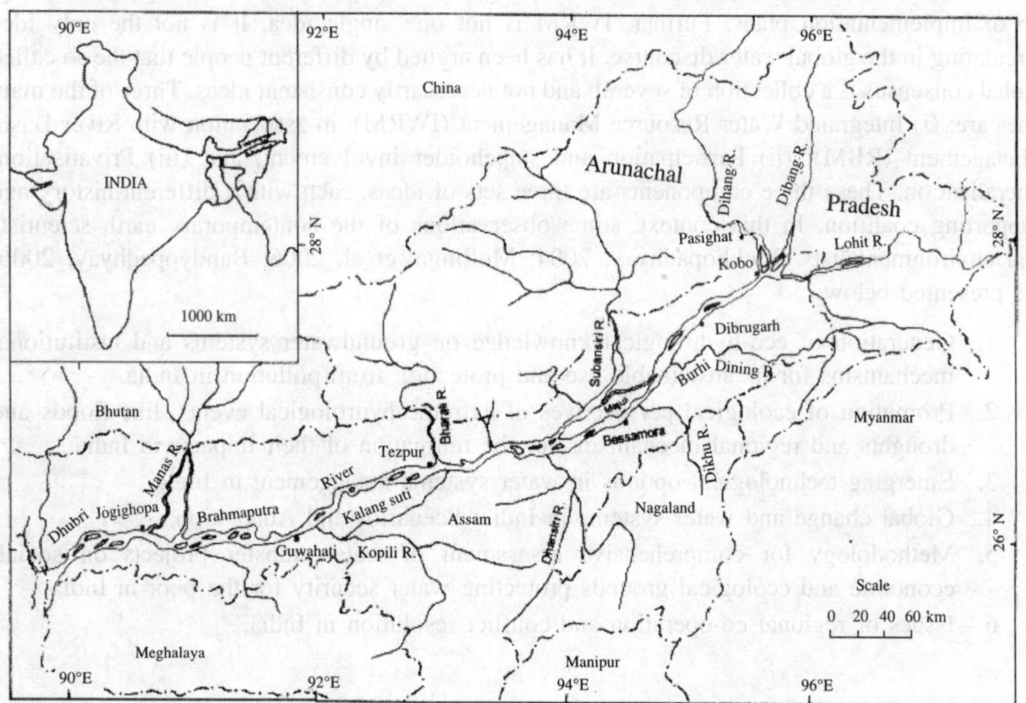

Figure 15.4 Drainage map of Brahmaputra basin.

physiography and drainage pattern of this basin. The sites selected for these dams are mainly in the outer and middle Himalayan uplands of Bhutan, India and Nepal. Over the last decade, an extensive public debate on the justification or otherwise of building these dams on the Himalayan rivers has been generated. A summary of the main elements of this debate is given by Bandopadhyay (2006).

Integrated Water Resource Management

We know that Integrated Water Resource Management as a global approach (IWRM) was laid at after the 1992 Conferences in Dublin (Integrated national conference on Water and Environment) and Rio de Janeiro (United Nations Conference on Environment and Development, or the Earth Summit). The Global Water Partnership (GWP) was established in 1996 and became the main social carrier of nations. The GWP promotes IWRM at global, regional and national levels. It is designed to support stakeholders in the practical implementation of IWRM. The concept rose to prominence in global water policy around the time of the second World Water Forum in March 2000. It was on this occasion that the GWP released its background paper No. 4 on IWRM, which sets out the 'basics' of the idea. IWRM may not be as universally supported as is sometimes claimed in global water debate.

It may be mentioned that IWRM is a process, which promotes the coordinated development and management of water, land and related resources, in order to maximize the resultant economic and social welfare in an equitable manner without compromising the sustainability of vital ecosystems (GWP 2000:22). Not surprisingly, a lot of global IWRM activity in developing countries is focused on promotion/awareness rising, networking, capacity building and drawing-up of implementation plans. Further, IWRM is not one single idea, It is not the only idea circulating in the global water discourse. It has been argued by different people that the so called global consensus is a collection of several, and not necessarily consistent ideas. Three of the main ones are: (i) Integrated Water Resource Management (IWRM), in association with River Basin Management (RBM); (ii) Participation and stakeholder involvement; and (iii) Privatisation/ liberalization. These three components are three sets of ideas, each with a different history and supporting coalition. In this context, some observations of the contemporary earth scientists and environmentalists (Mukhopadhyay, 2004; Mollinga, et al. 2006; Bandyopadhyay, 2006) are presented below:

1. Generation of eco-hydrological knowledge on groundwater systems and institutional mechanisms for its sustainable use and protection from pollution in India,
2. Promotion of ecological perspectives of extreme hydrological events, like floods and droughts and regional mechanisms for the mitigation of their impacts in India,
3. Emerging technological options in water systems management in India.
4. Global change and water systems in India: Scenarios and Adaptation,
5. Methodology for comprehensive assessment of water transfer projects on social, economic and ecological grounds protecting water security for the poor in India,
6. Issues of regional co-operation and conflict resolution in India,

7. Wider application of economics in the making of water policy and valuation of ecosystem services of water to promote conservation and sustainable use in India,
8. Generation of eco-hydrological knowledge on surface water systems in particular on the ecosystem services and assessment of environmental flows in India and social dimensions of water systems in South Asia.

Conclusion

The procurement of potable water—providing supplies to meet the essential water necessity for more than a billion population has become a great challenge in India. In connection with the emerging issues on water use it seems wise to refer to the stand of the Mardel Plata Conference in 1977 relating to the need to provide safe drinking water and sanitation and to reduce contamination of water, and UN General Assembly proclamation (1980) of the International Drinking Water Supply and Sanitation Decade (1981–90) emphasizing the basic questions of equity and protection of human health. Now, rapid growth of human population world over has given a con-committant boost to the technological solutions for water resource till need for an alternate integrated management has been felt. In other words, the technological solutions having reached to a saturation level in various terrains called for a rethinking and proposed to look towards traditional methods for successful advantageous marriage between the two, i.e. technology and tradition. In India, for example, traditional wisdom or education in water, harvesting and resource management were largely lost under the impact and social assimilation of technological education. The result has been the development of mind set proliferation amongst the vast population in urban, semi-urban and rural habitats for a technological solution of water resource problem. All education and enlightments centered around such thoughts for over last three to four centuries. The trend meets a reversal not totally banishing the technology but by using technology to the extent it can enrich the traditional systems: Due weightage should be given to; (i) Rainwater project harvesting from roof top (e.g., roof top rainwater harvesting for augmenting groundwater, etc.); (ii) Development of natural water sources like springs, rivers (by making them free from pollution); (iii) Development of terrain specific water harvesting structures to catch the run-off much of which goes to the sea, etc. Any suitable plan for water and land utilization is not just a function of terrain, slope, vegetation and precipitation but equal emphasis should be given to the dynamics of the processes involved in the build-up of the terrain concerned. The cultural landscapes in particular that might evolve during the process of development should especially harmonize with the physical environmental components like soil, vegetation, seismotectonics and geohydrolgical interactions. Therefore, an effective use of (a) modern methods and techniques, (b) active participation of people of the basin in the development schemes, (c) greater co-operation among the bordering states as well as countries are urgently needed.

References

Acharyya, S.K. (2005), North East India: A complex terrain of accreted continental blocks, *Proceedings of the Seminar on Minerals and Energy Resources of Eastern and North Eastern India*, Kolkata, 31–54.

Bandyopadhyay, J. (2006), *Integrated Water Systems Management in South Asia,* CDEP Occasional paper 09.IIM, Joka, Kolkata, 5–32.

Dasgupta, A.B and A.K. Biswas (2000), *Geology of Assam*, Geological Society of India, 17–31.

Goswami, D.C. (1985), Brahmaputra River, Assam, India. Physiography, Basin Denudation and Channel Aggradation, *Water Resource Research*, **21**(7), 955-957.

Mollinga, P.P. et al. (2006), *Integrated Water Resources Management*, Sage Publication, New Delhi.

Mukhopadhyay, S.C. (1982), *The Tista Basin—A Study in Fluvial Geomorphology*. K.P. Bagchi and Co. New Delhi.

Mukhopadhyay, S.C. (2004), Water Availability and Water Use in India, *Proc.Vol of the National Workshop cum Seminar on Water Security and Management of Water Resources*, NATMO, Kolkata, 262–270.

Mukhopadhyay, S.C. (2000), Basinal management of the Ganga–Brahmaputra Basin in India and Adjacent Countries, in: Prof. V.C. Jha (Ed.), *Geomorphology and Remote Sensing*, ACB Publication, Kolkata, 158–166.

Nandy, D.R. (2001), *Geodynamics of North Eastern India and the Adjoining Region*, ACB Publication, Kolkata.

Vaidyanadhan, R. (2002), *Geomorphology of the Indian Subcontinent*, ISRS, Dehradun.

16

Water Resource in Kashmir Valley A Scarcity in Plenty

Ali Mohammad and Abdul Bari Naik

Abstract: The distribution of water resources is extremely uneven in the valley of Kashmir. It is most plentiful in the low lying parts of the valley, while the uplands suffer from aridity imposed by its chronic deficiency. The valley has not been able to make optimal use of its water resources. This chapter highlights this issue by focusing on factors of water availability, surface and groundwater resources and the state of utilization of water resources.

Keywords: Bund, Cut-off, Torrents, Debris, Nambal, Outfall, Karewa, Kuhl

Introduction

Water in the Kashmir Valley is an extraordinary paradox. Considering the total run-off, area of water bodies and length of water courses, the Valley has no match in the Himalayas. In fact, its water features are the principal components in its scenic beauty. The geomorphic character of the Valley is, however, such that the distribution of water resources is extremely uneven—a situation which renders vast stretches of land totally or partially out of use either due to the excess of water or its deficiency. Water is most plentiful in the low-lying parts of the valley, which remain literally deluged, while the adjoining *Karewa* uplands suffer from aridity imposed by its chronic deficiency. In both these respects, the situation seriously constrains the optimal use of the Valley's land potential. The consequence is that the Valley presents the anomalous case of scarcity in the midst of plenty. The rivers carry large volumes of water which they cannot possibly contain as their channels get increasingly choked with silt, making floods a recurrent phenomenon with disastrous consequences on agriculture. Naturally, in the absence of any systematic scheme for water management, the spillover from the ever-rising channels spreads all over the low-lying tracts, which have been converted into extensive swamps, called the **Nambal.** The rest of the water flows out practically unharnessed, without being put to any substantial use before it escapes out of the Baramulla gorge. Recent data show that only a tiny fraction of this vast potential is being utilized for hydroelectric generation, the aggregate annual production from all power houses being about 20,000 kW The only other use of this enormous resource is in gradient irrigation, through the distribution system of *Kuhls*, in the making of which modern technology has hardly any contribution.

The above remarks are, however, relevant only in the context of the present understanding of the Valley's water potential, which is by no means complete. It is interesting to note that no serious attempt has yet been made to assess this potential, its mode of occurrence, spatial distribution and temporal variations in its availability. Evidently, no comprehensive planning is possible in the absence of such primary data, whether aimed at draining the swamps, augmenting water supply in agriculture or generating hydroelectricity. In fact, the present state of knowledge inhibits even the estimation of the gap between the water potential and the actual amount that is being used productivily.

An attempt will be made here to make an analytical study of the water resources of the valley, both surface and subterranean, temporal variations in its supply as perceived in the incidence of floods or droughts and the current level of its utilization.

Locational Characteristics of the Study Area

The valley of Kashmir is a unique geomorphic feature in the Western Himalayas. Lying in an elongated form (Figure 16.1), it presents the most picturesque view. The relative relief of the region varies between 1500–5000 m (Figure 16.2). Owing to its scenic beauty and moderately cool climate, this is known as Paradise on Earth. It compares well with Switzerland and Southern France as far as its climatic conditions are concerned. Drained by the Jhelum river system, this is about 135 km long and 32 km wide. Spreading over an area of about 17,670 km^2, it encompasses 7,100,382 people according to 2011 census. The 10 districts which make the valley are—Anantnag, Kulgam, Pulwama, Shupiyan, Budgam, Srinagar, Ganderbal, Bandipore, Baramula and Kupwara.

There are several depressions, lakes and springs in addition to the Jhelum and its tributaries. The valley may be divided into seventeen river basins (Figure 16.3).

Hydrological Network and Data

There is a great dearth of consistent hydrological data for Kashmir for any reasonable period of time. This makes a meaningful temporal study of local hydrological phenomena impossible. The meteorological observatory at Srinagar was opened in 1891 and at Gulmarg in 1897. The position has not substantially changed since then. Regular meteorological data are, however, available only for Srinagar, as the Gulmarg observatory functions only during the four summer months—June to September—for reasons best known to the IMD only.

The rainfall is measured at a number of places, though in many cases the records are far from consistent. Other than Srinagar, there are only four places—Wantipore (Pulwama), Anantnag, Uttarmachipura (Handwara), and Sri Partap Singhpura (Badgam)—which have rainfall records

Figure 16.1 Delineation of the Kashmir valley.

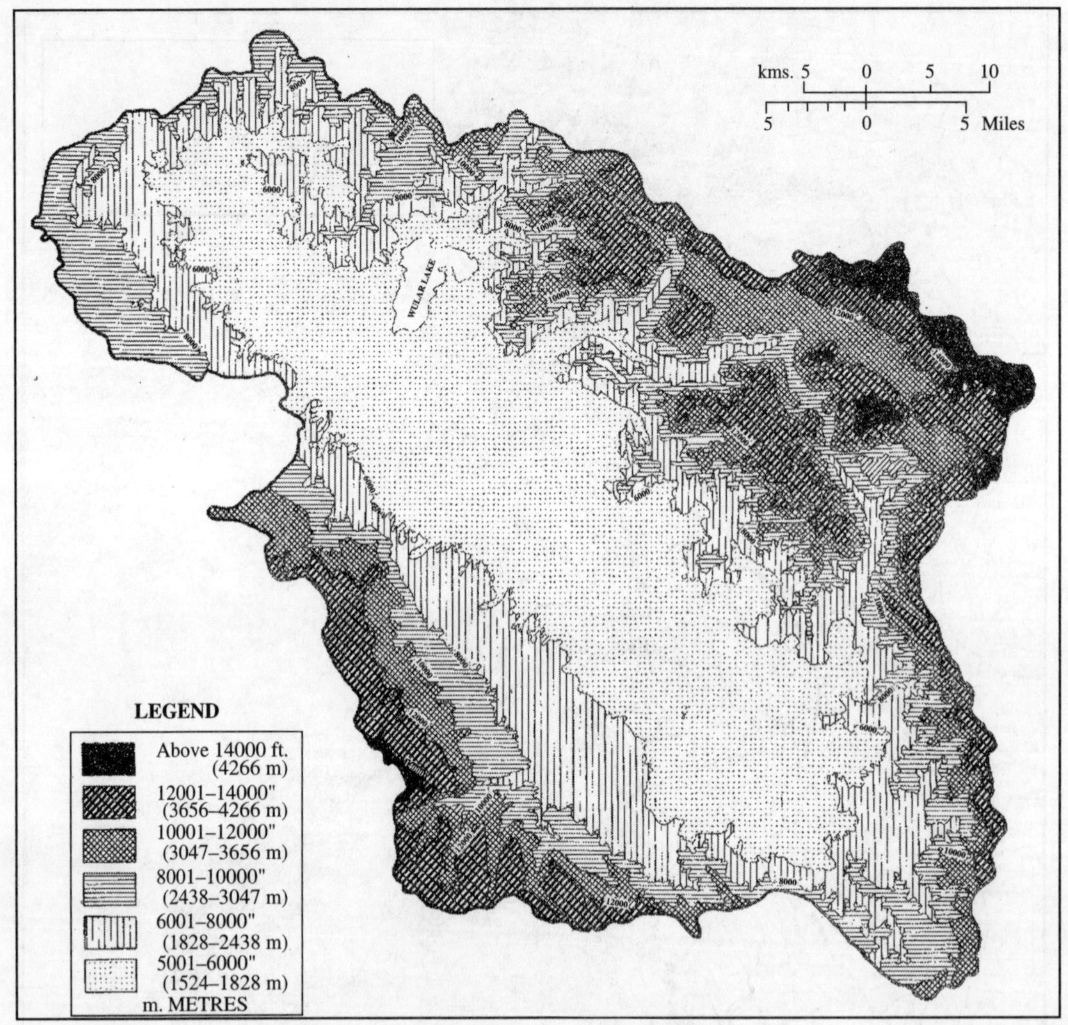

Figure 16.2 Relative relief of the Kashmir valley.

for at least seventy-four years. Kulgam and Baramulla have a record for seventy-two years; Langet fifty-eight years; Duru and Sopore fifty-eight years each. Mala Shahibag (Ganderbal) has a record for forty-four years only, beginning with 1924 and with a gap between 1933 and 1940.

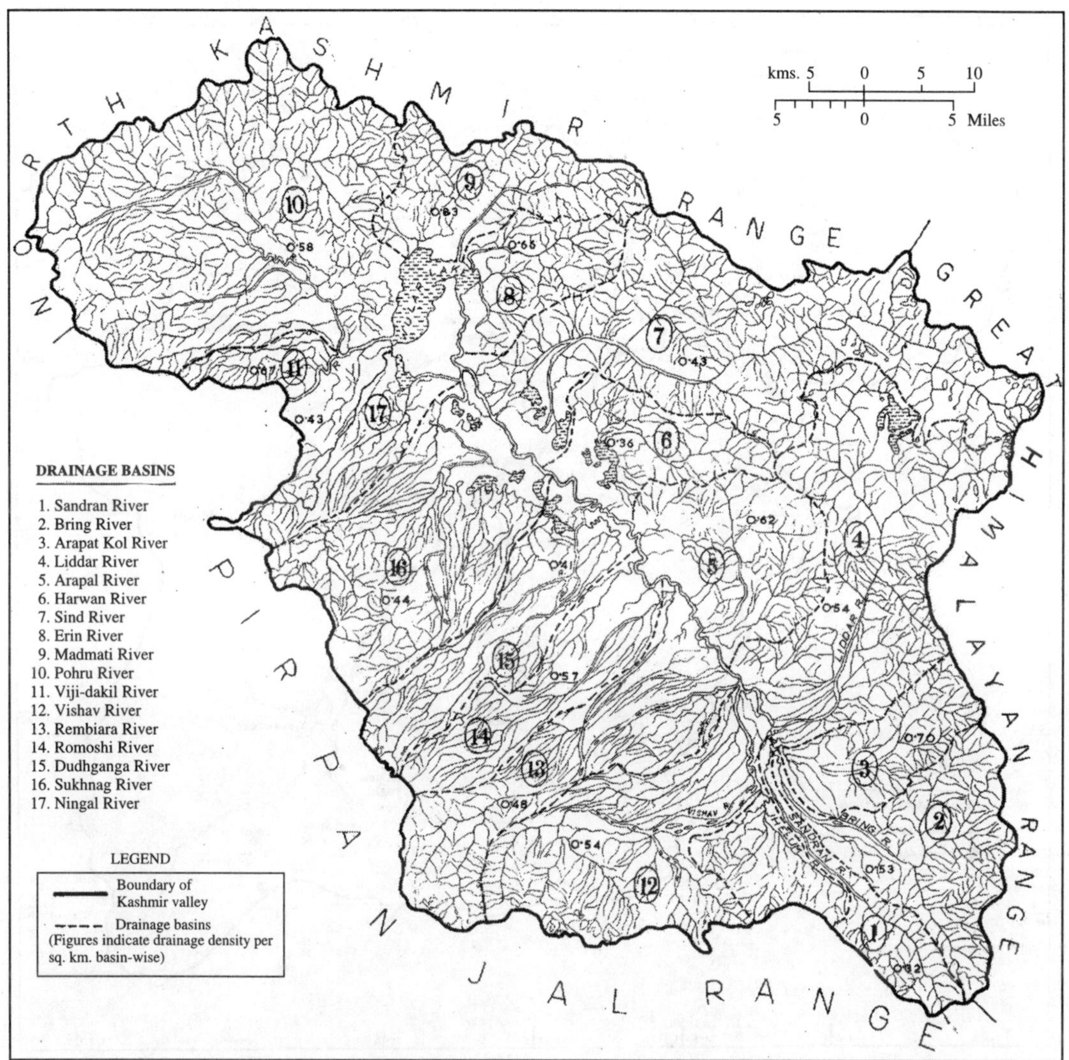

Figure 16.3 Drainage basins of the Kashmir valley.

Despite its heavy contribution to the valley's moisture supply, snowfall is only casually measured. There are snow gauges at the observatories of Srinagar city and aerodrome, and at Sonamarg, Gulmarg, Pahalgam, Qazigund and Banihal. Of these, the observations at the last five places are highly occasional (Figure 16.4).

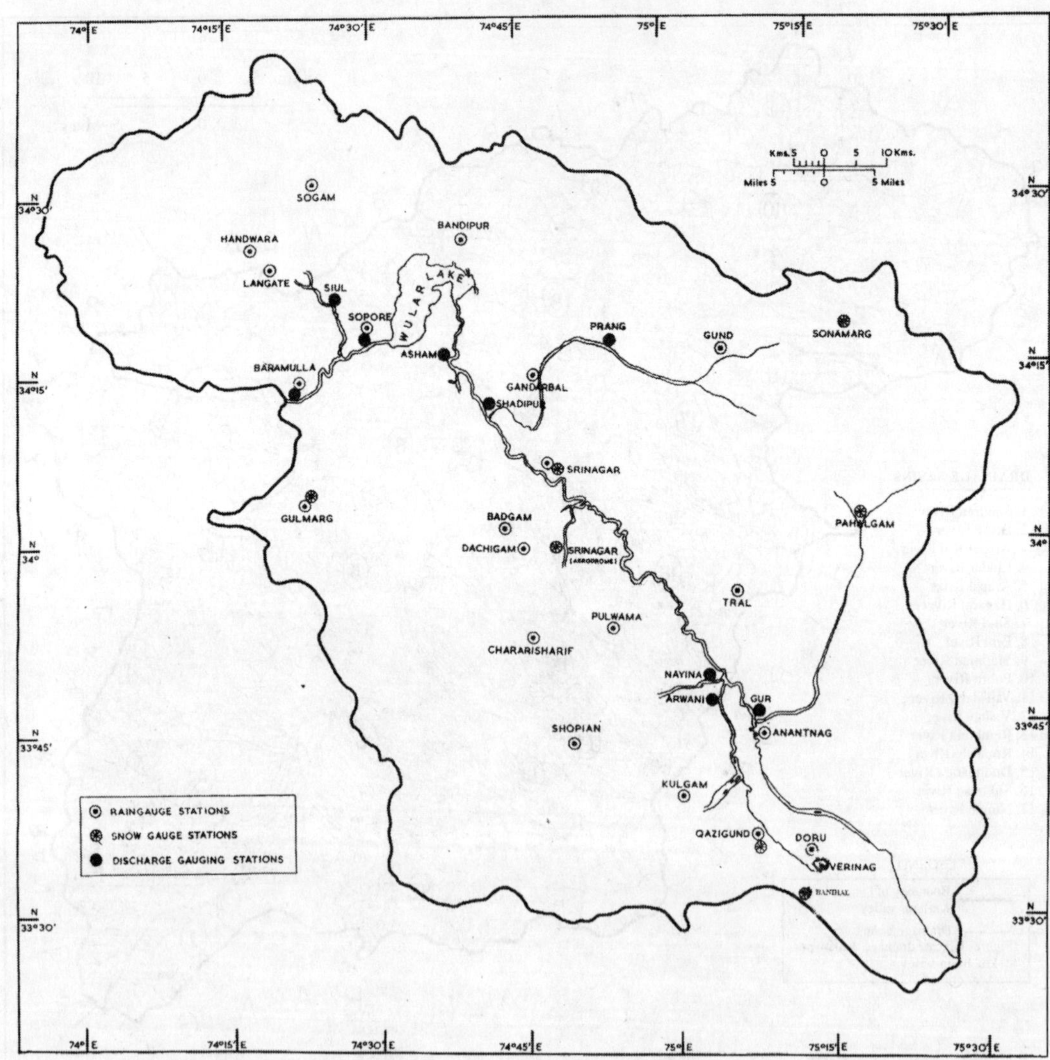

Figure 16.4 Hydrological network of the Kashmir valley.

Factors in Water Availability

The availability of water in a region is a function of the whole set of variables which determine the quantum of water inflow, outflow, and storage at a given point of time. While meteorological factors play a fundamental role in these processes, geological strata and topographical setting are decisive in determining the complexion of storage changes. The inflow of water, whether in the form of rainfall, snow or run-off over or through the surface, is of critical importance as later changes in its state or place are only consequential in nature.

Rainfall: The Kashmir Valley receives precipitation both in the form of rain and snow. It has been noted that the rainfall has a peculiar distribution pattern through the year. It is overwhelmingly concentrated in the winter and spring months in all parts of the Valley. The share of the winter and spring rainfall is, however, more than three-fourths of the annual total in the northwest (e.g., Handwara, Baramulla, Langet, and Sopore), while it is only about one-third in the central and the southeastern parts of the Valley (e.g., Srinagar, Pulwama, Anantnag, Kulgam and Ganderbal). The annual rainfall shows a regular increasing trend from Badgam and Srinagar in all directions. It is the lowest at Badgam (579 mm) and increases towards the northwest from Srinagar (663 mm) through Sopore (756 mm) and Langet (873 mm) to Handwara (1005 mm); and towards the southeast from Pulwama (592 mm) through Kulgam (898 mm) to Doru (1195 mm).

Intensity of rainfall: Another interesting feature of the rainfall of Kashmir Valley is its low average intensity per rainy day. An analysis of the fifty-year data (1950–2001) has indicated that the average intensity varies from 5.08–26.27 mm (Table 16.1). Doru has a consistent record of highest intensity throughout the valley which remains well above the other recording gauges in as many as nine months in a year. The rains are usually heavy in the southwest monsoon period in the central parts and in winter or spring in the rest of the Valley. There is a high expectancy of heavy rainfall in August or September which is often caused by a sudden cloudburst and is invariably followed by widespread floods in the Jhelum. Bhan (Bhan, 1965) has computed frequency of occasions with different 24-hour intensities of rainfall for Srinagar to show that there has been the highest frequency of occasions with an intensity of less than 12.7 mm of rain per day. There have been only three occasions in a fifty-year cycle when the intensity of rain exceeded 75 mm.

Table 16.1 Intensity of rainfall in Kashmir valley (mm per rainy day, based on average for 1951–2001)

Station	*Jan.*	*Feb.*	*March*	*April*	*May*	*June*	*July*	*Aug.*	*Sep.*	*Oct.*	*Nov.*	*Dec.*
Srinagar	11.00	11.71	12.47	10.76	17.08	5.08	9.53	13.81	11.48	13.44	10.71	10.80
Pulwama	12.81	18.85	17.27	13.12	12.27	15.70	14.95	14.80	14.71	14.42	14.15	14.23
Handwara	16.11	18.93	18.86	17.71	14.83	10.58	12.13	13.55	13.35	15.87	13.16	12.09
Anantnag	13.67	14.64	12.54	7.86	12.00	11.69	13.23	13.23	19.56	15.29	10.08	12.65
Kulgam	18.55	17.49	15.50	17.17	13.78	12.79	15.50	15.18	19.29	15.11	14.92	17.12
Dora	20.49	26.27	24.71	16.68	15.42	16.25	15.50	17.51	21.91	17.37	19.09	23.64
Ganderbal	12.34	14.00	12.57	15.14	14.07	10.69	18.83	20.54	17.61	12.36	11.18	13.64
Baramula	14.70	16.54	17.03	15.58	13.63	11.44	12.12	12.38	12.50	13.38	12.37	13.43
Langet	13.13	10.90	18.98	17.10	13.22	11.25	10.89	11.91	11.53	14.61	11.87	11.83
Sopore	13.32	13.66	14.97	12.69	11.90	10.25	9.37	4.66	11.76	10.58	11.13	12.95
Gulmarg	…	…	…	…	…	10.40	10.83	11.56	13.40	…	…	…
Badgam	10.96	15.21	12.86	12.63	11.37	9.18	12.18	11.41	17.21	14.53	11.54	10.39

Source: Based on actually monthly data in cents published in monthly and annual rainfall and number of rainy day, 1950–2001, India Meteorological Department, New Delhi, 2004.

Surface Water Resources

The surface water resources of Kashmir Valley are by any definition very large. The total run-off that escapes down the rivers or accumulates in a large number of lakes and marshes is a powerful indicator of this plentiful supply.

The river systems of the valley are fed both by rain and snow. Naturally, the flow is poor during winter months as most of the precipitation comes in the form of snow. The quantum of surface run-off increases with the onset of summer when the snow melts, and with the rain, generates a higher run-off. Normally, not less than three-fourth of the total annual discharge of the Jhelum flows during the summer months—April to August. In winter, the discharge falls down substantially—only 10 per cent of the annual discharge passes down during November–February, and not more than fifteen per cent during October–February.

As noted earlier, the major streams of the Jhelum system have their sources in the snow fields of the surrounding mountains which feed them during summer. The streams rising in the Pir Panjal have a lesser share of the snowmelt and their supplies are augmented by summer rains. The streams of the great Himalayan range, on the other hand, are dependent more on snow than on rain. This produces interesting contrasts between the flow pattern of the Pir Panjal and the Himalayan rivers. The discharge of Pir Panjal rivers is not only low; it is highly variable as the quantity of rainfall is the major component.

While the intensity of snowfall depends on the frequency and intensity of western disturbances which hit the valley during winter, the quantum of summer snowmelt depends on the amount and duration of sunshine and the total intake of solar energy. Summer discharge also depends on monsoon rains, which have a high variability and may be very heavy in the period of high discharge from snowmelt. As a consequence, the run-off in the summer is very high as compared to the discharge during the rest of the year. Thus, the discharge in May is 10–12 times that of December. The discharge rises with the rise in temperature from March onwards when low altitude snow starts melting. The volume of water supply in July and August is also dependent on rainfall and not on snow alone; the contribution of snow to river discharge gradually declines as autumn advances.

A study of the decennial averages (1990–2000) of the monthly discharge of Jhelum at Baramulla (Table 16.2) shows that only 11.65 per cent of the total annual run-off flows during

Table 16.2 Average monthly discharge of Jhelum at Baramulla (1990–2000) (Data in cusec) in Kashmir

Months	*Discharge*	*Per cent of the total discharge*	*Per cent of the total discharge in June*
January	148,985	3.48	22.16
February	214,583	5.10	31.91
March	368,565	8.60	54.81
April	578,480	13.70	87.37
May	665,498	15.52	98.98
June	672,382	15.68	100.00
July	514,356	12.00	76.50
August	503,680	11.75	74.91
September	286,413	6.68	42.60
October	189,565	4.32	28.19
November	73,685	1.72	10.96
December	62,340	1.45	9.27

Source: Based on actually monthly data in cents published in Monthly and Annual Rainfall and number of Rainy Days, 1990–2000, India Meteorological Department, New Delhi, 2004.

the four winter months (November–February). The five summer months (April–August) accounts for 68.65 per cent of the aggregate discharge. The maximum comes in June although May also does not lag far behind (Figure 16.5).

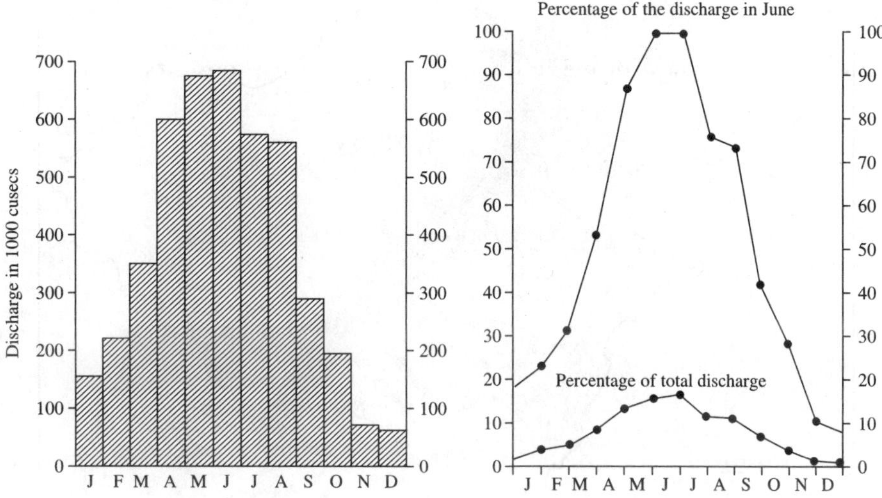

Figure 16.5 Average discharge of Jhelum at Baramulla.

Floods and Nambals: Plenty of Water

Floods have been a recurrent phenomenon in the Kashmir valley. Their frequency and the devastation caused by them are fairly understandable in the bowl that the Valley is. For one thing, the Jhelum is faced with the predicament of carrying the cumulative discharge of all its streams through a narrow passage down the valley, where silting goes on choking the channels infinitely, incapacitating the river from performing its primary function. The past behaviour of Jhelum shows that it has a maximum capacity of 'safely' carrying only half of a high flood discharges. The other half has but to spill over the banks breaching the embankments that have been constructed to contain floods. Thus, in the photographic situation in which the Jhelum is, the floods are but a natural phenomenon.

The magnitude of the flood problem can well be associated in that perspective. Even a casual look at history shows that the frequency of flood problem has been very high ever since the valley assumed its present form (Figure 16.6).

A heavy precipitation, usually coming during the end month of the summer monsoon and caused by a sudden cloudburst, leads to a severe flood. By now the catchment area of the river is already saturated and the high run-off swells the rivers beyond their capacity, with the result that the river bunds are breached and the whole Valley is converted into a big Nambal. The spillover from the rivers, particularly the Jhelum but also the Sind and the Pohru, flows to the depressions lying on the fringe of the rivers and inundates the agricultural lands with incalculable losses to the crops, livestock and human settlements. Not all the havoc is created by the nature; man has added to his predicament in a big way. With every increase in population,

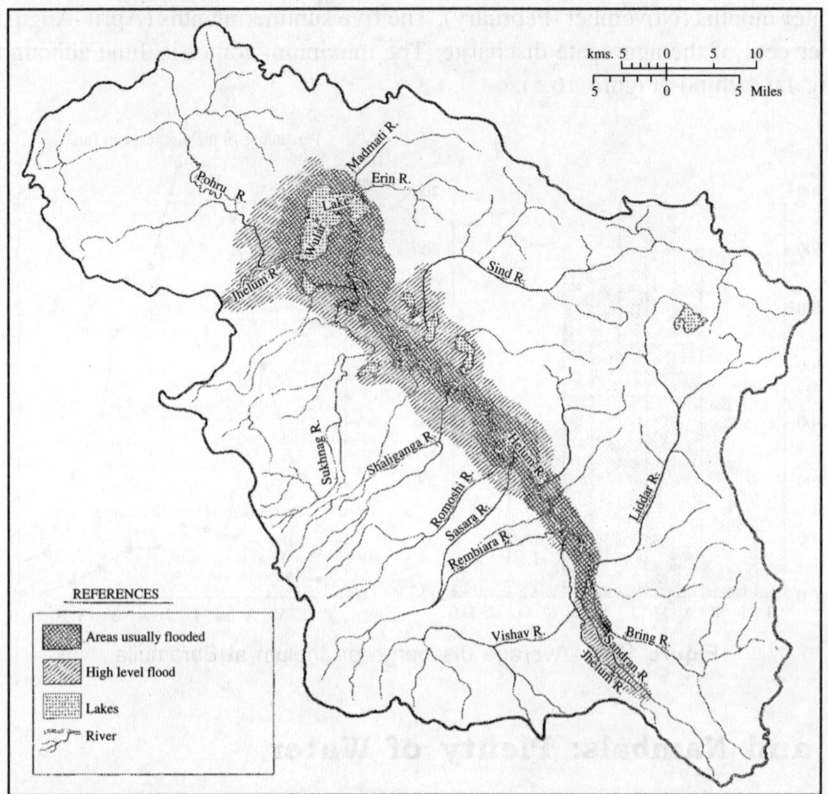

Figure 16.6 Areas liable to floods in Kashmir valley.

human settlements have grown and expanded, swallowing up new lands for agriculture and habitation. As cities have grown on the banks of Jhelum, its course has been narrowed and new embankments have been raised to contain its fury. The silting problem of the bed of the river goes on rising to the extent that no embankment can arrest the floods. The *bund* itself acts as a causal factor to floods. One consequence has been the emergence of extensive swamps on either bank of the river, particularly on the left bank.

The Jhelum in the Valley, especially at Awantipura, is bordered by a chain of these low-lying swamps, called **Nambals** and lakes which often act as natural absorption basins during floods. Significant among these are the Wular, the Nagin and the Anchar Lakes and the Batmalu, the Hokarsar, the Naugam and a host of other Nambals. They contain in them a good deal of the high flood discharges. It has been estimated that no less than 120,000 cusecs of the flood spillover is accumulated in these depressions every year. The actual run-off that can possibly pass down the Baramulla gorge is not more than 28,000 cusecs, which is perhaps the maximum volume the river can safely carry (Uppal, 1956).

It seems that the present precarious situation owes its origin to a number of factors which may be briefly listed. In the first instance, the general layout of the Valley is such that it is highly conducive to flooding. With the spread of settlement and growth of human population such measures as gradual encroachment on the water courses, reclamation of low-lying areas for agriculture, channelizing of rivers, creation of bunds along the river banks and construction of transport lines in the flood have further worsened the situation.

Flood control measures have been given top priority since the early stages of history. But effective steps to mitigate the damage caused by floods have all been taken in the 20th century. By 1930, a flood-spill channel however rejoins the Jhelum a few kilometers below the city. Other measures that have been adopted from time to time include construction of embankments along the river banks and of diversion channels, along with clearing silt from the river beds. The Irrigation Commission has recommended that the solution to this menace perhaps lies in:

1. Strengthening and realigning the bunds without raising them;
2. Improving the river channel by making cut-offs;
3. Providing a supplementary channel or floodway from Dogripura to Wular, and improving the outfall channel by diverting the Ningle (Ningal) and the Pohru rivers into the Wular lake; and
4. Stabilizing the torrents below Baramulla and clearing debris from the bed of the outfall channels

The Commission hoped that if these measures were properly implemented the Wular lake would be completely silted up and would be available for cultivation. The Commission's recommendation to silt up the Wular is, however, unrealistic. In the Wular lake, the Jhelum has a vast reservoir which plays a positive role in minimizing the load on the outfall channel during floods. The rise and fall of level in the Wular lake has a cause–effect relationship with the discharge at the point of outfall. Uppal (1956) estimated that during the floods the lake may receive about 60,000 cusecs, although it has the capacity to discharge 30,000–35,000 cusecs only. Undoubtedly the reclamation of low-lying tracts around the lake is likely to affect adversely its capacity of the lake to act as a moderator of flood in the outfall channel.

Groundwater Resources

There seem to be two main reasons for this lack of concern. First, an abundant supply of moisture from the surface sources, particularly in the floodplain of the Jhelum and other low-lying areas, ruled out the need to depend on underground water. Secondly, the political situation before and after the accession of the state of Jammu and Kashmir never aroused the rulers to care for an integrated development of the valley through optimally managing the land and water resources of the region. For most of the recent history, mounting pressure on land and a subsistence agriculture have been taken for granted, leaving the problem of dry Karewas as something lying out of the ambit of human effort. But it is on the Karewa uplands that the water problem is most acute and where agricultural development is contingent on the feasibility of successfully tapping groundwater reserves (Irrigation Commission).

Lately, the government of Jammu and Kashmir seems to have become conscious of this problem as the Central Water and Power Commission has been asked to launch a program to assess the groundwater potential of the Valley (Irrigation Commission).

The present study will, therefore, confine itself to casual observations regarding the availability and utilization of groundwater in certain parts of the Valley. Geologically, the strata that compose the low-lying areas of Kashmir valley are favourable for the occurrence of groundwater. Indirect evidence is provided by the natural springs which seem to draw their supply from the affluent seepage of groundwater to the fringe of the alluvial tract. These springs are known to have sufficient discharge of water which is often put to miscellaneous local uses, though the bulk of it remains unharnessed and unused. The scientists of the Central Groundwater Board have some data pertaining to the processes of recharging of aquifers for the state of Jammu and Kashmir as a whole. The estimates have little relevance to Kashmir Valley.

Utilization of Water Resources: Scarcity in Plenty

Water plays a limited though vital role in the economy of Kashmir. Its use is mainly in agriculture and to an average Kashmiri its plentiful supply means prosperity. The main uses are still traditional ones–gradient irrigation, navigation and primitive fishing-reminiscent of Neolithic times. The generation of hydroelectricity is only marginal, and, if compared with the available potential, infinitesimal.

Irrigation

The main use of surface water resources of the valley is in gravity irrigation with the help of primitive technology. There are, however, both political and environmental constraints on the optimal utilization of water potential. The Jhelum is one of the rivers covered by the Indus Waters Treaty which regulates the use of the Indus river between India and Pakistan. According to this treaty, while Pakistan is entitled to have a major claim on the waters of the Indus, the Jhelum and the Chenab and their tributaries, India can utilize their waters only to a limited extent. In its use of these waters, notably in the case of the Indus, India is further incapacitated by the difficult nature of terrain and communication problems.

The Kashmiri system of irrigation consists of *kuhls*[1] which take from water courses at convenient points. The *kuhls* far surpass the government canals in terms of area covered as well as length of channels. At the beginning of the first five-year plan, the area irrigated by *kuhls* was as much as sixteen times that of government canals (*Irrigation Department*). Although government canals have been consistently expanding their command area since 1950, there is no comparison between them and the *kuhls*. The Kashmiri *kuhls* irrigation system emerged under the feudal lords who were concerned with the construction and maintenance of these channels. With the abolition of the *zamindari* system the *kuhls* fell into negligence and proved to be a menace to the adjoining agricultural land as the spill-over from these channels caused recurrent floods.

The government has become conscious of this problem only recently and a comprehensive scheme has been chalked out to expedite their restoration and renovation (*J&K Annual plan,* 1070–71). Initially the scheme was designed to cover 2046 *kuhls* only, though it envisaged an eventual takeover of all the remaining *kuhls* with a command area of 1012 hectares. The government has, however, displayed little interest in the extension of irrigation to drier parts of

[1]*Kuhls* are irrigation channels in which river water is diverted by erecting weir or projecting snags.

the Valley, particularly the chronically dry Karewas. Nor will it be possible to extend irrigation to these uplands unless more complex technology is employed which ensures lifting of water to areas tens of metres higher from the river valley floors.

Domestic Uses of Water

One of the commonest uses of water is for drinking. Despite a plentiful supply of water in the Valley, there is no systematic distribution except in large urban centres. Among the districts of the Valley, Anantnag seems to the best served. A number of reservoirs have been constructed at different places in the district and tap water is supplied to the public. The towns of Pampore, Shopian, Awantipura and Sedov Tsotopora have water supply schemes. Of the nine urban centres in Baramulla district only four— Baramulla, Sopore, Bandipora and Gulmarg (Tangmarg)—have a regular water supply. So far as rural areas are concerned, only large villages of Wanigam and Bunagam in Baramulla tehsil; Nadihal, Tiyar, Seer and Ajar Aithmulla in Sopore; and Sogam in Handwara tehsil have been provided with a water supply system (Census, 2001).

Navigation

Watercourses also act as navigation channels. The Jhelum river and most of its tributaries in the floodplain as well as the Dal and the Wular lakes are navigable. Their role as arteries of transport can hardly be overemphasized.

Generation of Hydroelectricity

Although the Valley has a considerable potential for the generation of hydroelectricity, no major attempt has so far been made to exploit it substantively for either industrial or domestic use. There are very few urban areas and fewer villages which are served with electricity.

The Valley has two hydroelectricity stations at Ganderbal and Moharra with an installed generating capacity of 15,000 and 6000 kW, respectively. They cater to the needs of all urban centres besides important tourist resorts and a few villages. The villages so far electrified are few—2 per cent of all villages in Anantnag, 1.4 per cent in Baramulla and 8 per cent in Srinagar. Besides these two hydroelectric stations, work on the three projects—Chenani, Upper Sind and Lower Jhelum—is in progress. Of the three, Chenani was ready to be commissioned in 1972. A 220 kW transmission line will take the supply to Srinager and will be linked to an inter-regional grid augmenting to Ganderbal supply. It is further proposed that a 33 kW line will connect Pattan to Tanmarg, Sopore to Bandipora and Anantnag to Shopian.

One may expect that in the foreseeable future water will be put to more and more varied uses as the economy diversifies and new schemes of resource conservation and utilization receive increased attention. It is therefore necessary to fix priority at the very outset and chalk out a comprehensive strategy for the optimal utilization of the Valley's water resources.

From the aforesaid discussion, it is clear that the water resources in the Valley of Kashmir have not been optimally utilized, in spite of the fact that it is available in plenty. There are four methods which can be used to measure the scarcity of water amid plenty of water. These are: irrigated area as percentage of net sown area, hydroelectricity production, availability of potable water for people, and water for industrial use. Based on this criteria, if the water resource of the Valley of Kashmir is assessed, it proves the dictum of scarcity in plenty.

Conclusion

All the cultivated area in the Valley of Kashmir cannot be irrigated due to lack of infrastructure in transporting the water. An assured base of irrigation could have been achieved but this is not available especially in the Karewa region of the valley which possesses about 32 per cent of the cultivated area. It is a pity that in spite of plenty of water, Karewa looks like a desert.

The hydroelectricity plays significant role in overall development. Both social as well as economic development are dependent on hydropower. The Valley of Kashmir has potential to develop like Switzerland as far as power production is concerned; it could even export power. But it has not been achieved so far.

Likewise, the availability of potable water and industrial water are also posing serious problems. Almost, all the rural and urban settlements are located on the bank of rivers and water streams but they suffer from absence of water literacy. Seldom people realize that sometimes late snowfall and early melting of snow could be causes of scarcity of water in the Valley.

References

Bhan, S.N. (1965), *A Study of Fifty Year Rainfall of Srinagar (1901–1950) and Jammu (1893–1942),* Meteorological Department of India.

District Census Handbook of Srinagar (2007), Anantnag and Baramulla.

Reports of the Irrigation Commission.

Uppal, H.L. (1956), *Flood Control Damage and Reclamation in the Kashmir Valley*, Central Water Power Commission, New Delhi.

17

Groundwater Prospects in Panchkula District, Haryana

Surya Kant and A.C. Pandey

Abstract: The hydro-geomorphological maps depicting the groundwater prospect zones form the valuable data base to study the groundwater availability prospects in an area. In this chapter, the role of remotely sensed data and technology in the preparation of such maps and identifying the water deficit areas for planning and management have been examined. In this context, the groundwater quality, groundwater prospects and water resource development plans have been discussed with special reference to Panchkula district of Haryana.

Keywords: Hydrogeological Maps, Lithology, Aquifers, Mineralization, Bicarbonate, Fluoride, Surface Dykes, Lateral Groundwater Flow

Introduction

The present study attempts to map hydro-geomorphology of Panchkula district (Haryana) to identify the groundwater potential zones in the district, using data available from the high spatial resolution remotely sensed images. Data available from such kind of images have truly emerged highly useful to delineate groundwater prospect zones, especially in the regions composed of fluvial/denudational and structural geomorphic units. Earlier, hydrogeological maps, prepared by using conventional methods and mainly based on ground hydrogeological surveys, provided groundwater prospects by geological units, notwithstanding the fact that within each geological unit (rock type), the groundwater conditions vary widely due to differentials in relief, slope, intensity of weathering, nature of the weathered material, presence of fractures, surface water bodies, irrigated fields, etc.

In visual interpretation of satellite images, the keys to detect groundwater prospect zones are prepared on the bases of parameters, such as land forms, drainage, vegetation type and anomalies, soil tones, types of outcrop, and land use and land cover classes. The village level information collected for groundwater recharge, depth to water table and water quality, etc., also helps in the final preparation of groundwater prospect zones map (Hinton, 1996; Karanth, 1987; Todd, 1982).

The hydro-geomorphological maps depicting water prospect zones provide all the information required for proper evaluation of groundwater conditions. Such maps form a valuable database to help the user departments/agencies in identifying favourable zones (prospective zones) around the problem villages, thereby narrowing down the target areas (Baker and Panciera, 1990). Subsequently by conducting detailed hydrogeological and geophysical surveys within these zones, the most appropriate sites can be selected for drilling. Further, these maps will also be useful to identify suitable zones/sites for planning the recharge structures for improving the sustainability of drinking water sources.

The groundwater prospective zone maps will, thus, serve the twin purpose of: (i) quickly identifying the prospective groundwater zones for conducting site specific investigations, and (ii) selecting the sites for planning recharge structures to improve sustainability of drinking water sources in the lean season and in desired quantity.

Groundwater Regime

The groundwater regime is a dynamic system wherein water is absorbed at the surface of the earth and eventually recycled back to the surface through the geological strata. The groundwater regime is, however, influenced by a variety of factors including relief, slope, ruggedness, depth and nature of weathering, thickness and nature of the deposited material, distribution of surface water bodies, river/stream network, precipitation, canal command areas, groundwater irrigated areas, in addition to the geologic framework. Thus, the framework in which the groundwater occurs is as varied as that of rock types and the balance among the lithological, structural, geomorphic and hydrological parameters. The possible combinations, full of variety and complexity, are virtually infinite to conclude that the groundwater conditions at a given site are unique and not completely amenable to scientific understanding. Some of the conditions are often obscured and not readily apparent even from the field observations. However, factor-wise analysis, systematic mapping, and data integration and interpretation, based on conceptual understanding, help in overcoming this problem to certain extent.

For this purpose, all the variables controlling the groundwater regime have been grouped into the following four factors, which can be interpreted with the help of remotely sensed satellite images and integrated with to prepare the groundwater prospect zones map;

1. Geology/Lithology
2. Geological Structures
3. Geomorphology/Landforms
4. Recharge Conditions

Once, the information relating to the above listed four factors is precisely known, it is possible to understand the groundwater regime better by visualizing the gross aquifer characteristics of each unit. Systematic visual interpretation of satellite imageries in combination with existing geological/hydrogeological/geomorphological maps and literature supported by limited field checks/observations provide the following information related to these four factors, forming the valuable inputs in preparing the groundwater prospective zone map:

1. Geology/Lithology
   (i) Nature and distribution of different rock types
   (ii) Rock origin and their three-dimensional configuration
   (iii) Texture (porosity/permeability)
   (iv) Water holding and transmitting capacity of rocks
2. Geomorphology/Landforms
   (i) The assemblage of different landforms
   (ii) The shape, size and area extent of different landforms
   (iii) Relief, slope, ruggedness
   (iv) Depth of weathering and nature of weathered material
   (v) Erosion and deposition
   (vi) Thickness and the nature of deposited material
3. Geological Structures
   (i) Bedding
   (ii) Schistosity/foliation
   (iii) Faults
   (iv) Fractures
   (v) Shear zones, occupied by brecciated/milonitized chert/quartz/quartzite reefs
   (vi) Folds
   (vii) Circular features
   (viii) Structural trends
4. Hydrological Information
   (i) Major rivers and streams
   (ii) Surface water bodies like major reservoirs, tanks, lakes, canals, etc.
   (iii) Canal commands
   (iv) Groundwater irrigated areas
   (v) Groundwater over-exploited zones, etc.

Such kind of hydrological information in conjunction with (i) rainfall data, (ii) water table fluctuation data collected by regular monitoring of the network of observation collected from the wells, (iii) the data collected on yield estimates from the wells by conducting study of pump tests, and (iv) depth of water table and yield information collected from the inventory of wells form the valuable inputs for assessing the recharge conditions, estimating the groundwater resource and inferring the well yields in different geological and geomorphological assemblages.

The map of groundwater prospect zones prepared by integrating lithological, landform, structural and hydrological information provides a better understanding of groundwater regime in comparison to the conventionally prepared hydrogeological map.

Landform analysis often provides an excellent result for the probability of groundwater occurrence. If combined with other associated information like geology/lithology/structures/ brittle fractures, faults, joints lineaments, weathered zones and porosity and permeability of the strata, the results can vastly be improved.

Hydro-geomorphological Mapping

In the process of hydro-geomorphological mapping of Panchkula district, the different lithological, structural and geomorphic units interpreted and differentiated with the help of IRS ID/1C FCC digital data products, the Survey of India topographical sheets (scale 1:50,000) and existing literature form the basis for hydro-geomorphic interpretation. Table 17.1 provides the details on each unit along with their groundwater prospect in the district of Panchkula.

Table 17.1 Panchkula district: Depth of water table

Depth range (m)	*Area* (km^2)	*Per cent to total*
03–10	286.84	32.12
10–20	271.75	30.43
20–30	20.53	02.30
Outcrop area	313.98	35.15
Total	893.10	100.00

Source: Groundwater Cell, Haryana Government, Panchkula.

Aquifers and Groundwater Prospects

The groundwater in the district occurs under unconfined water table conditions in the upper aquifers, mainly formed of alluvium and semi-consolidated formations. In the deeper aquifer zones, where the water holding formations are the shale, silt and clay, the groundwater occurs in semi-confined to confined conditions (Table 17.2).

Table 17.2 Panchkula district: Area coverage of mapped hydro-geomorphic units and groundwater prospects

Hydro-geomorphic unit	*Map symbol*	*Description*	*Groundwater prospect*	*Area* (km^2)	*Per cent in total area*
A. Fluvial origin					
Channel Bar	CB	Small alluvial patch forming part of the riverbed.	Excellent	1.82	0.20
Valley fill shallow	VFS	Narrow depressions filled with alluvial and colluvial matter of shallow depth (<10 m)	Good	8.46	0.95
Flood plain deep	FPD	Narrow flat areas along the rivers formed of recent sediments (>20 m thickness)	Excellent	29.58	3.31
Flood plain deep ravenous	FPD-R	Highly dissected flood plain deep	Good	0.11	0.01
Flood plain shallow	FPS	Narrow flat areas along the rivers formed of recent sediments (<10 m depth)	Very Good	29.42	3.29
Flood plain shallow ravenous	FPS-R	Highly dissected Flood plain shallow	Good	0.08	0.01

(Contd.)

Table 17.2 Panchkula district: Area coverage of mapped hydro-geomorphic units and groundwater prospects (*Contd.*)

Hydro-geomorphic unit	*Map symbol*	*Description*	*Groundwater prospect*	*Area* (km^2)	*Per cent in total area*
Alluvial plain deep	APD	Very gently sloping plain of alluvial sediments >20 m thickness occupying southern part of the district	Very Good	115.72	12.97
Alluvial plain deep ravenous	APD-R	Highly dissected Alluvial plain deep	Good	14.04	1.57
Alluvial plain shallow	APS	Very gently sloping plain of alluvial sediment <10 m thickness occupying areas between APD and piedmont.	Good	67.13	7,52
Alluvial plain shallow ravenous	APS-R	Highly dissected alluvial plain shallow	Moderate	9.31	1.04
B. Denudational origin					
Piedmont alluvial deeply buried	FDD	Moderately sloping zone of colluvial and alluvial sediments at the foot of the hills >20 m thickness.	Moderate	55.51	6.22
Piedmont alluvial deeply buried ravenous	PDD-R	Highly dissected deeply buried piedmont alluvial	Poor	1.08	0.12
Piedmont alluvial shallow buried	PUS	Moderately sloping zone of colluvial and alluvial sediments at the foot of the hills >20 m thickness.	Moderate	63.25	7.08
Interrmon-tane valley	IV	Narrow linear valley of river Sirsa having widths of 2.5 to 7.5 km occupied by unconsolidated clastic sediments.	Very good	78.84	8.83
Denudational Hill	DH	Weathered, eroded & Denuded Hills generally made of boulders, sandstone showing rounded crests and attaining relief of about 300 m.	Poor	188.41	21.09
C. Structural origin					
Structure Hill	SH	High rising NW-SE trending hills, with prominent joints, occupying the NE part.	Poor-Nil	185.80	20.80
Water Bodies (Rivers, Ponds)				44.55	4.99
Total				893.10	100

In Panchkula district, the main aquifer is formed of alluvium and the piedmont zones, consisting of coarse sand, pebble, cobbles etc. This zone also forms the main recharge area in the district. The depth of water level in the pheratic aquifer varies from 8.3 to 30.1 m below the ground level (Figure 17.1). The range of fluctuation varies between 0.3 to 3.7 m and the rise is conspicuous in most parts of the district. The general slope of water table conforms to the topography of the area, which is in the southwest direction, with a gradient of around 1.5 m/km in the alluvial area. Generally the pheratic aquifers within depth of 50 m below ground level provide yields between 100–500 gallons per minute (gpm). The level of groundwater development in the district as a whole has not reached the optimum level. Nonetheless, Raipur Rani and Barwala blocks recorded the maximum development. The further

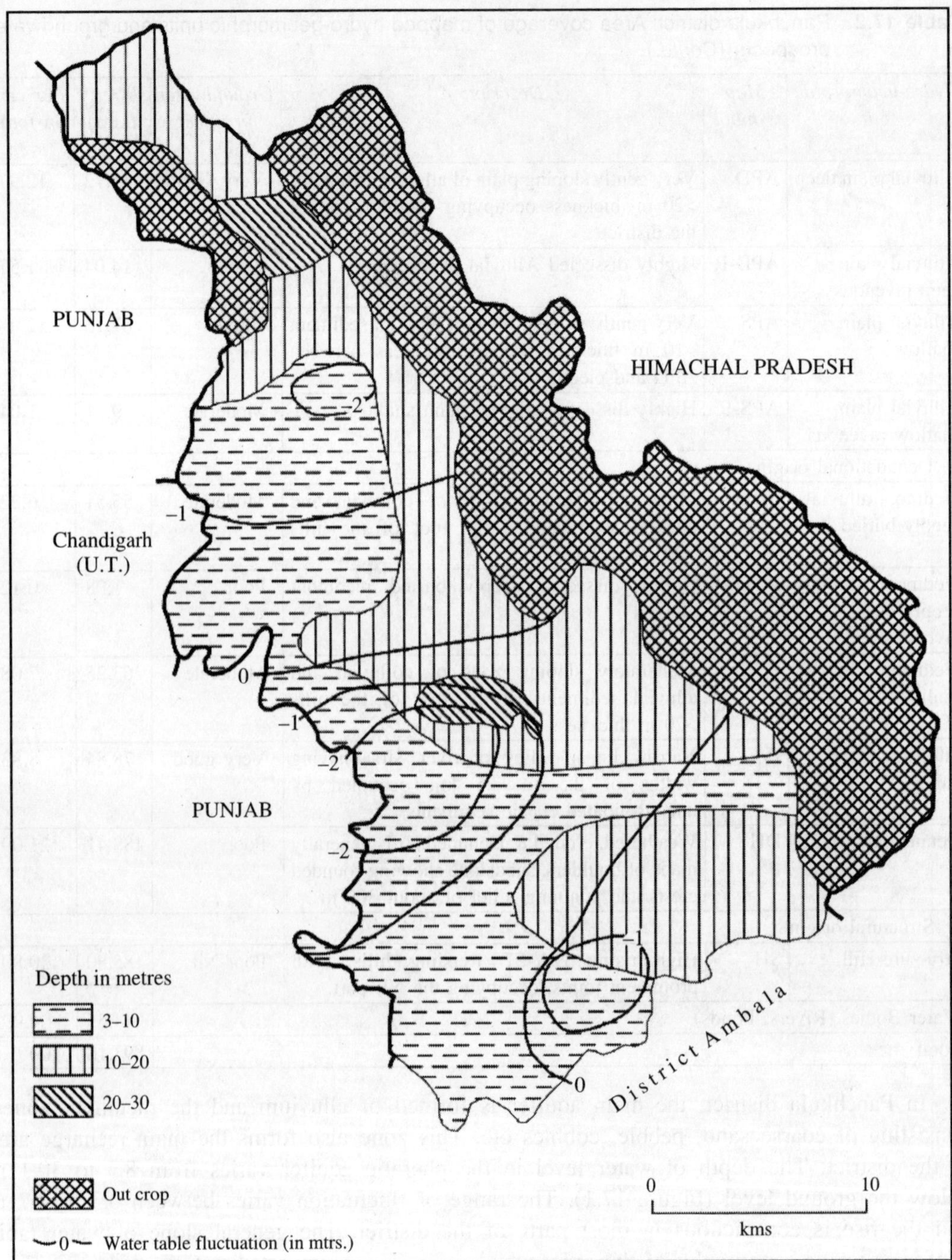

Figure 17.1 Depth to water table and water table fluctuation in Panchkula district.

development of groundwater in these two blocks must be restricted and the possibilities of recharging aquifer zones needs to be looked into on priority basis.

Groundwater Quality

In Panchkula district, industrialization, urbanization and intensive commercial agriculture have brought about significant changes in the quality of water (Figure 17.2). Additional concentration

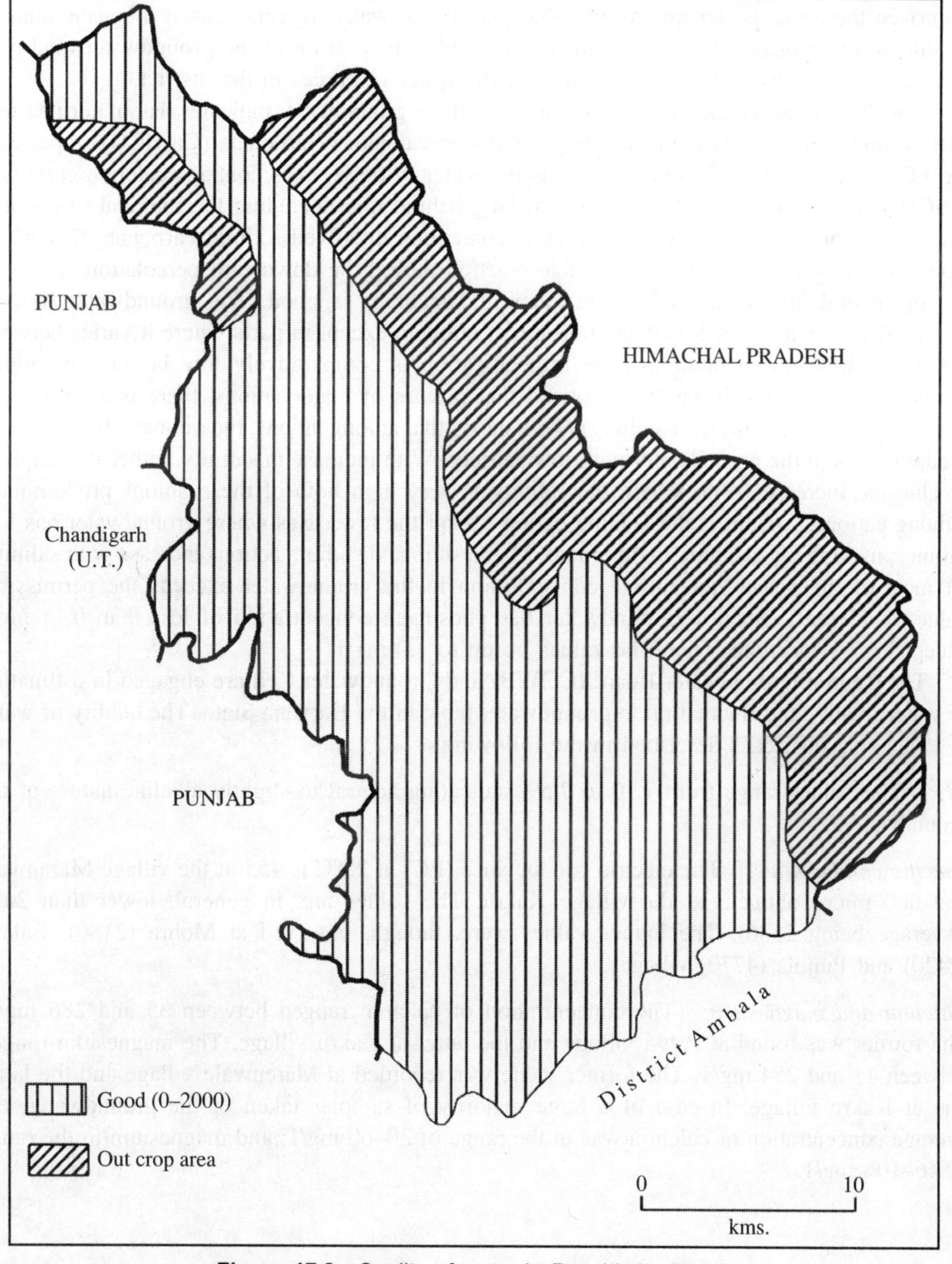

Figure 17.2 Quality of water in Panchkula district.

of chemical constituents brought in due to the weathering of rocks like limestone, shale, clay and other minerals in the northern parts of the district have also affected the quality of groundwater. Industrial effluents, sewage wastes, fertilizers, pesticides and insecticides have added a large number of pollutants to both surface and groundwater. In addition, the groundwater quality is also influenced by the seepage from canals and rivers. Such as dilution by canal water has improved the groundwater quality in some places, but water logging caused the accumulation of salts at other places. In view of all this, a regular monitoring of the groundwater quality is essential to stop any further deterioration of the water resources in the district.

A well-defined geochemical zoning of the shallow groundwater indicates that in northeastern part of study area, the groundwater is generally of calcium bicarbonate (Ca-HCO_3) type, with the EC values less than 2000 micro ohm/cm. Water in these areas contains calcium carbonate ($CaCO_3$). There can be several factors working behind this, including the removal of calcium (as $CaCO_3$) or the loss of Col or rainwater containing dissolved sodium carbonate ($NaHCO_3$) from the top soil layers, or ion-exchange reaction during the downward percolation.

In general, the quality of groundwater in Panchkula is good. The groundwater has the electrical conductivity of less than 2000 micro ohm/cm except in parts where it varies between 2000 and 3000 micro ohm/cm. The mineralization is comparatively low because of higher rainfall in the district. It has been noticed that in case of major anions, there is a strong and positive correlation with EC (Salinity). This shows that among anions, bicarbonate, by and large, predominates in the groundwater with low salinity. With increase in salinity, either the sulphate or chloride increases. But, where the salinity is very high both of these anions predominate. Among cations, sodium is the leading cation except the few cases where groundwater has low salinity; making the calcium predominant. Magnesium and sodium actions increase with salinity. At most of the places, the nitrate concentration in the groundwater exceeds the permissible value of 45 mg/1. Shallow groundwater has phosphate concentration of less than 0.15 mg/1 except in few locations where the values go up to 1.0 mg/1.

The Central Groundwater Board (CGWB) and Groundwater Cell are engaged in estimation of water quality and fluctuation in groundwater table in the Haryana State. The quality of water in Panchkula district is described in the following:

PH: The values range from 7.10 to 7.59, indicating neutral to slightly alkaline nature of the groundwater.

Specific conductance: The electric conductance (EC) at 25°C is 455 at the village Maranwala and 600 micro ohm/cm at the village Kakru. The values are, in general, lower than 2000 (Average being 1536). The higher values were, though, observed at Mohra (2180), Balana (2420) and Pinjola (4770) villages.

Calcium and magnesium: The concentration of calcium ranged between 35 and 286 mg/1. The former was found at Patwi village and the latter at Kakru village. The magnesium ranged between 11 and 254 mg/1. The former value was recorded at Marenwale village and the latter one at Kakru village. In case of a large majority of samples taken of the groundwater, the average concentration of calcium was in the range of 30–60 mg/1; and magnesium in the range of 46–106 mg/1.

Sodium and potassium: The sodium concentrations ranged between 27 (at Panchkula and Barwala) and 730 (at Kakru), the average value being 147 mg/1. In general, the groundwater has the concentration in the range of 50–200 mg/1. The concentration of potassium ranges from a negligible to 1160 mg/1. The latter value was recorded at Pinjola village. In a case of the large majority of samples analyzed, the potassium content was less than 20; the average value being 80 mg/1.

Chloride: The chloride concentrates in groundwater varied from 8–989 mg/1. The highest value (989 mg/1) of chloride concentrates in groundwater was recorded at Kakru village. This value was found 622 mg/1at Pinjola. In general, the shallow groundwater had chloride values lesser than 250 mg/1, the average value of concentration of chloride being 163 mg/1.

Sulphate: The sulphate content ranged from a negligible to 1410 mg/1. The highest value of sulphate contents in groundwater was recorded at Kakru village. In case of the large majority of groundwater samples, the concentration was found below 200, except in case of Mulana and Pinjola villages, where it was as high as 263 and 340 mg/1, respectively. The average concentration in the area was 141 mg/1.

Nitrate: Its concentration was generally less than 100 mg/1. High concentration of nitrate was observed in Raipur Rani (280) and Kakru (244) villages.

Fluoride: Its distribution in shallow groundwater was less than 1.5 mg/1 except in Shahzadpur (1.74) and Kakru (1.90) villages.

Bicarbonate: Bicarbonate concentration ranged from 239 (at Dharampur village) to 1619 mg/1 (at Pinjola village). The normal range of bicarbonate in shallow groundwater was recorded between 300 and 650 mg/1; the average value being 541 mg/1. Generally, the shallow groundwater in the district is of calcium bicarbonate (Ca-HCO_3) type. In Shahzadpur and Patwal areas, water was of sodium carbonate (K-HCO_3) type.

Suitability of Water

Domestic: Groundwater occurring in the shallow aquifers, by and large, was potable except in a few places, such as Kakru and Pinjola areas, where fluoride, salinity and nitrate have rendered the water unfit for drinking. At Raipur Rani nitrate content was 280 mg/1, which is beyond the permissible limits.

Irrigation: The water in most of the wells is suitable for irrigation purposes, except in Kakru and Pinjola areas, where the salinity level was too high, falling in class 4 (C4) category. Also water at Patwal, Mohra and Shahzadpur villages was marginally alkaline with high contents of sodium.

Groundwater Prospects

Panchkula district has about 224 km^2 or one-fourth of its total area under very good to good category of groundwater prospects. Good to moderate category have another 90.0 km^2 areas in Panchkula district. Besides this, more than one-seventh or 14.33 per cent area in Panchkula district falls under moderate to poor category of groundwater prospects. Poor to Nil has about 42 per cent or 375.0 km^2 area of the district (Table 17.3).

Table 17.3 Panchkula district: Groundwater prospect zones

Groundwater prospect zones	*Area* (km^2)	*Per cent to total*
Excellent to Very Good	76.0	08.51
Very Good to Good	224.0	25.08
Good to Moderate	90.0	10.08
Moderate to Poor	128.0	14.33
Poor to Nil	375.0	42.00
Total	893.0	100.00

Water Resource Development Plan

The economic development in an area is quite dependent on its natural resources. The land and water resources fall in category of the basic resources, forming the core of ecological system. These resources are now under the threat owing to depleting water table and increasing land-degradation. The challenge is, therefore, to develop these resources sustainable by making them more productive and their exploitation less hazardous. The economy of Panchkula is mainly dependant on agriculture and agro-industries. Groundwater situation is at a stage where its further development has to be judiciously planned and managed. The plan for the development of water resources in Panchkula district has been prepared on the basis of hydro-geomorphological characteristics, drainage, surface water availability, and status of groundwater exploitation and present land use.

Groundwater Development

The groundwater in the district occurs under unconfirmed water table conditions in the upper aquifers and under the semi-confined to confined conditions in the deep aquifer zones. The groundwater in the Panchkula district can further be developed with deeper wells except in the Raipur Rani and Barwala blocks where it should be restricted and possibilities of recharging aquifer zones should be looked into. The Piedmont zone (*Kandi* area) is being considered for further development of groundwater through deeper tubewells.

In Panchkula district, the development of water resources is mainly in 'safe' category except in Barwala and Naraingarh blocks, falling under the 'grey' category. Thus any further development of groundwater in the Barwala and Naraingarh blocks should be judiciously planned. The piedmont zone (*Kandi* area), which is the main recharge zone, can be explored with deeper tubewells to augment the groundwater resources.

Surface Water Resources Development Plan

Panchkula district has a well-developed network of drainage system, belonging to the river Ghagghar and its tributaries. Only a small part of Panchkula district is drained by tributary of the river Sutlej. A number of water harvesting structures to augment surface water resources as well as recharging of groundwater have been suggested. These include sub-surface dykes, check dams, and recharge pits. De-siltation of existing reservoir/tanks has been suggested as the main activity to increase their water holding capacity. These surface water harvesting structure and activities for Panchkula district have been marked on the map. Following criteria are considered as basic requirements for designing water-harvesting structures.

Check Dams

They are constructed, in general, on lower order streams (up to third order) with medium slopes. They are proposed where groundwater table is highly fluctuating; and the stream is influent or intermittently effluent. The area of catchments varies widely, but an average area of about 25 hectares is the minimum threshold requirement.

The parameters to be considered include slope, soil cover and its thickness and hydrogeological conditions such as rock type, thickness of weathered strata, fracture, depth to the bed rock, etc. There should be some irrigation wells in the downstream of the proposed structure (Table 17.4). The structure will serve for dual purpose. It reduces run-off velocity thereby minimizing erosion. Second, it allows the retained water to percolate down, resulting in increased recharge in the wells located downstream of the structure.

Table 17.4 Panchkula district: Suggested surface water harvesting structure

Suggested structure	*Location*	*Nearest village*	*Hydro-geomorphological unit*	*Slope (%)*
CD1	53B/13 B3-NE	1 km Dharmpur	PDS	3–7
CD2	53B/13 C3-NW	1 km Abclullpur	PDS	3–7
CD3	53B/13B3-SE	1/2 km Rampur	EPS	1–3
SD1	53B/14 B2-N	1 km Ramgarh	APD	1–3
SD2	53B/14 C2-NW	1 km Bila	APD	1–3
Dl	53B/14 C3-NW	Barwala	APD	1–3
D2'	53B/14 C3-W	Bharaili	APD	1–3
SD3	53F/2 A2-SW	2.5 km Raipurrani	APD	1–3
SD4	53F/2 A3-C	1.5 km Firazepur	APD	1–3
D3	53F/2 A2-SW	Raipur Rani	APD	1–3
D4	53F/2 A3-N	Sultanpur	APD	1–3

Subsurface Dykes

These structures are generally proposed to arrest the lateral groundwater flow (base flow in the stream) in the alluvial area. There should be considerable thickness of alluvium in that area with 2–5 m thickness of weathering mantle. Before constructing the subsurface dykes, the parameters such as thickness of sand, degree and extent of weathering and depth to bed rock need to be studied. The structure should be constructed up to the bed rock.

The areas suited to subsurface dyke construction can be delineated with the help of remotely sensed satellite images in combination with topographic sheets. The exact location can be fixed after field visits and ground verification. Wherever needed, the desiltation of tanks and recharge pits has also suggested.

Conclusion

Panchkula district exhibits diverse hydro-geomorphological conditions where the groundwater regime is controlled mainly by the topographical and geological features. Hydro-geomorphological mapping reveals that there are the excellent prospects of groundwater availability in area of the district, associated with alluvial and flood plain deposits. In contrast, the areas underlain by denudational and structure hills have poor to no prospects. Hence, these areas should be taken up for water resource management with development of water harvesting structures.

The economy of the Panchkula district, to a large extent, depends on agriculture and agro-industries, where the water constitutes an essential prerequisite. Therefore, the water exploitation especially in the alluvial plain areas has to be undertaken in a judiciously planned manner. Application of Remote sensing and GIS tools and techniques can effectively be applied for preparing water resource management plans.

References

Baker, C.P. and E.C. Panciera (1990), A geographic information system for groundwater protection planning, *Journal of Soil and Water Conservation*, **45**, 246–248.

Hinton, J.C. (1996), GIS and remote sensing integration for environmental applications, *International Journal of Geographical Information Systems*, **10**(7), 877–890.

Karanth, K.R. (1987), *Groundwater Assessment: Development and Management*, Tata McGraw-Hill, New Delhi.

Todd, D.K. (1982), *Groundwater Hydrology*, John Wiley, New York.

18

Declining Groundwater Level of Allahabad District, Uttar Pradesh

Archana Tripathi and Sunil Kumar Tripathi

Abstract: The role of groundwater is critical and crucial for variety of activities. Its declining tendency has been the cause of concern. This chapter analyses in detail the fluctuating water table in Allahabad District of Uttar Pradesh and concludes with several suggestions to restore and augment the situation of groundwater level for the welfare of the people and economy.

Keywords: Water Table Fluctuation, Groundwater Strata, Hydrological Characteristics, Groundwater Recharge, Horticulture, Key Wells, Permeability

Introduction

Water is indispensable for the existence and survival of life on earth. With the advancement of civilization, water has been found in large and progressively increasing list of uses. Water, whether it is ground or surface, is such type of resource endowment that requires careful attention for its proper utilization and management to fulfill the requirement of agriculture, domestic, industrial and miscellaneous uses. Allahabad district is at the junction of the Ganga and the Yamuna—the two mighty rivers. Here, one can see that there is ample source of surface water. But the water is polluted and it does not fulfill the needs of the district. This is why the dependence on the underground water has increased. On account of the excess exploitation of the underground water, the water level is declining day by day. In the Allahabad district, the problem of the underground water is prevailing mainly in the areas away from the rivers and in Shankargarh, Koraon, Jasra, Meja, and Manda blocks located in the south. In these places many wells become dry during the summer season and the same problem is with the handpumps. The water level decreases in the Ganga and the Yamuna rivers during summer and failure of monsoon. On account of this, the surrounding water also seeps into the Ganga river. As a result the wells and handpumps of the surrounding area become dry. The southern area of this district also suffers from water scarcity problem. In this area hard rocks are found and water can not be recharged. Therefore, water cannot be collected below the ground and this area suffers from the water problem. Of course, it is a concern of every sensible person. This chapter attempts to highlight this problem with some suggestions.

Objectives and Methodology

A set of four objectives has been kept in view in the research work:

1. To find out the spatial pattern of groundwater table in pre- and post-monsoon periods of the study area,
2. To identify the declining zone of groundwater table in the study area,
3. To evaluate the distribution pattern of groundwater recharge and discharge,
4. To chalk out a development plan for ensuring an optimal spatial utilization of groundwater resource on the basis of findings.

The study is mainly based on the secondary statistics. The literature survey covers wide range of publications such as journals, books, newspapers, and other published literature. Some of the works which have been especially taken into account are those of Alam and Kidwai (1987); Bhattacharya (1953); Bilas (1980); Khushlani and Khushlani (1984); Rao (1975); Mehta (1978); Singh (1997) and Tripathi (1996). Data concerning the groundwater table, recharge and draft have been taken from the groundwater department. For analysing the data suitable techniques such as average and choropleth methods are used.

Hydrological Characteristics of the Study Area

Allahabad District covers an area of 5437.2 km^2. It has a population of about 5,959,798 persons according to 2011 Census. The district is bounded by Sant Ravidas Nagar in the east, Mirzapur in the south east, Kaushambi in the west, Pratapgarh and Jaunpur in the north and the state of Madhya Pradesh, forms its boundary in the south. The district is situated between 24°47' to 25°47' N latitudes and 81°26' to 82°21' E longitudes. The district can be divided into three physiographic regions, namely, trans–Ganga plain, Doab and trans-Yamuna plain.

The major water bearing strata in the district are unconfined strata, confined strata and deep strata. Unconfined strata are found between the depth of 20 m to 150 m. This formation consists of fine and medium grained sand and groundwater occurs mainly in this strata. Confined strata are caused due to the presence of two clay layers, having the depth between 150 m to 250 m. In this strata, movement of water does not continue, that is why saline water occurs in this strata. In this zone, semi-confined strata is also found that have some clay or medium grained sand. Deep strata are found below 250 m and are rich of groundwater. This strata consists of medium grained sand in the northern part of the district while hard rock formation in the southern part. In hard rock formation, groundwater occurs only in the weathered or fractured zone.

Depth of Groundwater Table

Groundwater is found below the surface of earth. When rainfall occurs, some water goes down into the pore spaces in the soil and accumulates there. At certain depth the pore spaces in the soil get completely filled with water and the level which occurs is called **the water table**.

More simply the water table is the upper limit of groundwater. At present State Groundwater Department is monitoring water level in 211 hydrological stations in the district. Water level of different key wells of the district is shown in the Table 18.1.

Table 18.1 Allahabad district: Depth of water table in different key wells

Depth range	*Pre-monsoon*		*Post-monsoon*	
	No. of key wells	*Per cent of key wells*	*No. of key wells*	*Per cent of key wells*
0–5	38	21.11	88	48.89
5–10	80	44.44	42	23.33
10–15	40	22.22	36	20.00
15–20	17	9.45	13	7.22
20 and above	5	2.78	1	0.56

Source: State Groundwater Department, U.P.

The depth of water table in the district varies between 0.85 m to over 20 m below ground level. The minimum 0.85 m is found in Singhgarh village of Holagarh block and maximum is noted (20.25 m) in Dhanua village of Chaka block in the post-monsoon period. If we see the pre-monsoon period situation of the district, maximum water level is found in Shambhuchak village of Urva block while minimum (1.85 m) is observed in Kuthan village of Holagarh block.

The average water level of different key wells in the pre-monsoon period is maximum (16 m) in Urva block and between 10 m and 13 m in Handia, Saidabad, and Bahadurpur in the north and Urva, Karchhana and Chaka in the south (Figure 18.1). The same situation is found in the post-monsoon period (Figure 18.2).

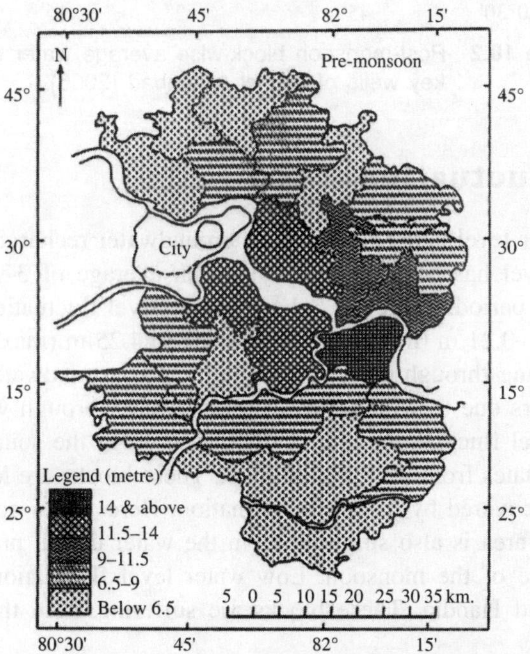

Figure 18.1 Pre-monsoon block-wise average water table of key wells of district Allahabad (2005).

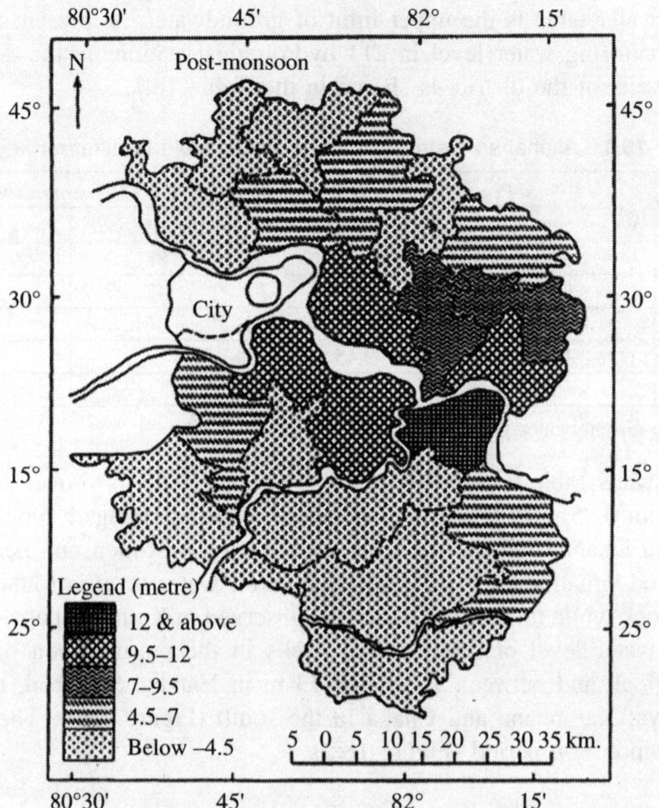

Figure 18.2 Post-monsoon block-wise average water table of key wells of district Allahabad (2005).

Water Level Fluctuation

The fluctuation of water level takes place due to groundwater recharge and draft. The average fluctuation of water level has been worked out on an average of 3-year water level data of pre- and post-monsoon period. Table 18.2 shows water level fluctuation by blocks. The water level fluctuation varies +0.21 m (minimum) in Baheria to 4.25 m (maximum) in Koraon block. All the blocks are passing through the stage of addition in groundwater storage. But lowering of the water level occurs due to withdrawal of groundwater through wells and tubewells.

The high water level fluctuation zone in the district is in the southern part of the district where water level fluctuates from 2.74 m to 4.25 m. These blocks are Meja, Urva, Shankargarh and Koraon which are covered by hard rock formation. Here, water accumulates in weathered or fractured zone. This area is also suffering from the water deficit problem especially during the period of the failure of the monsoon. Low water level fluctuation regions are Holagarh, Dhanupur, Saidabad and Handia. These blocks are suffering from the problem of declining water level.

Table 18.2 Allahabad district: groundwater table and water level fluctuation by blocks

Sl. No.	*Blocks*	*Average water table* (m)		*Water level fluctuation*
		Pre-monsoon	*Post-monsoon*	
1.	Kaudihar	6.08	3.36	2.72
2.	Holagarh	4.15	3.32	0.86
3.	Soraon	8.26	6.21	2.05
4.	Mau Aima	4.63	3.32	1.31
5.	Baheria	7.74	6.83	0.91
6.	Bahadurpur	12.0	11.64	0.36
7.	Phoolpur	5.36	3.67	1.69
8.	Pratappur	7.45	6.2	1.25
9.	Dhanupur	8.86	8.7	0.79
10.	Saidabad	10.3	9.04	1.26
11.	Handia	11.1	9.06	1.45
12.	Chaka	13	11.05	1.95
13.	Jasra	8.15	5.84	2.31
14.	Shankargarh	6.66	3.92	2.74
15.	Kaundhiyara	5.4	2.32	3.08
16.	Karchhana	12.12	11.91	0.21
17.	Meja	7.9	4.65	3.25
18.	Koraon	5.75	2.48	3.27
19.	Urva	16.5	13.32	3.18
20.	Manda	8.83	5.9	2.93

Source: State Groundwater Department, U.P.

Decline in Groundwater Level

Owing to excessive exploitation of water, groundwater level is declining day by day. The need for groundwater is increasing because of the fast growth of population, increasing area of irrigated agricultural land, industrial and other uses. According to the Statistical Year Book of Allahabad District (2003), about 47 per cent agricultural land in the district is irrigated by under groundwater. Table 18.3 shows the groundwater level of different key wells.

Table 18.4 shows the declining groundwater level of Allahabad district in pre- and post-monsoon period during 2003–2005. In the district, maximum groundwater level has decreased about 4.5 m in Imamganj village of Dhanupur block. Water level between 2.5 and 3.0 m has declined in many key wells of Meja and Manda blocks. In the district on an average water level has decreased by 1.08 m during this period.

Table 18.3 Allahabad district: Declining groundwater level of different key wells (2003–2005)

Declining water level (m)	*Pre-monsoon*		*Post-monsoon*	
	No. of key wells	*Per cent of key wells*	*No. of key wells*	*Per cent of key wells*
0–1	68	56.6	50	41.6
1–2	24	20.0	24	20.0
2–3	18	19.0	19	15.8
3–4	4	3.3	12	10
4 and above	6	9.0	15	12.6

Source: State Groundwater Department, U.P.

Table 18.4 Allahabad district: Decline of groundwater level by blocks

Sl. No.	*Blocks*	*Pre-monsoon*	*Post-monsoon*
1.	Holagarh	0.32	0.55
2.	Soraon		
3.	Kaudihar	0.79	0.53
4.	Mau Aima		1.04
5.	Baheria	0.61	1.96
6.	Bahadurpur	0.73	4.09
7.	Phoolpur	1.21	2.22
8.	Pratappur	1.98	3.37
9.	Dhanupur	2.89	4.59
10.	Saidabad	1.34	2.5
11.	Handia	1.01	2.36
12.	Chaka	0.71	1.84
13.	Jasra	0.25	1.37
14.	Shankargarh	1.62	1.37
15.	Kaundhiyara	0.49	0.34
16.	Karchhana	1.33	3.89
17.	Meja	1.63	0.49
18.	Koraon	0.99	0.26
19.	Urva	1.14	1.67
20.	Manda	1.57	1.16

Source: State Groundwater Department, U.P.

On block level the average maximum groundwater level (2.89 m) has decreased in Dhanupur block. In some key wells, the water level has declined at an alarming rate. In the post-monsoon period of the year 2003–2005, the water level went down 7.3 m in Veerpur village of Karchhana block and Chamanganj village of Bahadurpur block. Water level has decreased more than 4.5 m in Dhanupur, Handia and Pratappur. There are 14 blocks where table has been found to have declined between 1 to 4.5 m.

Groundwater Recharge and Discharge

The recharge of groundwater takes place from infiltration of rainfall water through geological formation. Obviously infiltration differs from one area to another area depending upon geological formation and outcropping of land surface. In the area where the clay caps land surface, the recharge from the infiltration is very less in comparison to those areas where coarse sand and gravel outcropping prevails. In the study region recharge from irrigational channel also takes place because of flowing perennial rivers, the Ganga and the Yamuna. Hence rainfall and infiltration channels are the principal sources of groundwater recharge in the district. About 90 per cent rainfall takes place between June and September and remaining 10 per cent is distributed during the rest of the year. The recharge is evidently reflected in the rise of groundwater table in the monsoon period. Thus the water table fluctuation between May and October is the dependable indicator of mean annual groundwater recharge.

The groundwater recharge (Table 18.5, Figures 18.3, 18.4, 18.5 and 18.6) in various blocks of the district ranges from 9142.05 mm^3 in Baheria to 2457.73 mm^3 in Chaka block. Comparing the average recharge of the Allahabad district (5606.06 mm^3) only 9 blocks are above this average where as the rest of the blocks are below this average. Figure 18.5 shows the distributional pattern of net recoverable recharge in various blocks. The per/km^2 recharge ranges from 6.85 mm^3 to 46.39 mm^3. It is very high in Baheria, Holagarh, Handia, Kaundhiyara, Mau Aima, Soraon and Urva whereas very low per km^2 groundwater recharge is found in Shankargarh, Chaka, Kaurihar, Koraon, Manda and Meja blocks.

Table 18.5 Allahabad district: groundwater recharge and discharge by blocks

Blocks	*Recharge* (mm^3)		*Discharge* (mm^3)		*Development* (%)
	Total	Per km^2	*Total*	Per km^2	
Kaudihar	6133.72	15.39	4245.13	10.65	69.21
Holagarh	6870.68	46.39	4568.53	30.84	66.49
Soraon	4798.12	35.46	2533.27	18.75	61.13
Mau Aima	5286.77	35.03	3248.09	21.52	61.44
Baheria	9142.05	36.74	6803.42	27.34	74.42
Bahadurpur	6051.43	22.86	5057.91	19.10	83.58
Phoolpur	6290.95	27.92	3583.06	15.90	56.96
Pratappur	5020.23	24.42	3056.02	14.87	60.87
Dhanupur	4765.63	27.49	3836.24	22.14	80.50
Saidabad	5146.14	26.02	3338.83	16.87	64.88
Handia	4910.98	30.59	3195.49	19.91	65.01
Chaka	2457.73	16.00	1996.1	12.99	81.22

(Contd.)

Table 18.5 Allahabad district: groundwater recharge and discharge by blocks (*Contd.*)

Blocks	*Recharge* (mm^3)		*Discharge* (mm^3)		*Development* (%)
	Total	Per km^2	*Total*	Per km^2	
Jasra	6247.35	23.17	3079.09	11.42	49.57
Shankargarh	3176.38	6.85	1039.18	2.24	32.72
Kaundhiyara	6879.78	34.31	2976.56	14.85	43.37
Karchhana	6215.78	26.7	4099.32	17.61	65.95
Meja	4720.51	10.56	2278.21	5.09	48.26
Koraon	8966.5	12.29	2696.12	3.69	30.07
Urva	5373.54	31.81	3031.39	17.94	56.41
Manda	3766.86	10.84	2401.91	6.91	63.76

Source: State Groundwater Department, U.P.

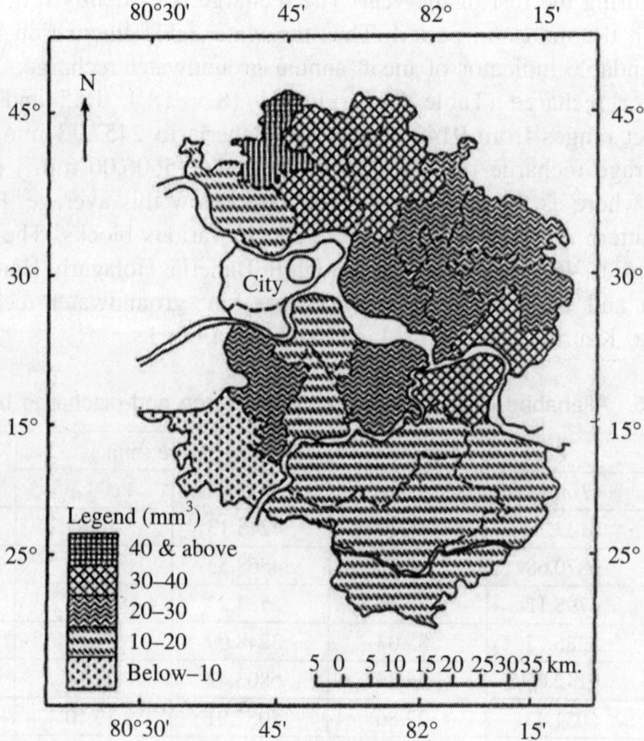

Figure 18.3 Block-wise groundwater recharge (per sq. km) in district Allahabad (2005).

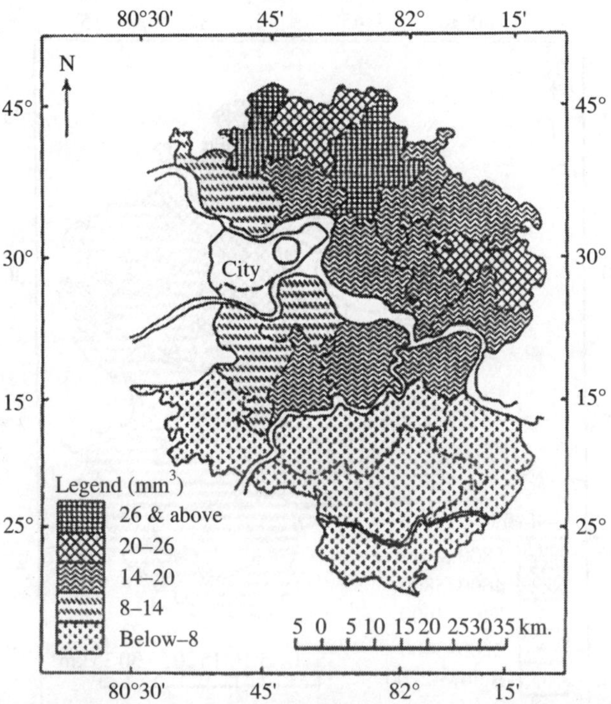

Figure 18.4 Block-wise groundwater discharge (per sq. km) in district Allahabad (2005).

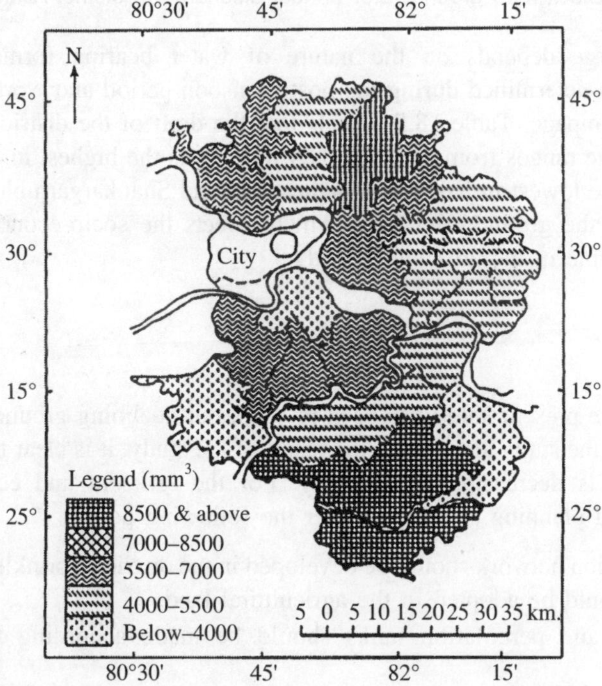

Figure 18.5 Block-wise groundwater annual recharge in district Allahabad (2005).

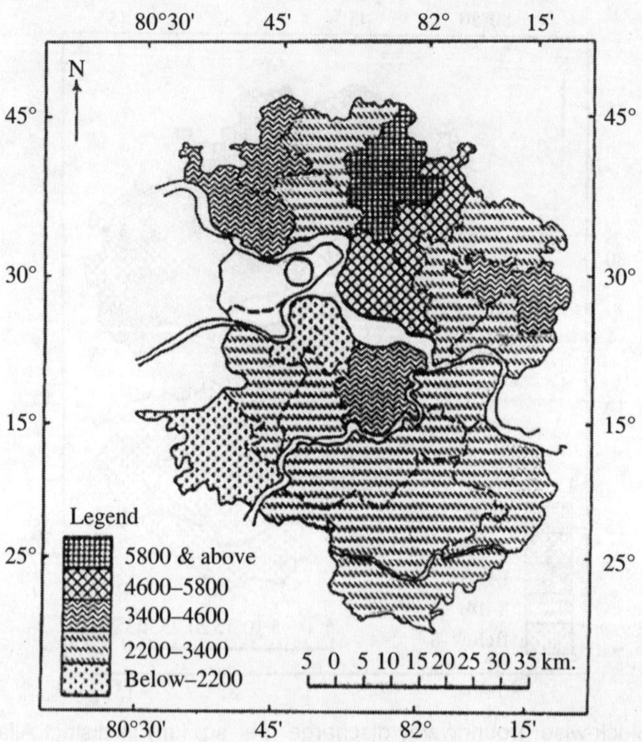

Figure 18.6 Block-wise groundwater annual discharge in district Allahabad (2005).

Draft or discharge depends on the nature of water bearing formation, porosity and permeability. Draft is determined during the post-monsoon period and worked out on the basis of the duration of pumpage. Table 18.5 reveals that the draft of the district is 67,481.87 mm^3. The per km^2 discharge ranges from 2.24 to 30.84 mm^3. It is the highest in two blocks (Baheria and Holagarh) and the lowest in Koraon, Manda, Meja and Shankargarh blocks. This discharge has great impact on the groundwater table which affects the socio-economic conditions and quality of life of people in the area under study.

Conclusion

The main focus of the present study has been to work out declining groundwater level, annual recharge and draft of the study area. From the result of the study, it is clear that the groundwater level of the district is decreasing day by day. For the efficient and economic use of the groundwater, a sound planning should consider the following points:

1. Micro irrigation network should be developed in the district. Sprinkler and drip irrigation practices should be adopted in the agricultural land.
2. Ponds, pits and percolation tanks should be made according to the flow of the rainwater.

3. Rooftop water harvesting system should be adopted. This system must be used in community centers, hospitals, educataional centers, other institutions and residential areas having larger space.
4. In the hard rocks formation, check dams and bandish should be made for collecting the rainwater. In bandish, water is collected in the slope side of the agricultural field.
5. Agro-forestry development may be promoted in order to allow the rainwater to percolate. Horticulture should be promoted in and near the barren land.
6. Cropping pattern of the irrigated area should be based on the availability of water. That is why we have to select crop variability and crop rotation.
7. Balance should be maintained between recharge and draft of groundwater. This balance helps in checking the depletion of water table.

References

Alam, S.M. and A.A. Kidwai (1987), *Regional imperatives in utilization and management of water resource, India and USSR*, Concept Publishing Company, New Delhi.

Bhattacharya, A.P. (1953), Penetration of rainwater to groundwater table in Doab, west of Ganga river in U.P. *I.R.I.* Tech. Memo.

Bilas, R. (1980) Groundwater resource of Varanasi district, U.P. India—An assessment, *The National Geographical Journal of India*, **26**(2).

Khushlani, K.B. and M. Khushlani (1984), *Irrigation Practice and Design,* Oxford and IBM Publishing Company, New Delhi.

Rao, K.L. (1975), *India's Water Wealth,* Orient Longman, New Delhi.

Mehta, M. (1978), *India's Water Wealth—Its Assessment, Uses and Projection,* Orient and Longman, New Delhi.

Singh, Tapeshwar (1997), Groundwater potential, quality and drinking water supply in India, *National Geographer*, **32**(1).

Tripathi, A. (1996), *Water resource potential, temporal utilization system and projection—A case study of Jaipur district, Rajasthan.* The thesis submitted to the university of Rajasthan, Jaipur.

19

Estimation of Run-off for Rainwater Harvesting in Haryana

Inder Jeet

Abstract: The surface run-off is one of the characteristic features of Haryana due to terrain. The present chapter attempts to focus on the methodology of estimating spatial and temporal run-off in the state. This helps in identifying the areas where rainwater harvesting is imperative for human survival and development.

Keywords: Stream Flow, Rate of Run-off, Percolation, Surface Gradient

Introduction

The moisture input in the form of rainfall is one of the major ecological influents on possible and actual farming system in an area. The reliance on it is more useful because it can express climatic complexes simply and quantitatively in terms of water balance. Haryana suffers from annual deficiency in water surplus. Water level fluctuations are common during pre-monsoon and post-monsoon seasons (Sharma, 1974). Annual rainfall varies between 1000 and 300 mm. Generally, 70–80 per cent is concentrated during three months of monsoon season. Rainfall, seepage by the Yamuna and the Ghaggar rivers and other streams, apart from drainage channels and recycled water are the main sources of water in this area. The short rainy season is succeeded by long dry season when soil moisture is rapidly depleted by high rate of evaporation. When rain comes, it may be of little use to the farmers since it is insufficient to recharge the depleted soil moisture (Singh, 1976). Basically, infiltration recharge is less than what is being lifted up for irrigation and, thus, water balance is disturbed.

Although rain is the main source of water globally, its distribution in both time and space is erratic. Developing rainwater catchment systems which can meet any given requirements depend therefore, on careful design. The maximum yield of rainwater is run-off from any system which is dependent upon two variables: the rainfall amount and the size of the catchment area. An intensive study by the US department of agriculture in a semi-arid area of Arizona (335 mm annual rainfall) carried out over two decades found that for every ten-fold increase in the catchment area the average run-off went down by about 36 per cent (Aggarwal, et al., 2003).

The run-off is generally considered in terms of the total flow carried by a stream during a month, season or year and accordingly it is termed as monthly, seasonal or annual run-off. The run-off is expressed either in millimeters or centimeters or meters of the water depth on the entire drainage basin or in hectare meter or cubic meter per unit area of the drainage basin. Further, the terms stream flow, discharge of a stream and rate of run-off are generally used to mean one and the same thing.

When the rainfall that has not been intercepted by the vegetation reaches the ground surface, part of it fills small depressions, part of it percolates into the soil, and remainder, if any, flows over the surface as overland flow. Each component of this equation is highly variable, and depends not only on the intensity of the rainfall but also on soil, vegetation and surface gradient. Rainfall reaching the soil surface has to fill the small depressions on the surface before any overland flow can occur, even on a totally impermeable surface. This depression storage does not vary with the amount of rainfall but with the nature of the surface, especially with slope gradient, vegetation cover, and land use practices.

In rainwater harvesting, the main interest is on the surface run-off which is the portion of rainfall that runs into rivers and finally into lakes and oceans. More accurately run-off is defined as that portion of rainfall which is neither absorbed into the ground, stored on the neither surface, nor evaporated but which flows over the land (Finkel et al., 1992). Run-off occurs only when certain thresholds are exceeded by rainfall. Either the rain intensity should exceed the infiltration rate, or the rainfall intensity or duration should exceed the storage capacity of the soil (Reij et al., 2001). Estimation or prediction of run-off is of primary importance in the design of conservation measures since the flowing water is both a cause of erosion and source of water supply. Two types of run-off are important in context of semi-arid zones: over land flow from the small watershed and intermittent streams. Perennial rivers in semi-arid zones generally have very large catchment area which does not yield significant amount of run-off.

Study Area

Rainfall is the main determinant of groundwater regime in the state of Haryana (27°50' N–31°6' N and 74°20' E–77°30' E), which occupies an area of about 442,12 km^2 (Figure 19.1) with a total population of 25,351,462.

Rainfall is markedly restricted in season and dry conditions usually prevail in the state. The short rainy season is succeeded by long dry season. The distribution of rainfall is irregular in both time and space and water deficiency is a problem everywhere. It is acknowledged that a very large amount of rainfall is received from monsoon during the months from July to August (Figure 19.2). Similarly, a good amount of rainfall is also received from a few depressions in January to March in the northeastern parts of Haryana. The monsoon rainfall decreases from east to west and northeast to southwest and cyclonic rainfall decreases from north to south and there is a significant variability in rainfall from month to month. The intensity of rainfall at any station can be very high to very low. In the northeastern parts, where the monsoon winds are strong as compared to the northwest, the intensity is high.

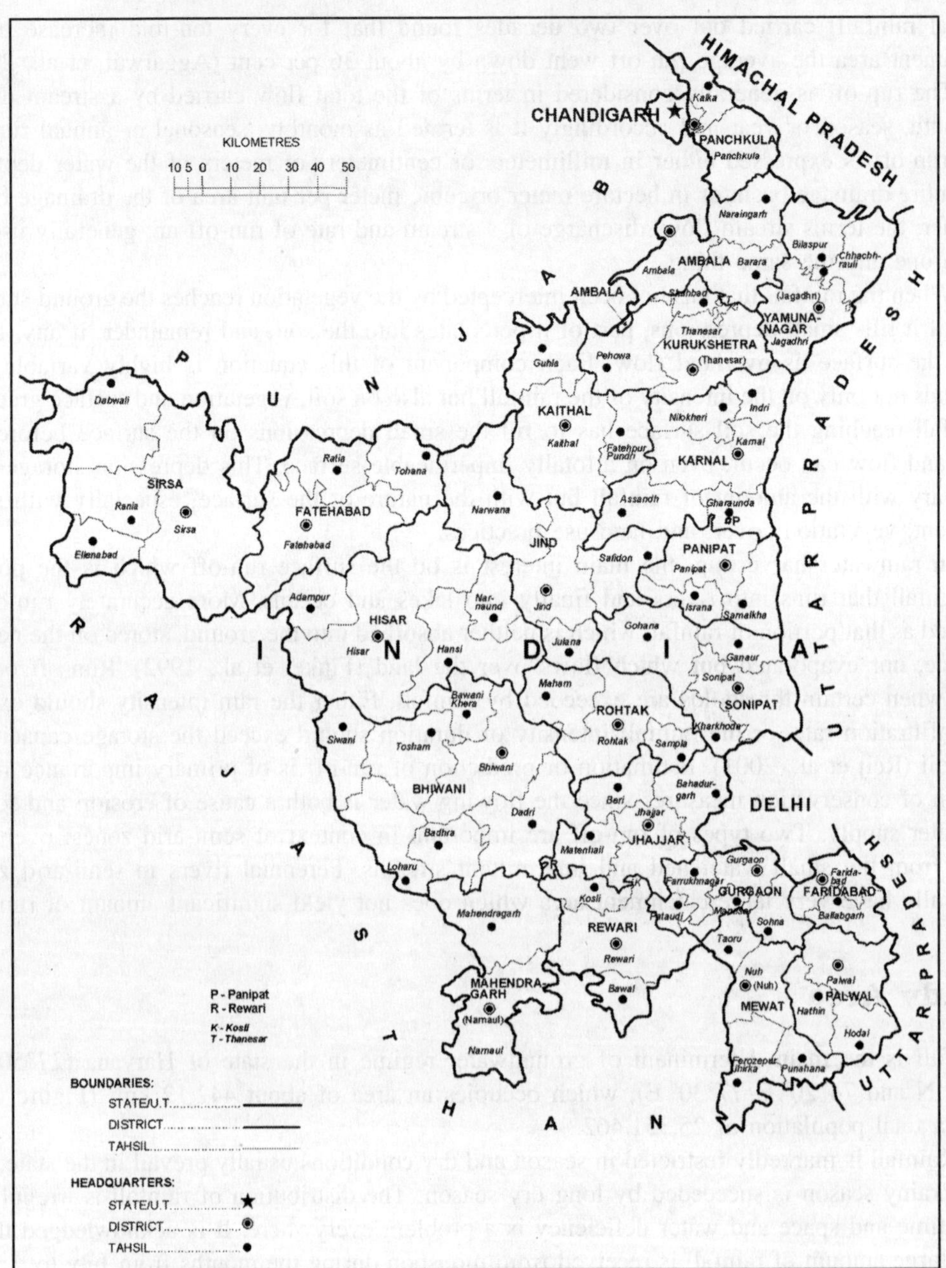

Figure 19.1 Administrative divisions of Haryana (2011).

Source: Administrative Atlas, Census of India, 2011.

The maximum values of annual rainfall are in the northeastern side with isohyets of 1100 mm passing through the administrative blocks of Naraingarh, Bilaspur and Chhachhrauli.

Figure 19.2 Percentage of the mean annual rainfall during the monsoon period in Haryana.

Rainfall reduces from northeast to southwest. In the southeast side of Haryana where Faridabad and Gurgaon districts are situated, the average annual rainfall increases considerably. Thus, isohyets through Faridabad, Gurgaon and Ballabgarh blocks gain a value of 650 mm rainfall. Table 19.1 shows mean standard deviation and coefficient of variability of rainfall of the selected stations of the study area.

It is evident from this table that coefficient of rainfall and dispersion from the normal is more in Narnaul and Hisar districts. These districts are situated in the southwestern and western parts of the state. As one moves towards the north and southern side of the state, the values of both standard deviation and coefficient of variability are smaller. But in Gurgaon district again these values are abnormally high. This abnormality might be due to the location of this district which is situated at the outcrops of the Aravalli hills. Moreover, everywhere rainfall is restricted in its seasonal distribution. Therefore, in the wide areas where average rainfall is marginal in amount, this variability is crucial. The coefficients of variability in monsoon and cyclonic rainfall are not identical in Haryana as the latter is highly variable. The cyclonic rainfall

Table 19.1 Mean, standard deviation and coefficient of variability of rainfall

Sl. No.	*Station*	*Mean*	*Std. error*	*Std. deviation*	*Coefficient of variability (%)*
1.	Ambala	875.1810	50.0814	229.5017	34.2
2.	Karnal	628.5857	49.5224	226.9403	36.1
3.	Gurgaon	764.5095	54.1031	247.9317	35.9
4.	Narnaul	536.7714	24.1563	110.6979	42.6
5.	Rohtak	588.0381	24.4871	112.2138	39.0
6.	Hissar	468.8238	20.8049	95.3399	40.3

Source: Computed

is least reliable and the same is true of monsoon rainfall in areas bordering the Rajasthan. Variability in excess of 20 per cent implies great risk in farming (Jeet, 2005).

The annual, seasonal and weekly coefficients of variation of rainfall are over 20 per cent in the State. The significance of variations in the amount of rainfall from year to year or season to season is difficult to assess unless these are related to defined water requirements of the area. This can be done by estimating the probability of specified amount of rain being obtained within a year. The variability of rainfall is inversely related to amount of rainfall. The areas of maximum variability experience the least reliability of rainfall. On the contrary, areas of least variability witness greater reliability of rainfall. As the state receives 80–90 per cent of its annual rainfall during the southwest monsoon season, variability of rain during this season indicates the trend of its annual variability.

From a hydrological viewpoint, precipitation constitutes almost entire water supply in any region; however, its water potential can never be assessed from precipitation alone. Therefore, it is necessary to know whether the precipitation is enough to generate surplus water in the form of run-off. Consequently, present study tries to evaluate the available run-off from the monsoon rainfall in volumetric term with the help of an empirical formula given by A.N. Khosla (1945) modified by Dhir (1960).

Methodology

A number of studies have been published in which different procedures and formulae of estimating run-off have been adopted by many scholars. None of them gives the satisfactory result. In the present study, Khosla's formula (1945) for run-off computation has been used. There are few points which support the choice of this method for present study. Probably the greatest merit of the formula lies in the fact that it does not involve the use of any numerical coefficient, the determination of value is left to individual judgment. The absence of this coefficient eliminates all likelihood of errors due to an incorrect estimation of its value.

The formula is as follows:

$$R_m = P_m - L_m \quad (19.1)$$

$$L_m = 0.481\ T_m \quad (19.2)$$

where,

R_m = monthly run-off (cm),

P_m = monthly rainfall (cm),

L_m = monthly evaporation losses (cm),

T_m = mean monthly temperature (°C).

A study of run-off estimation of the study area has been made. Five stations, namely, Ambala, Karnal, Gurgaon, Narnaul and Hisar were chosen for this purpose. Data relating to rainfall and temperature is available for these stations. Second, these stations represent different parts of the study area from north to south and southwest where over exploitation of groundwater has been taking place for the last many years. Run-off of these stations have been computed continuously for 30 years, i.e., from 1971 to 2010. Considering this time period an average value of run-off in terms of absolute and volumetric units have been estimated for each of these stations. Similarly, probability of occurrence of annual run-off for each of these stations has also been calculated. However, rainfall records are available for a long period and attempts have, therefore, been made to roughly appraise the water resources on the concept that the natural run-off (assuming that there is neither upstream development from the surface or the groundwater resources, nor any increment or decrement in the groundwater storage) is equal to the total volume of the precipitation minus the volume of water lost in the atmosphere through evapotranspiration.

Analysis of Result

Tables 19.2 and 19.3 (Figures 19.3, 19.4, 19.5 and 19.6) show the mean monthly rainfall, run-off and average annual run-off in different parts of the study area. These tables reveal that during the four months of rainy season, this area receives maximum of rainfall and consequently, this is the peak period of the year when maximum run-off is available for its storage through different kinds of water harvesting techniques. Although rain starts from the last weak of June, but during this month, rainfall only replenishes the soil moisture through infiltration or lost in the space in the form of evapotranspiration.

Table 19.2 Mean monthly rainfall and run-off (1971–2010)

Month	*Ambala*		*Karnal*		*Gurgaon*		*Narnaul*		*Hisar*	
	Rainfall (cm)	*Run-off* (cm)	*Rainfall* (cm)	*Run-off* (cm)	*Rainfall* (cm)	*Run-off* (cm)	*Rainfall* (cm)	*Run-off* (cm)	*Rainfall* (cm)	*Run-off* (cm)
January	2.3	0.6	0.8	0.0	1.8	0.0	0.9	0.0	0.5	0.0
February	2.6	0.8	3.0	0.0	2.4	0.0	1.0	0.0	0.9	0.0
March	2.3	0.0	2.03	0.0	1.0	0.0	0.6	0.0	0.0	0.0
April	1.8	0.0	0.1	0.0	1.3	0.0	0.3	0.0	0.0	0.0
May	1.7	0.0	1	0.0	1	0.0	2.7	0.0	0.0	0.0
June	12.0	0.3	4.9	0.0	6.2	0.0	8.1	0.3	8.0	0.0
July	27.8	14.0	19.2	7.2	27.6	12.9	17.1	5.3	22.8	3.4

(Contd.)

Table 19.2 Mean monthly rainfall and run-off (1971–2010) (*Contd.*)

Month	*Ambala*		*Karnal*		*Gurgaon*		*Narnaul*		*Hisar*	
	Rainfall (cm)	*Run-off* (cm)	*Rainfall* (cm)	*Run-off* (cm)	*Rainfall* (cm)	*Run-off* (cm)	*Rainfall* (cm)	*Run-off* (cm)	*Rainfall* (cm)	*Run-off* (cm)
August	19.0	7.4	20.2	5.6	18.4	4.9	15.7	0.3	12.5	1.2
September	12.0	2.0	12.6	1.8	10.3	0.5	7.1	3.6	4.8	0.0
October	4.5	0.0	2.5	0.0	3.6	0.0	0.9	0.4	2.5	0.0
November	0.9	0.0	0.8	0.0	0.3	0.0	0.1	0.0	0.8	0.0
December	1.7	0.0	1.6	0.0	1.9	0.0	0.2	0.0	0.0	0.0
Annual	85.2	23.9	70.5	14.5	75.8	18.3	53.7	9.9	52.0	4.6

Table 19.3 Haryana: District-wise average volume of rainwater available during monsoon season

District	*Area (Haryana)*	*Average monsoon rainfall* (mm)				*Volume of rainwater* (Ham)				*Total volume of rainfall*	*Average rainfall* (mm/ha)
		June	*July*	*August*	*Sept.*	*June*	*July*	*August*	*Sept.*		
Ambala	238,500	93.6	285.3	274.3	156	22,323.6	68,044.0	65,420.5	37,206.0	192,994.1	0.80
Yamunanagar	175,600	92.8	281.5	268.7	151.2	16,330.8	49,431.4	47,183.7	26,550.7	139,496.6	0.79
Kurukshetra	121,700	52.5	191.8	157.7	103.3	6389.2	17367.0	19,192.0	12,571.6	55,519.8	0.45
Kaithal	279,900	50.2	142.70	120.40	108.20	14,065.0	39,941.7	33,699.9	30,285.1	117,991.7	0.42
Karnal	196,700	52.2	191.8	191.8	115.4	10,267.7	37,727.0	37,727.0	22,699.1	108,420.8	0.55
Panipat	175,400	51.9	173.02	162.61	114.24	9103.2	30,344.2	28,520.0	20,030.6	87,998.0	0.50
Sonipat	138,500	42.7	168.7	161.9	99.1	5913.9	23,364.9	22,423.1	13,725.3	65,427.2	0.47
Faridabad	210,500	41.9	174.8	160.3	110.4	8819.9	35,511.3	33,743.1	23,239.2	101,313.5	0.48
Gurgaon	276,000	41.7	175.1	179.6	105.0	11,509.2	48,327.6	49,569.6	28,980.0	138,386.4	0.50
Mahendergarh	168,300	38.9	149.9	178.0	82.9	6546.8	25,228.1	2997.4	13,952.0	48,724.3	0.28
Rewari	155,900	47.40	140.86	135.17	112.56	7389.6	21,950.7	21,062.0	17,538.7	67,941.0	0.43
Bhiwani	514,000	30.7	128.5	133.8	68.1	15,779.8	66,049.0	68,773.2	35,003.4	185,605.4	0.36
Rohtak	258,100	34.9	150.5	140.9	78.8	9007.6	38,844.0	36,366.2	20,338.2	104,556	0.40
Jhajjar	183,000	45.79	143.00	115.06	101.00	8363.1	26,169.0	30,250.0	18,483.0	83,265.0	0.45
Jind	273,600	34.3	187.3	165.3	68.1	9384.4	51,245.2	45,226.0	18,632.1	124,487.6	0.45
Hisar	411,800	34.1	110.1	109.7	64.1	14,042.3	45,339.1	45,174.4	26,396.3	13,095.1	0.31
Sirsa	427,600	28.8	90.8	85.8	56.7	12,314.8	38,826.0	36,688.0	24,244.9	112,073.7	0.21
Fatehabad	216,000	31.12	91.41	87.99	60.47	6717.6	19,742.4	18,986.4	13,046.4	58,492.8	0.27

Source: India Meteorological Department, Government of India.

As rainfall continues in the coming months, at one point of time rainfall exceeds the infiltration rate during the month of July. Consequently, region shows extra water in the form of run-off. Similarly, as monsoon recedes from the last week of September, amount of run-off also comes down. More importantly, the significant characteristics of rainfall which may

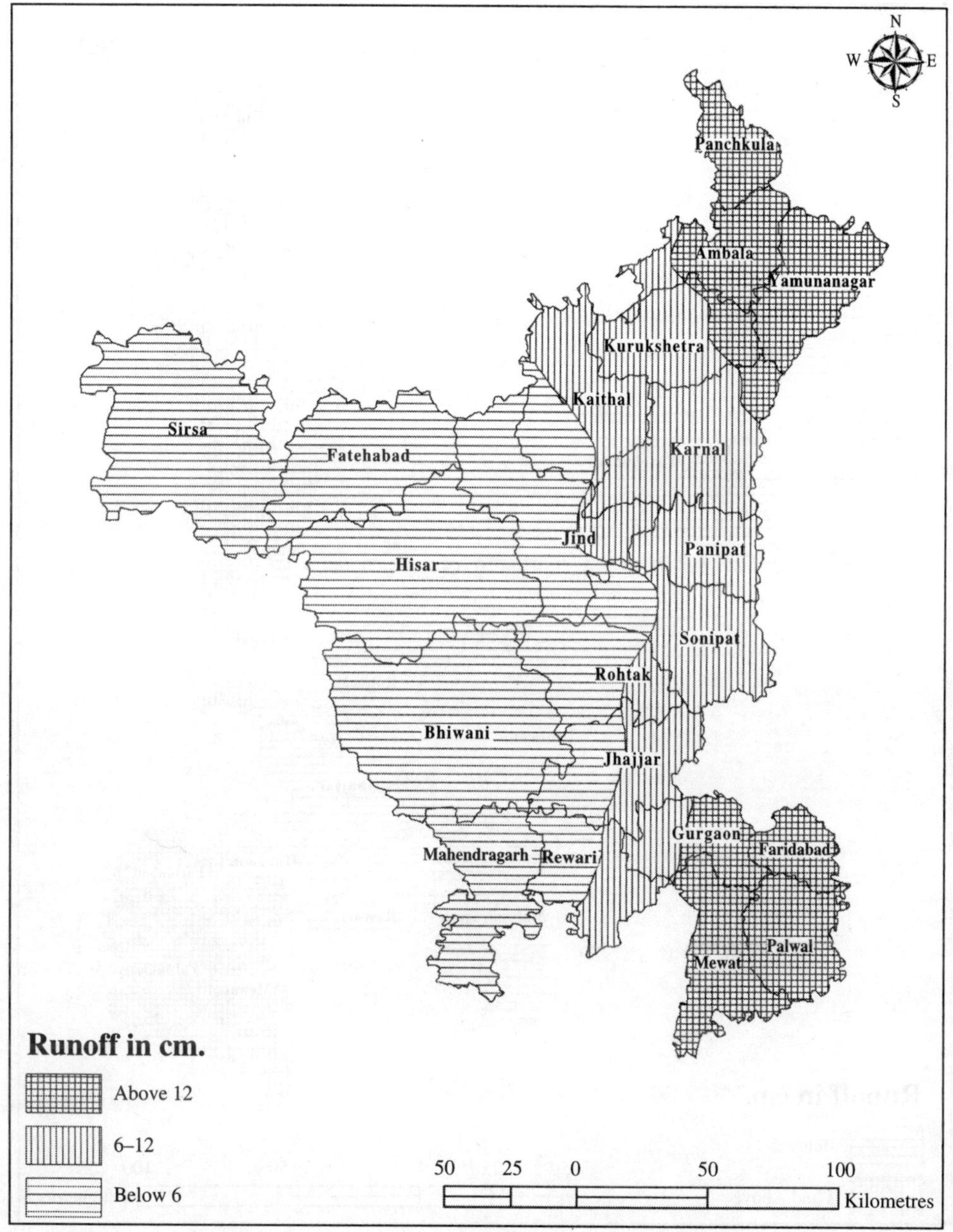

Figure 19.3 Average run-off during July in Haryana.

considerably affect the run-off are the types of rainfall, its intensity, extent and duration. Run-off increases with the increase of rainfall. This is so because an intense rainfall results in less evaporation and infiltration losses. During the monsoon season rainfall comes with intense storms at different frequencies which extend larger scope of run-off.

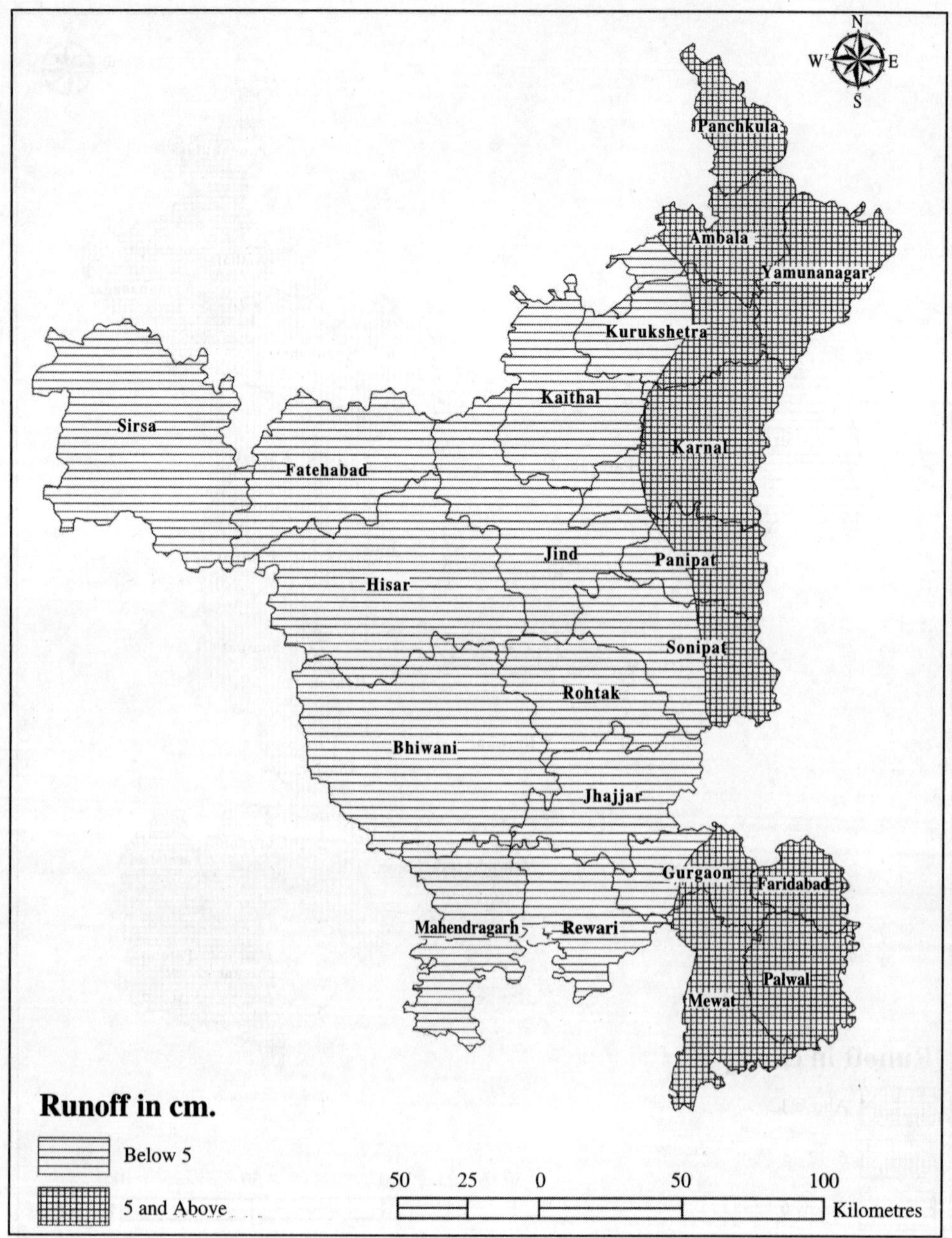

Figure 19.4 Average run-off during August in Haryana.

Northern Haryana which includes parts of Ambala, Punchkula and Yamunanagar districts experience more than 20 cm annual run-off. This amount of run-off is very significant from the harvesting point of view. Topographically, these parts have undulating slopes due to Shiwalik hills. These slopes provide rapid run-off down to the plain areas. The Markanda, the Tangri and other seasonal streams experience flash floods during the rainy season. The excess water during

Figure 19.5 Average run-off during September in Haryana.

the monsoon season has tremendous possibilities for storage in natural and artificial structures. Hence, the first rainwater harvesting structure was constructed in village Sukhomajari in 1978; it was followed by Nada in 1980, Bunga in 1885 and Relmajara in 1982.

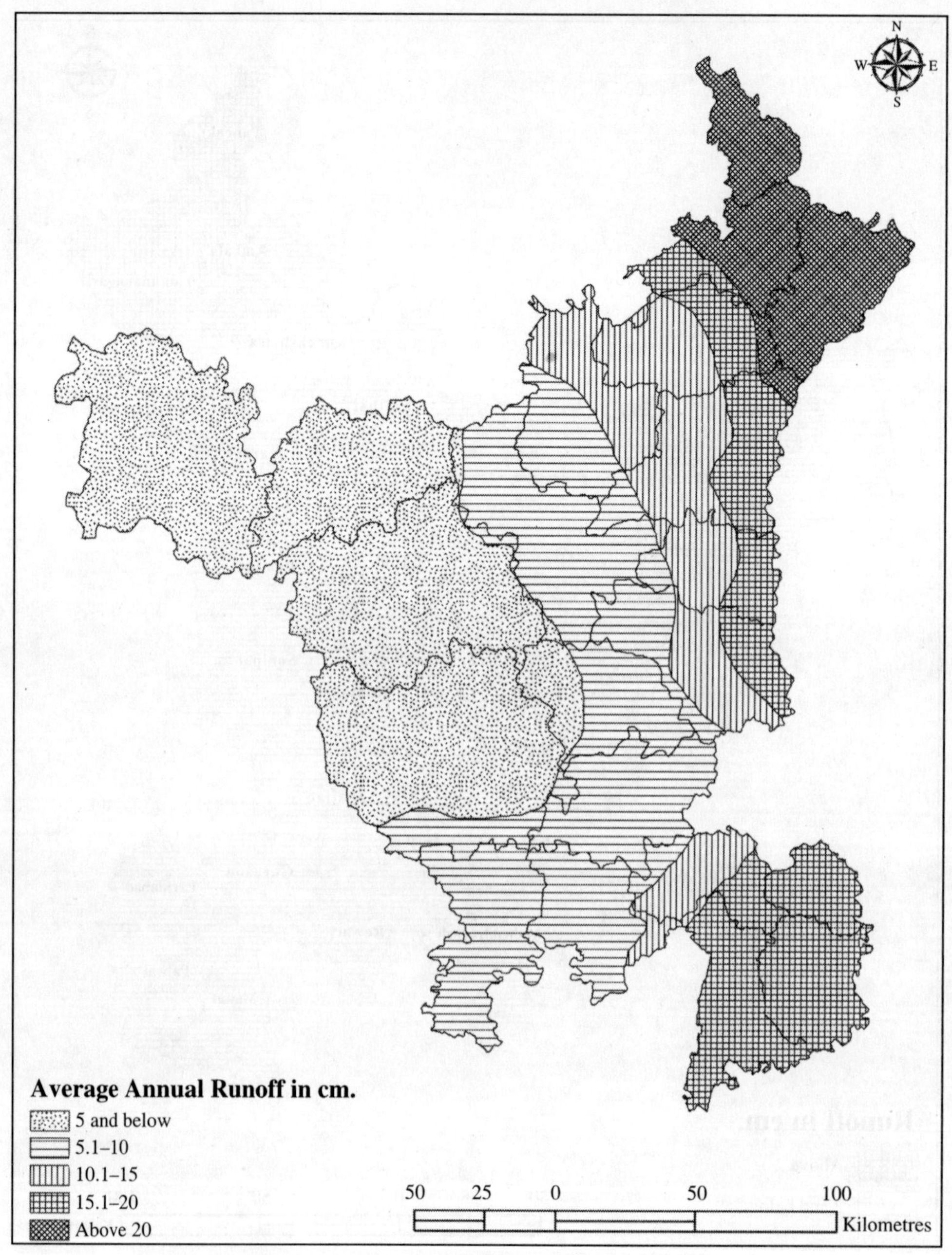

Figure 19.6 Average annual run-off in Haryana.

Moreover, Shiwaliks form main run-off zones in the Markanda and Tangri watersheds. Though the lithology in these geomorphic units (sandstones and conglomerates) has primary porosity, the predominance of shale and clays render them less permeable. High relief and steep slopes together with less permeable lithology result in loss of a major portion of the rainfall as surface run-off.

As one moves towards the southern parts of the state, quantity of run-off decreases (Figure 19.6) following the rainfall pattern. In the central and southwestern parts, which include districts of Kurukshetra, Karnal, Kaithal, Panipat, Sonipat, Jind, Rohtak, Faridabad, Gurgaon, Rewari, Mahendragarh and parts of Bhiwani district, amount of run-off varies from 15 to 5 cm. Run-off amount is less than 5 cm in the western parts especially in Sirsa, Hisar, Bhiwani and parts of Jind and Rohtak districts.

Similarly, if we take into account the monthly run-off, then July is the month when maximum run-off is available in the state. During this month, run-off varies between less than 6 cm in the western and south-western parts to more than 12 cm in the northern parts (Figure 19.3). In the month of August, run-off amount decreases and it concentrates around 5 cm which divides the state into two segments. Parts of Ambala, Yamunanagar, Karnal, Panipat, Sonepat, Faridabad and Gurgaon fall in the eastern side of 5 cm contour line and rest of the state falls in the western side of this line (Figure 19.4). Likewise, a very small amount of run-off is available during the month of September. More than 2 cm of run-off is available only in the hilly areas of Ambala, Punchkula and and Yamunanagar districts (Figure 19.5).

Conclusion

The aforesaid analysis reveals that the pattern of surface run-off is controlled by several factors such as duration and intensity of rainfall, surface structure and nature of slope. The estimation of surface run-off helps understand the potential areas of surplus and deficit of surface run-off.

For designing and developing water harvesting storage system, a reliable estimation of run-off is essential for a given soil and land use conditions. Analysis of data in this part of country has revealed that the maximum rainfall and run-off occur during monsoon period. No amount of run-off is reported in the months from January to April. However, in individual years, it can be as high as 72.3 cm due to high evaporation losses. This region has been designated as climatically water deficit zone. The maximum water deficit occurs during summer season, i.e. mid-March to mid-June. Hence, there is tremendous necessity to harvest rainwater into farm ponds or storage structures which can be either utilized during lean periods or for improving the groundwater regimes.

The empirical analysis presented here reveals that the state witnesses spatial and temporal patterns in run-off availability. The region is homogenous in topography, terrain, vegetation, geomorphology and soils with the result that the range of various interrelated variables affecting the availability of run-off is considerably reduced. It has been noted that the run-off is more in the northern parts of the state especially in the districts of Ambala, Punchkula and Yamunanagar. These districts have hilly terrain with the different magnitudes of slopes; consequently, the quantity of run-off is also high. As one moves southwards towards Gurgaon, Mahendragarh, and Rewari, run-off decreases with the decrease of rainfall. In these parts also due to the presence of Aravali hills again quantity of run-off is little bit more than the other parts of the region.

References

Agarwal, Anil, Narain, Sunita and Khurana, Indra (2003), *Making Water Everybody's Business*, Centre for Science and Environment, Delhi.

Dhir, R.D. (1960), *Rainfall-Run-off*, Central Water and Power Commission, Ministry of Irrigation and Power, Government of India.

Finkel, H.J., Finkel, Moshe and Naveh Ze'ev (1992), *Semiarid Soil and Water Conservation*, CRC Press Inc., Boca Raton, 93–101.

Jeet, I. (2005), *Groundwater Resources of India,* Mittal Publications, New Delhi.

Khosla, A.N. (1945), *Water Studies for Bhakra Storage Dam Project in Punjab*, Central Board of Irrigation of India.

Reij, Chris, Mulder, Paul and Begemann, Louis (2001), Water Harvesting for Plant Production, *World Bank Technical Paper Number 91.*

Sharma, V.K. (1974), Water Balance in Haryana–Punjab plain: A climatological approach, *The National Geographical Journal of India*, **20**(3), 145–159.

Singh, J. (1976), *Agricultural Geography of Haryana,* Vishal Publications, Kurukshetra.

20

Groundwater Resource Situation in Eastern Barddhaman, West Bengal

Mahamaya Laha (Mukherjee)

Abstract: The state of West Bengal is water surplus area. However, there is a great spatial variation in groundwater level depending upon season and use. This chapter attempts to present the groundwater situation of Eastern Barddhaman by highlighting groundwater reserve situation, seasonal variation in groundwater level, spatial distribution of groundwater abstraction structure, cropping pattern, groundwater budget, groundwater irrigation and spatio-social changes and finally groundwater irrigation and its adverse effects. This chapter hints at the remedial measures to meet the challenges of their adverse effects.

Keywords: Minor Irrigation (MI), State Water Irrigation Directorate (SWID), Principal Agricultural Office (PAO), Gross Irrigated Area (GIA), Gross Cropped Area (GCA), Lithology

Introduction

Development of groundwater reserve depends on geology, surface material, slope, soil, vegetation and rainfall of an area. Good rainfall, permeable rock, friable soil together make copious groundwater recharge in a region. Further seepage from surface water bodies also plays important role. District Barddhaman of West Bengal is located in Eastern India and eastern part of the district belongs to Lower Gangetic Plain. So the region is drained by a number of rivers and is rich in alluvial soil. Good annual rainfall, alluvial soil and seepage from surface water bodies are supposed to form good potential for groundwater reserve. Agriculture is main occupation in eastern Barddhaman and the district is well developed in agriculture since pre-British era. Hunter referred that Barddhaman used to contribute maximum revenue from agriculture in India (Hunter, 1877). Rich physical resource base has probably helped to sustain the pace of agricultural development of eastern Barddhaman.

Rich surface water resources like rivers, tanks and canals gear up agricultural development of eastern Barddhaman. As the use of groundwater irrigation starts, crop diversity increases and along with this some new problems crop up in agricultural sector.

The major objectives of this paper are to have an idea of lithological situation, spatio-temporal variation of groundwater level, spatial variation in groundwater abstraction structures, changing importance of irrigation sources, adverse effects of groundwater irrigation in eastern Barddhaman.

Methodology and Database

The study has been divided into two parts: (i) Study of groundwater reserve situation and (ii) groundwater irrigation and changes in agricultural scenario. For reserve situation 110 litholog data have been studied to know the thickness and depth of clay, coarse sand and fine sand layers, sand clay ratio, etc. A panel diagram has been prepared for eastern Barddhaman showing three units—coarse sand, fine sand and clay layers. Medium sand has been treated as coarse sand and 'fine to medium' as fine sand (Maitra and Ghosh, 1992). Instead of groundwater contour, map has been prepared for pre-monsoon and post-monsoon water level below the ground for the years of 1990 and 2008. For agricultural part block-wise study of irrigation sources (1991 and 2001), spatial distribution of shallow and deep tubewells during three minor irrigation census (1989–90, 1995–96 and 2000–01) and cropping pattern (1984–85, 2000–01 and 2007–08) have been studied and tabulated.

The data for lithology, groundwater level and number of tubewells during MI census have been collected from State Water Irrigation Department and Agri-Irrigation Department of Barddhaman.

Data of annual rainfall and block-wise cropping pattern have been collected from PAO, Barddhaman. Irrigation data have been collected from DCH, Barddhaman, 1991, 2001. Finally field survey has been conducted to explain the findings from secondary data analysis and to identify problems and prospects of growing use of groundwater irrigation.

Groundwater Reserve Situation

Groundwater recharge in an area depends on rainfall, soil, slope, vegetation cover, lithology, etc.

1. **Rainfall:** Being located in tropical monsoon climate 90 per cent rainfall occurs during monsoon (June–September). Winter and early summer being rainless groundwater level naturally goes down during that period. A study of annual rainfall from 1980 to 2008 shows that year of excess rainfall follows a deficient or scanty rainfall year. Scanty rainfall must lead to lowering of groundwater level. Average annual rainfall is 140 cm.
2. **Topography:** Topographically eastern Barddhaman is a level plain (10–60 m). Major slope of the district is from west to east. So, flow of groundwater will be eastward as per Darcy's law (Wisler and Brater, 1959; Todd, 1959). Again, secondary slopes to the Ajay and the Damodar rivers, though ill-defined, are also found. Seepage from rivers, however, may help to enrich groundwater reserve situation.

3. **Drainage:** There are three main rivers—the Bhagirathi-Hooghly, the Damodar and the Ajay and their tributaries—the Khari, the Banka, the Behula, etc., in eastern Barddhaman. Their shifting courses leave stagnant water bodies like ox-bow lakes, bils, decomposed linear channels, tanks, etc. Abandoned palaeo-channels of shifting courses are sites of potential aquifers.

4. **Soil and vegetation:** Soil comprises of river-borne alluvium. Natural vegetation of *sal* forest is found only in parts of Ausgram, Bhatar and Mangolkote police stations, the part of former Junglemahal district (Petterson, 1997).

5. **Lithology:** Litholog data shows the presence of sand and clay layers below the surface (Figure 20.1). Litholog data of eastern Barddhaman shows that all the blocks possess one thick (>20 m) coarse sand aquifer. Clay layer widens both at top and bottom in Ausgram, Bhatar, Mangolkote police stations towards west and coarse sand layer becomes thin in the east. In Galsi and adjacent Khandaghosh police stations, coarse sand layer is intruded by clay and fine sand layers and it gets fragmented into number of thin (<10 m) aquifers. Litholog sites are generally characterized by a thick clay layer at the top, followed by one or few thin aquifers of fine sand and coarse sand, then a thick coarse sand aquifer and again occurrence of clay layer at the bottom. So aquifer is mainly confined here. The fine sand aquifer is thick (20–40 m) only in parts of Manteswar, Katwa and Purbasthali police stations, moderately thick (10–15 m) in Ketugram, Kalna and parts of Purbasthali police stations and thin (<10 m) in all other police stations.

Table 20.1 compiled from the litholog data shows that tubewells are shallower (65–100 m) in Ketugram and Katwa police stations, i.e., to the north and deeper (150–350 m) in Ausgram and Mangolkote police stations, i.e., to the west. They are at 100–150 m depth in rest of the police stations. The availability of thick coarse sand aquifer determines the depth.

Coarse sand layer is very thick at Kalna, Purbasthali, Raina and Jamalpur police stations. All these police stations are located along two main rivers, the Bhagirathi-Hooghly and the Damodar. These coarse sand aquifers are sometimes 40–70 m thick and sometimes two thick aquifers (20 m or more) occur in a single log site. Such thick aquifers occur in case of 60 per cent log sites of Kalna, Purbasthali and Jamalpur police stations, 40–50 per cent log sites of Raina and Burdwan and 15–25 per cent log sites of Memari, Manteswar and Katwa police stations. In Memari, however, occurrence of one thick and two moderately thick (10–19 m) aquifers are more common. Westward in other police stations one thick and several thin coarse sand aquifers occur. In a single log site there may occur 4–5 aquifers in Memari and Burdwan, 6–9 aquifers in Ausgram, Galsi and Khandaghosh police stations. Like the thickness, depth of main coarse sand aquifer also varies. It occurs at 40–50 m depth in Ketugram, Katwa, Jamalpur and Khandaghosh police stations, at 60–75 m depth in Kalna, Manteswar, Burdwan, Memari and Purbasthali police stations, at 75–100 m depth in Galsi and at 150–250 m depth in Ausgram and Mangolkote police stations.

Gravel content in coarse sand layer enhances yield potentiality of aquifer and occurs specially at log sites near a river course. In eastern Barddhaman, all the police stations possess gravels, pebbles, shingles or kankars with coarse sand at least at 50 per cent log sites. Gravel

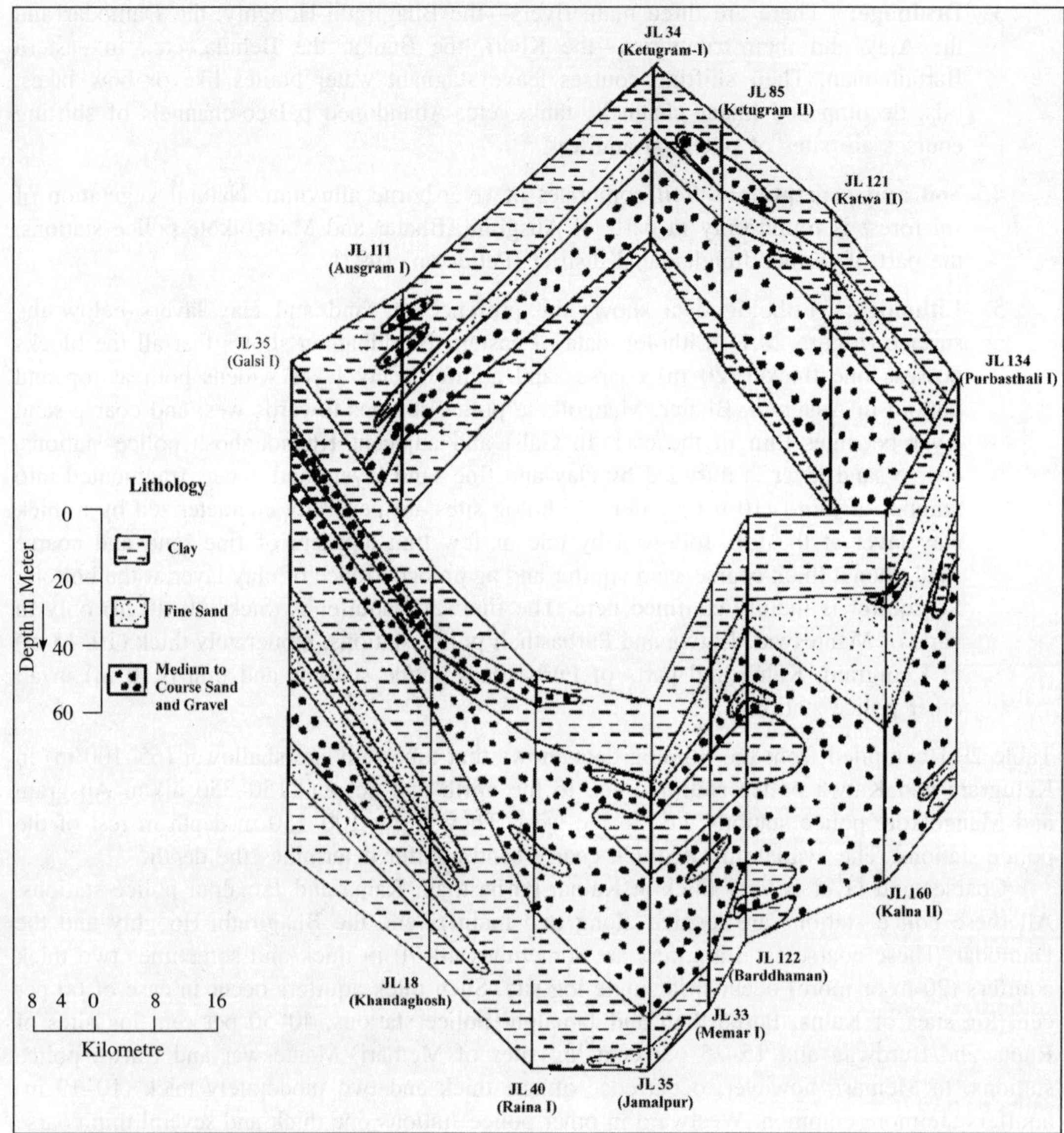

Figure 20.1 Panel diagram of eastern Barddhaman.

is found over 80 per cent log sites of Purbasthali, Kalna, Burdwan, Jamalpur, Raina and Galsi police stations. The total thickness of gravel containing aquifers is high to very high (25–60 m) in Purbasthali, Manteswar, Kalna, Jamalpur, Raina and Galsi police stations, both low and high (15–40 m) in Burdwan, Memari and parts of Khandaghosh police stations and very low (<10 m) in Ketugram, Katwa, Mangolkote, Bhatar and Ausgram police stations.

Table 20.1 Lithological characteristics of eastern Barddhaman

Sl. No.	*Police stations*	*Depth of tubewell* (m)	*Depth of thick* (>20 m) *CS* (m)	*Thickness of top Cl* (m)	*Per cent log sites with one* >40 m/ *two* >20 m *thick CS*	*Per cent log sites with GV/PB containing CS*	*Thickness of GV/PB containing CS* (m)	*Sand: clay*	*CS:FS*
1.	Ausgram	250–350	25–250	5–10	–	75	<10	0.5	3.7
2.	Burdwan	100–150	70–90	15–20	33	100	10–20	1.2	3.6
3.	Bhatar	100–110	30–40	25–30	–	–	20–30	1	3.0
4.	Galsi	130–150	80–90	10–15	–	85	25–60	1.6	3.33
5.	Jamalpur	110–125	30–50	20–30	67	100	40–50	2.1	3.6
6.	Memari	110–140	50–90	15–25	25	50	20–30	2.03	3.27
7.	Khandaghosh	100–130	30–40	5–10	–	67	15–25	0.92	4.1
8.	Raina	100–110	60–80	5–10	40	85	30–60	2.5	2.7
9.	Kalna	100–140	65–85	10–30	60	88	30–60	2.6	3.1
10.	Purbasthali	100–125	50–70	15–30	60	88	25–50	2.64	2.2
11.	Manteswar	100–125	60–75	5–15	17	67	20–40	2.14	2.14
12.	Katwa	75–100	40–50	15–25	25	60	<10	2.0	2.3
13.	Ketugram	65–85	25–35	10–20	–	75	10–20	1.5	3.13
14.	Mangolkote	100–250	80–180	9–12	–	75	<10	1.0	2.5

CS: Coarse sand, FS: Fine sand, Cl- Clay Gv- Gravel, Pb- Pebble.

Source: Agri-Irrigation Department, Barddhaman.

Like the main coarse sand layer, top clay layer is also very thick (20–40 m) in Katwa, Purbasthali, Kalna, Jamalpur and Bhatar police stations. But the top clay layer is often thin in Raina, Khandaghosh, Galsi, and Ausgram police stations and moderately thick (10–19 m) in Ketugram, Mangolkote, Manteswar, Memari and Burdwan police stations.

Owing to dominance of clay layer, sand clay ratio decreases towards west. The sand clay ratio is high (2.0–4.0) in the police stations of Purbasthali, Kalna, Katwa, Manteswar, Memari, Raina and Jamalpur, moderately high (1.0–2.0) in Burdwan, Galsi and Ketugram and low (<1.0) in Ausgram, Khandaghosh, Bhatar and Mangolkote in general. But coarse sand and fine sand ratio is high (2.0–4.0) in almost all the police stations of eastern Barddhaman. It is between 2.0 and 3.0 in Mangolkote, Katwa, Purbasthali, Manteswar, Raina and between 3.0 and 4.0 in Ausgram, Bhatar, Ketugram, Kalna, Memari, Burdwan, Jamalpur, Khandaghosh and Galsi police stations. In some log sites of Galsi, Khandaghosh and Memari fine sand is almost absent. It proves that along the rivers Ajay and the Damodar presence of coarse sand is higher than fine sand compared to the lithological situation along the Bhagirathi–Hooghly areas.

Groundwater Level Situation

Owing to rainfall, pre-monsoon groundwater level goes up in post-monsoon season. A spatio-tempoal variation is observed in pre-monsoon and post-monsoon groundwater level as well as in seasonal fluctuation of groundwater level (Figure 20.2).

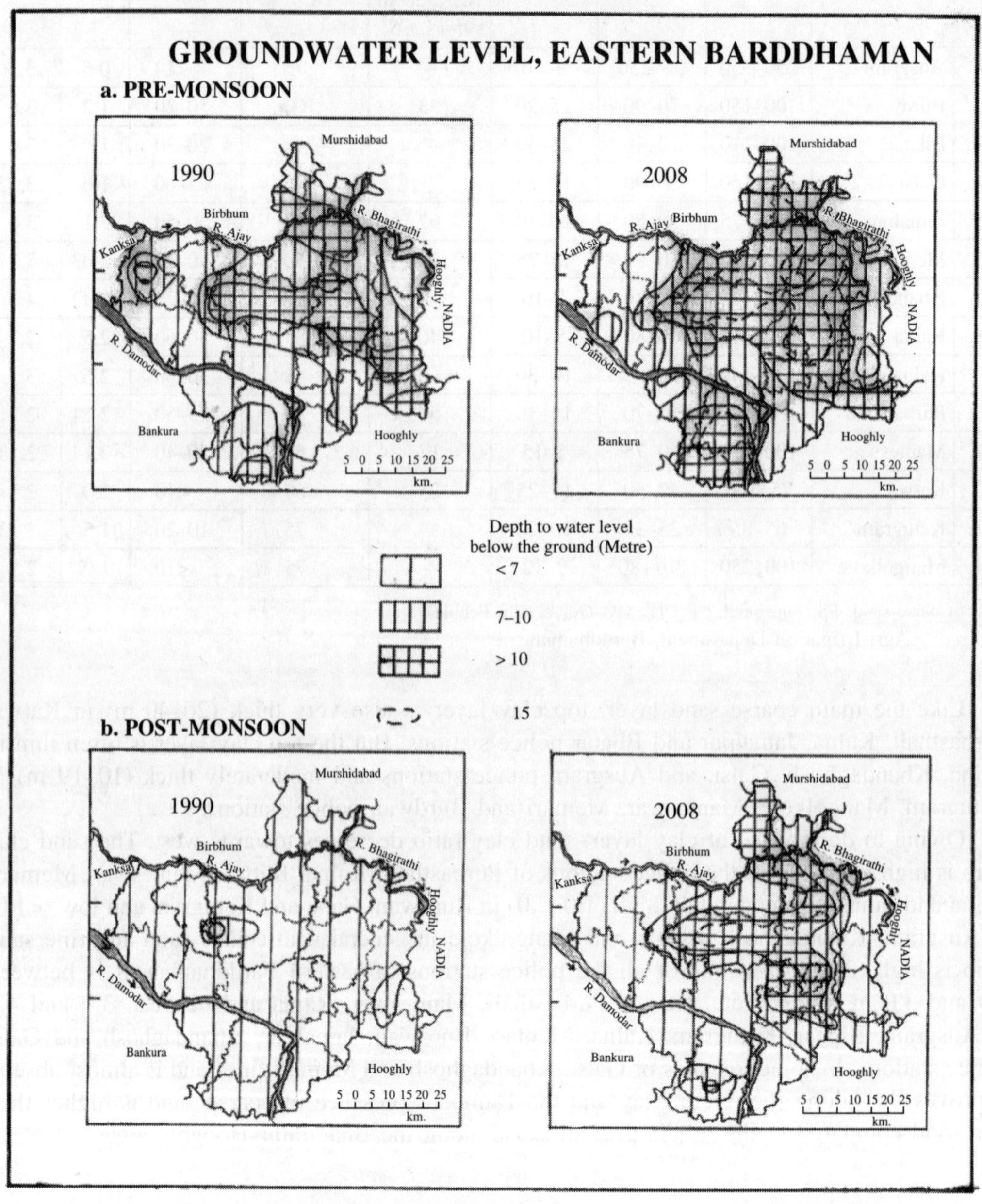

Figure 20.2 Pre- and post-monsoon groundwater level in eastern Barddhaman.

Eastern Barddhaman experiences an average seasonal fluctuation of groundwater level between 3 m and 7 m. There has been steady lowering of both pre–monsoon and post-monsoon water tables since 2000. Fluctuation of groundwater table is low (<5 m) in chronic low water table areas of Bhatar, Manteswar and even in high water table areas of Burdwan, Purbasthali-I, II, Galsi-I, II, Jamalpur blocks. Fluctuation is high (5 and 7 m) in Raina-I, II, Katwa-I, II and Kalna-II blocks. On an average groundwater level of the study area has been declining gradually but the rate of decline has been slow.

Irrigation Sources

In eastern Barddhaman tanks and rivers were main sources of irrigation in the beginning. Large scale canal irrigation started with the completion of DVC. Gross cropped area increased. The use of groundwater for irrigation started in late seventies and increased gradually. Availability of groundwater irrigation is ubiquitous in shallow water table areas of eastern Barddhaman. But canal has a space–time constraint. Again tubewell irrigation supplies controlled irrigation as required by crops other than paddy. A spatial variation of different irrigation sources has, however, been observed in eastern Barddhaman in 1991 and 2001 (Table 20.2).

Table 20.2 Source-wise irrigated area, eastern Barddhaman (1991, 2001)

Irrigation sources	*Per cent irrigated area*	1991	2001
Canal	>90	Bhatar, Raina-II, Galsi-I	Bhatar, Raina-II, Galsi-I
	70–90	Mangolkote, Ausgram-II, Khandaghosh, Raina-I	Ketugram-I, Mangolkote, Ausgram-I, Galsi-II, Raina-I, Khandaghosh, Burdwan-I, II, Memari-I, Manteswar
	50–70	Katwa-I, Jamalpur, Galsi-II, Ausgram-I	Ausgram-II, Jamalpur, Memari-II
Tubewell	>90		Purbasthali-II
	70–90	Purbasthali-II	Kalna-I
	50–70	Memari-I	Kalna-II, Purbasthali-I
	30–50	Purbasthali-I, Kalna-I, Manteswar	Katwa-I,II, Ketugram-II, Memari-II, Jamalpur
Other surface sources	30–50	Purbasthali-I, Ausgram-I	Ketugram-II, Ausgram-II
	20–30	Ketugram-I, Katwa-I, II	Katwa-II

Source: District Census Handbook, Barddhaman, 1991, 2001.

1. **Canal:** Canal, the major irrigation source shares >50 per cent of gross irrigated area in all the blocks of eastern Barddhaman except in Purbasthali-I and II blocks where there is no canal. Canal irrigation is the only important source in Bhatar, Galsi-I and Raina-II blocks. It is also of prime importance in Mangolkote, Burdwan, Raina-I and Khandaghosh blocks. It shared 50–70 per cent area in Ausgram-II and Jamalpur blocks in 1991 and 2001. From 1991 to 2001 canal irrigated area markedly increased

(25–40 per cent) in Memari-I, Manteswar, Ketugram-I, Ausgram-I and Galsi-II blocks and covered 70–90 per cent area in 2001. But in Ausgram-II, Mangolkote and Katwa-I and II blocks, i.e., northward from Damodar river, canal irrigated area decreased by 10–20 per cent during 1991–2001. In 2001, Kalna-I block was almost devoid of canal irrigation.

2. **Tubewell:** Tubewell irrigation is only important source in Purbasthali-II block covering 88 per cent of GIA in 1991 and 96 per cent in 2001. In 2001, tubewell irrigation covered 85 per cent of GIA in Kalna-I block and 50 per cent and 70 per cent in Purbasthali-I and Kalna-II blocks respectively. It also shared >50 per cent of GIA in Memari-I block in 1991. This minor irrigation also had significant share (30–50 per cent) in Ketugram-II, Katwa-I, II, Memari-II and Jamalpur blocks in 2001. From 1991 to 2001 share of tubewell irrigation increased in Jamalpur, Purbasthali-I and Katwa-II blocks by 10–15 per cent and in Kalna-I and Katwa-I blocks by 30–40 per cent. But its share decreased by 10–20 per cent in Memari-I and Manteswar blocks due to spread of canal irrigation there. Therefore, tubewell irrigation is important eastward away from Damodar and it serves a nominal area (<5 per cent) in canal dominated blocks of Bhatar, Galsi-I, Raina-II.

3. **Other surface water sources:** Tank, river, bil, etc. are other surface water irrigation sources which are important in the riverside blocks of Ausgram-I, II, Ketugram-II, Katwa-II and Purbasthali-I covering area between 20–40 per cent. During 1991–2001 share of this irrigation source increased by 20 per cent in Ausgram-II and decreased by 20–25 per cent in Purbasthali-I and Ausgram-I blocks. This irrigation is also significant in parts of other riverine blocks like Katwa-I, Manteswar, Memari-II, Kalna-I, Jamalpur and Khandaghosh sharing 10–15 per cent of GIA both in 1991 and 2001. But it is insignificant (<5 per cent) in canal dominated blocks of Bhatar, Galsi-I, II, Burdwan and Raina-I, II.

Spatial Distribution of Groundwater Abstraction Structures

Private irrigation development is slow in eastern India (Vaidyanathan, 1989). But this is not true for eastern Barddhaman. Groundwater abstraction structures (shallow tubewells and deep tubewells) rapidly increased here from first minor irrigation (MI) census (1989–90) to second MI census (1995–96) as groundwater irrigation was largely adopted by small farmers during mid-nineties. During 1989–90 number of shallow tubewells were limited (250–1000) in most of the blocks, but only Jamalpur block had >3000 shallow tubewells. Number of shallow tubewells increased by >400 per cent in the blocks of Katwa-II, Ketugram-II and Memari-II and between 100–300 per cent in the blocks of Katwa-I, Manteswar, Ketugram-I, Galsi-II and Raina-I during 1995–96. Growth of shallow tubewells from second to third MI Census narrowed down. In most of the blocks growth was <20 per cent only and in Katwa-I, Raina-I, Khandaghosh, Bhatar, Galsi-I and Purbasthali-II blocks it was between 20 and 55 per cent. Negative growth was observed in Jamalpur, Kalna-I, II and Ketugram-II blocks due to disfunctioning of tubewells.

As per third MI census the highest density of shallow tubewells (18.62 tubewells/km^2) has been found in Purbasthali-II block.

During first MI (Minor Irrigation) census there were no deep tubewells in canal-dominated blocks of Bhatar, Ausgram-I,II, Galsi-I and II. In most of the blocks there were only 1–15 deep tubewells. Only Burdwan, Mangolkote, Khandaghosh and Raina-II blocks had 20–40 deep tubewells. During 2000–01, number of deep tubewells were 50–60 in Purbasthali-I, II, Kalna-I, II, Katwa-II blocks in the eastern margin and also in Raina-I block. There were 30–46 deep tubewells in Manteswar, Katwa-I, Raina-II, Khandaghosh blocks and 20–30 in Jamalpur and Memari-II blocks. Deep tubewells decreased in number noticeably from 1989–90 to 2000–01 in Burdwan, Mangolkote and Memari-I blocks where extraction had started earlier.

Cropping Pattern

In Barddhaman district, paddy is main crop. Paddy used to cover 78 per cent of gross cropped area in 1984–85 and its share has declined to 70 per cent in 2007–08. Share of boro paddy has increased from 12 per cent in 1981–82 to 21 per cent in 2007–08. However, from 1970–71 to 2007–08 areal coverage of boro paddy in the district has increased by 500 per cent over 37 years. Next to paddy important crops are potatoes, vegetables and oilseeds, which have increased their share between 3 per cent (1981–82) and 7–8 per cent (2007–08) each. Other crops (jute, wheat, pulses, onion) have negligible share. Though paddy is main crop, spatial variation is found in cropping pattern.

During mid-eighties (1984–85) boro paddy had large areal coverage (>5000 ha) in Burdwan, Jamalpur, Galsi-I, II, Purbasthali-I blocks. During 2007–08 boro paddy covered >10,000 ha area in Burdwan, Bhatar, Galsi-I, II, Manteswar and Memari-I blocks. Share of boro paddy has been as high as 30–45 per cent to the block's gross cropped area in Galsi-I, II and Bhatar blocks and 20–30 per cent in Burdwan block since eighties. But the importance of boro paddy has decreased in two pioneer bocks, Jamalpur and Purbasthali-I due to growing importance of potato in the former and vegetables in the latter. Area under boro paddy has shrunk in general except in Bhatar, Raina-II and Ketugram-I blocks. Field survey shows that small farmers have markedly reduced the boro paddy cultivation mainly due to rising diesel price and consequent increase in cost of groundwater irrigation. Boro paddy requires watering of 40–50 hours or more per bigha from a shallow tubewell.

Potato is yet another important crop which depends on groundwater and requires 10–12 hours of watering per bigha. In 2007–08, potato covered 8.42 per cent area in the district. Potato cultivation was important in Jamalpur, Kalna-I, II and Memari-I, II blocks even in mid-eighties (1984–85). However, area has considerably increased during 2007–08.

Vegetable also depends on groundwater and it requires 8 hours of watering per bigha. In the district vegetable cultivation covers 7 per cent area (2007–08), but it is concentrated largely in Purbasthali-I, II (>15 per cent) followed by Katwa-I, II, Kalna-I, II, Burdwan and Khandaghosh blocks (7 per cent). Purbasthali-II is the pioneer block where vegetable cultivation increased from 13 per cent (3000 ha) in 1984–85 to 30 per cent in 2000–01 and 33 per cent (14,000 ha) in 2007–08. During 2007–08, share of vegetables outmatched that of paddy in this block. It is to be noted that Purbasthali-II wholly depends on groundwater irrigation.

Field survey shows that variety of vegetables grow at riverine islands, e.g., Gaitanpur (JL 165, Khandaghosh), Begunkola (JL 121, Ketugram-II), etc., which depend mainly on groundwater irrigation (Bhattacharya, 1998). This perishable cash crop needs constant inspection from sowing to marketing and so it is often grown in small holdings.

Oilseed, a dry crop of rabi season covers 7.7 per cent of GCA of the district (2007–08). Among various oilseeds sunflower is highly remunerative. In spite of government encouragement sunflower cultivation is not popular here. But the char village of Gaitanpur (Khandaghosh) is successfully growing this crop and selling at Barddhaman town.

Fruit culture and floriculture became popular in the area in late nineties. Cooperative farming of mango, rose, tuberose at Purbasthali (JL 80) and guava plantation at Srirampur (JL 135) in Purbasthali police station can be mentioned in this respect. Both flowers and fruits are cultivated in many char villages having easy access to urban market.

Groundwater Budget in Eastern Barddhaman

Differential access to canal and other surface water irrigation and variation in crop culture in the blocks lead to various level of development of potential groundwater reserve across the study area. Groundwater budget calculated by SWID in eastern Barddhaman shows that maximum irrigational development of potential reserve has taken place in groundwater dependent Purbasthali-I,II blocks (69 per cent) followed by Kalna-I, II (50–60 per cent), Katwa-I, II, Manteswar, Ketugram-II, Jamalpur and Memari-II blocks (30–50 per cent). Level of groundwater development is low (10–25 per cent) in canal dominated blocks of Ausgram-I, II, Bhatar, Mangolkote, Ketugram-I, II, Memari-I, Burdwan, Raina-I, II, Khandaghosh and Galsi-I, II blocks. Supply of canal irrigation lessens the demand of groundwater and perhaps seepage from unlined canal enriches groundwater reserve situation there.

Groundwater Irrigation and Spatio-social Change

Groundwater irrigation has made every piece of land cultivable. But to sell the surplus access to market or cold storage is necessary. At Bamunia village (JL 124) in Manteswar road condition improved after the installation of mini deep tubewell and submersible pump. Contrarily the use of groundwater and vegetable cultivation increased with the improvement of road condition or introduction of bus or rickshaw service at Sasanga (JL 58) in Khandaghosh, Belkas (JL 21) in Burdwan, Nirol (JL 27) in Ketugram-II block, Mandra (JL 98) in Purbasthali-I, Chaknara (JL 134) in Memari-I block, etc. So extension of groundwater irrigation and betterment of transport facility are interdependent.

Boro paddy cultivation has risen after eighties by using groundwater irrigation. This labour-intensive crop absorbs local scheduled caste people and the tribal people of Bankura, Purulia and adjacent districts of Jharkhand as agricultural labourers. Groundwater irrigation also makes multiple cropping possible and so gives year round employment opportunity. New employments are generated for pumpset-seller, generator-seller, van-rickshaw puller (from field to market), etc.

In areas having tubewell facilities, marginal farmers and landless labourers take lease of land from big farmers, till the land, make profit and ensure daily meal to their families, e.g., at Kuchut (JL 33) in Memari-II block.

Groundwater marketing is well known in Gujarat and Tamil Nadu (Saleth, 1996). In Barddhaman also it has become common in many villages like Nirol in Ketugram-II, Baharpur (JL 22) in Burdwan block. Big farmers install mini-deep tubewells or number of shallow tubewells and small farmers hire irrigation water from them at higher cost. Under similar situation social tension has widened in Punjab (Shiva, 1997). But the scenario is sometimes reverse in Barddhaman. In low water table areas big farmers who can afford to install submersible pump, provide irrigation water to small farmers in their need and get assured labour from them during boro paddy cultivation. Such friendly relationship has been found to develop among farmers in some villages of Manteswar block.

Groundwater Irrigation and Its Adverse Effects

In spite of lot of benefits excessive groundwater irrigation brings many adverse impacts:

1. The seasonal lowering of groundwater level in pre-monsoon is further activated due to widespread groundwater irrigation for potato in winter and boro paddy in summer. Based on declining water table and other related factors five blocks, Bhatar, Manteswar, Mangolkote, Ketugram-I and Memari-II were designated as 'critical zone' by SWID, Barddhaman in 2006. It's an alarm to the district. Over extraction of groundwater leads to an average fall of water table by 8–10 m a year in Punjab and Haryana and about 60 per cent tubewells do not function there in summer months (Tripathy, 2011).
2. Beyond 7 m depth centrifugal pumps of shallow tubewells do not work properly. Discharge of tubewell decreases in summer. The farmers combat the situation by lowering the pumpset around 2–5 m in different parts of eastern Barddhaman.
3. In some pockets of Khandaghosh and Manteswar blocks declining water table forces the farmers to lower the pumpset by 8–10 m. It results into subsidence of land in many villages of these blocks.
4. Big farmers often escape the hazard of subsidence. They replace shallow pumpsets by submersible pumps in mini deep tubewells. Small farmers cannot afford the cost and groundwater resource becomes mere reserve to them.
5. Potato cultivation increases after assured irrigation supply from tubewells. But sometimes over production reduces the market price and farmers incur loss due to distress sell.
6. Greater yield from boro paddy attracts the farmers to bear the cost of cultivation but damage of crop sometimes makes them economically depressed.
7. Rising tubewell irrigation indirectly causes deterioration of natural surface water bodies and that in turn impedes seepage of water.
8. Exclusive dependence on groundwater irrigation in multi-crop zone of Purbasthali leads to lowering of water table and it may be a reason of arsenic pollution of groundwater in Purbasthali and parts of Kalna and Katwa police stations along the Bhagirathi-Hooghly river.

In spite of the problem of disfunctioning of shallow tubewells and increasing cost of groundwater irrigation, farmers prefer groundwater irrigation for its assured supply and try to survive by developing indigenous techniques.

Conclusion

Eastern Barddhaman is rich in sandy aquifer. Everywhere there is at least a 20 m thick aquifer. Thickness of aquifer increases eastward and clay content westward. Shifting river course and flood deposit help to form good sandy aquifers and many potential aquifers like palaeo channels in eastern Barddhaman. In eastern Barddhaman groundwater level occurs at 5–20 m depth and experiences gradual declining both in pre- and post-monsoon seasons. Bhatar, Manteswar, Katwa-I blocks in the eastern Barddhaman are the chronic low water table areas. Mangolkote, Ketugram-I, II, Memari-II, Raina-II and Kalna-II blocks are now also experiencing low water table (10–20 m depth) during pre-monsoon season. Though costlier, groundwater irrigation is preferred to canal for its assured supply and nature of controlled irrigation supply. Extension in groundwater irrigation has increased crop diversity by increasing vegetables, oilseeds, fruits and flowers cultivation. But crop combination undergoes little change as these crops cover very less area compared to paddy. Even after increase in groundwater irrigation paddy is only crop in Bhatar and Galsi-I blocks and boro paddy still very important there. In the areas of declining water table mini-deep tubewells with submersible pumps replace the shallow tubewells. In low water table areas, sometimes mutual understanding of big farmers and small farmers make groundwater available to the small farmers also and a good social relation develops among them. Continuous abstraction of groundwater leads to lowering of water table. Arsenic pollution has taken place probably due to lowering of groundwater level.

Though eastern Barddhaman is rich in groundwater resource, constant extraction of groundwater may cause steady lowering in future and water crisis in summer. So, this is high time that boro paddy cultivation should be restricted. High remunerative dry crops like sunflower and peanuts can be cultivated with proper guidelines of agro-scientists. To encourage flower and fruit cultivation easy access to urban market should be ensured. Strong agro-industrial sector should be developed by government or private entrepreneurs for paddy, potato and fruits. For direct control of groundwater extraction existing rules of tubewell spacing should be strictly followed to preserve groundwater resource for future generation. Deteriorating tanks and bils should be renovated to practice conjunctive use of surface water and groundwater for irrigation. Mass awareness programmes should be carried out to conserve groundwater.

References

Bhattacharya, K. (1998), *Applied Geomorphological Study in a Controlled Tropical River, the Case of the Damodar between Panchet Reservoir and Falta*, Unpublished Ph.D. thesis, The University of Burdwan. Barddhaman.

Hunter, W.W. (1877), *A Statistical Account of Bengal: District Burdwan, Bankura, Birbhum*, 1st reprint, **4** (1973), D.K. Publishing House, Delhi.

Maitra, M.K. and N.C. Ghosh (1992), *Groundwater Management: An Application,* Ashish Publishing House, New Delhi.

Petterson, J.C.K. (1997), *Bengal District Gazetteer, Burdwan*, Govt. of West Bengal.

Saleth, R.M. (1996), *Water Institutions in India: Economics, Law and Policy*, Commonwealth Publishers, New Delhi.

Shiva, V. (1997), *Violence of Green Revolution: Third World Agriculture Ecology and Politics*, The Other India Press, Research Foundation for Science Technology and Ecology, New Delhi.

Todd, D.K. (1959), *Groundwater Hydrology*, John Wiley & Sons, Inc., London.

Tripathy, K.K. (2011), India's agricultural growth and stagnation: A review, *Kurukshetra.* **60**(2), New Delhi.

Vaidyanathan, A. (1989), *India's Agricultural Development in a Regional Perspective*. Centre for Studies in Special Sciences, Kolkata, **43**.

Wisler, C.O. and E.F. Brater (1959), *Hydrology,* John Wiley, London.

PART IV

Natural Resources Management

21

Natural Resources Management in a Mountainous Environment

The Case of Solan District, Himachal Pradesh

D.D. Sharma and H.N. Misra

Abstract: The management of natural resources is assuming greater importance as human population continues to grow unchecked and these resources are squeezing. The State of Himachal Pradesh is blessed with nature's bounty but at the same time it faces marginality, inaccessibility, fragility, and extremity in weather phenomena. The optimal management of these resources with minimal adverse impact is, therefore, essentially required for sustainable development. Based on the case study, the present chapter attempts to propose some useful strategies in maintaining and managing these precious natural resources which are vital for the survival of mankind on the earth surface.

Keywords: Land use/Land cover, Change Detection, Vulnerable Ecology, Sensitive Ecosystem, Land use Inventory, Replenish, Contour Bunding, Terrace Cultivation

Introduction

Himalayas present a very vulnerable ecology and sensitive environment where land, water and forest are only very delicately balanced. Even small disturbance in any of these is likely to cause very large scale repercussion and implications in all of them. The increasing pressure of human population on these resources has been only worsening the situation. Obviously, the per capita availability of land, water and forests has declined and the technology to meet the challenges emanating from this is so expensive that it is beyond the reach of common man. There is unbreakable relationship between human beings and natural resources. Any human action leads to some changes; some are of very short duration and of exploitative nature, while other may be long term and stable. The present case study of Solan district in Himachal aims at focussing these issues by discussing the state of land, water and forest in the study area. The paper also hints at reorienting the management practices for more sustainable use of natural resources.

Study Area

The State of Himachal Pradesh is divided into twelve districts. Solan (30°45' to 31°21' N latitudes and 76°36' to 77°15'20" E longitudes), is one of the twelve districts of Himachal Pradesh, which extends over an area of 1936 sq. km bordering the Punjab plain in the west. In view of administrative convenience, the district has been divided into five tehsils and two sub-tehsils (Figure 21.1). According to 2011 census the population of the district is 576,670, the density of population being 297 person/km^2. The pace of urbanization during the last two decades has been accelerated and there are eight small and intermediate urban centres housing more than 20 per cent population of the district. Interestingly, this is much higher than the urban population of the state. The urban centres of the district are growing so rapidly that it has great bearing on the hilly terrain and mountainous environment.

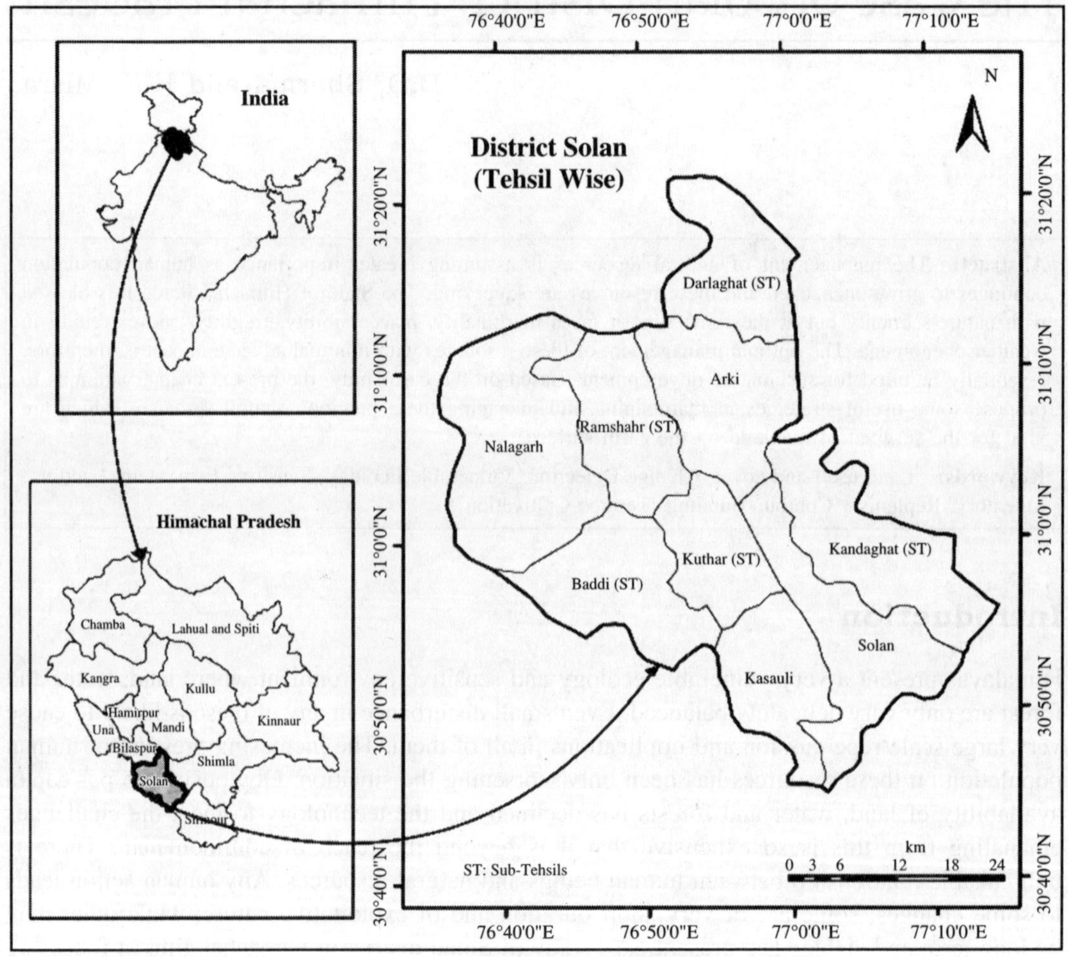

Figure 21.1 Location map of Solan district.

The soils of the region are young and thin which vary from light to sandy heavy and in the valley area it is sandy and sandy loam. The climate of the district is mostly sub-tropical in the lower reaches and the moist temperate in the upper reaches.

The terrain of the district varies from hilly to mountainous punctuated by three valleys—Saproon valley in Solan tehsil, Doon valley in Nalagarh tehsil and Kunihar valley in Arki tehsil. The elevation varies from only a little less than 300 m to more than 2100 m above mean sea level (Figure 21.2).

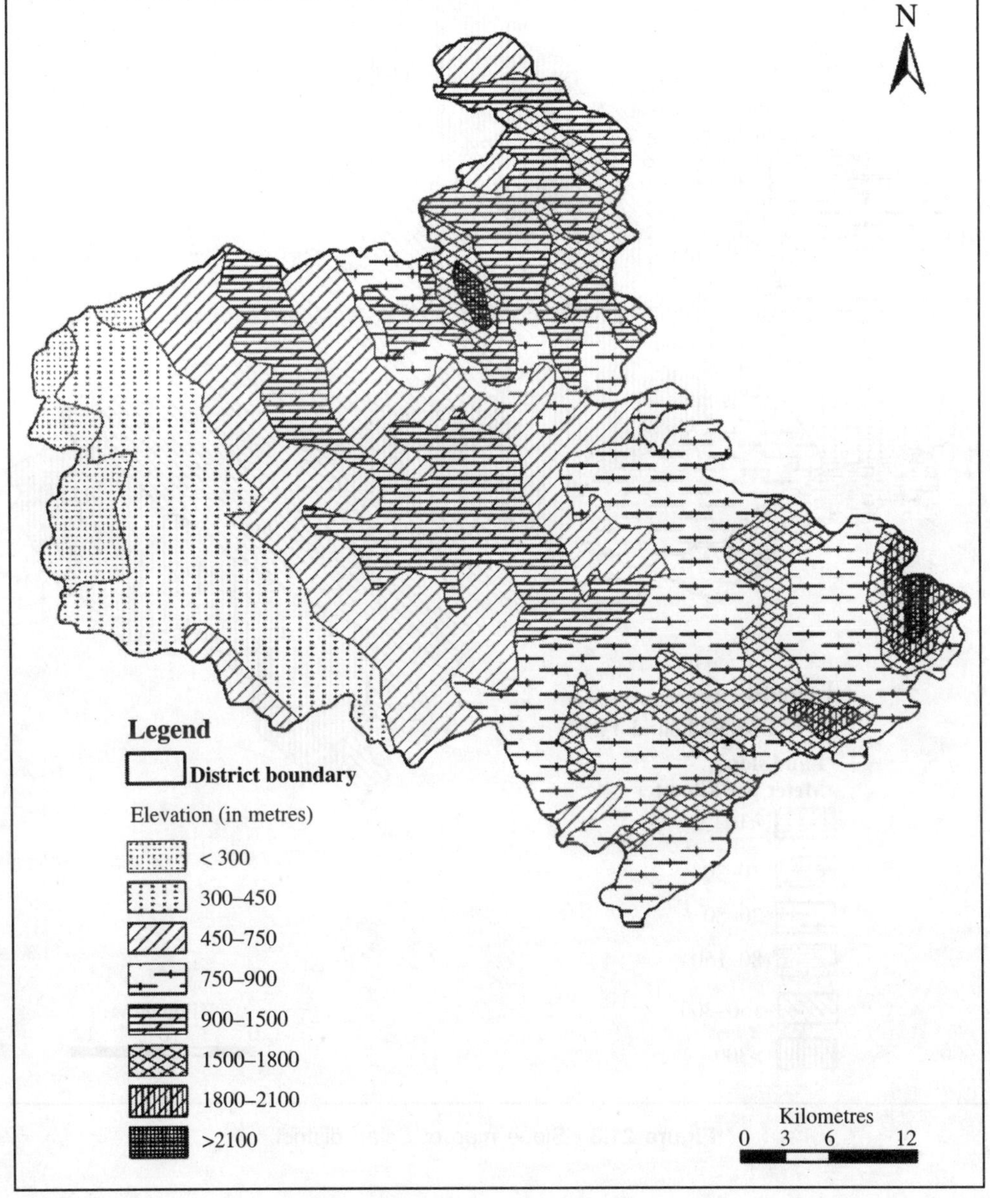

Figure 21.2 Relief map of Solan district.

The area is characterized by steep slope as major portion records slope above 150 m/km. There is only a small portion where slope is below 10 m/km. Thus the major part of the area is not suited to agriculture (Figure 21.3).

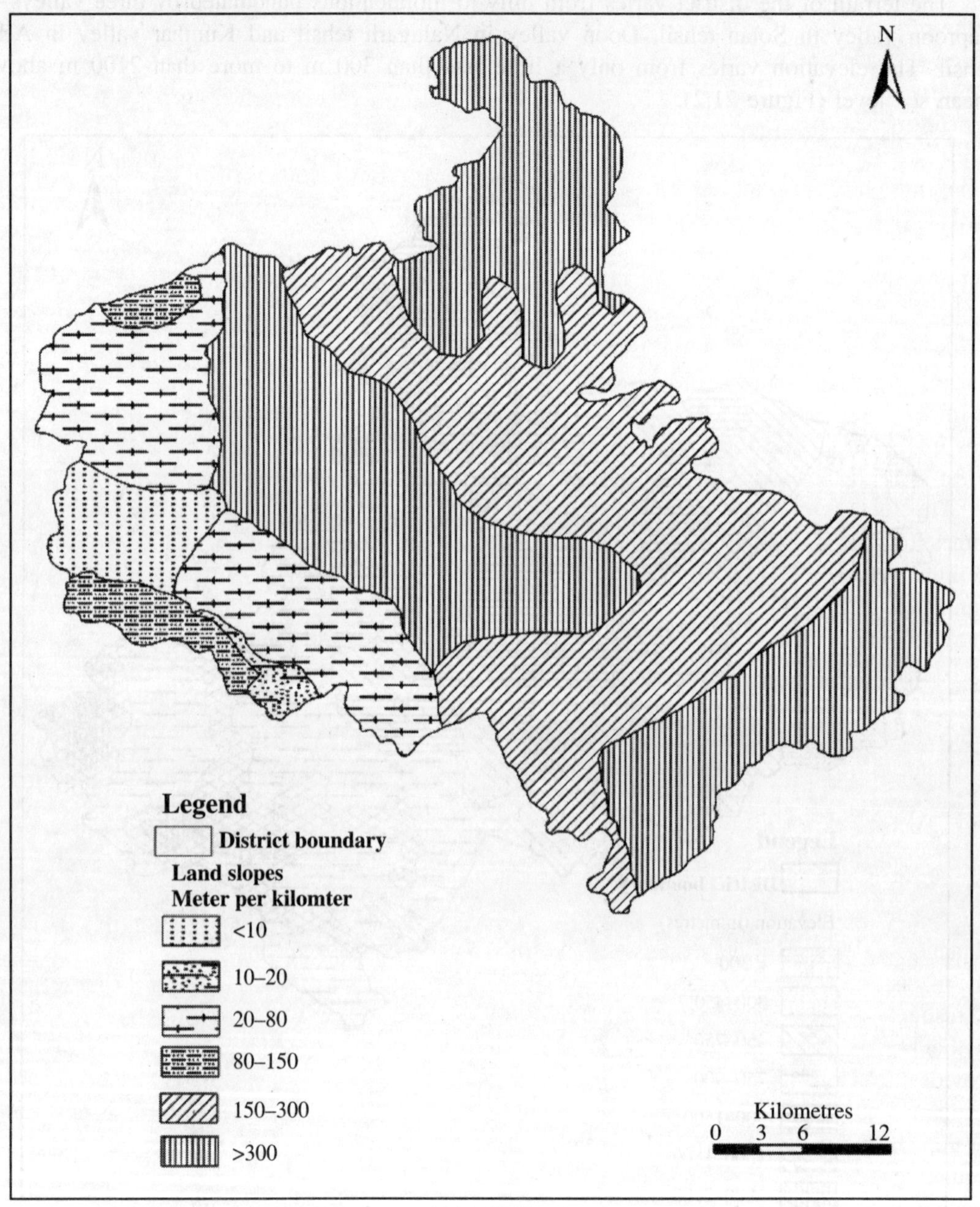

Figure 21.3 Slope map of Solan district.

The Present State of Natural Resources

The terrain of the district is mostly hilly and the fragile soils sit on the top of the soft and cleavable rocks. The forest cover has been protecting this fragile land for long, but mounting anthropogenic activity and peoples' greed cleared the forest and took away the protective cover leaving the skin of the earth exposed and vulnerable. This may also be attributed to poor economic conditions of the farmers who operate their farms at a subsistence and marginal agricultural land and they compensate their loss by extending crop to new areas by clearing forests (Negi, 2006). The cultivated and uncultivated lands are equally important as the food comes primarily from the cultivated land while the fodder, fire woods, water, building materials, agricultural and domestic implements and other natural products come from the uncultivated land, and forest protects these lands. Therefore, land, water and forests must be maintained and managed to meet the basic needs and to preserve the environmental quality and ecological balance in the sensitive hilly terrain. The district Solan is also facing the problem of land degradation, water scarcity and depletion of natural vegetation. It is a well established fact that inappropriate land use leads to decline of soil productivity and ultimately poorer quality of life. The change detection in the land use/land cover during 2001–09 clearly indicates how area under agricultural land has increased and forest cover has declined (Figure 21.4). In fact forest area has been encroached by settlements and agricultural land.

The inhabitants of the district face a great difficulty because of lack of water for drinking, domestic and agricultural needs. In 2008–09 the percentage area having assured irrigation facilities was only 24.43 per cent whereas more than three-fourths of the net sown area was completely rain fed (Annual Season and Crop Report, 2008–09). In the recent few years, the district has been facing drought like situation and natural drinking water springs are drying up. The town of Solan often suffers from water shortage. There is great water crisis especially during summer. The tap water often comes after 4–5 days. The forest land, grazing land and other common lands have been increasingly degraded, leading to deforestation and ecological imbalances on one hand and the unemployment, poverty, deterioration in the quality of life on the other.

Resource Management Strategy

Management of resources is a very complex issue and there are several variants of management. The management has to seek compromise between optimal use and preservation and conservation of resources. There are different approaches of resource management such as (i) top down, (ii) bottom up, (iii) adaptive and (iv) integrative. It is basically the integrative approach which provides the workable solution as it combines public-private partnership through peoples, participation. Management of resources aims at judicious and optimal use with adequate scope for replenishing and renewal of resources. Since all natural resources are interdependent, it requires an inclusive approach of management. Inclusive approach emphasizes on sustainable development of all the natural resources together.

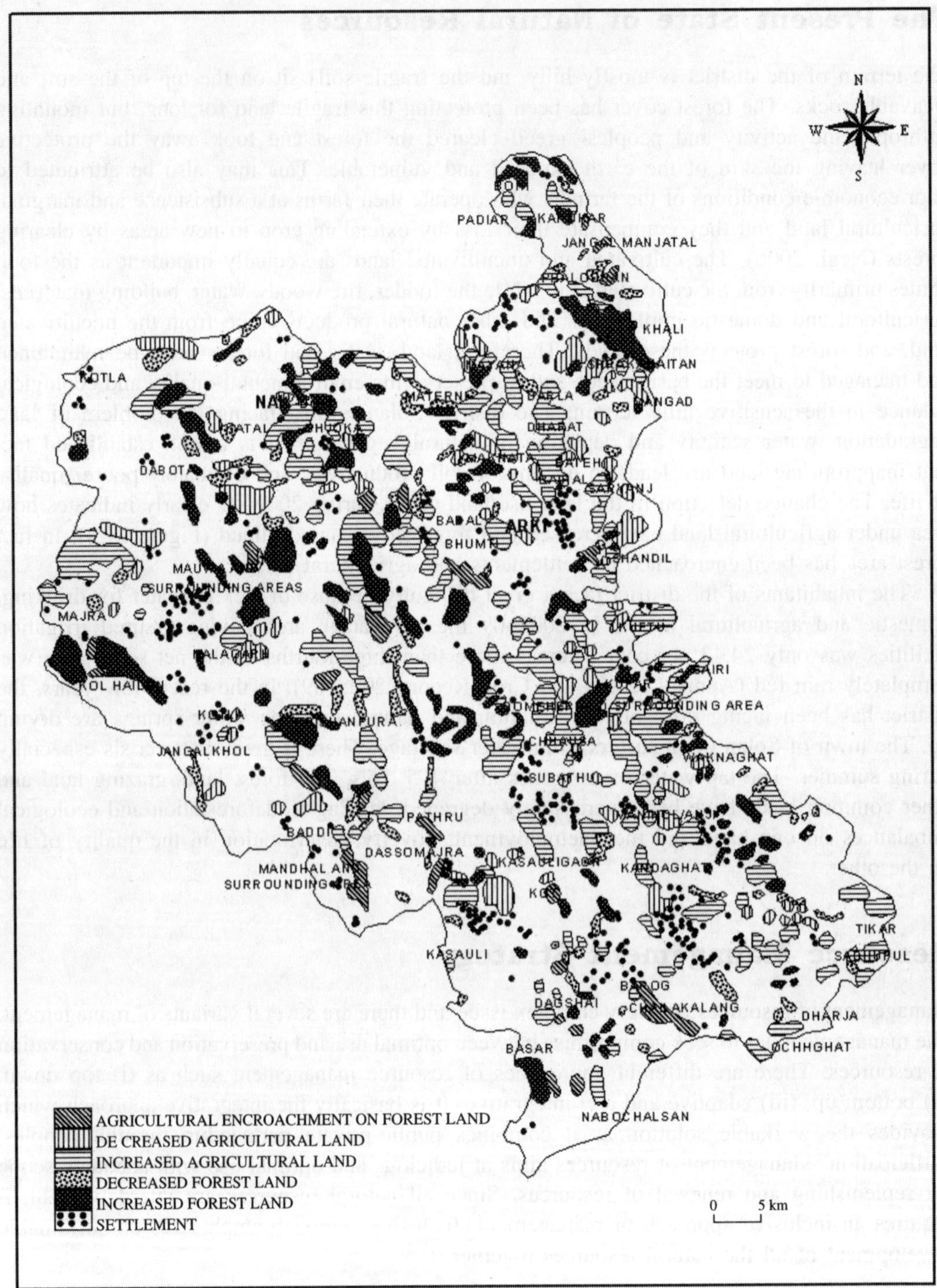

Figure 21.4 Land use and land cover changes in Solan district.

Land Resource

The land resource of an area may be assessed from the land cover/land use and land utilization. A perusal of the land utilization (Table 21.1) clearly reveals that the net sown area has declined from 39,807 hectares (21.6 per cent) to 37,600 hectares (20.8 per cent) during a span of 10 years (2000–09). Area put to non-agricultural use has gone up. The forest area remains static. But barren and uncultivable land has declined and has been put to uses other than agriculture (Table 21.1). This is because the roads, buildings and other construction activities have accelerated. What is clearly evident is the pressure of growth of population on resources, i.e., land. The population has gone up from 303,280 persons in 1981 to 576,000 in 2011.

Table 21.1 Land utilization pattern of district Solan, 2001–2009 (Area in ha.)

Year	2000–01	2008–09
Total geographical area (by village paper)	180,923	180,900
Forests	20,290(11.2)	20,300(11.23)
Barren and Unculturable land	15,251(8.4)	11,600(6.42)
Net sown area	39,807(21.6)	37,600(20.8)
Land put to non-agricultural uses	9682(5.4)	12,900(7.13)
Permanent pasture and other grazing land	77,698(42.9)	77,300(42.74)
Land under misc. tree crops groves not included in area sown	823(0.5)	600(0.33)
Culturable waste	11,958(6.6)	14,900(8.23)
Other fallow land	1193(0.6)	2400(1.30)
Current fallow	5021(2.8)	3300(1.83)

Figures in parenthesis show per cent

Source: Directorate of Land Record, Himachal Pradesh, Shimla.

It is needless to say that population is an important resource for any development, yet it is a major source of environmental degradation when it exceeds the limit of carrying capacity of the support system. The mounting population pressure and increased use of new technology have resulted in an increase in agricultural production but without any efforts for soil conservation. This has led to a progressive loss of soil fertility. Transport network developed rapidly in the district during the past two-three decades. The total length of the roads in the district during 1973–74 was only 817 km, which increased to 2301 km, in 2000–01. Today all towns and most of the villages are connected to the district and tehsil headquarters by a network of motorable roads. The construction of these roads and buildings has resulted in depletion and degradation of forest, soil erosion, and land degradation.

The proximity of agriculturally advanced State of Punjab and spread effect of green revolution technologies have been responsible for the stunning progress that the district achieved in agricultural production. The production of food grain has increased phenomenally. The farmers of the district have been using HYV seeds. The district has become leading producer of mushroom, tomato and ginger. The use of pesticides in the study region has increased several fold. Similarly the consumption of chemical fertilizers has accelerated the contamination of soil. This has degraded the organic matter and physical properties of the soil.

The overgrazing of natural grass lands by domestic animals and migratory sheep, indiscriminate cultivation on steep slopes combined with poor agricultural practices and construction of roads especially badly designed roads by felling of trees for domestic purposes and lopping for fodder, etc. eventually lead to even more severe land degradation in the form of soil erosion and land sliding in the study area. This situation calls for some urgent steps to be taken to overcome these problems:

1. Each and every parcel of the land should be surveyed and a comprehensive land use inventory based on the quality and suitability should be prepared. Based on this environment and people friendly land use plan may be prepared which should be strictly followed and any uncalled for aberration should not be allowed.
2. There is need to bring down the area under the categories of culturable waste, barren lands, fallow lands and waste lands. The efforts are to be made to reclaim such areas in such a manner that all the waste lands are utilized to their optimum level for the development of agriculture and forests so that soil erosion and degradation can be checked. This will help reduce the pressure on existing land resources.
3. Bench terracing, terrace farming and contour ploughing may also be encouraged to overcome the problem of soil erosion.
4. Chemical contamination of the virgin soil and water resources is major hindrance in the maintenance of soil fertility. This has come as a byproduct of modern agriculture which has induced the excessive use of chemicals without realizing the fact that these chemicals are ultimately harmful. The farmers should be encouraged to use organic manures (cow dung and green manure) in the fields.
5. In order to meet the challenges of growing demand on limited resources, it is necessary to grow more food through intensive but modern cultivation methods.
6. The open grazing system is causing a serious damage to the soil and, therefore, stall feeding needs to be promoted.
7. The practices of cultivation on very high slopes need to be stopped to avoid the erosion and landslide.
8. Horticulture provides very viable alternative to traditional cropping pattern because that is economically profitable and environmentally eco-friendly. Apple orchards and vegetable production have, of late assumed great significance in the economy of mountainous environment in general and area of study in particular.

Water Resource

Water is an essential natural resource for sustaining life on the surface of the earth. The increasing rate of population and deforestation and thoughtless use of water resource have led to its depletion at an alarming rate. The water resource of the study area is found in the form of rivers, streams, lakes, ponds, and springs and also in the form of groundwater. But most of these surface water resources get dry during summer season and level of even groundwater goes deep down resulting in scarcity of water both for drinking as well as irrigation. There are several rivers which form the major sources of water in the district, but most of these are seasonal. The Gambhar, the Ashwani, the Kaushalaya, the Blad, the Sirsa, the Baliana and the

Sutlej are a few perennial rivers in the district but during the summer, the discharge of water in these rivers is very low (Figure 21.5). The field survey reveals that several water springs, which once were the sources of fresh water, are disappearing. The drinking water crisis has not only assumed alarming proportion, it has become chronic in the entire state of Himachal Pradesh in general and Solan area in particular.

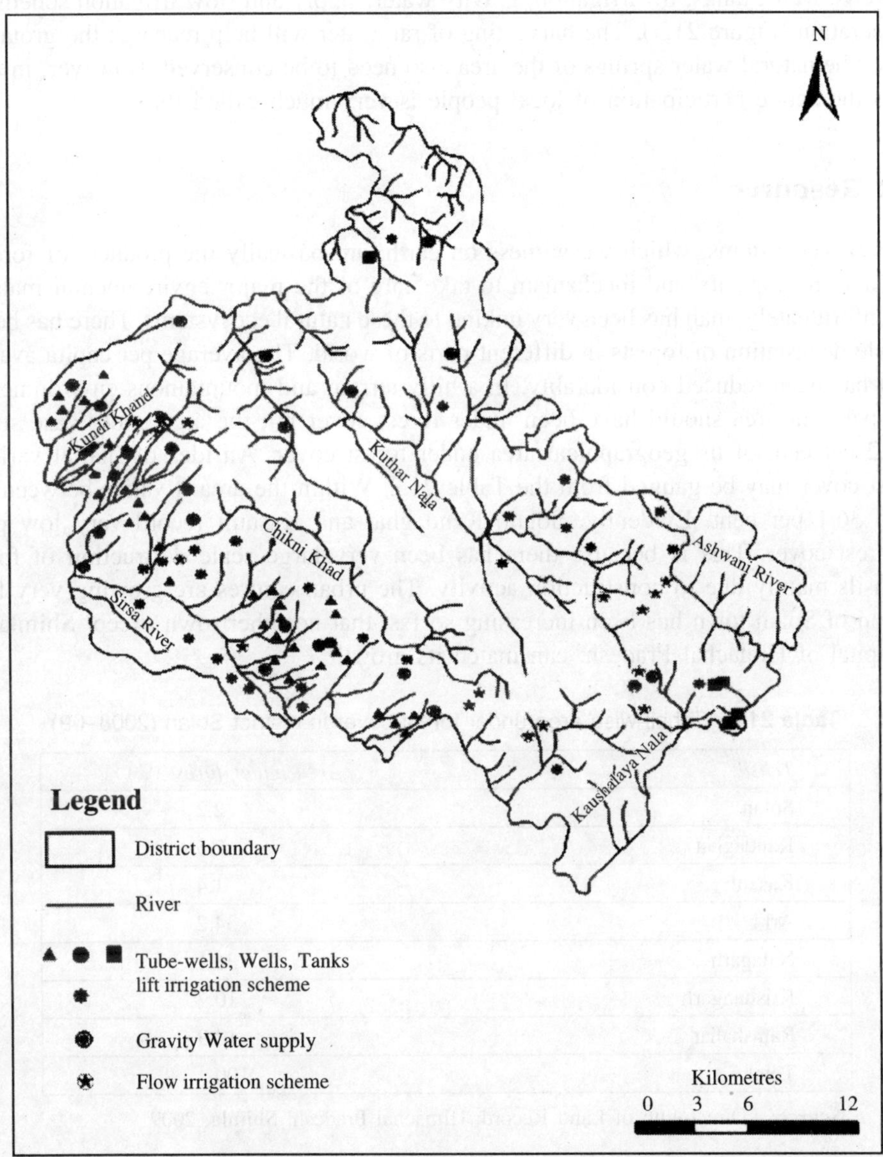

Figure 21.5 Water resources of Solan district.

Source: Central Groundwater Board, Irrigation Dept. Govt. of India.

There are several ways by which the supply of water may be retained for the longer period. For example, there is immediate and urgent need to control the surface run-off. The surface run-off may be checked or at least slowed down by quick growing vegetation and grasses. This will also prevent soil erosion, improve water availability and increase fuel and fodder besides agricultural production through irrigation. There are different sources of irrigation such as tubewells, wells, tanks, lift irrigation, gravity water supply and flow irrigation scheme which are in operation (Figure 21.5). The harvesting of rainwater will help recharge the groundwater. Likewise, the natural water springs of the area also need to be conserved. However, in all these activities the active participation of local people is very much called for.

Forest Resource

Varieties of ecosystems, which we witness on earth, are basically the products of forest. The forests have the capacity and mechanism to take care of the major environmental maladies of world. Unfortunately, man has been very unkind to these natural ecosystems. There has been very large scale devastation of forests in different parts of world. The average per capita availability of forest has been reduced considerably. In a hilly terrain and mountainous environment more than 60 per cent area should have been under forest cover but the area under case study has only 11.2 per cent of its geographical area under forest cover. An idea of spatial variation in the forest cover may be gauged from the Table 21.2. Within the area it varies between 1.4 per cent and 36.1 per cent. Evidently, Solan, Kandaghat and Kasauli record very low per cent under forest cover. This is because there has been very large scale destruction of forests in these tehsils mainly due to construction activity. The urban centres are growing very fast; the population of Solan town has been increasing so fast that no other town except Shimla, which is the capital of Himachal Pradesh, can match its growth.

Table 21.2 Tehsil-wise area under forest cover in district Solan (2008–09)

Tehsil	*Area under forest* (%)
Solan	2.2
Kandaghat	2.5
Kasauli	1.4
Arki	34.2
Nalagarh	36.1
Krishangarh	10.7
Ramshahar	12.9
Total	100

Source: Directorate of Land Record, Himachal Pradesh, Shimla, 2009.

Interestingly, this little area under forest is also facing serious threat from forest fire, overgrazing, and illicit felling of trees every year. There is an utmost need to manage the forest resources. This situation calls for some management strategies to be adopted to restore the forest cover and thereby the ecosystem:

1. The forests are highly vulnerable to fire and this causes great loss of the forest wealth every year. There is a need to apply both structural and non-structural measures to control the forest fire. A special task force may be established to mitigate the loss and manage the menace.
2. The formulation of afforestation projects and projects implementation should be done in consultation with local people. The private–public cooperation needs to be formalized and strengthened.
3. In view of the very low area being under forest cover, there is a need to increase the forest cover through effective implementation of afforestation programmes. There is a large area under permanent pasture and other grazing land (42.7 per cent) and barren and uncultivable land (6.4 per cent), part of which can easily be brought under afforestation programmes. Social forestry, agro-forestry and horticulture may also be encouraged by providing technical guidance and encouraging peoples' participation in a big way.
4. Policy initiatives with a built in mechanism to meet the demands of local people for fuel wood, fodder, minor forest produce, small timber and other domestic needs must be encouraged both for short as well as long-term solution of the forest-related problems.

Conclusion

It is evident from the aforesaid discussion that land and water as also forests are under great stress due to increasing population and thereby anthropogenic activities. Colossal damage is being done to environment due to too much interference in the land and water ecology. Forests, which are the links and bind the land and water, are being destroyed at a very large scale in the name of developmental activities only to accommodate rapidly expanding urban population. This situation, therefore, calls for an integrated and inclusive approach to manage land, water and forests. Each and every parcel of land should be surveyed and a comprehensive land use inventory may be prepared.

The land use allocation may be done on the basis of characteristic, quality and suitability with adequate care to environment. The land use planning should be so designed so that it has adequate provision for preservation and conservation of water and forests. It is this integrated and inclusive approach which may help solve the problem of natural resource crunch and pave the way for sustainable development. Frequent water crisis and unwanted deforestation will be a thing of past, if the land use plan is strictly adhered to.

References

Annual Seasons and Crop Report (2008–09), Office of the Commissioner (Revenue), Shimla, Himachal Pradesh.

Census of India (1991), *District Census Handbook*, Solan District, Series-9, Part XII-A & B, Village and Town Directory, Directorate of Census Operation, Shimla, Himachal Pradesh.

Census of India (2001), *Provisional Population Total, Paper-3*, Series-3, Directorate of Census Operation, Himachal Pradesh.

Census of India (2011), *Provisional Population Total,* Directorate of Census Operation, Himachal Pradesh.

Kumar, A. (1998), *Mountain Ecosystem: A Scenario of Unsustainability*, Indus Publishing Company, New Delhi.

Negi, S.S. (2006), Management of Land Resources in Himalayas in Raina, K.K. et al., (Eds.) *Sustainable Land Resource Management in Himalayan Region*, Bishen Singh Mahendra Pal Singh, Dehradun.

Report of the National Commission on Agriculture, 1976, Part IX, Forestry, 33.

Statistical Abstract of Solan District (2009), Statistical Department, Solan, Himachal Pradesh.

22

Water Resource Potential and Its Management in Arunachal Pradesh

Vishal Gupta and A.A. Ansari

Abstract: The state of Arunachal Pradesh is a water surplus region and therefore has a great potential but difficult terrain and topography prohibit the potentialities to be realized. Geologically, the entire area is composed of sedimentary, meta-sedimentary and intrusion at places. The sedimentary rocks have provided a good aquifer in this region. The syntaxial bend and the extension of Himalaya towards north, east and south traps the moisture laden winds resulting into huge amount of annual rainfall. Water being one of the essential commodities for survival of mankind, is considered as a prime natural resource and precious asset of each nation. Evergreen forests cover more than 70 per cent of the state with its numerous turbulent streams, roaring river, deep valleys, lofty mountains, snow-clad shining peaks, hundreds and thousands of flora and fauna. This chapter highlights the need of managing water resources in this hilly terrain by suggesting the development of several multipurpose small hydroelectricity generating plants which may meet the requirements of power crisis within and outside the state.

Keywords: Water Resource Potential, Perennial River, Mountain Terrain, Hydro Power, Water Resource Management

Introduction

This chapter is written in the wake of growing concern about effective utilization of water resources in particular and all other resources in general. It was in the early 2000 that the wave of environmental concern started propagating from a pioneering landmark, i.e., Rio Earth Summit in 1992 and consequently the entire globe came into its grip resulting into the unprecedented increase in the discussion related to sustainable utilization of resources from almost each and every part of the world. Several organizations and bodies were formed to chalk out the effective utilization of water resources such as Global Water Partnership (GWP), World Water Connect (WWC), World Water Forum (WWF) International Commission on Irrigation and Drainage (ICID) in 1996. The Indian government also constituted a National Commission on Integrated Water Reserve Development (NCIWD) so as to keep a pace with global awareness as well as to regulate the water resource for its effective and sustainable utilization. Apart from governmental organizations, there are several non-governmental organizations such as NABARD, National Tree Growers, and PRADAN, which also focus on the proper utilization of water resources. The issue of linking of rivers is being taken care of by the National River Commission (NRC).

The overall growth and development of a region depends on an effective management system which utilizes land and water resources. India has great disparities in terms of the water resource potentiality. This water resource is distributed all over the country in the form of either run-off or in the form of gravitational water or underground water in several major and minor watersheds. The major problem faced by the people is the scarcity or unavailability of water during the required time and flooding at another point of time. Arunachal Pradesh has a bounty of water resources in the form of run-off water. Almost all the rivers and streams are perennial with a very high intensity of discharge fluctuation. However, the flooding situation is a rare phenomenon in the Arunachal Pradesh because of its mountainous and undulating terrain which facilitates the smooth drainage. The spatial and temporal variation in the availability of water resources has necessitated its sustainable utilization with proper planning and management.

The conceptual framework of this paper was synthesized through literature pertaining to water resource management and allied topics (Singh, 1999; Singh et al., 2004, Mishra, 2001; Murthy, 1975; Maji, 2007; Jose et al., 1981; Doolette and McGrath, 1990, Sen, 1984). The statistical data was acquired from secondary sources. Further, the field observation in the three districts of Arunachal Pradesh, i.e., West Siang, East Siang and Papumpare districts was also carried out (Ansari and Gupta, 2006).

Study Area

The state of Arunachal Pradesh is a land of the dawn-lit mountains lying between 26°40' to 29°25' latitudes and 91°35' to 97°35' longitudes occupying an area of 83,580 sq. km (Figure 22.1).

This is the largest state in north-east. The state stretches from the snow capped eastern Himalaya at an altitude of 6000 m to the plains of Brahmaputra valley. Arunachal Pradesh is surrounded by Bhutan, China and Burma. The Kangto, the Nyegi Kangsang and the Gorichen are some of the highest peaks in this part of Himalaya. The major rivers that flow through the state are the Siang, the Kameng, the Subansiri, the Lohit and the Tirap. These rivers have created broad valleys in these areas. The Brahmaputra enters Arunachal Pradesh from Tibet and flows into Assam and then to Bangladesh before falling into the Bay of Bengal.

The state is inhabited by several tribes (Burman, 1970). According to 2011 census the population of Arunachal Pradesh is 1,382,611 registering a growth of 25.92 per cent during 2001–11. The sex ratio is 920 and the density of population is 17 per sq. km. The state is divided into 16 districts and the density varies between 1 (Dibang Valley) and 47 (Tirap) (Table 22.1).

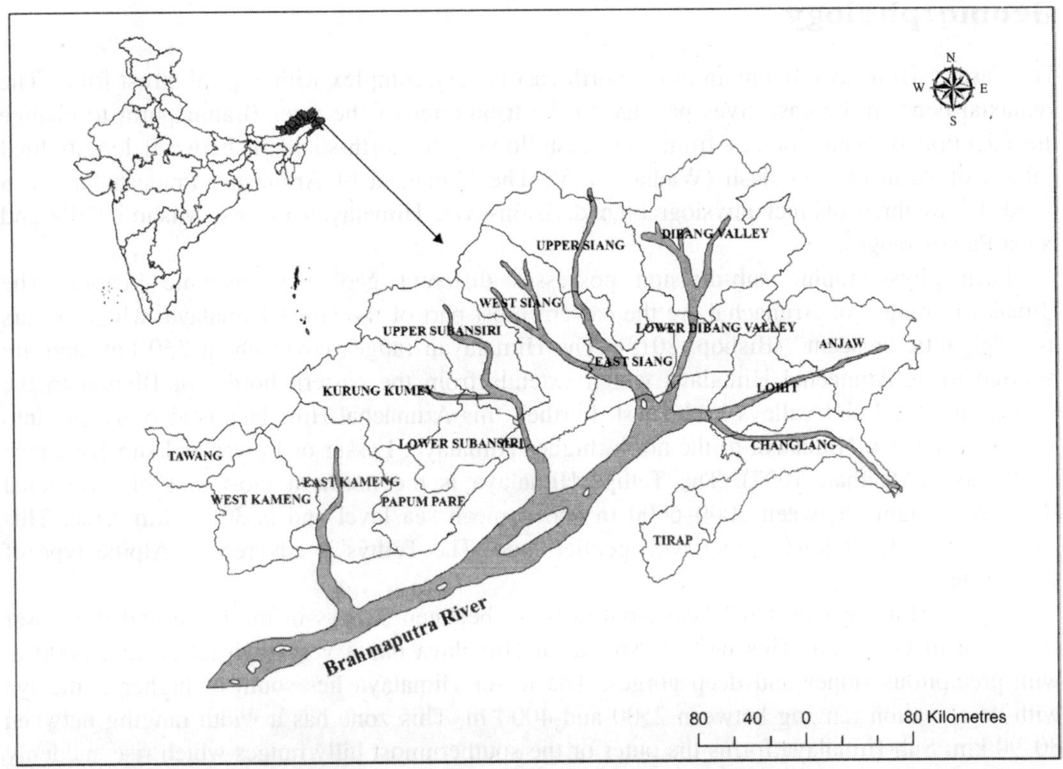

Figure 22.1 Location map of Arunachal Pradesh.

Source: Administrative Atlas, census of India, 2011 (Modified).

Table 22.1 District-wise population statistics of Arunachal Pradesh

Sl. No.	*State/District*	*Population*	*Population growth (%)* 2001–2011	*Sex ratio* 2011	*Population density* 2011
	Arunachal Pradesh	1,382,611	25.92	920	17
1	Tawang	49,950	28.33	701	23
2	West Kameng	87,013	16.64	755	12
3	East Kameng	78,413	37.14	1012	19
4	Papumpare	176,385	44.57	950	51
5	Upper Subansiri	83,205	50.34	982	12
6	West Siang	112,272	8.04	916	13
7	East Siang	99,019	13.3	962	27
8	Upper Siang	35,289	5.77	891	5
9	Changlang	147,951	17.96	914	32
10	Tirap	111,997	11.63	931	47
11	Lower Subansiri	82,839	48.65	975	24
12	Kurung Kumey	89,717	111.01	1029	15
13	Dibang Valley	7948	9.3	808	1
14	Lower Dibang Valley	53,986	7.01	919	14
15	Lohit	145,538	16.44	901	28
16	Anjaw	21,089	13.77	805	3

Source: Census, 2011.

Geomorphology

The Eastern Himalaya mountain in the north-east is very complex with several thrust folds. The syntaxial bend in the east gives passage to the tributaries of the river Brahmaputra to change the direction of their courses from west-east flowing to north-south in between longitudinal valleys of Arunachal Pradesh (Wadia, 1975). The Himalaya of Arunachal Pradesh has been divided into three distinct physiographic divisions viz. Himalayan ranges, Mishmi Hills and Naga-Patkoi ranges.

Each physiographic sub-division possesses different geological tectonic history. The Himalayan ranges of Arunachal are the eastern most part of the Great Himalaya, which occurs as a "gigantic crescent" (Bishop, 2013). The Himalayan ranges cover about 350 km. and are referred to as Arunachal Himalaya which extends from the eastern border of Bhutan to the Dibang and the Lohit valleys in the east. Further, this Arunachal Himalaya is also divided into Tethys or Tibetan Himalaya to the north, higher Himalaya, Lesser or Lower and sub-Himalaya to the south (Kumar, 1997). The Tethys Himalaya is the northern most part of Arunachal Himalaya ranging between 3000–6000 m above mean sea level and is 30–40 km wide. This part is relatively of lower relief with gentle slope. The Tethys is covered by Alpine type of vegetation.

Higher Himalaya runs northeast-southwest in between Tethys in the north and the lesser Himalaya in the south. This part of Arunachal Himalaya has a very high relief, i.e., 6000 m with precipitous slopes and deep gorges. The lesser Himalaya lies south of higher Himalaya with its elevation ranging between 2500 and 4000 m. This zone has a width ranging between 80–90 km. Sub-Himalaya forms the outer or the southernmost hilly ranges which rise suddenly from the Brahmaputra plain. There is wide variation in the width of this range which varies from 10–20 km in the west to 1–2 km in the extreme east.

The Mishmi Himalaya forms the eastern most part of Arunachal Pradesh. It runs from northwest to southeast and further continues in the form of parallel ranges of Burma. This range has an elevation ranging between 2500 and 6000 m. Rivers like the Siang, the Dibang and the Lohit drain this area. The Naga-Patkai ranges act as the water divide between the rivers draining the Brahmaputra plain and the Burma. This range runs in the direction from east-west to northwest-southeast. The main rivers which drain this area are the Nao Dihing, the Tirap and the Namphuk.

Such physiography of Arunachal Pradesh always pushes the southwest monsoon winds up along the slope and results in rapid moist adiabatic cooling that causes condensation and precipitation. This is a very usual phenomenon particularly during April to October (Table 22.2). Since these moist air are trapped in between the southern, eastern and northern extension of Himalaya, it keeps on continuing rainfall in the states of Arunachal Pradesh, Nagaland and Manipur. Besides these factors, there are numerous rivers, marshes, lakes in the valleys of Arunachal Pradesh which supply enormous evaporated water even during the dry periods.

The Brahmaputra river is a powerhouse of both water resource and sediment load. It appears to be a fresh sea starting from Sadiya in the east to Dhubri in the west and is navigable throughout its length. The Brahmaputra drainage system is described as unique in the world as it provides the only living example where the drainage pattern runs in a diametrically opposite direction as it flows from west to east in Tibet and further flows east to west in India and is an antecedent river. The Brahmaputra is considered as the lifeline of North-East India which includes Assam, Meghalaya, Tripura, Manipur, Mizoram and Arunachal Pradesh (the largest state of north-east India). The total basin area of Brahmaputra is about 58,000 sq. km of which India has only 33.6 per cent, the China has the largest share of it which is 50.5 per cent, while Bangladesh and Bhutan have 8.1 and 7.8 per cent respectively. The drainage area of this river in the states of India is: Arunachal Pradesh (41.88 per cent), Assam (36.33 per cent), Meghalaya (6.00 per cent), Nagaland (5.55 per cent), Sikkim (3.75 per cent) and West Bengal (6.47 per cent). The river Brahmaputra originates in Kailash Range in Tibet at an elevation of about 5300 m above mean sea level and exhibits a wide range of slope variation from 4–17 m/km in the George section, 27 cm/km at Pasighat where it enters the Assam plain and 10 cm/km at Guwahati. In its total length of 2880 km, 1625 km is in Tibet, 918 km in India and 337 km in Bangladesh.

Table 22.2 Average annual rainfall in Arunachal Pradesh (mm)

Sl. No.	*Rain gauge station*	*Year*		
		2001	2002	2003
1	Tawang	1291.40	NA	1543.30
2	BomdilSeppaa	1384.60	2362.60	2048.90
3	Seppa	2641.30	1703.00	2143.00
4	Itanagar	2289.20	2921.60	3300.80
5	Zero	522.41	878.56	681.50
6	Daparijo	1208.90	1839.60	1803.60
7	Along	1628.00	2374.40	2333.92
8	Pasighat	405.00	NA	NA
9	Yingkiong	3116.70	2241.89	2970.30
10	Roing	4723.70	3484.00	4420.13
11	Tezu	2659.62	2775.20	3889.80
12	Changlang	1482.20	2142.10	2644.20
13	Khosna	3194.40	3711.20	2347.90
14	Anini	2327.60	1678.00	NA

Source: Directorate of Economics & Statistics, Arunachal Pradesh.

Water Resource Management

The water management deals with the regulated supply system, allocation of water flow, treatment of water, interlinking of river basins, etc. Water resource management is the integrating concept for a number of water sub-sectors such as hydro power, water supply, sanitation, irrigation, drainage and environment. An integrated water resource perspective ensures that social, economic, environmental and technical dimensions are taken into account in the management and development of water resources.

Management of water resource is interdisciplinary task, which requires an integrated approach, i.e., it involves both science (geography, climatology, geomorphology, geology, soil science, environmental science, ecology, agriculture, etc.) and humanities (social structure, politics, society, economics, administration, etc.). It is essentially an interdisciplinary in approach because it has a great deal of relation with physical character of catchment area, land use cover, policies and land regulation system and the traditional methods of water harvesting and management.

The amount and intensity of precipitation received in India is related to the monsoon rainfall. India receives more than 80 per cent of its rainfall through southwest monsoon while the rest of 20 per cent is received during northeast (retreating) monsoon and cyclonic depression, etc. There is a huge variation in the amount of water received in various parts of India and, therefore, it is very much essential to manage the available water resources for round the year utilization in agriculture and other usages and to harvest its latent potentiality through the hydro power projects (Table 22.3).

Table 22.3 Water resource potential of Himalayan river basin in India (In billion cubic metres)

River basin	*Catchment area* (sq. km)	*Average water resource potential*	*Surface water resources*
Indus	321,289	73.31	46.0
Ganga	861,452	525.02	250.0
Brahmaputra	194,413	537.20	24
Barak & others	41,723	48.40	NA

Source: NCIWRD, New Delhi.

There is a great variation in the availability of water in the different river basins of India (Table 22.4). The average annual run-off of all the rivers of India has been assessed as approximately 1869 cubic km, out of which only 690 cubic km is utilizable portion through diversion, storage and reservoir. The gravity water potentiality of the country has also been estimated at 432 cubic km. However, there has been a decreasing trend as far as the availability of water is concerned. It has gone down to 1869 cubic meters in 2001 from 5177 cubic m in 1951.

Table 22.4 Basin-wise strength of Himalayan rivers in India (in billion cubic metres)

Name of the river basin	*Catchment area* (sq. m)	*Average annual flow*	*Live storage capacity*		
			Complete projects	*Projects under construction*	*Projects considerations*
Indus	321,289	73.31	13.89	2.45	0.27
Ganga	861,452	525.02	36.84	17.12	29.56
Brahmaputra and Barak	236,136	585.60	1.09	204	63.35

Source: NCIWRD, New Delhi.

Water Resource Management through Hydro Power Projects

Though there is a huge potentiality of hydro power development in Arunachal Pradesh, little has been tapped because of combination of factors. However, at present 64 per cent, i.e., 2469 villages have been electrified out of total 3863 villages. During annual plan (1990–91) some seven micro hydro schemes i.e., Yingkyong (0.2 MW), Sessa (1.5 MW), Sille (0.5 MW), Yambung (0.5 MW), Sissiri (0.5 MW), Tago (4.5 MW) and Jugddin (1.5 MW) were installed. The water reservoir of these hydro power projects can also meet the demand of water in the lean season. This reserved water is regulated in the agricultural fields and is supplied as drinking water. As per the statistics derived from Ministry of Non-Conventional Energy Sources, New Delhi, Arunachal Pradesh has 492 identified small hydro sites each one of which can generate electricity up to 25 MW (Table 22.5). The total capacity of hydro power in Arunachal Pradesh is 1059.00 MW. A sum of ₹ 3888.32 crores was pumped in 2002–2007 as against 3 crores during first five year plan (1951–1956) in order to augment the production of hydro-electricity. However, the potential yet remains to be tapped. Arunachal Pradesh has been focusing on deveopment of huge hydro power potential (IBEF, 2010). The hydro electric power potentiality of Arunachal Pradesh has been assessed to be around 50,000 MW. (WAPCOS International Consultants). The government of Arunachal Pradesh has signed a Memorandum of Understanding with central sector power generators and integrated power developers in order to develop 135 hydroelectric power plants with an aggregate capacity of 25,722 MW. (IBEF, 2010). In the Central Sector, 405 MW has been developed by North East Electric Power Corporation (NEEPCO) by commissioning the Ranganadi Hydel Project. Other projects such as 10 MW Dikrong Project and 11,000 MW Upper Siang Project are at different stages of commissioning (Human Development Report, 2005). The four big projects currently under construction included 2000 MW Subansiri Lower, 600 MW Kameng, 110 MW Pare

Table 22.5 Identified small hydro sites up to 25 MW in selected states drained by Himalayan river

Name of the state	*Identified no. of sites*	*Total capacity* (MW)
Arunachal Pradesh	492	1059.00
Assam	46	118.97
Bihar	171	367.97
Himachal Pradesh	323	16,424.78
Jammu and Kashmir	201	1207.27
Manipur	96	105.63
Meghalaya	98	181.50
Mizoram	88	190.32
Nagaland	86	181.39
Punjab	78	65.26
Uttar Pradesh	445	1472.93

Source: Ministry of Non-Conventional Energy Sources, New Delhi.

and 1750 MW Demwa Lower hydroelectric projects (Table 22.6). The projects are targeted for completion by 2013–2017.

Table 22.6 List of hydro projects under execution (Excluding projects under Ministry of New and Renewal Energy) as on 31/7/2013

Name of project (MW)	*Unit No.*	*State/agency*	*Capacity* (MW)	*Likely commissioning*
Subansiri lower 8 × 250 = 2000	U-1 to U-8	Arunachal Pradesh/ NHPC	2000	2016–18
Kameng 4 × 150 = 600	U-1 to U-4	Arunachal Pradesh/ NEEPCO	600	2016–17
Pare 2 × 55 = 110	U-1 to U-2	Arunachal Pradesh/ NEEPCO	110	2014–15

Source: Central Electrical Authority website: www.cea.nic.in.

In order to encourage local participation, State Government has also introduced Small Hydro Power Policy–2007 to develop 2000 MW of hydro power from small projects (1 kW to 5 MW) to be built by private developers under Built Own Operate and Transfer. (Department of Power, Government of Arunachal Pradesh, 2008.)

In the recent move, 91 new hydroelectric power projects (35,987 MW) are proposed to come up. Projects with the capacity of above 25 MW have been allotted to the government of Arunachal Pradesh as per the report of Cabinet Committee of Investment (August, 2013).

Conclusion

The present study justifies that the geological diversities have provided a unique geomorphological setting to entire Arunachal Pradesh. Being entirely the hilly area from east to west and north to south, there is great variation in the height and slope of the ranges. Geologically, the entire area is composed of sedimentary, meta-sedimentary and intrusion at places. The sedimentaries have provided a good aquifer in this region. The syntaxial bend and the extension of Himalaya towards north, east and south traps the moisture laden winds resulting into huge amount of annual rainfall. But the major problem associated with such type of physiographic unit is that much of precipitation water gets wasted in the form of run-off. Thus, to utilize the water resources to its fullest, the water management is very much required. The water resources management can be effectively accomplished through the construction of multi-purpose projects. A lot of development in the field of hydro power plants in the study area is taking place which is evident from the statistics and governmental initiatives. Local people have also taken considerable initiative towards providing environmental friendly water resource utilization and energy generation. The traditional way of water harvesting and management are also being practiced here by people through personal and community participation. In fact, these traditional practices of water management in small watershed areas are playing important role in the sustainable development of the region.

References

Ansari, A.A. and V. Gupta (2006), Indigenous Technique of Soil and Water Conservation in the Siang Region of Arunachal Pradesh, India, Published in, *Hydrology and Watershed Management*, edited by Rao, B.V. & Giridhar, M.V., B.S. Publication, Hyderabad, Andhra Pradesh, India

Bishop, Barry C. (2013), *Encyclopaedia Britanica*, Inc.

Burman, B.K.R. (1970), *Demographic and Social-Economic Profile of Hill Areas of Northeast India*, Department of Publication, Census of India, New Delhi

Department of Power, Government of Arunachal Pradesh, 2008, January 24, *The Arunachal Pradesh Gazette*, Vol. 15, Naharlagun, February 7, 2008. Retrieved on August 2013 from http://westkameng.nic.in/Actsandnotifications/NotificationfromPower.pdf

Doolette, J.B. and W.B. McGrath (1990), *Watershed Development in Asia: Strategies and Technologies*, World Bank Technical paper-27, Washington

Human Development Report (2005), *Itanagar,* Government of Arunachal Pradesh.

IBEF. (2010), *Arunachal Pradesh*, Indian Brand Equity Foundation

Jose, C.S. et al. (1981), Run-off/ Watershed, *Indian Journal of Soil Conservation*, **5**, 251–265.

Kumar, Gopendra (1997), *Geology of Arunachal Pradesh*, Geological Society of India, Bangalore, India.

Maji, Debabrata (2007), Hydropower Development and Environmental Issues in Reference with Arunachal Pradesh, *Proceeding of WMEC'O7*, edited by Viswanadh, G.K. and M.V.S.S., Giridhar, Hyderabad, 472–484.

Mishra, Archana (2001), *Watershed Management*, Author Press, New Delhi.

Murthy, J.V.S. (1975), *Watershed Management in India*, Wiley Eastern Ltd., New Delhi.

Sen, D. Purandare, A. (1984), *Management of Watershed Projects in Northeastern region: Problems and Perspective*, Workshop, Watershed Management NIRD Pub.

Singh, S. (1999), *Atlas of Arunachal Pradesh*, Publication of Govt. of Arunachal Pradesh, India

Singh, V.P. et al. (Eds.) (2004), *The Brahmaputra Basin Water Resources*, Springer Publication.

Wadia, D.N. (1975), *Geology of India*, Tata McGraw-Hill, New Delhi

WAPCOS International Consultants, Studies of Kalai Hydro Electricity Project.

http://www.infraline.com/Details/Cabinet-Committee-on-Investment-approves-2-Arunachal-hydro-power-projects-204751.htm

23

Water Supply in Nagpur City Management Based on Peoples' Perception

Subhangi Girgaonkar and Nanda Charthad

Abstract: Indian urbanization is in the process of metropolitanization. According to 2011 census, there are 53 metropolises and 160.7 million persons (or 42.6 per cent of the urban population) live in these Million Plus cities. These metropolises, due to overcrowding of population, have been facing several problems. However, all of them are very severely hit by the water crisis. The present chapter highlights several issues of water problem being faced by the residents of the Nagpur city. Interviews, surveys and questionnaires reveal that water crisis is basically the product of lack of management. A judicious use of surface and groundwater coupled with water harvesting under the joint venture of public and private partnership can go a long way in the sustainable solution of water supply problem.

Keywords: Perception, Geohydrology, Water Distribution System, Groundwater Potential

Introduction

In the modern society demand of water remains on the rise. Along with the population growth, the recent spurt of constructional activities and ever growing need of non-domestic sector has led to an increased demand of water in recent years in the metropolitan cities in India. Consequently most of the municipal corporations are concerned over the declining per capita availability of water. The situation has called for better water management and water conservation by all possible means to tackle water shortage on a sustainable basis. To achieve sustainability however, conservation measures are felt more necessary than turning merely to supply side of the problem. It is because in future the investment to capture additional surface run-off will become increasingly expensive (Chadha, 2004). Therefore, conservation measures through public participation are the logical option to reduce water demand and to achieve sustainability in water supply. This chapter aims to examine present water supply position including groundwater potentiality and level of public awareness on various water issues.

The study is based on both the primary and secondary data and confined to domestic use of water only. The primary data collection involved questionnaire and interview survey of one hundred households. Discussions and interviews were also organized with the officials of the Department of Water Works, N.M.C., Nagpur and experts, with aim to understand current problems of water distribution system.

A comprehensive questionnaire comprising of both open and close ended questions has been used for conducting the survey. This has been supplemented by data obtained from various secondary sources which include municipal, geohydrological, meteorological and census publications. The collected data from all the sources have been compiled, tabulated and analysed.

Study Area

Located on 21°09' N and 79°09' E in the Vidarbha region of Maharashtra (Figure 23.1), Nagpur is indeed in the heart of India. It is the capital of Vidarbha region and the district's headquarter. It has the pride of being the second capital of Maharashtra and the winter home of the Legislative Assembly. Sprawling over an area of 217.16 sq. km, it housed 2,129,500 persons (2001) with decadal growth rate of 26.22 per cent, which is much higher than the national average (21.34 per cent). According to 2011 census, the population of the city is 2,497,777 registering a growth of 17.29 per cent during 2001–2011.

The climate of Nagpur is characterized by dry sub-humid type with hot summer and mild winter. The annual rainfall average is 1112 mm distributed over 60–70 rainy days. The middle of June to the end of August is the period of high rainfall. High temperatures of 45°C or more are witnessed during May, while low temperatures of 8°C to 10°C are reported in the month of December and January. The city does experience a condition of drought. There is possibility of drought in every 5.5 years (Jain and Jain, 2003). The city comes under the moderate drought prone zone (Girgaonkar, 2002).

Status of Municipal Water Supply

Today, the Water Works Department of Nagpur Municipal Corporation looks after the water supply of the city. It has 10 sub-divisions functioning in the city. The first public water supply system started in 1936 and since then the authorities have been constantly in search of newer sources. At present the water is brought to the Gorewada Tank situated in the north-west of Nagpur through an open canal from Navegaon Khairi located at a distance of 48 km north of Nagpur. Water is filtered at Gorewada and treated for distribution. However, the distance factor and the whole supply of treated water have made the entire process uneconomical. Consequently, Water Works Department of NMC suffers from heavy losses.

The total supply from all the sources is about 500 MLD. After accounting distribution losses of about 30–35 per cent due to leakage and non-domestic supply of 35 MLD, the per capita, per day availability of water in the city is about 135 l. This falls short of 150–200 l per capita per day as recommended by Central Health Engineering Organization (CHEO). Hence, there is an apparent gap between the demand and supply. The city authorities have also constructed open wells and handpumps in various localities of the city. Besides this, civic authorities are thinking

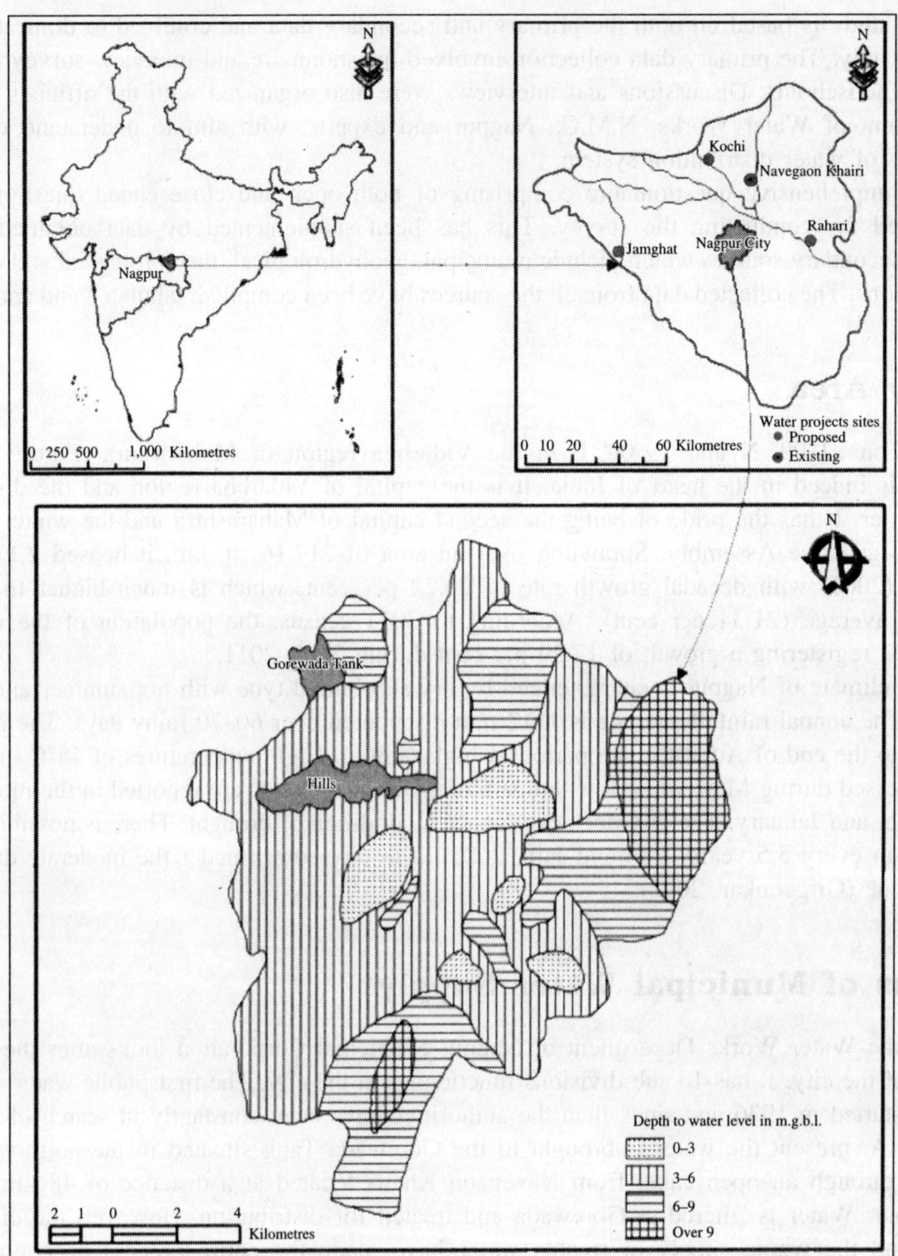

Figure 23.1 Location map of Nagpur city.

of moving to distant areas in search of potential sources, which are located still farther from the city and this may naturally create an additional economic burden. Some of the current problems of water distribution system have been summarised in Table 23.1. The experts stress on a better plan and efficient system, where losses could be minimised, consumption checked and recovery improved.

Table 23.1 Current problems of water distribution system, Nagpur city

1	Heavy loss of water through pipe line network and canal
2	Internal distribution losses in water supply (30–35 per cent)
3	Pipe line network is 50 years old and even Blue Print is not available with the department
4	Citizens connect high power pumps to NMC taps, consequently water shortage due to pilferage
5	NMC spends about 85 crores in water distribution. Total demand from consumers against water works out to be ₹ 72 crores and the total recovery from water is about 50 crores, creating a deficit of ₹ 25 crores. Consequently entire process is uneconomical
6	If not tackled properly, the city will face severe water shortage in the next few years

Source: Outcome of interviews with the officials and experts.

Groundwater Potential

In the city depth of water level ranges between 3 and 9 mbgl. There are many areas in the central part where shallow groundwater level (0–3 m) occurs. Here groundwater use is negligible due to excessive supply of water through NMC taps resulting into shallow water level. Deeper water level more than 6 mbgl occurs in the northern, western and southern parts of the city, where groundwater use is maximum either due to non-availability of corporation water supply or very limited duration of supply. In the major parts of the central and eastern Nagpur, groundwater level ranges between 3 and 6 m. The study conducted by CGWB officials has revealed that those areas, where groundwater level is rich, get regular and 24 hours supply and where groundwater level is poor, have no drinking water network (Hitavada, 2004) or very limited water supply.

Peoples' Perception on Water Issues

A questionnaire was served to know various dimensions of water supply and water use. The questions were based on the issues like awareness about the sources of water to Nagpur city, sources of water to household, period and intensity of groundwater use, period of water shortage, duration of water supply, total requirement of water for drinking and cooking, perception about previous days unused drinking water, natural behaviour while using water for various household activities, public perception about rainwater harvesting and compulsory roof-top water harvesting. Such type of awareness and behaviour searching questions and dialogues were of great help in understanding public perception and consciousness about various issues of water. Many questions were thought provoking for the respondents. Table 23.2 is an outcome of such an investigation.

What follows is a brief description of the findings of household survey. A larger percentage of respondents were highly educated (57). Females, who are responsible for managing water in the households, dominated the sample. From the total sample group, 55 respondents were living in the independent houses.

Table 23.2 Behavioural response of residents of Nagpur on water issues

Sl. No.	*Type*	*Number of respondents*	*Sl. No.*	*Type*	*Number of respondents*
1	Education		9	Consent for compulsory roof top water harvesting	
	Undergraduates	43		Positive response	65
	Postgraduates	57		Negative response	12
2	Sex			Not answered	23
	Male	22	10	Period of shortage of water	
	Female	78		Throughout the year	05
3	House type			In summer	51
	Independent	55		Never	23
	Flat	18		Some times	21
	Rented	27	11	Water supply hours	
				1–2	23
4	Awareness about water			2–5	31
	Sources to the city			5–16	26
	Correct response	26		16+	08
	Partially correct	50	12	Views about previous days drinking water	
	Wrong response	01		95 respondents considered it as a stale water	
	No idea	23	13	Nature of water waste	
5	Sources of water to household			Run the tap continuously up to the end of routine household activities	22
	Corporation tap	31		Use tap water for watering gardens	37
	Tap + Well/Tubewell	57		Use tap water for washing vehicles	57
	Only Well/Tubewell	12		Use tap water for cleaning courtyard	43
6	Intensity of groundwater use				
	Throughout the year	40			
	In summer	10			
	When shortage of tap water	19			
7	Awareness of water harvesting			Total Respondents—100	
	Positive response	39		Age of Respondents—20 to 60 years	
	Negative response	61			
8	Purpose of water harvesting				
	Aware	23			
	Not Aware	77			

Source: Based on the response to the questionnaire of the household survey in Nagpur.

When asked about the sources of the water to the city, it was found that very few respondents (26) had the correct knowledge about the sources of water and their distance from the city, thus, they are unaware of the economics involved in getting water from distant sources. It was revealed that most of the surveyed households (69) had their own water resources, either in the form of wells or tubewells. Out of this about 40 respondents use groundwater throughout the year. Thus, total water need of the residents is not met from the corporation water supply alone and they have to cater their needs from the sub-surface sources. It was revealed that about 12 households had to depend on groundwater sources only because, there was total absence of water network in the peripheral zone and water supply in the city could not keep pace with the population increase. However, 31 households depended only on the corporation tap water. Their total water requirement is easily fulfilled by the corporation supply. This highlights the wide disparity in water allocation.

Following observations were made in interview with the respondents:

1. The wells have to be dug deeper frequently (once in four-five years) in order to maintain supply of water.
2. During 7–8 years of occupancy of their households, they observed continuous fall in the water level of their own wells.
3. Water level declines sharply in summer. Consequently they could not run the pump more than 15 minutes at a time.

This throws light on the fact that the surface water level is deepening every year and yearly natural replenishment of water is poor.

In this backdrop, it was necessary to know people's perception regarding water harvesting. Out of the total respondents, only 39 found to be aware about the concept of rainwater harvesting. Further when the same respondents were asked about the purpose of water harvesting, only 23 respondents could be able to explain correctly the purpose of water harvesting. This shows poor level of awareness on this major issue. When the importance of compulsory roof top water harvesting was explained to them and when asked whether they are ready for the same, nearly 65 respondents responded positively in favour of compulsory roof top water harvesting.

In general water shortage was not felt by the residents throughout the year, because they supplement municipal water supply by sub-surface sources. However, water deficiencies are most common in summer months, when the water level is at its lowest and municipal water supply dwindles with feeble pressure. About 51 respondents suffered from water shortage in summers.

Severe disparity in the duration of water supply has been revealed in the household survey. It varied from 1 to 24 hours. It was found that households located in the established old colonies and civil lines areas get dependable and adequate water supply, while households of newer colonies and areas of peripheral zones are the most badly affected parts. Households survey revealed that on an average 10 to 15 l of supply of water per capita per day is the optimum, which can meet the average demand for drinking and cooking. Urban communities are supplied with filtered and treated water. However, 95 respondents felt that previous days drinking water gets stale and, therefore, not used.

Water is made available at the doorsteps of the urban community. Consequently they use water more lavishly. In the investigation, it was revealed that about 22 respondents run the tap continuously up to the end of the activity while performing the routine domestic work. In the survey, it was observed that 43 respondents use tap water in the court yard, while 37 use it for watering gardens, and larger proportions of respondents (57) use tap water for washing their vehicles. It has been rightly observed that in India good quality water suitable for drinking is generally used in gardening, car washing, etc., which can be easily performed by non-potable water (Banerjee, 2004).

Conclusions and Suggestions

The overall picture that emerges from this survey is that water shortage in the city is confined to summer season and is caused by highly uneven allocation of municipal water. The distribution system of water suffers from the lack of management. It does not take into consideration the groundwater potentiality. The example of Nagpur city clearly shows that crisis today is more of water management than that of water itself. Some of possible measures which may help achieve the sustainable solution of water problem may be as under:

1. Real solution lies in the judicious combination of the surface and groundwater with planned use of water harvesting techniques. It is the first step towards achieving the sustainable water supply in the city. Public participatory water harvesting programmes should be pursued in various parts of the city.
2. Now the time has come to achieve the sustainability in the water supply through stringent measures, particularly in the context of deficit financial budget of the Water Works Department. Water should be supplied with high pressure for short duration to minimise the wastage and misuse of water instead of long duration and 24 hours supply.
3. Limited short duration municipal water supply for drinking purposes and sub-surface sources for other domestic activities may give better results, especially in areas where groundwater use is minimum. People should be encouraged to use groundwater for routine domestic work. This may lessen the burden on municipal supply.
4. Creating awareness among residents is yet another effective way of solving water problem. The urban community needs to be made water conscious. Reducing demands through water consciousness and inculcating conservation attitude in urban community is an urgent need to achieve sustainability in water supply. It is essential to make the people aware of the status and various issues in water sector including distance of water source and economics of treated water supply through print and electronic media, film shows, charts, models, road side hoardings and through regular sharing of information.

References

Banerjee, B. (2004), Sustainable Management of Water Resources, *Transactions*, **26**(1), 5–11.

Chadha, D.K. (2004), Status of groundwater development and management in India, in: Tapeshwar Singh (Ed.), *Resource Conservation and Food Security*, Concept Publishing Company, New Delhi, 9–29.

Girgaonkar, S. (2002), Drought assessment for Vidarbha and rural development, *Unpublished Research Paper.*

Hitavada (2004), Daily newspaper, 19th May, *City Line*, 1.

Jain, S.K. and P.K. Jain (2003), Rainwater management for water recharge in Urban inhabitation: A case study of Nagpur city, in: *Rainwater Harvesting,* C.G.W.B., Central Region, Nagpur.

24

Urban Water Supply and Groundwater Management
The Case of Allahabad City

D.S. Pandey

Abstract: Indian cities are facing water crisis both in terms of availability and quality, mainly due to lack of appropriate management of groundwater. It is significant to point out that groundwater plays the dominant role in urban water supply. The present chapter focuses on the system of water supply in Allahabad city and concludes with several recommendations in order that Indian cities in general and Allahabad city in particular do not encounter the problem of water supply in terms of quality as well as quantity in future.

Keywords: Doab, Kankar, Acquifer, Flood Plain Reservoirs, Conjunctive Use of Water

Introduction

Groundwater plays an important role for water supply in many urban centers of India. Nearly 50 per cent of total water supply is being catered from groundwater. It plays even more dominant role in cities/town located in the Indo-Gangetic alluvial plain. The city of Allallabad, located in doab of the Ganga and the Yamuna rivers, depends on groundwater for its domestic consumption from historic past (Figure 24.1). The city is spread over 82 km^2 with a population of 12.17 lakh as per 2011 Census. In addition, the city provides shelter to a sizable floating population, which settles temporarily for its livelihood.

Initially the city was spread in an elongated fashion along the natural levee of the Ganga river. Subsequent pressure of growing population and other developmental activities compelled the expansion of the city southward by encroaching the flood plains of the Ganga and the Yamuna rivers. The area receives about 958.8 mm rainfall in a year through southwest monsoon.

Geomorphologically the area falls in the flood plain of the Ganga and the Yamuna in the doab area. The general slope of the area is towards the east. The elevation of the area ranges from 89.30 to 93.57 m. The Ganga channel is braided during its lean flow and meandering

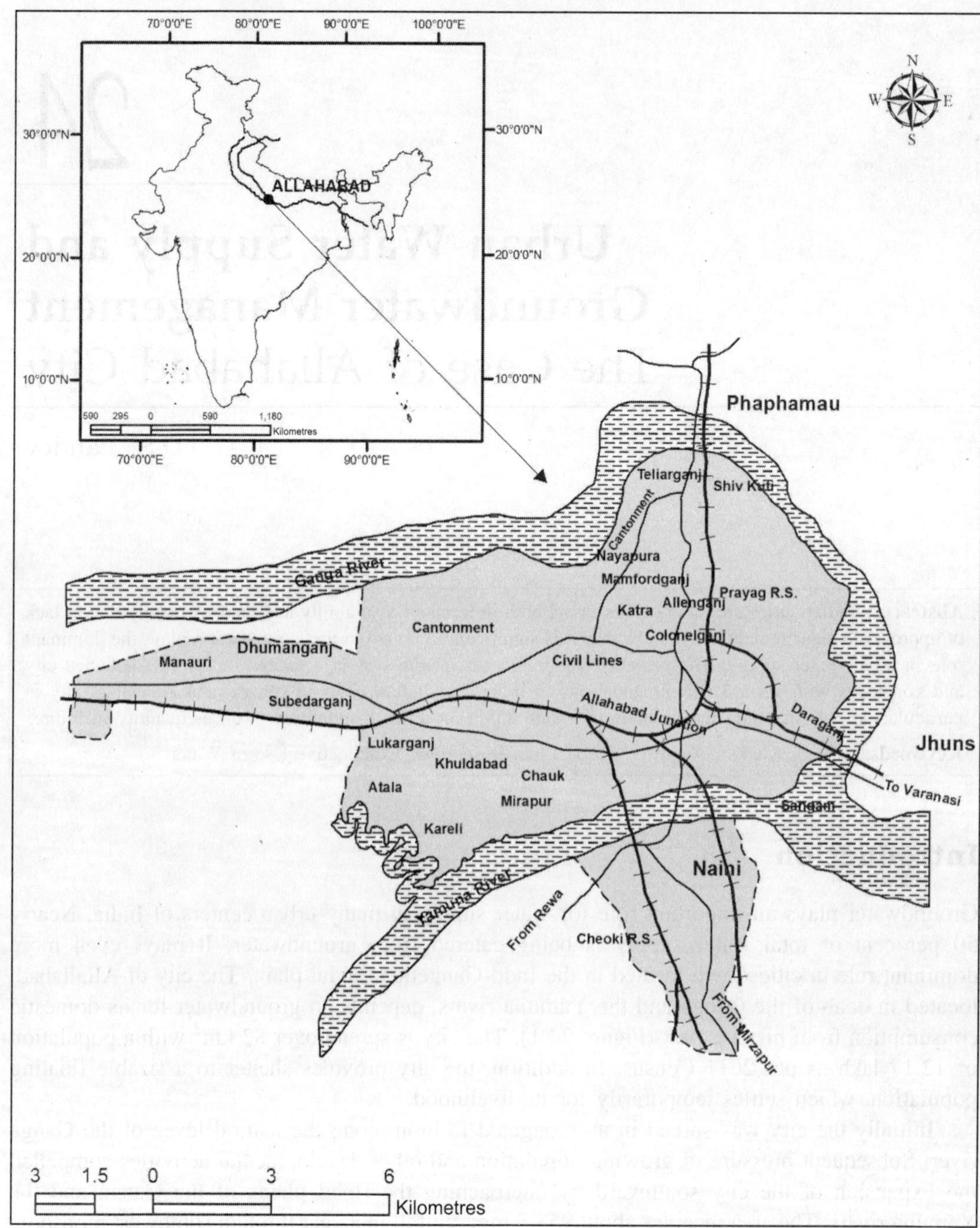

Figure 24.1 Location map of Allahabad city.

during high flow. However, the channel pattern shown by the Yamuna river is of strictly meandering type. Braid bars/sand flats, vegetated permanent bars/island bars are active flood plain characteristics of the surface.

Geology

A generalized geological succession present in and around Allahabad city is given in Table 24.1. The city area is covered by Gangetic Alluvium of Quaternary age. The thickness of sediments is about 247–264 m. The Quaternary sediments are underlain by Vindhyan Supergroup of rocks (Kaimur Sandstone and Bijaigarh Shales) which belong to pre-Cambrian period.

Table 24.1 Geological succession in Allahabad

Age	*Lithology*
Quaternary	Alluvium comprising silt, clay and kankar
Pre-Cambrain	Vindhyan Sandstone and Bijaigarh Shale

Hydrogeological Framework

In the Allahabad city and its environs, the groundwater occurs in a thick zone of saturation within the thick unconsolidated sediments. The aquifer underlying the area is made up of medium to coarse grained sand, gravel and pebble bed. Deepest bore hole drilled by Central Groundwater Board in this area at Sulemsarai is down to depth of 278.12 m. The first aquifer is encountered at 20 m depth below the top clay blanket and continues down to 120 m depth (Figures 24.2 and 24.3).

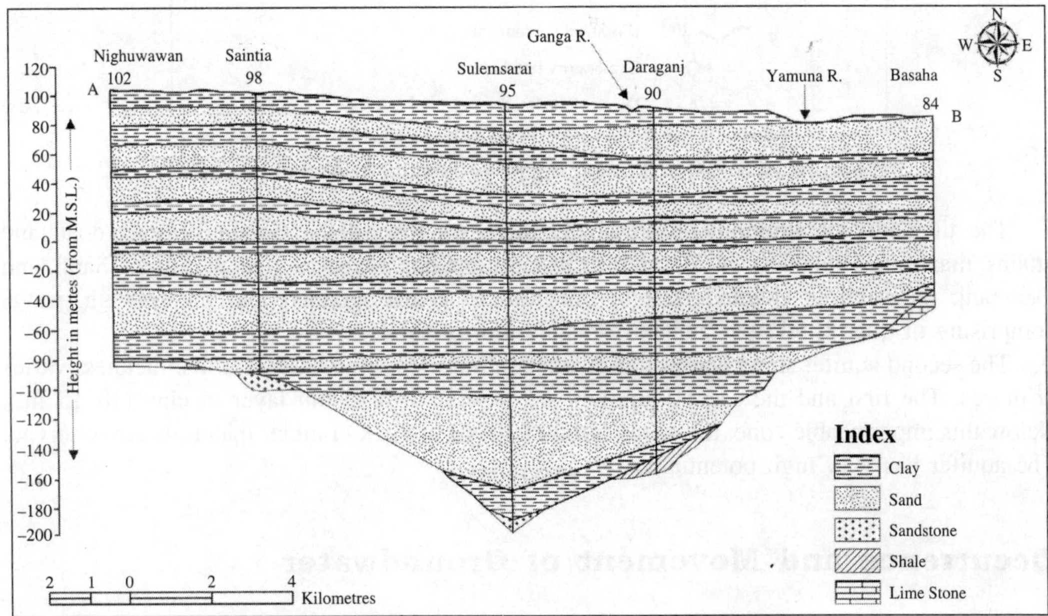

Figure 24.2 Sub-surface cross-section map of Allahabad city.

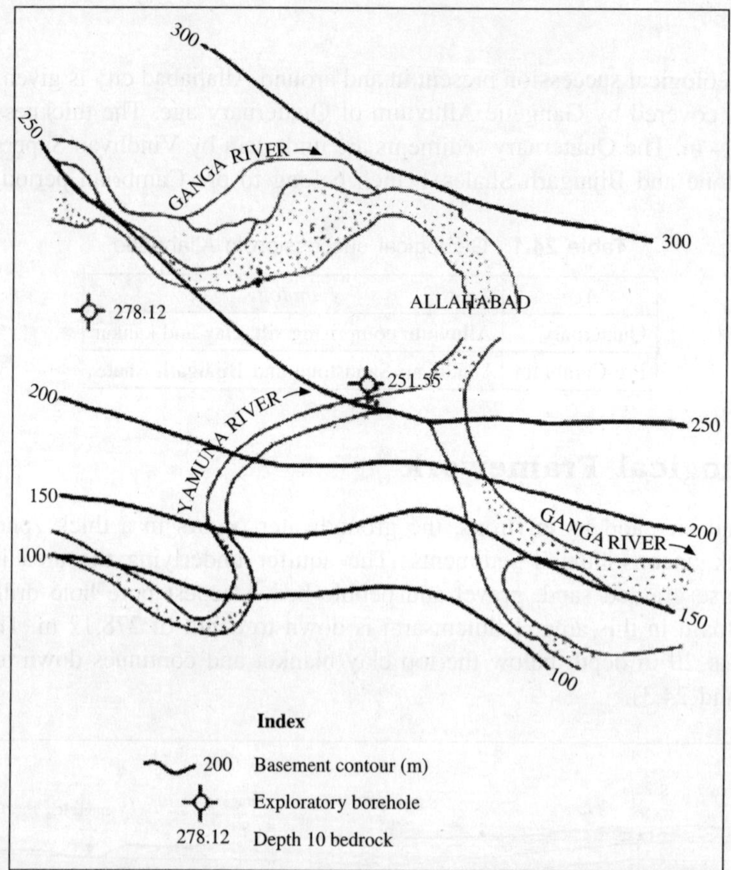

Figure 24.3 Map showing depth to bedrock in Allahabad city.

The thickness of alluvium progressively increases toward the Ganga-Yamuna doab and attains maximum thickness at Basahari. Observation has revealed that at Sulem Sarai and Daraganj, the sand is characterized by medium to coarse grained and mixed with gravel comprising of quartz, feldspar and ferro-magnesium minerals.

The second aquifer starts below 150 m and continues down to basement. Its thickness varies at places. The first and the second aquifers are separated by a thin layer of clay (10–15 m.). Below this impermeable zone, the sandy horizon 30–40 m thick granular materials are observed. The aquifer has very high potentiality.

Occurrence and Movement of Groundwater

Shallow Aquifer

Groundwater occurs under unconfined condition in shallow aquifers and semi-confined to confined in deeper aquifers. The pre-Monsoon depth of water varies from 1.85 to 23.40 m, whereas the depth of the well varies from 7.8 to 40 m. During the post-monsoon period, however, depth of water level changes and ranges between 2 and 20 mbgl. The shallow water level has been observed along the Ganga and the Yamuna rivers.

Deeper Aquifer

The piezometric head of deeper aquifers ranges between 6 and 20 m and roughly coincides with that of the shallow and unconfined units, suggesting that within alluvial pile-up different aquifers are interconnected regionally. The study of the water table elevation in the city indicates that the groundwater flow is towards the rivers Ganga and the Yamuna in the alluvial part.

However, a well-defined groundwater divide does exist, which trends roughly NW-SE. Groundwater elevation contour shows that the flow is in north direction towards the Ganga river and south along the Yamuna river. Both the rivers are effluent in nature. The gradient of water table is 0.4 m per km.

Status of Urban Water Supply System

The water supply system was first introduced in Allahabad town in the year 1891 to cater the need of small population, i.e., only 1.7 lakh. With the growth of population and rapid urbanization, the water supply system was strengthened in view of the ever increasing demand of water in the city area in 1925, and is being extended till date. The demand of water supply is fulfilled by Allahabad Jal Sansthan, Allahabad Development Authority and Jal Nigam by handpumps and tubewells. Presently the water supply of Allahabad has been divided into 11 zones with respect to population and its water demand projection in future which has been presented in Table 24.2 and Table 24.3. The groundwater availability is worked out considering 82 sq. km. area; 10 per cent specific yield in phreatic zone with 2.2 m water level fluctuation comes around 18.2 MCM.

Table 24.2 Water requirements in river water districts of Allahabad city

Lukerganj Zone		
Description	*Years*	
	2010	2025
1. Population	43,900	62,700
2. Water demand	11.85	16.93
3. Water availability (MLD)	15.00	15.00
(a) River water	–	–
(b) Tubewell water	15.00	15.00

(Contd.)

Table 24.2 Water requirements in river water districts of Allahabad city (*Contd.*)

Khusroobagh Zone		
Description	*Years*	
	2010	2025
1. Population	–	–
2. Water demand	–	–
3. Water availability (MLD)	30.00	30.00
(a) River water	–	–
(b) Tubewell water	30.00	30.00

Atala Zone		
Description	*Years*	
	2010	2025
1. Population	1,77,900	2,33,800
2. Water demand	48.03	63.13
3. Water availability (MLD)	55.00	55.00
(a) River water	–	–
(b) Tubewell water	55.00	55.00

Kydganj Zone		
Description	*Years*	
	2010	2025
1. Population	1,12,600	1,19,300
2. Water demand	30.40	32.31
3. Water availability (MLD)	25.00	25.00
(a) River water	–	–
(b) Tubewell water	25.00	25.00

Civil Lines Zone		
Description	*Years*	
	2010	2025
1. Population	86,500	1,26,000
2. Water demand	23.26	34.02
3. Water availability (MLD)	10.00	10.00
(a) River water	–	–
(b) Tubewell water	10.00	10.00

Table 24.3 Water requirements in groundwater districts of Allahabad city

Colonelganj Zone		
Description	*Years*	
	2010	2025
1. Population	1,36,500	1,67,600
2. Water demand	36.86	45.25
3. Water availability (MLD) (a) River water (b) Tubewell water	NA	NA

Sulemsarai Zone		
Description	*Years*	
	2010	2025
1. Population	42,300	96,500
2. Water demand	11.42	26.05
3. Water availability (MLD) (a) River water (b) Tubewell water	NA	NA

Rasulabad Zone		
Description	*Years*	
	2010	2025
1. Population	68,600	74,000
2. Water demand	18.52	19.98
3. Water availability (MLD) (a) River water (b) Tubewell water	NA	NA

Daraganj Zone		
Description	*Years*	
	2010	2025
1. Population	98,000	1,06,700
2. Water demand	26.46	28.81

Phaphamau Zone		
Description	*Years*	
	2010	2025
1. Population	42,300	96,500
2. Water demand	11.42	26.05

Naini Zone		
Description	*Years*	
	2010	2025
1. Population	24,200	54,800
2. Water demand	65.34	147.96

Future Water Requirements

Though water availability in Allahabad city is sufficient, even then the overall situation of water supply in various zones is not satisfactory due to various reasons. The supply zones are broadly divided into two categories—River Water District and Groundwater District (Figure 24.4).

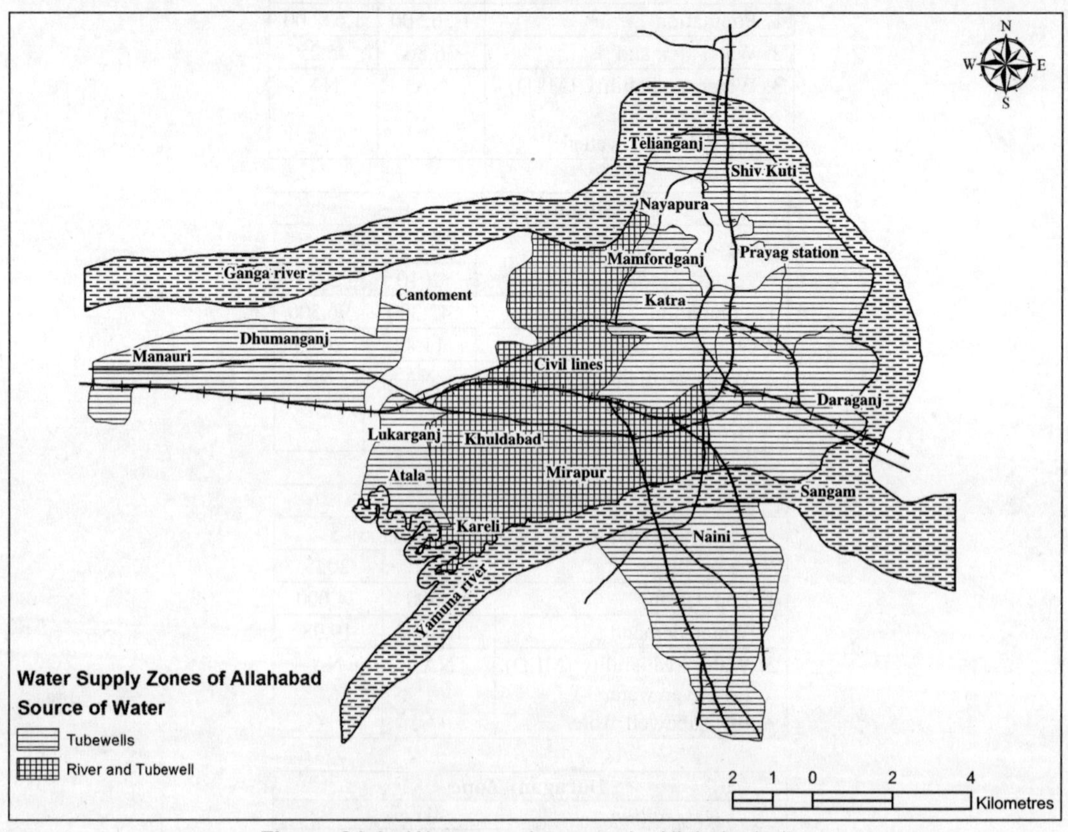

Figure 24.4 Water supply zones in Allahabad city.

The scarcity of water is being experienced even at this time in groundwater districts. The reason for the scarcity is that the tubewells are not giving sufficient discharge. This part of Allahabad is growing rapidly due to several new industries. Hence, detailed proposal may be prepared for this area based on the demand of the industries. There is, therefore, an urgent need to promote the idea of second water works. Accordingly, the city may be divided into the following four sub-zones in order to meet the water requirement through groundwater supply (Pandey, 2002; Allahabad Jal Sansthan, 1997; U.P. Jal Nigam, 1991). The four sub-zones are as under:

Sub-zone A

Allahabad Jal Sansthan opines that the construction of further tubewells will not be possible due to land getting scarce in congested locations. The area beyond Lajpat Rai Road towards north, consisting of locations like, Mamfordganj, Balrampur House, Nayapurwa, etc. comes under Sub-zone 'A' based on groundwater supply.

Sub-zone B

The area beyond Allahabad-Prayag Railway track (Rampriya Road, Jawaharganj, Dhareriya, Chota Baghara, etc.) having groundwater supply lie in this zone.

Sub-zone C

The Katra locality and parts of University Road come under this sub-zone. This is presently fed by the existing zonal pumping stations at Mayo Hall.

Sub-zone D

The localities of Coloneganj, Allenganj, Tagore town, Bank Road and part of Allahabad University etc. come under this zone.

The water supply in these sub-zones may be made as per the Table 24.4.

Table 24.4 Utilization of Khusroobagh water works after construction of new water works

Name of Zone	*Water to be supplied from Khusroobagh water works* (MLD)
Lookerganj	15.00
Khusroobagh	30.00
Atala	25.00
Kydganj	25.00
Civil Lines	25.00
Colonelganj	15.00
Total	135.00

Groundwater Management

Sustainable management of water resource is a major challenge at present. Groundwater conservation and augmentation have been a matter of major concern for sustainable supply of drinking water. This can be achieved by recharging the aquifer system. Different artificial recharge techniques may be adopted to augment the groundwater condition:

1. **One channel storage and recharge by storm water channels:** The Ganga and the Yamuna, two major rivers, become more active during Monsoon, which provide outlet to flood water as well as local area run-off. However, with careful planning the flood and rainwater can be stored in the channel itself. Deepening and widening them can enhance the surface capacity of channels, wherever possible. The stored water can be used from the surface or extracted from the aquifers after their recharge.

2. **Off-channel storage of flood water:** Storm water can be stored in channels but possibilities exist to create the off-channel reservoirs linked to main channel. This is possible through the creation of off-channel reservoirs, especially wherever the suitable recharge area exists, e.g., abandoned channels, oxbow lakes, etc. in the flood plain of the Ganga and the Yamuna rivers. It is a useful method to store flood and rainwater for lean period.
3. **Flood plain reservoirs for conjunctive extraction:** Generally, fresh water aquifers with copious discharge underlie the flood plains. Reservoirs on the flood plains can be created by scooping out the earth at appropriate locations and let these reservoirs to be filled up by the Monsoon flood water. The recharged water can be extracted from the aquifer by battery of shallow tubewells during the lean season.

Conclusion

The aforesaid discussion reveals that the city's water supply may be endangered with the pace with which the population has been increasing. The groundwater district areas are already experiencing the water shortage. Following steps may be taken for maintaining the sustainable water supply in the city:

1. Possibilities should be explored for construction of collector wells in the present flood plain area of the Ganga and the Yamuna rivers.
2. To control declining trend, there is an urgent need to recoil and conserve all the available surface water into groundwater through artificial recharge measures.
3. Owing to rapid urbanization of the area major quantity of rainwater goes as surface run-off and very little scope is left for groundwater recharge. Rainwater harvesting and its collection in low area in suitable reservoirs will improve the groundwater regime.
4. The roof top rainwater harvesting method for recharging the groundwater horizon may prove much beneficial.
5. The old handpumps and open wells should be rejuvenated for water supply development program.
6. Necessary precautions should be taken while selecting new sites for groundwater structures to avert pollution hazards.
7. It is imperative to educate the people about their responsibilities and attitude towards water resources utilization and conservation for its sustainable development in future.

References

Jal Sansthan, Allahabad (1997), *Technical Feasibility Report*.

Pandey, D.S. (2002), *Report on Urban Groundwater Management Studies in Allahabad City*, Uttar Pradesh, C.G.W.B., Unpublished Report.

U.P. Jal Nigam (1991), *Approach Paper on Allahabad Water Supply*.

25

Role of NGO in Water Conservation and Village Development

Abdul Shaban

Abstract: This chapter highlights the success story of water conservation, ecological protection and enhanced agricultural production at the initiative of a NGO called Pani Vikas Team, an offshoot of Narmada Bachao Andolan (NBA). The construction of small check dams has not only helped in water and ecological conservation, this has also led community participation. It also focuses on changing paradigms of village development due to globalization, privatization, and liberalization and suggests the sustainable development of village resources through Gandhian model of development.

Keywords: NGO, NBA, Gram Swaraj, Small is Beautiful, Shramdan, Paradigm, Pani Vikas

Introduction

Southern and south western part of Madhya Pradesh has a semi-arid type of climate with annual rainfall of about 80 cm. This rainfall is concentrated in Monsoon period during June–September. The terrain is dominated by Satpura and Maikal hill ranges. It is a source region of many important rivers flowing in all directions, most important being the Narmada, the Tapi and the Son. The soil in this area is largely gravelly and reddish, with lower content of humus, except in valleys and rivulets. Semi-thorny vegetation with dotted patches of trees in valleys are other peculiarities of natural landscape. This area is also a part of mid-Indian tribal belt, where tribal population has been pushed due to repeated incursion by other communities from north in the process of peopling of India. To meet the national and regional electricity demand and demand of water for irrigation, a master plan was prepared to dam the Narmada at several places in 1960s and early 1970s. In that period the population in those areas was lower (which increased considerably subsequently) and was thought to displace only a few thousand families. However, the plan of damming the river with monumental dams for electricity generation and irrigation could start in early 1980s. From that time, as mentioned above, the population density in the area has increased considerably and displacement became a major issue, besides ecological concerns. The Narmada Bachao Andolan (NBA) which was working in Dhule district of Maharashtra for proper rehabilitation package for oustees of Sardar Sarovar Project also started working in Nimar District of Madhya Pradesh in 1987 against the displacement of people and for their proper rehabilitation. The agitation by NBA after 1987 became consistent, coherent and broad-based against the Narmada Valley Project.

The growth of population in the semi-arid area over the years has led to increase in agricultural practices and number of animals. This has an impact on environmental components in terms of decreased surface and groundwater, increased soil erosion (by water and wind) and loss of vegetation (due to grazing and exploitation for other uses). The ecological destructions led to stagnation and often decline in agricultural production of main crops: rice, cotton, maize and bajra. The available ecological services and products like vegetation, grazing land, water availability, soil production and wild animals also declined. This created a crisis in the area which is still amplifying and deepening in many villages. The decline in agricultural production and ecological products (vegetation, soil quality, wild animal, grazing land, underground and surface water) and services led to the migration of people from the area and also in villages Roopkheda, Mordhar, and Jamali of Khangone districts, situated in south western part of Madhya Pradesh.

The Task Force on Development Options

Repeated hunger strikes and agitation by NGOs (like NBA), civil society groups, and those displaced by dams and their arguments for alternative models of development and electricity generation rather than only from big dams, which displace people and damage environment, forced the government of Madhya Pradesh to constitute a Task Force to study Narmada valley Development Options in January 1998. The Task Force was to submit its report by the end of June in that year. Besides, the government officials, the Task Force also included members of NBA, Alok Agrawal and Medha Patkar. The immediate concern was submergence of 13 villages due to Maheshwar Hydel-Power Project. In the report against the Madhya Pradesh Electricity Board's argument, NBA presented alternative methods and questioned the role of big dams in sustainable development. The argument of NBA was in Gandhian (Village Swaraj, 1963) and Schumacherian (Small is Beautiful, 1973) framework. There were no differences of opinion about the need of electricity and development, but the method to generate the electricity by damaging environment and displacing people was questioned. It was argued by NBA that irrigated areas can be increased by small dams or watershed methods. Further, the run of river type approach was argued would be less destructive than impounded dams. NBA also argued for hybrid-solar-biomass-fossil fuel thermal electricity generation systems in place of hydroelectric power through big dams. However, the Task Force Report could not get its due importance and the 'big dam approach' remained only alternative for those in government.

Formation of Pani Vikas and Water Conservation

The NBA was convinced with the efficacy and sustainability of the alternative methods of development. They found government discouraging and following more conventional approach than alternative and non-conventional methods of development or electricity generation and water management. To chart out the alternative path of development, two of the members (Bhagwan Dada and Sangeeta Kenara) of NBA went to an NGO named Samaj Pragati Sahyog at Bagli, M.P., in 2001 for watershed training and formed a new offshoot of the NBA 'Pani Vikas Team'. Equipped with watershed training, Bhagwan dada with his four other colleagues wandered in villages of Khargone district to find out suitable location to start watershed work. It was also a task to convince people that they should start conserving their own environment and water for their development. The lack of fund was a problem and Pani Vikas could only start work if villagers get convinced and start work of water conservation through Shramdan. The Pani Vikas team stayed in village Roopkheda as they could convince the villagers about their idea of development and intervention. The team found that the village is inhabited by tribals (Barela and Bhilala) who used to migrate for work to Khargone town and other places for work due to degradation of environment (vegetation, soil and water). The soil was pebbly and could dry up very quickly and therefore without regular irrigation agriculture could not be practiced on most of the 600 ha land of total 100 families in the village. They also found that gram panchayat was not doing much development work and villagers were left to fend for themselves.

Initially, Pani Vikas Team member did not tell villagers that they are from NBA. NBA was opposed and attacked in areas which were only benefiting but was supported where displacement was to happen. Many political parties were also antagonistic to NBA as they thought that NBA was antidevelopment. In February 2001, even police raided their office at Roopkheda and took away their utensils and maps of the villages including toposheets. The police was suspecting that Pani Vikas Team members could create violence in the area and make people rise against the government. Further, they feared that NBA could breed naxals, as people were unhappy because of displacement and drowning of their settlements and fields. Further suspicion rose because of the young girls (Sangeeta and Paro) in the team. The rural and conservative society could not convince itself that girls can stay with someone else or without their family members. Another suspicion was that some of the team members are Christian and they are on proselytizing mission. People from nearby villages used to clandestinely watch their gods/images and the ways the members used to pray/worship (as they doubted them for belonging to Christianity). So all the 'naxal', 'young girl', 'anti-dam', and 'religious' angles were against them, besides lack of finances. The outsiders (people from other villages), police and CID were against them but the villagers in Roopkheda were convinced about the sincerity, dedication and honesty of Pani Vikas Team members.

Mobilization of Villagers

Initially, Pani Vikas Team won the confidence of sarpanch and slowly of all the inhabitants in village Roopkheda. The team also ventured out to nearby villages to convince people about the importance of in situ water management as water from canal was a distant dream and also harmful for their brethren somewhere else. In January 2002, Pani Vikas Team had taken some of the villagers of Roopkheda and other neighbouring villages, Mordhar and Jamali, to Alwar District to show them the work of water management by an NGO named Tarun Bharat Sangh.

After seeing the success of the water management in Alwar district and its impact on economic and social life, the villagers were encouraged and planned to implement water management plans in their own villages.

Meanwhile Pani Vikas Team created 'Village Water Development Committee' (VWDC) in each of the three villages, Roopkheda, Mordhar and Jamali. The committee comprised of 8–10 members and compulsorily the representation of women was kept as 50 per cent of the total members in each of the three villages. The task of the committee was to (1) mobilize the villagers for water management through Shramdan and (2) to oversee the work so that quality construction can be done. The motivation of the members in Roopkheda village where Pani Vikas Team was staying was relatively higher and so they started progress on work quite fast. The villagers, old, young, women and men along with members of Pani Vikas Team surveyed their own village and identified site for construction of boulder checks and earthen dams. On the first day (30 March, 2002) of work in Roopkheda, total 80 persons came out for Shramdan and the first day itself they created 6 boulder checks. On the next day 6 more boulder checks were created by the same number of persons and on third day 70 persons created 4 boulder checks. After this, the villagers celebrated Vasant Panchami festival and then got together to decide about construction of earthen dams.

Achievements

The work on an earthen dam started on April 4, 2002 and 170 people constructed the same in 4 days. After this the villagers constructed another earthen dam in 4 days. This earthen dam was 13 m in length and 3 m high.

The villagers again constructed a 40 m and 2 m high earthen dam (Table 25.1). The importance of this latter dam lies in that some of the villagers contributed their land for the dam, and this was beginning of new thinking in the village Roopkheda. Given that concentration of Pani Vikas Team remained in village Roopkheda in order to make it a success to demonstrate other villages the benefit of water and environmental conservation, the work in two other villages remained slow. Table 25.1 presents the progress of work in the three villages during 2002–03.

Table 25.1 Water and environmental conservation works completed in three villages (M.P.)

Year	*Village*	*Border check*	*Earthen dam*	*Dug wells*	*Repair of earthen dams*	*Plantation* (No. of tree planted)*	*Bori Bandhan***
2002	Roopkheda	16	4	–	–	500	2
	Mordhar	–	–	1	–	250	2
	Jamli	–	–	–	–	250	–
2003	Roopkheda	16	4	–	4	1200	3
	Mordhar	–	–	–	–	–	6
	Jamli	–	–	–	–	–	5
2004	Roopkheda	25	1	–	–	–	–
	Total	57	9	1	4	2200	18

Source: Field Work

*Trees included bamboo, mahua, amla, karanj and neem.

**Bori-bandhan dams are dams constructed with sacks filled with earth/soil.

Sharamdan

The participation of farmers in the villages, particularly in Roopkheda towards water conservation through Shramdan was encouraging. The average land holding in the village was about 2 ha and the big farmers, about 10 families, had 20–30 ha each. There were no landless families. The big farmers in general avoided joining the Shramdan work as they had tubewells through which they could mine the water and irrigate their field. The small farmers and medium farmers were suffering lots as their tubewells/dugwells were drying up and in non-monsoon season there were hardly sufficient yield to irrigate their fields. As all the families in the village belonged to tribal group, there were no caste issues in work participation and Shramdan. The women participation was also quite high; Sangeeta and Paro from Pani Vikas team became their role models. In Shramdan, mainly women participated. Male used to dig soil and women used to carry and put it on dam. The participation of male was lower as they used to migrate to towns and cities for wage earnings. The participation was from all age groups: old, young and children.

Situation Before and After the Intervention

The water and environment conservation work led to considerable improvement in economic and social situations of the inhabitants in Roopkheda. The groundwater level increased substantially and in the village hardly any well or handpump remained dry by 2004. As water yield of the wells increased, so the irrigation in the village. The irrigated area, which was about 20 acre earlier increased by 30 per cent in 2004. The net sown area in the village increased from about 40 acre to 150 acre between 2002 and 2004. In the village, there used to be only one cropping season, the Monsoon, and rest of the seasons the fields used to lie vacant for the lack of sufficient water. However, after the water conservation work, the rabi crop also started to be cultivated by almost all the families. The number of domesticated animals also increased in the village. Villagers used to mostly rear goats as it used to give good and quick returns which they used for buying cloths, medicines, fare in case of migration, fee for children, buying bicycles or other consumer goods, besides having small savings. The main reason behind increase in number of goats was increase in grazing land or grass land. Increased moisture in soil on slopes and undulating lands led to growth of grass which goats could then graze. The number of trees and smaller bushes also increased which further provided fodder for such animals. Growth of trees largely remained around the earthen dams where moistures were available throughout the year. Soil erosion stopped and soil productivity increased leading to increased production of crops. The rainy season used to support crops like rice, cotton, bajra and maize, while after the conservation works, rabi season has wheat and gram. The diet of the villagers also improved. Earlier due to lack of water, vegetable used to be grown only in Monsoon season. However, after the conservation work, vegetables are also grown in winter season. There were no water borne diseases in the villages. However, women and children used to suffer a lot due to decline in groundwater level resulting in drying of handpumps and wells, the sources of drinking water.

The drinking water used to be fetched from some far off wells (from a distance of 500 m to 1 km) and there used to be quite a lengthy queue. The collection of water used to be the task of women and mostly of school going girls. They used to collect water before school time and so they used to awake early in morning. In collecting water, they used to get exhausted and in that state they also used to go to school. Migration of people from the village in search of wage employment also considerably stopped. This led to better enrolment and attendance of children in the village school. The villagers recognized the importance of conservation of water and started recharging groundwater through collection in developed structures. They did not withdraw too much of water from their wells and surface bodies and leave water for wild animals and ecology (tree, grass and soil). Thus they recognize ecology as another sector that demands water besides human and irrigational needs. A comparative summary of the improvement in the village before and after the water conservation work is given in Table 25.2.

Table 25.2 A few indicators before and after water conservation work in village Roopkheda (M.P.)

Indicators	*In* 2002 (*before start of work*)	*In* 2004 (*December*)
Out-of-district migration	180 persons (60 families)	8 persons
Migration to Khargone town for work	40 persons	10 persons
Net sown area of wheat	25 acre	150 acre
Grass and vegetation on hills	Grassless	Grass on hills and planted plants growing
Well irrigation	Insufficient water in off-monsoon season	5–6 ft higher level and sufficient yield
Water in wells in summer	Insufficient/dry	Sufficient
Wheat production per acre	5–6 quintal	12–15 quintals
Rabi season	No significant crop	Wheat, gram and vegetables cultivated
Awareness about trees	Low	High, felling trees stopped

Source: Field Work.

Community Development

An important development that took place in the process of water conservation was that community and family ties got strengthened within the village and also between neighbouring villages (Mordar and Jamali). People started visiting from one village to other to learn from each other and exchange ideas. There was hardly any fight within and between the villagers. The villagers realized that community cooperation can reverse the process of degradation and underdevelopment in the villages. They collectively made water structures, managed drinking water, and surface and groundwater for irrigation and planted trees. They decided collectively in consultation with Pani Vikas Team and implemented the decisions collectively. The Pani Vikas Team always remained with them, and guided, galvanized and educated them.

Sustainability of Programme

What came to fore on several occasions was the lack of initiatives by villagers. Without consultation of Pani Vikas Team they could hardly initiate work. Pani Vikas Team admits that they tried to create capacity, ability and leadership among the villagers to take up the initiatives by their own, but have not succeeded much in this. Further, the changing lifestyle, demand and necessities in the villages have made the availability of cash with individuals a necessity. They need cash for education of their children, for their health spending and conspicuous consumer goods like bikes, radios, television, mobile phones, etc. The agricultural production can hardly provide sufficient income for such demands. People from the villages, therefore, have started demanding wage labour from the Pani Vikas Team. The Pani Vikas Team during years 2002–04 largely managed with minimum funds available with them (collected from contribution of sympathizers of the NBA). Government hardly provided any help and in fact remained antagonist to the NBA on Narmada Dam issues.

Broader Context

The case highlights both the process and products. Process or means sometimes assume more importance than product itself. We can see that both the NBA and the government were agreeing on need of electricity, water and development, but their argument for means to achieve the same was/is quite different: the government adopting 'big is efficient' model while NBA argued for 'Small is Beautiful' and Gram Swaraj or Gandhian model of development.

The 1980s and 1990s were decades of transition in development thinking in India. The decades were the meeting times of modernization and neo-classical economics of 'big is efficient' and Soviet thinking of planning 'big' with newly emerged environmental consciousness and sustainable development paradigm. In the former paradigm, demand for certain commodities and services somewhere could be satisfied by the production from elsewhere. In general, change in geographies, sociologies and ecologies were of hardly any concern before 1980s. Planners used to think the land as tabula rosa, and plan on the same as they liked. The environment was least cared and economic development was given the highest priority. Social constraints were ignored and only physical constrained were thought of relevant for planning. In 1980s and 1990s, the concept of sustainable development arose and it came to be largely accepted that societies are embedded in their physical environment and without the sustainability of environment, sustainable social and economic systems cannot be created. Since late 1990s, the thinking of planners and policy makers has largely changed in favour of planning for sustainable development. The protest by civil society, NGOs and those being victim of such plans, as in the case of Narmada Valley Project, has played important role in shaping such thinking in planners and policy makers. In this context, NBA has been a leading NGO to voice for 'alternative model of development'.

The role of village development in a country like India is acknowledged by all but practiced by a few, largely non-seriously by the government. The government plans have been for villages but the concentration of economic activities somehow has taken place in towns and cities. A few committed civil society organizations and NGO's have attempted to take up the cause of village development with such approach as water resources management. The paradigms 'small is beautiful' and 'Gram Swaraj' advocated by some NGO's (like that of NBA) have often come in conflict with government schemes of 'bigs'. The rights of inhabitants and environmental destruction were the main points on which NBA protested against dams. The contribution of

NBA in village development, prevention of migration and poverty has been immense. However, being a NGO, its role and capacity in development interventions have always been limited.

The case also brings forth many other important points such as (a) equity of benefits/ losses between those who lose land, settlements, environment and socio-economic systems and those who benefit located somewhere else without losing anything, (b) The problems of biases against certain religion and manufactured and innovated fears of proselytisation, (c) the manufacturing of fear and hatred against NGO groups by political class and police repression on suspicion for NBA members creating naxals, (d) the differences in perception of villagers with whom the Pani Vikas Team lived and other villagers who doubted them, (e) the role of outsiders, NGO members (including the two young girls who were labeled in many ways) in mobilization of people for village water conservation despite of all odds, (f) the role of Shramdan in initial stages of development to cultivate sense of sacrifice, pride in the work, enhancement of community belongingness, sense of ownership and responsibility, (g) IWRM and its socio-economic and environmental benefits: poverty alleviation, migration decline, water availability, and water sustainability, (h) villagers recognizing the role of water conservation in sustainable development, and environment as one of the sectors which too requires water, (i) role of environment in overall development of village, (j) the impact of water conservation on women and children (mainly young girls who used to awake early in morning to collect water and then go to school exhausted—which must have affected the learning ability), and (k) relatively better social position of women in tribal societies than those in 'caste' and religiously dogmatic societies.

The case also highlights the dilemmas and demand of villagers in present day development paradigm. The unleashing of information, advertisement of products, demand of health and education, aspiration for conspicuous consumption, language and culture of those of middle and higher classes in cities, have increased the demand for wage/cash earning. In fact, Pani Vikas Team struggled to keep the villagers together due to lack of sufficient funds to provide wage employment to them during 2005–06. The case, thus, also shows the inherent nature of problem with village development paradigm of those of Mahatma Gandhi and Schumacher in present context (too powerful capitalist and consumerist forces). The powerful forces of capitalism with globalization are developing homogeneities in aspiration and lifestyles, and rural societies depending on only agriculture can hardly satisfy them and so there is an increasing demand for money. For money, one has to migrate to cities, and also to learn and enjoy the new lifestyles. The consequence is demographically burgeoning and exploding cities. This in turn necessitates more investment in cities and towns, leaving villages starved for funds. And this vicious process is keeping on reinforcing itself.

Notwithstanding this, many agree that sustainable development can only be brought through Gandhian and Schumacherian models of development (Bhole, 2007) and essentially through the process of ecological and water conservation (like IWRM). It is argued that the sooner we realize this, the better.

Conclusion

The role of NGO's continues to be significant as it works within frame of local conditions and contexts. The approach of development pursued by the NGOs is much less harmful to the ecology and environment. The NGOs also ensure local participation which is essential for the success of plans, policies and programmes. One way implementation from top without local community participation does not fulfil the objectives. The dictum that local problems have local solutions continues to be very valid in resolving the problems of water shortage, irrigation, soil erosion and deforestation. In spite of the fact that globalization has accelerated the aspirations of villagers, the Gram Swaraj model of Gandhi or Small is Beautiful of Schumacher is the only alternative of sustainable development at the end.

References

Bhole, L.M. (2007), *Collected Papers on Gandhian Thoughts*, Amani International Publisher, Keil, Germany.

Cap-Net, Global Water Partnership, and IJNDP (2005), *Integrated Water Resources Management Plans: Training Manual and Operational Guide*, The Netherlands.

Gandhi, M.K. (1963), *Village Swaraj*, Navjivan, Ahmedabad.

Government of Madhya Pradesh (1998), *Report of the Task Force to Study Narmada Valley Development Options*, Office of the Governor, Bhopal.

Schumacher, E.F. (1973), *Small is Beautiful: Economics as People Mattered*, Hartley and Marks, Vancouver, Canada.

26

Drought Management in India

P.S. Tiwari

Abstract: This chapter highlights the impact of drought as a disaster and suggests several ways to tackle the problems such as change in cropping pattern, promotion of drip/sprinkler irrigation, reforms in water pricing, watershed management, conjunctive use of water and change in organizational structure. This chapter also discusses the merits and demerits of national water grid, which is being talked as a preferred solution for combating the problem of water crisis in India.

Keywords: National Water Grid, Drip Irrigation, Land Care Policy, Watershed Management, Natural Hazards, Spat, Grandiose Dream, Vagaries of Indian Monsoon

Introduction

The natural hazards like floods, droughts, cyclones, earthquakes and volcanic eruptions take heavy toll of life and property each year all over the world (Gupta et al., 2011; Alexander, 1993). Their impact is, however, much more severe in the developing countries than it is in the developed world. Whereas the impacts of floods, cyclones, earthquakes and volcanic activity are sudden and severe, the ill-effects of droughts are gradual, all-pervasive and long lasting. India faces a severe drought almost after every 3–4 years particularly in the southern, northern and central parts (Nagarajan, 2003, Gupta and Gupta, 2000). This chapter focuses on droughts and tries to indicate how droughts can be managed with available resources and technology.

Droughts have been recorded since times immemorial. In fact, the economic history of India has largely been the history of droughts and famines. Large-scale movements of population from western and northwestern India to the more rainy central and eastern parts were mostly caused by droughts and famines. The stories of the great famine of 1896 are still fresh in the minds of the people of the north Indian society when human beings competed with animals for the scarce tree leaves for their survival. The repressive measures of the alien Government in forcefully collecting land revenue and confiscating movable property added immensely to the misery of the people.

How do droughts occur? Droughts result from failure of the monsoon. The vagaries of the Indian monsoon are well known. In fact, nothing is certain about the monsoon—its onset, continuance and retreat, or the amount of rainfall and its areal coverage. Sometimes floods and droughts are reported the same time in different parts of the country or in the same area at different times of the monsoon period. The torrential nature of monsoon rainfall results in flash floods and wastage of water. The flash flood at Nagaur in Rajasthan desert in 1972 is well known, when a buffalo, washed away with the flood, was stranded on the roof of a building and had to be rescued with the help of a crane.

The mechanism of monsoon has not been fully understood so far. Scientific research, including the Monex Experiment and study of EL Nino effect, has given us valuable insight into the working of the monsoon. With the help of the scientific data and sharper analytical tools, weather forecasting in India has become much more accurate than it was about a decade back. Looking to the scientific advancement, there is reason to believe that our scientists shall be able to solve the mystery of monsoon very soon and shall provide us clues to prepare in advance to meet the challenge of droughts and floods. Till that time we have to live with the vagaries of the monsoon.

The ill-effects of drought are of far-reaching nature and lead to economic, social and political hardships and upheavals. The first and the foremost victims of drought are the farming community, particularly the small and marginal farmers, land less labourers, rural artisans and small traders who constitute more than two-thirds of our society. The farmer, having invested all his resources in the field in form of seeds, fertilizers, and cultivation costs, looks to the rain God praying for His mercy in vain. His crop fails, his plans for the future go topsy turvy, his dreams are shattered, and hunger and starvation stare in his eyes. The rural artisans loose their jobs, and the small traders in the local market loose their business and livelihood. The drought has its cascading effects on the urban economy as well. The demand for manufactured goods and services is drastically reduced, leading to unemployment and economic recession. Many towns and cities face shortage of water even for drinking purposes.

The demand for limited water supply in drought years, many times, leads to social and political upheavals. River water disputes gather momentum, resulting in strife and tension in the riparian states. The Kaveri water dispute between Karnataka and Tamil Nadu and the recent show down between the two states bear testimony to the political fall-out of droughts. The two states have been fighting for greater share of the Kaveri water for the last four decades but the fight turns ugly and disastrous only in drought years. So long as there is good monsoon, the dispute is forgotten to be remembered again when the rain fails.

How to Manage Drought?

Drought management has two perspectives—the short term and the long term. Short-term management focuses mainly relief and rehabilitation. Most of the state governments keep ready baskets of projects to be undertaken in such eventualities. The problem in short-term measures arises not so much because of lack of ideas or well-formulated projects, but because of tardy implementation of the programmes. The implementation is related to the efficiency of the state government and quality of governance, which vary widely from one state to another.

The long-term strategy to mitigate and minimize the ill-effects of droughts hovers around two main issues: rational utilization of available water resources, and augmentation of water resources. We shall outline briefly some of the measures to manage the water resources effectively.

Change in Cropping Pattern

The water requirement of different crops varies widely. When water is in short supply, it is prudent to consider the water efficiency of different crops, and promote crops with better water efficiency. Rice and sugarcane, which consume lot of water, should be allowed only during the rainy season and in wet areas only. Drought resistant varieties should be promoted in drought-prone areas and grain farming should be discouraged in non-irrigated areas in favour of tree crops, which can withstand droughts better.

Promotion of Sprinkler/Drip Irrigation

Flood irrigation, commonly practiced in India, results in wastage of precious irrigation water. Water required to irrigate one hectare in flooding system is enough to irrigate three hectares in sprinkler system and nine hectares in drip system. Sprinkler and drip irrigation have received patronage of the Government for quite some time, still these systems do not find favour with the farmers. Efforts should be made to find the impediments in adoption of these systems, and corrective measures, including practical demonstration, should be undertaken.

Reforms in Pricing of Water

One reason why sprinkler and drip irrigation have not gained popularity is the fact that water has not been priced properly. In most of the states, the water charge is related to the area irrigated, and not the amount of water used. This results, many times, in over irrigation and that, in turn, leads to water-logging and salinity. If water is charged according to the volume used, cropping pattern will automatically change and less water efficient crops will give way to the more water efficient ones. The myth that water cannot be measured at the field level has to be exploded with research and extension.

Comprehensive Land Care Policy and Watershed Management

Land and water resources, the two basic requirements of our agricultural economy, are finite in nature. Both these resources are inter-dependent. The country should adopt a comprehensive land care policy, which should naturally include efficient water management. Reckless deforestation and expansion of cultivation to undulating grasslands and steep slopes have played havoc in the last five decades after Independence. Due to extensive soil erosion in catchment areas, most of our reservoirs and tanks have silted much faster than stipulated. This has resulted in reduced storage of water as well as in substantial evaporation loss due to spread of water over larger surface. In olden days, water storage capacity was maintained by annual deepening of tanks and ponds. The humus-rich silt of the tank bed was used as fertilizer in the fields and gainful employment was created for the farmers when there was no other farming operation left for them after the harvest of the Rabi crop. Unfortunately, the practice has disappeared for various reasons with the passage of time.

One major hurdle in maintaining the storage capacity of large reservoirs is the mismatch between the interests of the watershed and that of the command area. The farmers of the watershed are in no way compensated for their efforts to check soil erosion to maintain the storage capacity of the reservoir by the beneficiaries in the command area. Some viable system should be devised to tie-up the interests of the two groups. Our irrigation systems are managed very poorly, to say the least. The reservoirs and canals are managed by technocrats with little training in management techniques. The irrigation department has no mechanism to oversee land use and agricultural practices in the watershed or to prevent deforestation, check soil erosion and promote soil conservation. The irrigation charges are collected by the revenue department and not by the irrigation department, which supplies the water. Irrigation in the country is heavily subsidized and invariably every irrigation project is a loss-making proposition. The cost–benefit analysis undertaken in the initial stages to assess the viability of the project is forgotten once the project is approved and construction starts.

This is certainly not a happy situation and cannot be sustainable. It is high time that serious thought is given to corporatize irrigation works. Corporations, with equity participation of the farmers of both the watershed and the command area, should be entrusted with the responsibilities of maintenance of the irrigation works including the reservoirs and the canals, and management of the watershed and command area. They should be professionally managed, should generate their own revenue, and should be self-sustaining.

Conjunctive Use of Water

Conjunctive use of surface and ground water has been talked about in our country for long, but precious little has been achieved so far. In fact, no serious efforts have been made in this direction. A few states, like Tamil Nadu, have initiated some legislation. Water harvesting is being promoted in metropolitan areas, particularly those facing water problems. Check dams and percolation tanks have been encouraged in some areas. All these efforts are, however, too inadequate.

Organizational Structure

Drought management requires an organizational set-up to oversee the efforts of different agencies involved in various aspects of the problem. Such organization should ideally have three tiers: district, block/mandal, and village panchayat, and should involve the government agencies, NGOs and public institutions. The district council, headed by a senior bureauocrat, should include:

1. the heads of all government departments dealing with land and water,
2. all NGOs working in the districts,

3. a technical expert in the field of civil engineering/irrigation, working in the local university/college, and
4. a social scientist, preferably a geographer or an economist.

The council should be responsible for formulation of projects, procurement and management of financial resources, technical guidance to the block/mandal and village units in implementation of programmes, project monitoring and evaluation, and for coordination. The block/mandal and village councils, organized on the model of the district council, should basically be responsible for implementation of the projects.

The projects should be formulated and implemented in the spatial frame of watersheds. The size of the watershed should be determined by the terrain of the region. The watershed should be delineated following village boundaries, as far as possible, for the sake of administrative convenience. The valuable experience gathered in the on-going projects in various states should be fully utilized. The most prestigious programme in drought management, the Drought Prone Areas Programme (DPAP) has been in operation in a large number of districts throughout the country for more than three decades now. The Janmabhumi Programme of the Government of Andhra Pradesh and the Village Development Plans formulated and implemented by the Government of Kerala are some other innovative programmes. The experience of the Water User Cooperatives of the Maharashtra Government could also be considered. Frustrated over the failure of these cooperatives, set up two years ago, in managing the state owned canals and ensuring equity in irrigation water distribution, and payment of water rates, the Maharashtra Government is edging towards a decision to auction such rights and responsibilities to some private franchisee. The evaluation studies of such programmes can provide valuable insights in constitution of organizational structure of district, block and village councils and in formulation and implementation of specific programmes.

National Water Grid

The National Water Grid or the plan of linking major rivers now seems to be the preferred solution for combating recurring droughts in the country. The plan visualizes transfer of 1500 cubic m of water per second from the Ganga during the flood season to the Kaveri through a chain of canals, linking the Mahanadi, the Godavari, the Krishna and the Pennar. A link between the Ganga and the Brahmaputra is also planned. This plan seeks to end the flood problems of the Ganga and the Brahmaputra, while at the same time solving the drought in southern India by diverting the excess water of these Himalayan rivers to the monsoon-fed peninsular ones. It requires construction of more than 1000 km of link canals, 10,000 MW of electricity for lifting water to highlands, and over 200 storage reservoirs to enable this water transfer. M.S. Reddy, former Secretary, the Union Ministry of Water Resources, estimates that this plan will cost over ₹ 500,000 crores, much higher than the official estimate of ₹ 185,000 crores.

The idea of linking major rivers of India was first mooted by K.L. Rao, when he was irrigation minister in Nehru's cabinet and was later on taken up as Garland Canal by Dastur in the 1970s. The ruling Bharatiya Janata Party re-affirmed the commitment to the scheme in 2000. In response to a public interest litigation, the Supreme Court has now directed the Central Government to consider linking all major rivers within 10 years. The Government of India plans to link the peninsular rivers by 2035 and the Himalayan rivers by 2043 and integrate the two networks thereafter. The Prime Minister has announced the Government's resolve to go ahead with the project on a war footing, and has constituted a task force to plan feasibility studies.

The proposed inter basin water transfer linkages of Himalayan and Peninsular segments have been shown in the maps (Figure 26.1). The project is being undertaken without proper debate pre-conditional to a decision of this magnitude, and with no specifics of the project made available to concerned citizens and people's organizations to peruse. The inter-basin transfer of water has come under criticism since the Irrigation Commission of the British days. Inter-linking of rivers as proposed by Dastur was rejected long back by the Central Government on the advice of experts. The politics that comes with any human intervention in rivers flowing since generations from one administrative unit to another is well known. With the recent spat between Tamil Nadu and Karnataka fresh in our minds, it is difficult to take seriously a grandiose dream of linking all the rivers.

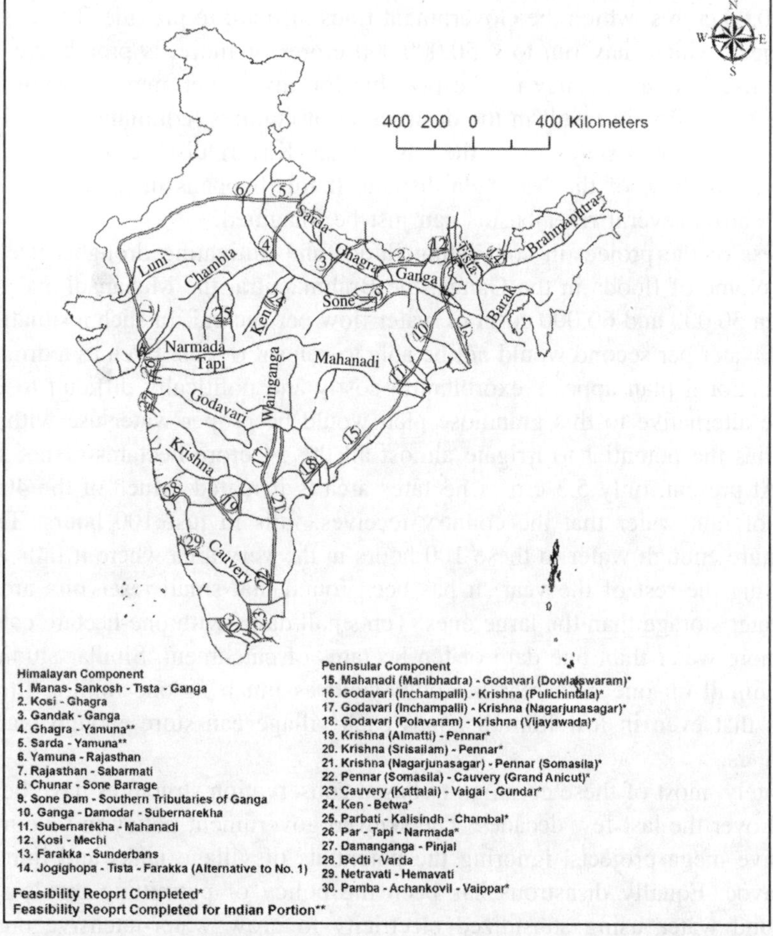

Figure 26.1 Proposed inter basin water transfer links of Himalayan and peninsular components in India. (Based on National Water Development Agency, India.)

The construction of huge reservoirs on the Ganga and the Brahmaputra, and the canals to link these reservoirs to the southern rivers will submerge vast fertile lands and village communities in the densely populated northern plain, and will displace millions of families in rural and urban areas. Apart from the colossal economic loss due to submersion of fertile lands and forests, and prohibitive cost of rehabilitation of displaced people, the social and political costs will be insurmountable.

The project will lead to serious ecological disorders. The construction of reservoirs will impoverish the lower reaches of the rivers. The expansive canal system will lead to water logging and salinity in the absence of proper drainage, and will fragment wild life habitats.

Lifting of water from the Ganga–Brahmaputra plains to the Deccan plateau will require enormous amount of energy. In the present scenario of energy crisis and ever increasing gap between demand and supply, it appears almost impossible to make such energy available for the purpose.

The incomplete, unused and under-utilized existing irrigation projects in the country require about ₹ 80,000.00 crores, which the Government finds difficult to provide. The cost of this new river grid project, which may run to ₹ 50,000,000 crores or more, is prohibitive, and looking to the current fiscal situation, may not be possible for any Government to arrange.

The project may finally result in the destruction of cultures, communities and ecosystems, creating conflicts between states as in the case of the Kaveri dispute, or between states and the people as in the case of the Narmada dispute. If this happens in just one river basin, the consequences across several river basins can just be imagined.

The success of the project in controlling floods and mitigating droughts itself is suspect. The normal volume of floods in the Ganga, the Brahmaputra, the Mahanadi and the Godavari ranges between 30,000 and 60,000 cu m of water flow per second. In such a situation, lifting of 1,500 cu m of water per second would not be able to control floods. Even as a drought proofing measure, the national plan appears exorbitantly costly and politically difficult to operate.

A feasible alternative to this grandiose plan would be proper water use within each river basin, which has the potential to irrigate almost all the 14 crore hectares of net sown area in the country. At present, only 5.3 crores hectares area is irrigated. Much of the 400,000 crores cubic meters of rain water that the country receives, falls in just 100 hours. Therefore, the trick is to capture enough water in these 100 hours in the very area where it falls and conserve and use it during the rest of the year. It has been found that small reservoirs are much more effective in water storage than the large ones. Ten small dams with one-hectare catchment each would store more water than one dam of ten hectares of catchment. Similar studies show that 100 mm of rainfall on one hectare plot could yield as much as one million litres of water. This indicates that even in low rainfall zones each village can store enough water to last in the drought years.

Unfortunately, most of these community based conservation structures have been neglected and destroyed over the last few decades. The skewed government policy in favour of cash and cement-intensive mega projects, ignoring the potentials of village tanks and minor irrigation, has played havoc. Equally disastrous has been the policy of permitting reckless drawing of bountiful ground water using subsidized electricity to grow water-intensive crops for high cash returns. It is instructive to know that the recent row for the Kaveri waters was over the contesting claims of Karnataka farmers who wanted the water for their second sugarcane crop as against Tamil Nadu farmers who had been growing three crops of paddy.

Raining Opportunities for Geographers

Geographers can play very important role in drought management. Their integrated training in physical and social sciences and their skill of spatial analysis, synthesis and interpretation make them eminently suited to work for drought management. They can contribute substantially in project formulation, implementation, monitoring and evaluation. Vast opportunities are awaiting them.

Conclusion

The traditional methods of water conservation could be more effective in overcoming the problems of droughts. The construction of large dams or linking of rivers does not seem to be very feasible proposition in the long run. The National Water Grid or the plan of linking major rivers, which seems to be the preferred solution combating recurring droughts, may finally result in the destruction of cultures, communities and ecosystems sparking conflicts between states and between people and states. They are likely to run counter to the objectives. In fact local problems need local solutions and, therefore, the traditional wisdom should be given due weightage besides, of course, strengthening the new technologies of saving water for fighting the calamity caused due to droughts. The proper water use within each river basin and community-based conservation structures need to be given priority in combating the droughts and water scarcity.

References

Alexander, D. (1993), *Natural Disasters*, UCL Press, London.

Gupta, A. and A.K. Gupta (2000), Integrated water management and guiding elements of national water policy, *Yojna*, 16–20.

Gupta, A.K., P. Tyagi and V.K. Sehgal (2011), Drought Disaster Challenges and Mitigation in India: Strategic Appraisal, in, *Current Science*, **100**(12), 1795–1806.

Nagarajan, R. (2003), *Drought: Assessment, Monitoring, Management and Resource Conservation*, Capital Publishing Company, New Delhi.

27

Drought Mitigation in Rajasthan

Monika Kannan

Abstract: Drought mitigation poses a great challenge especially in the state of Rajasthan which experiences the occurrence of drought almost every year. The mitigation measures include drought prediction, drought monitoring and drought management. This chapter focuses on the utility of space born multi-spectral measurements in identification and mitigation of droughts. These techniques have very high degree of accuracy as far as the collection of data is concerned.

Keywords: Mitigation, Agro-met, Prediction, Monsoon Trough, Jet Stream

Introduction

Remote sensing is science and art of collecting data of most inaccessible areas and GIS helps in mapping. The techniques are very useful even in monitoring and managing the disasters such as droughts and floods. Drought is the single most important weather related natural disaster often aggravated by human actions. According to the Indian Meteorological Department (IMD), meteorological drought is defined as occurring when seasonal rainfall received over an area is less than 75 per cent of its long-term average value. The beginning of drought is subtle, its progress is insidious and its effects can be devastating (Mathur and Jayal, 1993). The EL NINO phenomenon occurring in the Pacific Ocean may provide fairly short-term prediction of drought in some areas. Space borne multi-spectral measurement holds a great promise in providing information and mitigating the drought in arid regions (Khan and Narain, 2003; Kogen, 1990). Six major causes of droughts are; (a) late onset and early withdrawal of monsoons, (b) less rainfall during absence of depression (low pressure system) passing India, (c) prolonged breaks in the monsoon rainfall, (d) re-establishment of southern branch of Jet stream, (e) upwelling of cool water over the Arabian sea and extension of cool Somalian current over Arabian sea and, (f) the movement of Monsoon trough closer to the Himalayan zone.

A perusal of 80 years data on drought shows that extent and impact of drought is getting reduced. During 1930–1940, nearly 73 per cent of the country was affected by the drought. However, currently only 35–40 per cent area gets affected by droughts. This is particularly because the technology to monitor and manage drought has improved and the Remote Sensing and GIS have been playing significant role in this direction.

The purpose of this chapter is to examine the relevance of Remote Sensing and GIS techniques in studying the droughts in the state of Rajasthan.

Study Area

The state of Rajasthan (23°3' to 30°12' lat. and 69°30' to 78°17' long.), spread over an area of 342,239 km^2, is the largest state in the country with a population of 68,621,012 according to 2011 census. It has grown by 21.44 per cent during 2001–2011. It is the hottest region of India with the temperature reaching 50°C (summers) in Marusthali and 0–1°C (winters) in Ganganagar–Churu districts. The mean cloud formation is highest in July and August, varying between 2 and 6 (0 being cloud free sky).

The state is divided into 32 districts and based on the recurrence of drought, these may be placed into five categories (Figure 27.1). The most frequently affected districts are—Jaisalmer, Barmer, Jalor, Sirohi and Jodhpur.

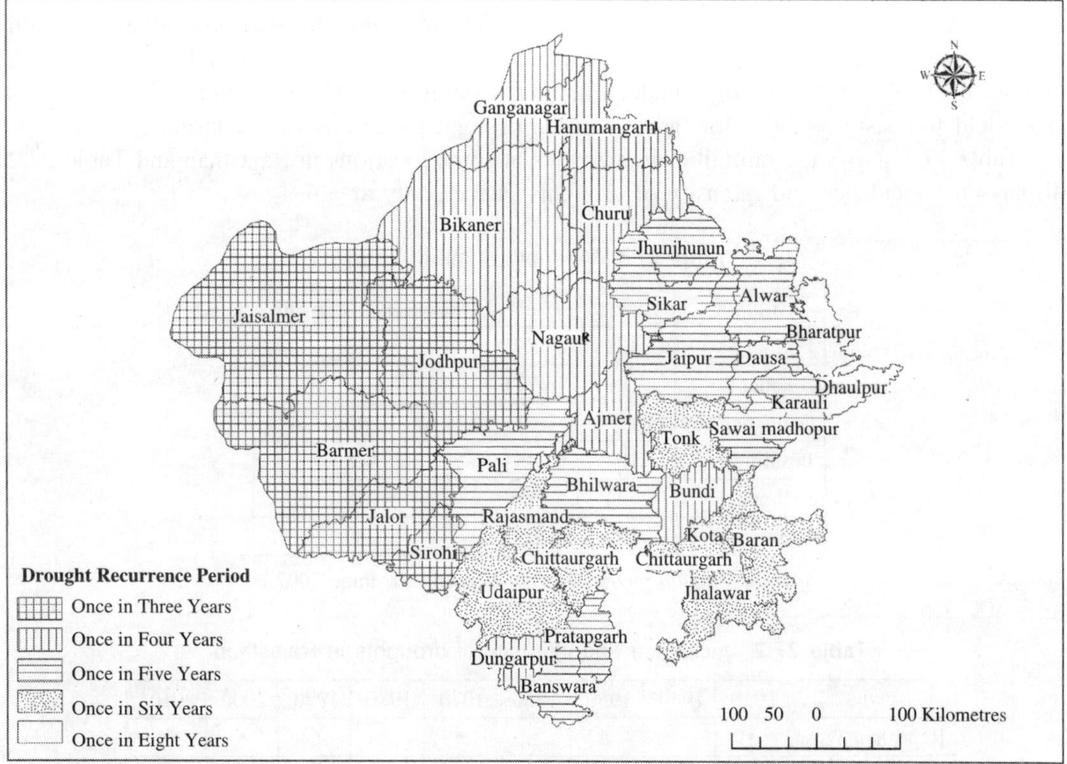

Figure 27.1 Drought affected areas in Rajasthan.

Methodology and Data Base

Geo-Stationary Satellites provide continuous and synoptic observations about the drought conditions in Rajasthan. The Central Research Institute for Dryland Agriculture (CRIDA) has 6 agro-meteorological observatories in its regional stations at Jodhpur, Jaisalmer, Bikaner, Pali, etc. The drought prediction for the period beginning from June to the end of September comes from Long Range Forecast (LRF). The 1st operational LRF for seasonal monsoon was based on the Himalayan snow cover. Presently the IMD issues LRF based on statistical techniques. The long-term rainfall predictions are given by INSAT and NOAA, the geo-stationary and polar orbiting satellites, respectively, by generating global and regional atmospheric parameters. The medium range rainfall predictions are given through the data provided by NCMRWF (The National Centre for Medium Range Weather Forecasting). This is done by vertical sounding and radio sounding data on water vapour, pressure, temperature and vertical profile data in the T86/NMC model. In short range rainfall prediction INSAT based visible and thermal data is used. A project named National Agriculture Drought Assessment and Monitoring System (NADAMS), sponsored by the Department of Agriculture and Department of Space (DOS) had been taken up by NRSA in collaboration with IMD. This focuses on the assessment of agriculture drought in terms of occurrence, relative severity and persistence. The NDVI derived from NOAA-AVHRR data is used for drought monitoring through bi-weekly bulletins. Multi spectral scanning system is used to acquire images from aircrafts and satellites. Drought research unit set up by IMD, Pune works under Planning Commission, Govt. of India. This provides crop yield forecasting (CYF) for farmers in the drought prone areas of Rajasthan.

Table 27.1 shows the rainfall characteristics at some locations in Rajasthan and Table 27.2 displays the incidence and intensity of droughts in the study area.

Table 27.1 Annual rainfall (in mm)

Station	*Lowest*	*Highest*	*Rainy days* (25 mm)
Barmer	129	895	13
Bikaner	29	771	17
Ganganagar	123	641	15
Jaisalmer	104	454	8
Jodhpur	24	1176	18
Sikar	269	632	30

Source: *Indian meteorological department*, Pune 2007.

Table 27.2 Incidence and intensity of droughts in Rajasthan

Years	1930	1940	1950	1960	1970	1980	1990	2000	2010*
Rajasthan West	•	□	□	□	•	□	□	•	•
Rajasthan East	•	□	○	○	□	○	□	□	□

○ No drought □ Mild drought • Severe drought 2010* predicted

Drought Mitigation

Drought is a reoccurring and devastating feature in Rajasthan and, therefore, it is imperative that it should be studied well in advance in order to combat the potential onslaught of droughts. There are three stages of drought mitigation programme which are as mentioned below:

1. **Drought Prediction:** Remote sensing data provides major input in rainfall prediction through weather maps. NDVI and AVHRR data identify areas of dry vegetation. Thermal infrared images record the radiant temperature of land.
2. **Drought Monitoring:** Monthly reports on crop and seasonal conditions during *Kharif* season (June–October) have been brought out since 1992. These reports are brought out at district level. With the availability of IRS, WIF data with 188 mm spatial resolution, the methodology is being updated to provide quantitative information on sowing of crops, surface water spread and crop conditions at taluk and block level. Seasonal spatial variations are also monitored.
3. **Drought Management:** Severely drought affected regions (Figure 27.1) of western Rajasthan experience water shortage for drinking, irrigation and food crops. To address this issue, a nationwide project, Integrated Mission for Sustainable Development (ISMD) was taken up in collaboration with DOS and State Remote Sensing Application Centre, Jodhpur. This aims at generating local specific action plan for development of land and water resources on a micro watershed basis in drought prone areas. Farmer's weather bulletins are regularly issued by the state and regional meteorological centres. The bulletin contains the onset, scarcity and intensity of rainfall. An Aridity Anomaly Index (AAI) developed on the lines of Thornwaite (1948) concept is used to monitor the incidence, spread, intensification and recession of drought. These anomalies are used for crop planning and in early **warning** maps during droughts.

To provide safe drinking water to rural masses during droughts, National Drinking Water Technology Mission has been launched by DOS. Groundwater potentiality maps showing ground projects are being prepared at 1:125,000 scale in the state in order to help solve the problem of water shortage.

Conclusion

The conventional methods of identification and mitigation of droughts are being replaced by latest and accurate data observation of remote sensing. Agro-met parameters estimated from remote sensing data are used to validate ground based observations and the same are being turned to usable products. Space born multi-spectral images have facilitated the accuracy and precision of prediction. Polar orbiting satellites have an advantage of providing much higher resolution imageries, even through at a low frequency which can be used for detailed drought monitoring. The efforts are on to locate the underground lost channels of the river Sarashwati. It is said that the location of such water sanctuaries may serve great deal in meeting the challenge of water shortage.

References

Khan, M.A. and P. Narain (2003), Integrated watershed management for sustainability, In: *Human Impact on Desert Environment*, Scientific Publishers, Jodhpur, India.

Kogen, F.N. (1990), Remote sensing of weather impacts on vegetation in Non-homogeneous Areas, *International Journal of Remote Sensing*, **11**.

Mathur, K. and N. Jayal (1993), *Drought, Policy and Politics: The Need for a Long-term Perspective*, Sage Publications, New Delhi.

Thornthwaite, C.W. (1948), An approach toward a rational classification of climate, *Geographical Review*, **38**(1), 55–94.

28

Rainwater Harvesting
An Answer to Depleting Groundwater

Zubaida Farooqui, Amna Farooqui and Qutub Jahan

Abstract: Uttar Pradesh, which is largest in terms of total population among Indian states, suffers severely due to rapid depletion of groundwater. This chapter traces the status of groundwater in Eastern, Western, Central and Bundelkhand regions of the state besides a few cities, and suggests different ways of rainwater harvesting for benefit of the masses.

Keywords: Irrigation, Capturing Run-off, Rooftops, Eco-friendly, Water Harvesting, Ponds, Tanks

Introduction

We live in a water challenged world today, one that is becoming more so each year as 80 million additional people stake their claims to the earth's water resources. Unfortunately all the projected 3 billion people to be added over the next half century will be born in countries that are already experiencing water crisis. Even today a large population of these countries does not have access to safe drinking water. India is one such country and is estimated to have 1.5 billion people by 2050 AD.

Water resources are one of the most vital national assets and hold the key to the nation's economy, prosperity and stability. The varying availability of this resource calls not only for its judicious uses but also for planning for its conservation and further development.

Water is a priceless national asset and must be used properly to meet the basic needs of the people. Recognizing water as a resource the United Nations General Assembly in December 2003, declared the decade 2005–2015 as the International Decade for Action "Water for life" and the 22nd March as the World Water Day. These commitments inspire the people to save drinking water and stop exploitation of water resources (DGW, 2005).

Groundwater Resources

Groundwater is the most important and most harnessed of water resources due to its easy availability and common use for different purposes throughout the year. India has vast groundwater resources. The underground water resources are affected by the climatic conditions, topography, geological structure and hydrological conditions of the area. The average rainfall over the country is about 120 cm as a whole and the rainfall over India's area of 328 million hectare gives a total precipitation of 3700 billion cu m. Only 22 per cent of this total rainfall percolates under the ground. Of this total amount, about 430 billion cu m reaches up to the upper surface of the soil. Remaining 384 billion cu m reaches the previous strata which could be obtained by digging well. But only 70 per cent of this amount can be exploited economically.

The development of groundwater resource, in order to meet various requirements, has received an accelerated emphasis during the past two decade. In many areas overexploitation has resulted in falling groundwater level and deterioration of water quality. Over pumpage due to excess withdrawal of water for irrigation has been found to be a prime reason for depletion of groundwater especially in rural area. Another noticeable problem in cities is the lack of space available for seepage of water underground. Moreover the capacity of the soil to infiltrate the precipitation into groundwater to make up the storage are limited, large quantity of rainwater is lost to surface run-off and evaporation during the monsoon period. It has been observed that percolation of rainwater into the ground is decreasing due to high rate of deforestation and soil erosion. Again with the development of agriculture, more irrigation water will be required by the farmers to increase the production. Groundwater is the source of four fifth of the domestic water supply in rural areas and half of that in urban and industrial areas. However, it is important to mention that only 30 per cent of the actual groundwater potential has been harnessed in India.

Position of Groundwater in Uttar Pradesh

Uttar Pradesh has the highest groundwater potential because of a large number of rivers having high prospect for groundwater potentialities.

Table 28.1 shows the availability of groundwater and its present level of development in the state of U.P. But at present, gradually the rainfall is declining and the level of groundwater is reducing.

Table 28.1 Availability of groundwater and its present level of development in the state of U.P.

Region	*Net groundwater availability* (Lac. ha m)	*Annual draft for all uses* (Lac. ha m)	*Net groundwater availability for future irrigation* (Lac. ha m)	*Stage of development* (%)
Eastern	2.95	1.36	1.59	46.20
Western	2.77	1.84	0.93	66.40
Central	1.89	1.05	0.84	55.50
Bundel Khand	0.47	0.13	0.34	27.60
Total	8.08	4.38	3.70	54.20

Source: Groundwater Department, U.P. 2005.

In Uttar Pradesh, high decline in underground water level during the last 15 years has occurred due to increasing demand and excessive pumpage of water. The declining trend of water level has gripped almost one-third of the state. In various parts of the state, the groundwater situation is alarming as the water table has depleted by 8–10 m within the span of only 10–12 years. In the urban areas, this situation is even more alarming (Irrigation Dept., 2003).

Table 28.2 shows that the depletion in groundwater level is the highest in Lucknow followed by Kanpur, Agra, Aligarh and Mathura cities. One of the main reasons for groundwater depletion in these areas is the excessive pumpage from the deeper aquifers (Govt. of U.P., 2003). This stresses the need for conserving every drop of rainwater or else, the entire country will encounter acute water shortage in future. Moreover declining groundwater level is reducing the base flow in the rivers and in turn threatening the very existence of groundwater for the rivers like the Gomti.

Table 28.2 Depletion of groundwater in various cities of U.P.

Name of cities	*Depletion in groundwater* (cm/year)
Lucknow	56
Kanpur	45
Agra	40
Varanasi	23
Aligarh	40
Ghaziabad	22
Mathura	36

Source: Under Groundwater Department, U.P. 2005.

The water crises being faced by the country is mainly due to gross mismanagement of available water resources. From 19th century onwards, the state took the sole responsibility of water management, which led to communities and households to be no longer the primary agent of water provision and management. The use of rainwater and flood water declined and resulted in heavy reliance on surface water and groundwater. At present, the adverse effect of this type of management is clearly visible. The level of extraction from rivers has been so much that most of India's river basins have severely degraded and the rivers are badly polluted.

Water Conservation through Rainwater Harvesting

Rainwater harvesting may be adopted to overcome the problems of water crisis. Water harvesting means capturing the rainwater where it falls, or retaining the run-off in one's own village and town.

Experts suggest various ways of Rainwater Harvesting like capturing run-off from roof tops and from local stream and conserving water through watershed management. Rainwater harvesting is a simple, economical and eco-friendly method of water conservation. Rainwater can be harvested for two purposes: firstly, storing it for ready use, and secondly, for groundwater recharging. The decision whether to store or use the water for recharge, depends on the rainfall and also the sub-surface geology.

In the roof top harvesting process, the water is collected from roof of the building and stored in groundwater reservoir for beneficial use in future. There are so many benefits to harvest roof top rainwater, as this is an ideal solution to resolve the groundwater problem and again to use the rainfall runoff. Table 28.3 shows the estimated potential benefits of roof top rainwater harvesting. The roof water harvesting can easily meet the requirement of a family consisting five members if it is collected in the expanse of 100 sq. m. of area. There are several other benefits. It is supposed to be bacteria free and it also helps in reducing the flood hazards.

Table 28.3 Estimated potential/benefit of roof top rainwater harvesting

Roof Top area	100 sq. m
Annual Rain Fall	900 mm (0.9)
Run-off coefficient of cemented roof top	0.85
Total available water for recharge from cemented roof (Area*Rain*Run-off coefficient)	100 × 0.9 × 0.85 = 76.5 cu m = 76,500 l
Consumption of drinking water for five member family (150 l per person/day)	150 × 5 = 750 l per day
In this way recharged underground sources from Roof Top (100 sq. m/year)	76,500 l
Roof water harvesting can fulfill the need of water of a five-member family	102 days

Source: Department of Groundwater, Uttar Pradesh.

For reducing the cost of rainwater harvesting from roof top in urban areas, lakes and ponds can be used as storage basins for rainwater to recharge the groundwater table. For this, low lying open areas should be identified and should be used as storage basins for rainwater to recharge the groundwater table. Existing ponds and lakes should be properly maintained while ensuring that they keep receiving the rainwater in the form of surface run-off. As a precautionary measure no raw sewage should be allowed to go into these storage basins.

In rural areas, barren and uncultivable land can be used for rainwater harvesting. This will help in solving the problem of water scarcity and will also reduce the risk of severe floods. If the rainwater can be detained in the field itself, it will result in the recharge of groundwater. This will involve the making of bunds around the fields if these do not exist and also raising the height of existing bunds to a suitable level. It will depend upon the local condition, such as terrain type, cost and pattern of rainfall and characteristics of soil, etc.

Rainwater harvesting has been in practice in India for long time to meet the domestic and irrigational water need of the local communities. In the past rainwater was harvested directly as it fell on the ground and from flooded streams. Traditional rainwater harvesting systems are known by different names in different parts of India like Kunds, Baories, Tankas, Baoli, Bandh/Bandhi, Talab, Saza Kava, etc.

At present, immediate steps are needed to practice rainwater harvesting at a large scale. Most of the domestic water needs of the country can be met successfully by adopting rainwater harvesting. Our government has enacted certain laws for rainwater harvesting. The Central Groundwater Board issued directive to the state municipal authorities to undertake roof top rainwater harvesting on a large scale and also to amend city bye-laws for mandatory participation of every dwelling unit towards groundwater recharge.

The Uttar Pradesh Government has made it compulsory for the buildings, which have plinth area greater than 300 sq. m, to have made provision for water conservation and rainwater harvesting (Govt. of U.P., 2003). The U.P. Government has modified the previous law and according to new policy (G.O. 25, April 25 2006) the buildings having 200 sq. km area are also required to have the provision for rainwater harvesting. Underground recharging system has been made compulsory in public buildings in the government layout plan having less than 200 sq. m area.

Conclusion

There is a large scale depletion of groundwater and that is a cause of great concern. The need of the hour is to conserve every drop of rainwater to encounter acute water shortage in future. Rainwater harvesting is an economical and better answer to the problems of water scarcity, floods, irrigation and other water requirement of our country. The government has enacted certain laws for rainwater harvesting but there are several shortcomings.

It is essential to develop the technique of rainwater harvesting for recharging the level of underground water not by enforcing the policies of the government, but by awareness in the general public about the alarming situation and by motivating the people to conserve every drop of water.

Following suggestions may be useful for future action and consideration:

1. Roof top rainwater harvesting and recharge should be made mandatory in urban areas.
2. All the public buildings should be provided with such type of facility and for this sufficient fund should be allocated.
3. This concept should be further extended to surface pavement rainwater harvesting and recharge, so that maximum amount of surface run-off from urban area can be harvested or recharged into groundwater.
4. All the existing ponds and tanks should be made free from illegal possession.
5. The importance of water conservations and its techniques should be taught to the primary and secondary level students by making it part of the syllabus.

References

Dept. of Groundwater, U.P. (2005), *Bhoo Jal Sandesh*.

Government of U.P. (2005), *Experimental Project on Roof Top Harvesting*, Dept. of Miner irrigation.

Government of U.P. (2003), *Rainwater Harvesting in Urban Areas*, Notification.

29

Watershed Development Model and The Case of Bihar

H.N. Misra and Ashutosh Mishra

Abstract: Currently, there is a great emphasis on sustainable development. The objectives of sustainable development can, however, be achieved in real sense of the term only when planning is done at watershed level. A watershed is a homogenous unit in terms of lithological structure, geographic terrain, socio-economic conditions and cultural-ecological settings. Land, water, soils and forest which form the basic environment have optimum interaction in a watershed. The objective of this chapter is to propose watershed development model and suggest its application for the socio-economic development of Bihar, which is one of the most poverty stricken states of the country. There are altogether 19 watersheds in Bihar. The spatial and functional planning of these watersheds within the frame of watershed development model may herald a new era of socio-economic transformation in the state.

Keywords: Homogenous Unit, Supra Local Region, Lithology, River System and Tributaries, Leopold Matrix, Monitoring and management, Simulation

Introduction

The environmental monitoring and management have become the sine qua non in the contemporary regional development processes. This is necessary in order to have development without destruction—a development which is eco-friendly and sustainable in nature. The sustainable development, which is the major goal of any developmental planning, can be achieved only when the natural environment, i.e., its carrying capacity and potentials, are given due attention. This is possible through proper mapping, monitoring and management of different kinds of natural resources such as land, water, minerals, flora and fauna and the entire biospheric components. This is not an easy task. Besides, if the size of the area is large, task is further complicated. This, therefore, calls for micro-level planning.

The micro-level planning is the planning at the sub-regional level. There are different indicators and parameters to determine the areal units best suited to micro-level planning. However, what is most important in this context is the homogeneity in terms of natural endowments and social and economic environments. Planning cannot succeed if this homogeneity is not built into the process of regional planning. It has been established that river basins, catchment areas or for that matter watersheds provide the areal units best suited for environmental monitoring as well as for management and development.

A watershed or hydrological unit is a supra local region which is considered to be very appropriate for the purposes of planning and management. A watershed is a homogenous unit in terms of lithological structure, geographic terrain, socio-economic conditions and cultural-ecological settings. Land, water, soils and forest which form the basic environment have optimum interaction in a watershed. The concept of river-basin planning and watershed management is not new. The planning of Damodar Valley Corporation (DVC) in India is basically the outcome of the idea culminating from the success story of Tennessee Valley Authority. It is, however, unfortunate that over a period of time the importance of river-basin planning was relegated to an inferior position in view of a number of other imperatives and parameters used for regionalization. The metropolitan planning, sectoral planning, multilevel planning and subsequently the integrated area development planning became much more powerful concepts. But now it is being realized that the basic objective of the planning is economic development by protecting environment and retaining social and cultural value systems. Identification of watersheds is, thus, an important method of regionalization for planning purposes. A watershed is defined as the entire area drained by a river system, or one of its major tributaries. It may be either a water surplus area or water deficit area. In both the cases there is a problem of resource management. The basic purpose of watershed development is to raise the income level, generate employment, encourage peoples participation and promote the concept of judicious use of water and land. There are several scholars who have done reasonably very good work to highlight the importance of watershed planning (Deshpandey and Reddy, 1991; 1999; Farrington and Deshpandey and Thimmaiah, 1997; Farrington, et al., 1999; Samra, 1997, Rao, 2000).

The objective of this chapter is to propose a watershed development model and suggest its application in the case of Bihar which happens to be the most backward state of the Country.

Watershed Management: National Programmes

Historically the conceptual foundation of watershed management in India started in 1880 with the Famine Commission and then with the Royal Commission of Agriculture in 1928. There are several programmes which were launched from time to time to promote the watershed development. Some of these programmes which are listed below are mainly watershed development programmes:

1. Soil conservation in the catchment of River Valley Project in Third Five Year Plan.
2. Integrated Watershed Management of Flood Prone Rivers (FPR) During Fourth Five Year Plan.
3. Soil, Water and tree conservation in the Himalayas (Operation Soil Watch) during 1980–81.
4. Operational Research Project on Integrated Watershed Management during 1983–84.
5. National Watershed Development Programme for Rainfed Agriculture (NWDPRA) during 1986–87.

As at present 263 districts of the country have been identified under Watershed Development Programme (WDP). The watersheds are of three types—micro watershed falling in the range of 500–1000 ha, mini-watershed comprising several micro-watersheds and covering around 5000 ha and macro-watershed equivalent to a river basin and encompassing several thousands of hectares.

Watershed Development Model: Analytical and Explanatory Structure

Model is normally said to be an abstraction of reality. The three hierarchical levels of abstraction are iconic, analogue and symbolic. Normally models are classified into these three categories. However, there are some models which are deterministic and probabilistic in nature. Models are also classified as graphical and mathematical. In the present case, an effort has been made to present the graphical model of watershed development. The watershed development model for sustainable development proposed here is based on the fieldwork and review of literature. The analytical structure of the model has been presented in Figure 29.1 (Misra, 2001). There are six boxes. These are: (1) Identification of watershed, (2) Contour mapping, (3) Identification of emerging issues and problems, (4) Problem solving, (5) Management and (6) Impact assessment.

Box-1 focuses on identification of watershed which may be of different sizes and shapes, such as micro watershed, mini watershed and macro watershed. Each one of these has different hydrogeomorphological structure and socio-economic characteristics.

Box-2 is meant for contour mapping of the hydro-geomorphological changes, socio-economic transformation and people's perception/human behaviour. Man is not necessarily a perfect economic man but a great satisficer. He does not work in a phenomenal environment. He takes decisions in behavioural environment, and, therefore his perception in decision making is quite important to be taken into account.

Box-3 is devoted to identifying the major issues and problems which exist and are likely to emerge. These problems may be environmental/physical such as loss of water and soil, soil degradation, loss of biomass, landslide, earthquake, water logging, pollution, siltation, desertification, etc. The economic problems may be related to unemployment, low productivity and poor per capita income. Social problems may pertain to low literacy, family planning problem, poor health and diseases, and cultural problems may relate to loss of cultural value systems, language problems and loss of other mental and moral values and abstract things.

Box-4 presents the problem solving approaches, which are of two types: spatial and sectoral. While spatial approach emphasizes on the overall planning in the forms of service centres and market centres for smooth flow of goods and commodities within a watershed, the sectoral approach emphasizes on the preservation of common property resource (CPR) such as forests and grasslands for fuel, fodder and timber (agro forestry and social forestry, etc.), diversification of agriculture, promotion of horticulture, floriculture, pisciculture, conservation of minerals and mining, eco-tourism and recreational planning besides promoting secondary sector such as cottage and household industries based on local resources such as agro based and food processing industries. It is, however, important that the planning should get feedback from the perception of people. The historical, social and cultural contexts should also be properly taken care off for the satisfaction at the emotional levels.

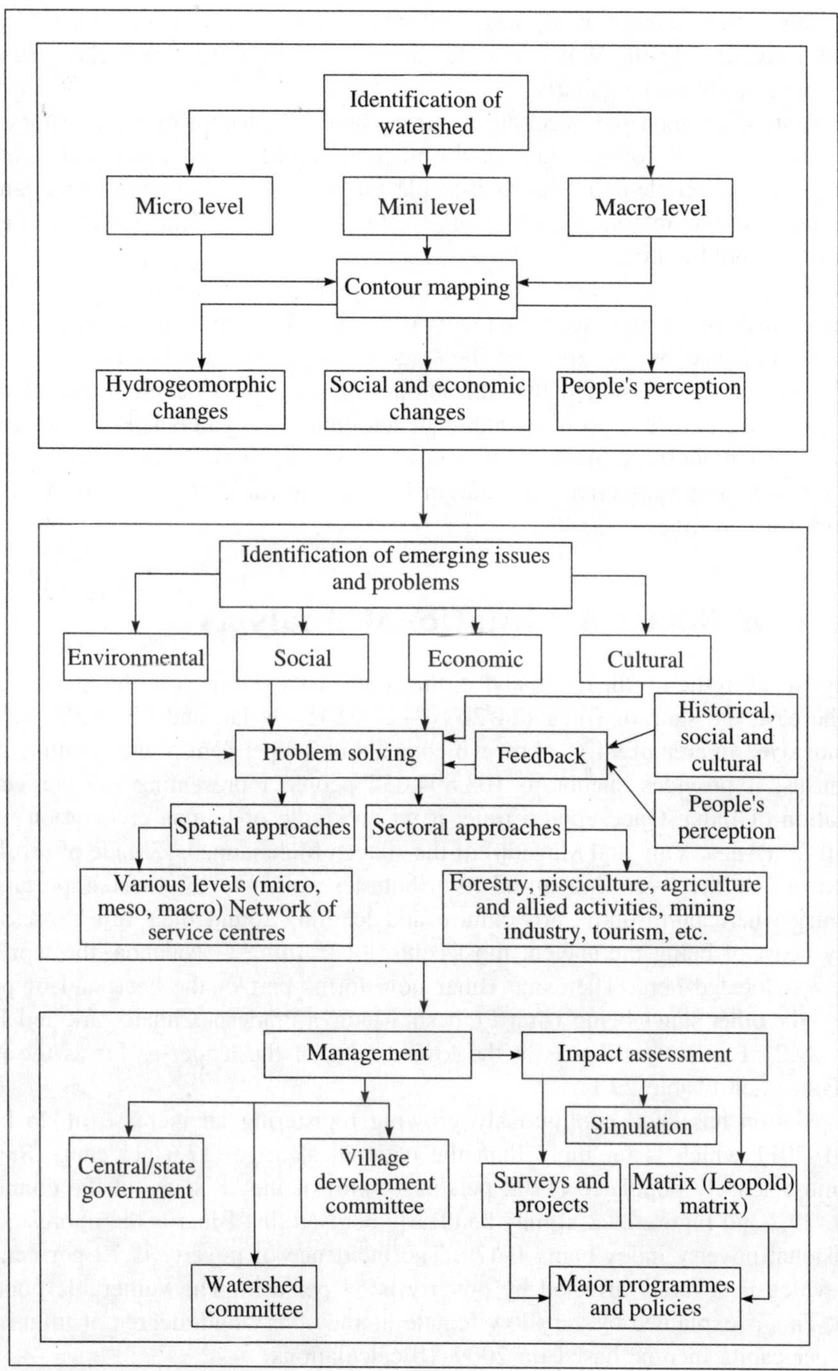

Figure 29.1 Explanatory structure of watershed development model.

Box-5 shows the management stage in which three-tier structure—(a) Central/State Government Bureaucracy, (b) Watershed Development Committee, (c) Village Development Committee, need to interact regularly.

Box-6 emphasizes upon the necessity to strengthen the concept of participatory planning. There is, however, need for constant environmental impact assessment and simulation in order to pre-empt the problems in the foreseeable future. The impact assessment can be made possible through survey, interviews, observations, field immersion, quantification, ranking and application of Leopold matrix.

All the above six boxes have been put into the form of analytical model for a little more explicit analysis at the overt and covert levels. The first two boxes represent the stage I model. The next boxes represent the stage II model and the last two boxes represent the stage III model. It is assumed that this model of watershed development, if applied in proper perspectives, can lead to sustainable development of watersheds in the country. In order to make the model operational, there is a need to have some infrastructural facilities which pertain to building effective information base in the form of data bank for monitoring changes from time to time.

The Case of Bihar: A Situational Analysis

Bounded by Nepal in the north, Jharkhand in the south, Uttar Pradesh in the west and Paschim Banga in the east, the state of Bihar (24°20'10"–27°31'15" N lat. and 82°19'50"–88°17'40" E long.) spreads over an area of 94,163 km^2 which is about 2.8 per cent of the country. According to 2011 census, it provides shelter to 103,804,637 people representing 8.6 per cent of the total population of India. Once upon a time, it was a cradle of human civilization which was fulcrum of three (Anga, Vajji and Magadh) of the sixteen Mahajanpadas. Made of fertile alluvial plain carved out by the river Ganga and its tributaries, this was the most important granary of the country where philosophy, art, culture and learning found their full expression. This could easily boast of being the ancient most centre of learning as Nalanda, the world famous University, was located here. The same Bihar now forms part of the heartland of poverty of the country—the other states being Uttar Pradesh, Madhya Pradesh, Chhatisgarh and Jharkhand (see Figure 29.2). Evidently Bihar is at the lowest rung of the ladder as far as the per capita income is concerned (Table 29.1).

The population has been continuously growing registering an increase of 25.1 per cent during 2001–2011 which is far more than the national average (17.6 per cent). Surprisingly this is the most densely populated (1102 person/sq. km) of the 28 states of the country. From Tables 29.1, 29.2 and Figure 29.2, it may be clearly perused that Bihar is the poorest state, with multidimensional poverty index being 0.479. The incidence of poverty is 79 per cent and the population which is severely affected by poverty is 54 per cent. The vulnerable population is 10 per cent. This is explained by very low female literacy, very high degree of infant mortality and lowest per capita income based on 2009–10 calculations.

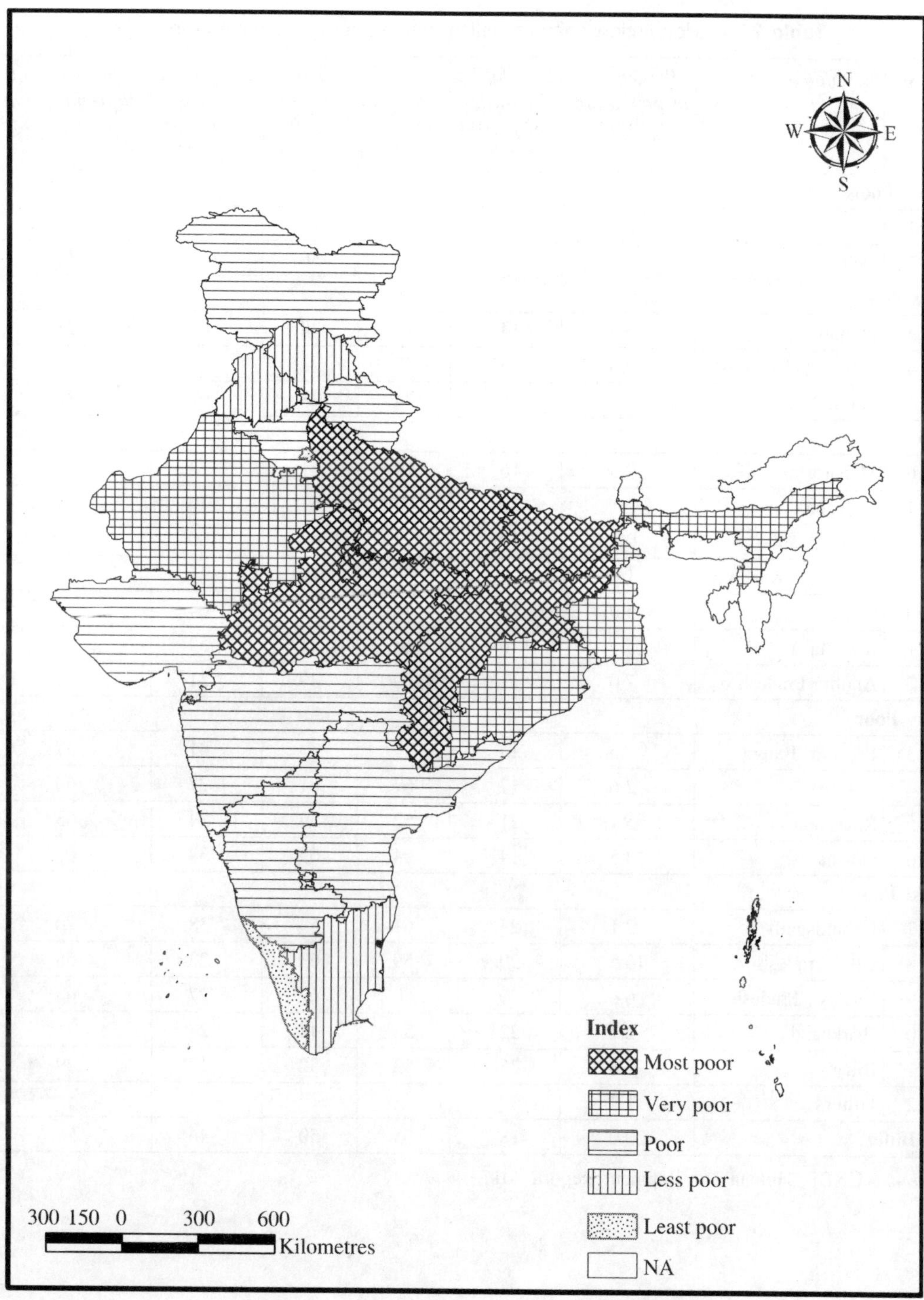

Figure 29.2 Level of poverty in Indian states.

Table 29.1 Population characteristics and incidence of poverty in India

Sl. No.	*State/Union territory*	*Percentage of population* 2011	*Population growth* 2001–2011 (%)	*Female literacy* 2011 (%)	*Infant mortality* 2009	*Per capita income* 2009–2010 (₹ 1000)	*Incidence of multi-dimensional poverty* (%)
Least Poor							
1	Kerala	2.8	5	92	12	59	13
2	Delhi	1.4	21	81	36	117	12
Less Poor							
3	Punjab	2.3	14	71	38	61	25
4	Himanchal Pradesh	0.6	13	77	–	50	30
5	Tamil Nadu	6.0	16	74	28	64	31
Poor							
6	Maharashtra	9.3	16	75	31	74	38
7	Haryana	2.1	20	67	51	79	39
8	Uttarakhand	0.8	19	71	41	60	40
9	Jammu & Kashmir	1.0	24	58	49	31	41
10	Gujarat	5.0	19	71	48	64	41
11	Karnataka	5.1	16	68	41	52	43
12	Andhra Pradesh	7.0	11	60	49	51	45
Very Poor							
13	Paschim Banga	7.6	14	71	33	41	57
14	Assam	2.6	17	67	61	27	60
15	Rajasthan	5.7	21	52	59	34	63
16	Odisha	3.5	14	64	65	33	63
Most Poor							
17	Chhattisgarh	2.1	23	61	54	38	70
18	Uttar Pradesh	16.5	20	59	63	23	68
19	Madhya Pradesh	6.0	20	60	67	27	68
20	Jharkhand	2.7	22	56	44	27	75
21	Bihar	8.6	25	53	52	17	79
22	**Others**	1.3					
All India		100.0	18	65	50	46	54

Source: UNDP, Human Development Report, 2011.

Table 29.2 Multi-dimensional poverty index and vulnerable population in India

Sl. No.	*State/Union territory*	*Multi-dimensional poverty index* MPI = H*A	*Incidence of poverty (%)*	*Average intensity across the poor (%)*	*Per cent population vulnerable*	*Per cent population in severe poverty*
Least Poor						
1	Kerala	0.051	13	40	22	2
2	Delhi	0.054	12	44	14	3
Less Poor						
3	Punjab	0.112	25	46	19	9
4	Himanchal Pradesh	0.125	30	42	26	7
5	Tamil Nadu	0.130	31	43	20	9
Poor						
6	Maharashtra	0.180	38	48	20	15
7	Haryana	0.186	39	47	21	16
8	Uttarakhand	0.185	40	47	20	16
9	Jammu & Kashmir	0.194	41	47	21	17
10	Gujarat	0.201	41	49	17	19
11	Karnataka	0.206	43	48	19	19
12	Andhra Pradesh	0.209	45	47	18	19
Very Poor						
13	Paschim Banga	0.304	57	53	16	31
14	Assam	0.316	60	53	18	33
15	Rajasthan	0.338	63	54	15	36
16	Odisha	0.339	63	54	16	34
Most Poor						
17	Chhattisgarh	0.367	70	53	13	38
18	Uttar Pradesh	0.369	68	54	15	39
19	Madhya Pradesh	0.374	68	55	14	41
20	Jharkhand	0.441	75	59	12	51
21	Bihar	0.479	79	60	10	54
22	**Others**	–	–	–	–	–
All India		0.283	54	53	16	29

Source: UNDP, Human Development Report, 2011.

The condition is really precarious. There are a host of factors which have been responsible for this, such as poor governance, lack of management of natural resources, absence of infrastructure and low investment in health and education. The natural resources especially land and water have been particularly ignored both at the policy as well as implementation levels. Much needed land reform has been completely absent and most of the fertile land is being washed out every year due to recurrence of floods.

The purpose here is to focus mainly on land and water which are the two invaluable natural resources of Bihar and which play catalytic role in the economic development of this state. The management of these resources in the past was basically responsible for economic uplift of Bihar. The fact of the matter is that the management and planning of both the natural resources has been ignored over a period of time. Nearly 36 per cent of the area and 63 per cent of the total population has been constantly under threat of flood. This is a recurring feature almost every year (Sinha, 2008). These floods have been doing colossal damage to the land as the fertile top soil is being drained by the rivers and the process of siltation in river beds has been accelerating. Almost all the districts of North Bihar are affected by flood every year (Figure 29.3).

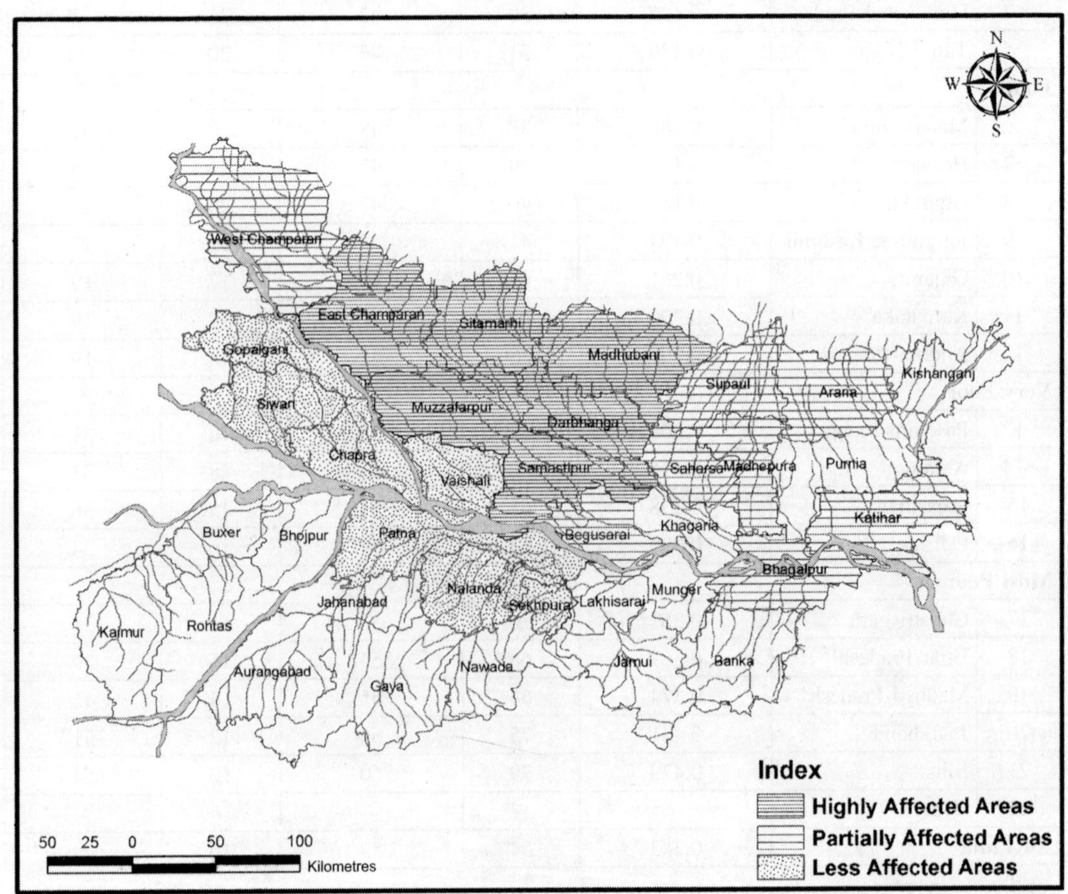

Figure 29.3 Flood affected areas of Bihar.

The floods of Bihar are further intensified by the rivers coming from Nepal but the river Ganga and the Kosi and their tributaries drain most of the area of Bihar. As at present there are nineteen river basins/sub basins (Table 29.3, Figure 29.4) which need to be carefully monitored for implementing the different programmes and schemes of development pertaining to infrastructure, agro-processing industries, spatial arrangement of markets and service centres besides the sectoral development based on the characteristics of each watershed.

Table 29.3 Watersheds of Bihar

Sl. No.	*Name of the main river/rivers*	*Allotted basin number*	*Outfall of the main river*
1	Ghaghra	1	Ganga
2	Gandak	2	Ganga
3	Burhi Gandak	3	Ganga
4	Bagmati–Adhwara	4	Kosi
5	Kamla–Balan	5	Kosi
6	Kosi	6	Ganga
7	Mahananda	7	Ganga
8	Karmnasa	8	Ganga
9	Sone (Stem)	9	Ganga
10	Punpun	10	Ganga
11	Kiul	11	Ganga
12	Harahar	111	Kiul
13	Badua–Belhama	12	Ganga
14	Chandan–Bilasi–Chir	13	Ganga
15	Ganga–Stem	14	Bay of Bengal
16	Kao–Gangi, etc.	141	Ganga
17	Baya	142	Ganga
18	Koa–Bhena, etc.	143	Ganga
19	Mahi	144	Ganga

Application of the Model

Each one of the 19 river basins of Bihar needs to be developed within the frame of watershed development model proposed earlier. The hydro-geomorphological dynamics and socio-economic changes taking place in the watershed need to be mapped, and the emerging issues and problems should be identified. The problems may be social, economic and cultural in nature. The next step is problem solving, which can be done through spatial and sectoral planning.

Spatial planning should take care of the links among villages, markets, service centres, growth points and growth centres. The transport network—rail, road and the water—should be strengthened in order to connect these centres. This will accelerate the smooth flow of trade, traffic, goods and services. The sectoral planning should take care of the promotion of the primary, secondary, tertiary and quaternary sectors. It is significant to mention that all the 19 watersheds are traditionally very rich in primary sector produce especially because of the availability of fertile soil and plenty of water. There is need to take the full advantage of this situation by introducing crop diversification through modernization giving greater boost to cash crops. There is a very good scope for promoting agro-based industries in all the watersheds. In addition, there is a need to promote a massive investment in health and educational sectors in order to achieve the goal of social transformation.

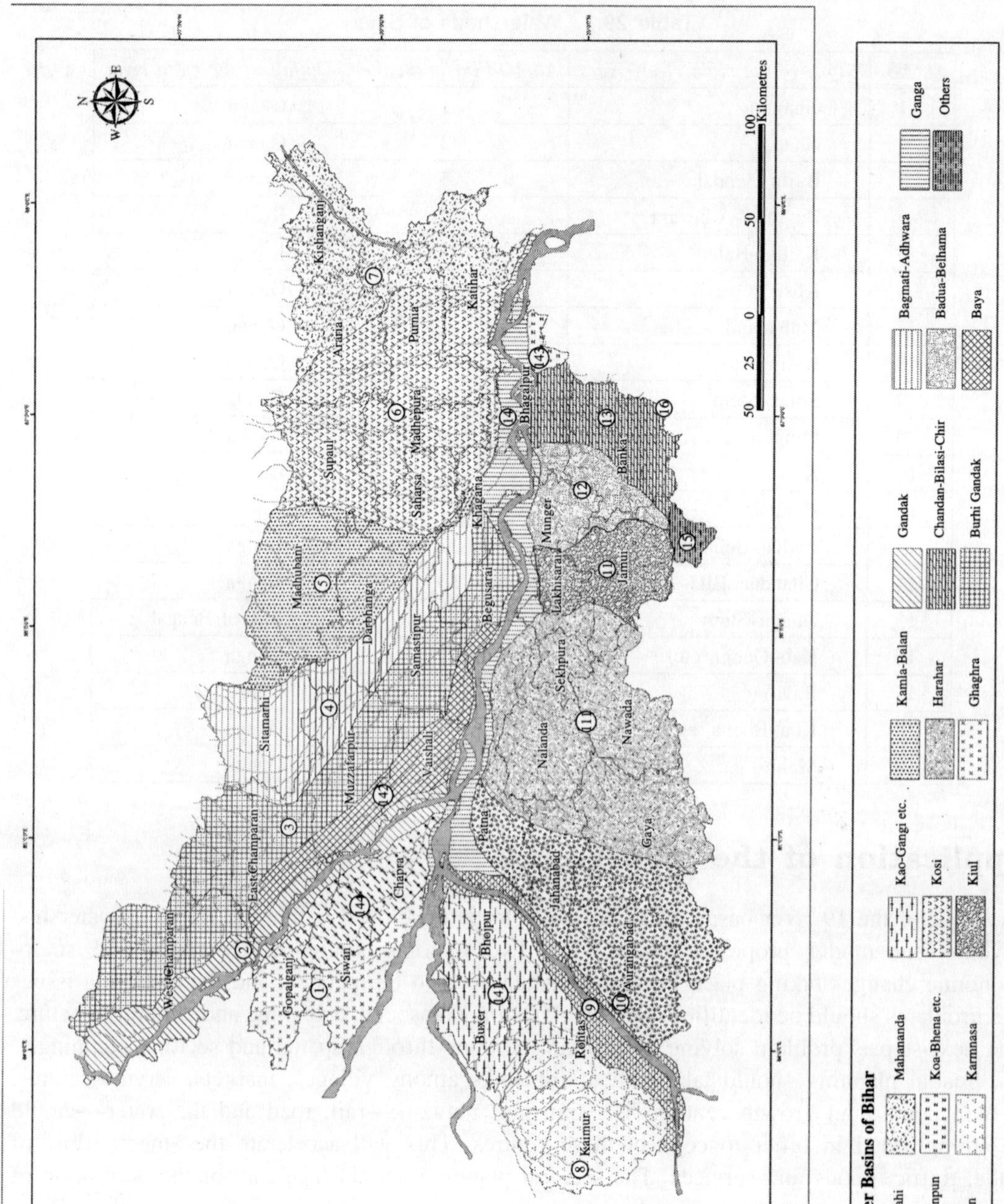

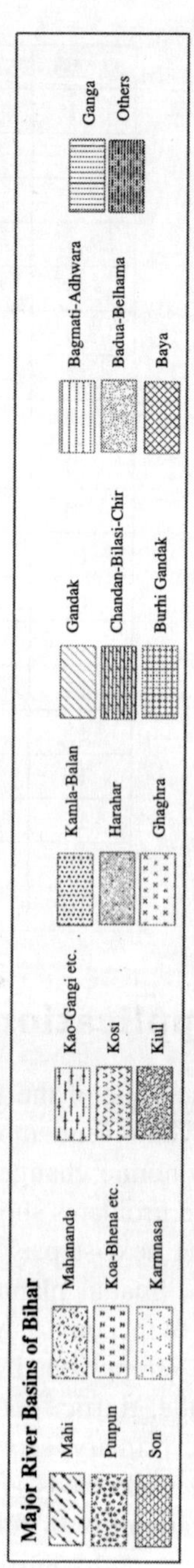

Figure 29.4 River basin map of Bihar.

Desilting of rivers, promoting the concept of check dams and small dams for irrigation, pisciculture, hydroelectricity, water resistant crops and extending the scope for navigation are some of the potential areas to be looked into to manage the water for productive purposes. Land reform needs to be given special priority besides controlling soil erosion. Selection of crops best suited to soil needs, should be taken up in a big way for improving the economy at grass root level.

Conclusion

The Watershed Development Model proposed here envisages six steps which are: (i) identification of watershed—mini, micro or meso, (ii) contour mapping/monitoring of watershed, i.e., hydro-geomorphological changes, socio-economic changes and behavioural perspectives, (iii) identification of emerging issues and challenges of the different categories of watersheds which could be of social, economic, environmental and cultural nature, (iv) problem solving through spatial and sectoral approaches with feedback mechanism, (v) management and monitoring jointly by state/central committee, watershed development committee and village development committee (these committees will ensure participation of all stake holders), and (vi) impact assessment both quantitatively and qualitatively by independent organizations and individuals.

The socio-economic conditions in Bihar are in deplorable state and development processes are very slow. The natural resources especially land and water have not found due focus in the development plans and policies. The interplay of these two resources can be gauged into nineteen river basins or watersheds which are easily identifiable in the state of Bihar. These natural regions create the environment for major anthropogenic activities. The application of this Model, it is hoped, will provide the much needed impetus/fillip required for socio-economic transformation of the nineteen watersheds. For a sustained development, it should continue to be supported by appropriate policies, institutions and technological researches. The model may be replicated elsewhere in similar situations if the objective is to promote sustainable development.

References

Deshpandey, R.S. and G. Thimmaiah (1999), Watershed development approach and experience of national watershed development programme in the country, *Journal of Rural Development*, **18**(3), 453–469.

Deshpandey, R.S. and V.R. Reddy (1991), Differential impact of watershed based technology: Some analytical issues, *Indian Journal of Agricultural Economics,* **46**(3) 261–269.

Farrington, J. and C. Logo (1997), Scaling up participatory watershed development in India: Lessons from the Indo-German watershed development programme, *Natural Resource Perspective*, No. 17, Overseas Development Institutes, London.

Farrington, J. et al. (1999), *Participatory Watershed Challenges in the Twenty First Century*, Oxford University Press, New Delhi.

Misra, H.N. (2000), *Monitoring and Management of Watershed in Himachal Pradesh: A Case of Sirkhad*, Project Report, G.B. Pant Institute of Himalayan Environment and Development, Almora.

Rao, C.H. Hanumantha (2000), Watershed development in India: Recent experience and emerging issues, *Economic and Political Weekly*, **35**(45), 3943–3947.

Samara, J.S. (1997), *Status of Research in Watershed Management*, Central Soil and Water Conservation Research Institute, Dehradun.

Sinha, C.P. (2008), Management of Floods in Bihar, *Economic and Political Weekly*, Nov. 15, 40–43.

Index